CONTEMPORARY ITALIAN FILMMAKING:
STRATEGIES OF SUBVERSION

Pirandello, Fellini, Scola, and the Directors of the New Generation

Contemporary Italian Filmmaking is an innovative critique of Italian film-making in the aftermath of World War II, as it moves beyond traditional categories such as *genre film* and *auteur cinema*. Manuela Gieri demonstrates that Luigi Pirandello's revolutionary concept of humour was integral to the development of a countertradition in Italian film-making that she defines as 'humoristic.' She delineates a 'Pirandellian genealogy' in Italian cinema and culture through her examination of the works of Federico Fellini, Ettore Scola, and many directors of the 'new generation,' including Nanni Moretti, Gabriele Salvatores, Maurizio Nichetti, and Giuseppe Tornatore.

A celebrated figure of the theatrical world, Luigi Pirandello (1867–1936) is little known beyond Italy for his critical and theoretical writings on cinema and for his screenplays. Gieri brings to her reading of Pirandello's work the critical parameters offered by psychoanalysis, poststructuralism, and postmodernism to develop a syncretic and transcultural vision of the history of Italian cinema. She identifies two fundamental trends of development in this tradition: the 'melodramatic imagination' and the 'humoristic,' or comic, imagination. With her focus on the humoristic imagination, Gieri describes a 'Pirandellian mode' derived from his revolutionary utterances on the cinema and narrative, and specifically, from his essay on humour, *L'umorismo* (*On Humor*, 1908). She traces a history of the Pirandellian mode in cinema and investigates its characteristics, demonstrating the original nature of Italian filmmaking that is particulary indebted to Pirandello's interpretation of humour.

(Toronto Italian Studies)

MANUELA GIERI is Associate Professor of Italian and Cinema Studies at the University of Toronto.

Contemporary Italian Filmmaking:
Strategies of Subversion

Pirandello, Fellini, Scola, and the Directors of the New Generation

MANUELA GIERI

UNIVERSITY OF TORONTO PRESS
Toronto   Buffalo   London

© University of Toronto Press Incorporated 1995
Toronto Buffalo London
Printed in Canada

ISBN (cloth) 0-8020-0556-X
ISBN (paper) 0-8020-6979-7

∞

Printed on acid-free paper

Toronto Italian Studies

Canadian Cataloguing in Publication Data

Gieri, Manuela
  Contemporary Italian filmmaking: strategies of
subversion: Pirandello, Fellini, Scola, and the
directors of the new generation

  (Toronto Italian studies)
  Includes bibliographical references and index.
  ISBN 0-8020-0556-X (bound) ISBN 0-8020-6979-7 (pbk.)

  1. Motion pictures – Italy – History.
  2. Pirandello, Luigi, 1867–1936 – Influence.
  I. Title. II. Series.

  PN1993.5.I73G54 1996   791.43′0945   C95-932709-6

Photos courtesy of the Museum of Modern Art, New York; Letizia Messina
and Intrafilms; Gabriele Salvatores and the Colorado Film; and Nanni
Moretti and the Sacher Co.

University of Toronto Press acknowledges the financial assistance to its pub-
lishing program of the Canada Council and the Ontario Arts Council.

A mio padre, il cui ricordo sempre mi rasserena e mi da coraggio.
A mia madre la cui forza e gaiezza sono fonte costante di ispirazione.
A tutta la mia famiglia che ha sempre rasserenato e incoraggiato
il mio cammino verso la maturità.

Contents

Acknowledgments

There are many roads one has to travel before getting to the end of a journey. There are many people one meets on those roads, and each one of them brings something unique to one's journey. At the end, one sits back and recollects the roads and the encounters, but it is hard at times to recall the faces of all those who counted. It is easy instead to remember a feeling, a vague and dear remembrance of things past that will accompany you for your entire life. To all those who gave me such a precious gift, I say 'thank you.'

At the beginning of this journey, there is one and only one person who then accompanied me all the way. He is the one who brought me to North America and to my Ph.D. He is the one who encouraged me to work on a dissertation on Pirandello and the cinema. He is the one who always believed in and supported me in my journey to professorship and scholarship notwithstanding our many differences. He is Peter Bondanella, and to him go my warmest thanks.

Many other fine scholars have played a major role in my journey, and have constantly been a source of inspiration and support: Gian Paolo Biasin, Glauco Cambon, Robert Dombroski, Guido Fink, Harry Geduld, Enzo Lauretta, Edoardo Lebano, Romano Luperini, Millicent Marcus, Paolo Puppa. I would also like to thank all those friends who stood by my side in the happy as well as in the difficult times, who constantly encouraged me, and who inspired me in more than one way: Cinzia Bianchi, Cristina Degli Esposito, Paolo Fasoli, Andrea Fedi, Davide Gasperi, Corrado Paina, and Andy Stein. A special thank you goes to Donato Santeramo, whose relentless support and unconditioned friendship made this journey not only possible but thoroughly rewarding.

To Nanni Moretti, Gabriele Salvatores, and Giuseppe Tornatore goes my gratitude for their willingness to share with me their experience and knowledge. The final stage of this project is entirely indebted to the many suggestions they gave me during our conversations. I must also thank Moretti's Sacher Film, Salvatores' Colorado Film, and Letizia Messina of Intrafilms for most of the photographic material on the new Italian cinema we have used for the volume. My unlimited gratitude also goes to Ron Schoeffel, who is unquestionably responsible for the realization of this project with University of Toronto Press. His encouragement in the initial stages, his advice on practical matters, and his warm support made it all an easy and happy journey.

Last, but not least, my entire family deserves special mention for their unlimited love and trust. With and because of them, my dreams have become reality.

CONTEMPORARY ITALIAN FILMMAKING

Luigi Pirandello

Introduction:
Why Pirandello and the Cinema?

To begin a critical investigation by posing from the outset a question that could undermine the validity and the very existence of the whole work might seem foolish, or at least not strictly orthodox. However, to confront the question 'Why Pirandello and the cinema?' – that is, to consider the complex problem of the relationship between Pirandello and the 'Seventh Art' – has become essential to an understanding of Luigi Pirandello's place and role in the development of twentieth-century narrative and dramatic arts, and, more importantly here, in the birth and growth of the new medium in an Italian context. The investigation of Pirandello's desultory utterances on the cinema may cast new light on an important segment of Italian filmic discourse as it developed in the second half of this century.

A celebrated figure of the theatrical world, Luigi Pirandello (1867–1936) is almost unknown beyond Italy for his novels and, even more so, for his critical and theoretical writings.[1] Almost unfamiliar to the English-speaking world are Pirandello's many 'encounters' with the cinema. Just as most intellectuals and artists who themselves experienced the turn of the century and its many revolutions, Pirandello developed an interest in the new medium of cinematography as both a technology and a means of artistic expression quite early in his life.[2]

To appraise his 'encounter' with cinema, it is important to remember that Luigi Pirandello was a controversial and eclectic persona; his life spanned nearly seventy troubled yet almost 'miraculous' years, and his work traversed many genres and media. He was a dramatist, of course,[3] but also a novelist,[4] an essayist,[5] a poet,[6] even a painter.[7] Because of his interest in the diverse artistic discourses, he was equally engaged in investigating the linguistic possibilities offered by their meeting and interaction.[8] Like many of his contemporaries, Luigi Pirandello could not avoid being affected by the appearance of the cinema, which soon engaged the other well-established art forms in a close debate. It is not by chance that as early as 28 March 1911, Ricciotto Canudo[9] published a pamphlet entitled *Manifeste des sept arts* in which he defined cinema as the 'Seventh Art.'

Even though Pirandello's initial relationship with the 'moving pictures' was that of a spectator,[10] he soon became involved in a discourse with the cinema that never took the form of a monologue, regardless of what a number of critics maintained for so many years. Pirandello understood as early as 1904 the marvels the new technology was bringing forth. Quite surprisingly for the time, he then decided to write a novel on the world of the moving pictures and on the cinematic apparatus itself.[11]

In Italy, Pirandello was not alone in his interest in the poetics and potentiality of the cinema. As Pierre Leprohon once remarked, 'L'Italie est la première à susciter sur le cinema des études théoriques et critiques dont certaines anticipent même sur son avenir'[12] ('Italy is the first to provoke theoretical and critical studies on the cinema, some of which anticipate some of its future developments'). In fact, as early as 1907, several essays were published on the cinema. Giovanni Papini's article 'La filosofia del cinematografo' ('The Philosophy of the Cinema') appeared in the daily paper *La stampa* published in Turin, and Edmondo De Amicis' famous essay 'Cinematografo cerebrale' ('Cerebral Cinema') was published in *Illustrazione italiana*. In the same year, Ricciotto Canudo himself, as reported by Leprohon, made a revealing statement as he wrote in *Vita d'Arte*, 'Le rêve des féeries est achevé pour le théâtre et un nouveau merveilleux, imposé par la science, inspirera les artistes de demain' ('The dream of the fairies is over for theatre and a new dream of the marvellous, imposed by science, will inspire the artists of tomorrow'). And so it did, as proven by the many statements on the new medium that crowded both official and avant-garde publications in Italy thereafter.

The debate on the artistic nature of cinema was feverish, as was the discussion of its social function and the moral issues it raised for the artists and the men of letters asked to work for it. Many collaborated with the industry primarily for economic reasons, and soon imposed over the new and not yet codified medium prefabricated aesthetic beliefs – for example, the futurists, and even the famous Italian poet Gabriele D'Annunzio. D'Annunzio maintained cinema to be the art of the marvellous, and thus felt that set/stage elements needed to be emphasized and elaborated. On the contrary, other artists and intellectuals such as Luigi Pirandello comprehended quite early that cinema needed to elaborate its own language, its own grammar and syntax, emphasizing the issue of rhythm, and thus the importance of montage. It may be relevant to remember here that in later film theories these elements came to qualify the so-called 'specifico filmico' ('filmic specificity'). It may also be important to note, as Guido Aristarco, the prominent film critic and historian, once remarked, that 'Di un linguaggio cinematografico specifico e del tutto autonomo, Pirandello fu sempre un fervido sostenitore'[13] ('Pirandello was always a fervid supporter of a specific and totally autonomous film language').

Pirandello's reaction to the 'moving pictures' has been variously defined as conflictual, negative, and problematic. Even though his initial attitude was one of 'suspicion/caution,' he entertained with the 'moving pictures' a 'love-hate relationship'[14] that lasted nearly thirty years. Although his interest in the cinema began in 1904, only in 1913 did he initiate an active participation in the industry, continuing his 'discourse' with the new medium up until his death. These are facts every scholar now acknowledges, even though for a number of years a prejudiced attitude characterized many critics' observations on this particular area of Pirandellian studies. Even a scholar so notoriously reluctant on this matter as Gaspare Giudice, Pirandello's famous biographer,[15] had to admit the existence of a sincere interest in the cinema in the Sicilian author. Although his biography is an accurate and valuable source of information for any student of Pirandello,[16] Giudice is one of the scholars primarily responsible for the persistence of a prejudiced judgment about Pirandello's attitude toward the new means of expression. In fact, in the beginning of the chapter devoted to the question of Pirandello and cinema, Giudice states:

Dalla iniziale avversione, durante tutta la fase del cinema pionieristico, Pirandello passa all'avversione e all'aperto disprezzo nell'epoca contrassegnata da film come *Quo vadis?* e *Cabiria*, e a una forse più avvertita e diversamente avversa partecipazione nel periodo del trionfo del sonoro.[17]

From the initial distraction during the whole phase of pioneeristic cinema, Pirandello moved to aversion and overt contempt in the period characterized by such films as *Quo Vadis?* and *Cabiria*, and then to a perhaps more alert and differently averse participation in the epoch which witnessed the triumph of sound.

It is now a common understanding that, contrary to what Giudice states, and as I mentioned earlier, Pirandello was, in fact, drawn to the new medium as early as 1904. From that moment onward, he regarded cinema in a complex and not merely confrontational manner. Further- more, Giudice's comments on Pirandello's reaction to films such as En- rico Guazzoni's *Quo Vadis?* (1913) and Giovanni Pastrone's *Cabiria* (1914) appear quite general and vague. Needless to say, even his re- marks on Pirandello's 'more alert' and yet 'averse participation' in the debate at the advent of sound does not really bring insight to Piran- dello's elaborate and fully articulated position on the use of sound in film.[18]

Giudice continues by listing the several encounters that occurred be- tween Pirandello and the cinema of his day, even though he constantly emphasizes the negative elements of the various events, and often openly 'censors' the Sicilian artist's reaction to the cinema, which, ac- cording to the critic, was either polemic or decisively confrontational. Giudice believes that, especially with the introduction of sound in film, Pirandello's position resulted in a simple and powerful defence of the- atre against cinema. As Jennifer Stone argues, Giudice gives the im- pression that 'Pirandello both misjudged the potential of the talkies and had a conservative regard for the traditional elements of the the- ater.'[19] Although Pirandello's initial response to the talkies may not have been entirely positive and was certainly problematic, his attitude cannot be described as totally dismissive and confrontational. Like many of his contemporaries, such as Charlie Chaplin, Charles Vidor, and Sergei Eisenstein, to mention only a few, he regarded the introduc- tion of sound as 'problem-posing.' Giudice, then, goes as far as includ- ing in his discussion a truly 'unfortunate' comment on the non-produc- tion of a film project Pirandello wished to realize with Max Reinhardt and that was inspired by one of his most famous plays, *Sei personaggi in cerca d'autore* (*Six Characters in Search of an Author*, 1921):

Per fortuna questo *Sei personaggi – venti anni dopo* non si potè realizzare, e Rein- hardt non potè fare grande, nè fare bello, a spese di un Pirandello invecchiato, che forse troppo adesso cedeva alle suggestioni degli altri, e che certo non avremmo ben visto nei panni dell'attore cinematografico.[20]

Luckily this *Six Characters – twenty years later* could not be realized, and Rein- hardt could not accomplish big and beautiful things at the expense of an aged Pirandello, who perhaps then would far too easily surrender to others' sugges- tions, and whom we could not really see suited for the role of the film actor.

Aside from its limited vision, this statement also contains unforgivable omissions – for instance, the fact that Pirandello had for many years wanted to realize a film adaptation of *Six Characters*, his most famous and controversial play. As Francesco Càllari argues, the history of Pirandello's many attempts to succeed in this film venture begins in 1926, and it can hardly be described as a manifestation of senile weakness.[21]

Giudice concludes his argument by citing in a strongly prejudiced manner – that is, only as an extreme example of Pirandello's many 'defences' of theatre over cinema – a few remarks from a long and otherwise perceptive speech Pirandello made in 1934 at the Convegno Volta, in which he analysed the health of the *teatro drammatico (dramatic theatre)*. I shall return to this speech later, since I believe that on that occasion Pirandello provided an important contribution to a full redefinition of the idea of 'spectacle,' and, therefore, enunciated the roles theatre and cinema should have in society. At any rate, Pirandello's discourse, even in that particular event, was far more articulate than a mere defence of theatre against cinema, as Giudice would have us believe.

One should also bear in mind that by the time the cinema became popular, the theatre was already experiencing one of its most devastating crises. Some of the reservations Pirandello might have harboured do not necessarily constitute a stance against film per se, but rather mirror a concern over the conditions of the theatre, reservations about the non-synchronous aspects of the talkies, and a reluctance to renounce the physical presence of the actor. In any case, Pirandello's critical and theoretical utterances on cinema should be interpreted as stages of a wilful participation in a debate current among the period's filmmakers as well as other artists and intellectuals involved in narrative and dramatic arts.

As Nino Genovese has recently remarked, Pirandello's attitude toward the new technology and the avenues it opened to narrative and dramatic arts was unquestionably more complex than that of many of his Italian contemporaries, such as D'Annunzio himself and Giovanni Verga.[22] This attitude was not a contradiction to Pirandello's concept of life; as a matter of fact, it was quite harmonious with his entire *Weltanschauung*.[23] I do agree with those who maintain that his relationship with the Seventh Art was multifarious and intricate; I do not believe it was contradictory, as others have stated. There is nothing in Pirandello's creative and 'scientific' writings that can truly support the hypothesis of his being uncompromisingly against the new medium. On

the contrary, as Leone De Castris maintained as early as 1962,[24] by looking at the whole constellation of his many works on and for the cinema,
one comprehends that Pirandello was never hostile to the new means of
expression, but he certainly railed against 'la civiltà che lo asservisce e
lo deforma a suo modo' ('the civilization that enslaves and deforms it at
its pleasure'). In particular, Pirandello condemned 'l'aberrazione natu-
ralistica che le prime poetiche del cinema ingenuamente ri-
proponevano'[25] ('the naturalistic aberration which the early poetics of
cinema ingenuously reproposed'). Thus, Pirandello was never an antag-
onist of the cinema itself; however, as he rapidly moved away from naturalism in theatrical and narrative works, he undoubtedly became a
strong opponent of the naturalistic use of the cinematic apparatus,
which was growing prevalent in the film industry. According to Pirandello, as he expresses himself through one of his characters, the cameraman Serafino Gubbio in the novel *Si gira ...* (*Shoot!*, 1915–16), cinema
was becoming nothing but a 'sconcia contaminazione' ('obscene contamination') of reality and poor fiction because of naturalistic practice.[26]

Over a nearly thirty-year period, Pirandello not only wrote essays on
cinema as an institution and as a means of artistic expression, he also
penned several screenplays. Although some screenplays have yet to be
brought to light, and new findings are still taking place, we have evidence of Pirandello's inquisitiveness and involvement in both the technical and theoretical aspects of the new medium.

As I mentioned earlier, there has always been disagreement about
the nature and true significance of Pirandello's relationship with the
cinema, as some of his utterances on this matter have been substantially misread, and his participation in various film projects has all too
often been interpreted as exclusively motivated by money. Quite recently, though, a partial consensus has been reached among critics,
who finally recognize that Pirandello was truly and profoundly interested in the artistic possibilities of the new means of expression. However, most studies still insist on Pirandello's problematic 'regard' toward cinema. Quite recently, Nino Genovese has argued that
Pirandello's apparently contradictory attitude can be explained from
both a practical and a theoretical perspective. On the one hand, it was
imputable to the economic pressures that haunted Pirandello for his
entire life; on the other, it was certainly motivated by his concept of humour, that is, the 'sentiment of the opposite' that constitutes the foundation of his complex *Weltanschauung* as well as of his aesthetics.[27]

Over the years, a number of studies have investigated Pirandello's
many encounters with the film industry. In particular, two volumes

edited by Nino Genovese and Sebastiano Gesù have enriched this field of research with new insight. The first is a collection of essays on Pirandello and the cinema; the second is dedicated to adaptations for the screen of Pirandello's narrative and dramatic works. I must also mention the long-awaited volume by Francesco Càllari, a scholar who has dedicated his life to study and research in this area.[28] Although preceded by a plethora of brief studies on the subject in various languages, these two significant achievements in the broad field of Pirandello studies offer a comprehensive investigation of the Sicilian author's relationship with the world of the 'moving pictures.' They have also sanctioned the change in the critical response toward this particular issue.

Given that these publications are in Italian, and no similar work exists in English, with the exception of a few good yet non-exhaustive essays, in the first section of my work I briefly discuss Pirandello's concrete interest in the movie industry, his collaboration on a number of film ventures, and some of his unrealized projects. I will not pursue a close analysis of the film adaptations of Pirandello's works, since Genovese and Gesù already devote the second volume of their work to this, and Càllari also provides us with an exhaustive, well-annotated filmography. Furthermore, such investigation would require an entire volume, since many films have been adapted from Pirandello's narrative and dramatic works from his lifetime to the present. Incidentally, to discuss the various cases of adaptation seems an idle undertaking at present, since this is certainly not the most fascinating aspect of Pirandello's encounter with the cinema.

Most studies suggest that an intriguing area of research would be the so-called *Pirandellism* in the cinema. This term was first used in France to define the general feeling of uneasiness that permeated French society after World War I. Over the years, it came to signify such concepts as relativism, cerebralism, and the general and widespread sense of alienation in the early twentieth-century machine age. The term, however, soon came to be slightly derogatory, and this is primarily the reason why it eventually became obsolete. This is also the reason why this perspective did not produce a good analysis of so-called 'Pirandellisms' in the cinema, with only few exceptions, such as, Maurizio Del Ministro's inspiring analysis of Ingmar Bergman and Orson Welles in his *Pirandello scena personaggio e film.*[29]

Even though it would be hard to disregard the value of Del Ministro's contribution to our discussion, one has to acknowledge some of the methodological problems this important work still displays. It is difficult to understand, for instance, why the entire first section of the volume is devoted to Pirandello's theatre and the second to a close analysis of a number of films by Bergman and Welles, while no conclusion is drawn either on Pirandello's 'influence' on contemporary forms of filmmaking or on the particular *'taglio* prettamente cinematografico' ('specifically cinematographic *style*') that some of his theatrical works unmistakeably bear, as Nino Genovese suggests,[30] or as, before him, Arcangelo Leone De Castris stated in his *Storia di Pirandello*.[31] De Castris goes as far as maintaining that one of Pirandello's plays, *Sogno (ma forse no)* (*I Dream (Perhaps Not)*, 1929), is 'una vera e propria sceneggiatura cinematografica, concepita secondo un preciso linguaggio filmico' ('a true screenplay, conceived according to a precise filmic language').[32] Del Ministro also fails to draw meaningful conclusions about Pirandello's possibly 'active' contribution to the definition of a theory and/or an aesthetics of the cinema. Other works have explored this area of Pirandello studies better, as will be discussed in the second chapter of the present volume. To point to the limitations of Del Ministro's work by no means implies a reproach of his investigation. On the contrary, it is because of that book and other pioneering investigations of this particular segment of Pirandello studies that this work is now possible.[33]

It is imperative, however, to redirect the discussion by introducing another definition, in many ways opposed to the now well-established term *Pirandellism*, which served to define the indirect influence Pirandello exercised on twentieth-century artistic discourses, and thus on the cinema.[34] This influence, though, has been frequently characterized as a set of themes and motifs, that is, in terms of content. In fact, very little attention has been given to the 'linguistic' – the particular meeting of linguistic and psychological implications contained in most of Pirandello's utterances on the theatre, on narrative expression in general, and on the cinema in particular. Within this perspective, an important reference is Pirandello's essay on humour, since here the author provides us with a true 'manifesto' for twentieth-century poetics and aesthetics.

To comprehend the contours of Pirandello's 'influence' on subsequent forms of cinematic narrative, one ought to discuss a Pirandellian *mode* – that is, not only a set of themes and motifs, but a specific way of 'articulating' the filmic discourse itself, its syntax as well as its grammar. The theoretical and ideological justification of the Pirandellian mode can be found in Pirandello's utterances on the cinema, in his revolutionary overturn of traditional theatrical and narrative strategies, and, above all, in his essay on humour, *L'umorismo* (*On Humor*, 1908).

Many scholars have suggested Pirandello's influence on directors such as Ingmar Bergman and Alain Resnais,[35] Jean-Luc Godard and Alain Robbe-Grillet, Akira Kurosawa and Woody Allen, and, in an Italian context, Michelangelo Antonioni, Federico Fellini, and even Pier Paolo Pasolini.[36] As mentioned earlier, most works focus on a set of themes and motifs that can be generally defined as 'Pirandellian' and that can be detected in different films. Little has been done in terms of verifying whether or not one can suggest the existence of a true 'Pirandellian mode' in contemporary filmmaking. This kind of cinematic discourse is obviously characterized by specific themes and motifs, but also, and more importantly, by a specific 'articulation' of the discursive practice. To provide a profitable definition of such mode of discourse, one ought to discuss Pirandello's intriguing concept of humour as he expressed it in his essay *On Humor*. In that work, Pirandello gives a full definition as well as a true 'history' of the 'humoristic' genre. This genre is obviously in a constant and critical dialogue with the so-called 'classical' genres, comedy and tragedy. Humour, as Pirandello defined it, is a linguistic response to the specific psychological and existential condition modern man experienced and, to a certain extent, still experiences, a condition defined by specific motifs such as fragmentation, division, and thus alienation or estrangement. The 'Pirandellian mode' produces metadiscoursive narratives that are self-reflexive, eccentric, and hypercritical, and pursue a true repositioning of the various 'parties' involved in the discoursive practice.

It is only through such a perspective, I believe, that one can truly account for the differences between filmmakers and still place them one next to the other. A simply thematic approach would be quite insufficient to interpret and understand the inner similarities between forms of cinematic discourse apparently so different from one another. Moreover, an approach that only indicates common themes and motifs cannot fully explain Pirandello's 'influence' on different directors. In the second chapter of my work, I discuss Pirandello's numerous and diverse utterances on the cinema and define the contours of his contribution to the founding, or rather to the development, of an aesthetics of the Seventh Art. Furthermore, I investigate the characteristics of the 'Pirandellian mode' as it developed in a general history of cinema, beginning in the fifties and reaching full maturity in the sixties and seventies, still enduring in a sort of 'vulgarized' form in the present. The last three chapters of this book will be devoted to a discussion of this cinematic discourse in an Italian context, specifically in the works of directors such as Federico Fellini, Ettore Scola, and a few representatives of the so-called 'new Italian cinema.'

Feu Mathias Pascal by Marcel L'Herbier (1925)

1 He Lost It at the Movies: A Love-Hate Relationship of Over Thirty Years

The French film historian Pierre Leprohon opens his *Le cinéma italien* by reminding us of the prominent role Italy played in the birth and growth of the cinema. He argues that Italy had nourished an interest in the mechanical reproduction of images since Leonardo da Vinci's conception and description of the *camera oscura*, built for the first time by the Neapolitan Giambattista Della Porta in the seventeenth century.[1] It was also in Rome where a German Jesuit, Father Athanasius Kircher, elaborated a model for the Magic Lantern, which he described in his *Ars Magna Lucis et Umbrae*.[2] As Leprohon observes, even though these events can be placed better in a general history of photography, they still constitute a necessary premise for the invention of the cinema, which was born in France and Italy almost contemporaneously.

A fledgling Italian cinema had its beginnings in 1895 when, on 11 November, Filoteo Alberini was granted a patent for his Kinetograph, a device for photographing and projecting quite similar to the Lumière Cinématographe, which had seen the light only a few months earlier. Thereafter, interest in cinema grew rapidly in Italy, and in 1905 the first film studio was established in Rome by Alberini himself.[3] Less than a year after its founding, the studio Alberini and Santoni became the famous Cines. Alberini remained as its 'direttore tecnico' ('technical director'), and it continued to exist to the outbreak of the Second World War. However, other studios soon appeared all over the country, and by 1910 yearly production reached impressively high figures for the era.

The year 1913 constituted the apex of the early Italian film industry. Figures show that approximately 738 films were produced, together with 127 documentaries.[4] This was also the year during which Pirandello's long-sustained interest in the cinema 'openly' began.[5] It is also roughly the period in which Pirandello became 'actively' involved in the theatre. His interest in the theatre dates back to his youth, as an extensive and detailed chronology recently compiled by Alessandro D'Amico has proved. Yet it was only in 1910 that one of his works was finally brought to the stage.[6] Pirandello thus began to move decisively into the world of drama in that year, when Nino Martoglio, the Sicilian dramatist, convinced him to transform the short story 'Lumíe di Sicilia' ('Lights in Sicily') into a one-act play, which Martoglio then staged together with a play from Pirandello's youth, La morsa (The Grip),[7] at the Teatro Metastasio in Rome on 9 December with his company Teatro Minimo. In 1912, Pirandello published Il dovere del medico (The Doctor's Duty), written the year before. The play was staged a year later by Lucio D'Ambra and Achille Vitti. From that point on, Pirandello continued almost without interruption to work both in the theatre and for the cinema.[8]

Nino Martoglio and Lucio D'Ambra came to be mediators in Pirandello's first encounters with the film world. According to D'Ambra, as early as 1911 Pirandello promised to submit a screen adaptation of Ippolito Nievo's Le confessioni di un ottuagenario[9] to the Film d'Arte Italiana, the Italian branch of the French studios Pathé.[10] At the time Martoglio founded the Morgana Film Studios with clear artistic intentions: one of his ambitions was to make cinema and good literature merge. In that studio, one of the best Italian silent movies, Sperduti nel buio (Lost in the Darkness, 1914), was produced. Although a number of Italian artists were drawn to the new medium primarily for economic reasons, Martoglio hoped to enact a reasonable compromise between artistic demands and economic needs. In 1913 he was about to direct films adapted from works by such famous writers as Giovanni Verga and Salvatore Di Giacomo. As a consequence, Pirandello felt he could work for the cinema as well, as is evident from a letter he sent to Martoglio: 'Verga, Bracco, Salvatore Di Giacomo ... A gonfie vele! Non potrei fare qualcosa anch'io?'[11] ('Verga, Bracco, Salvatore Di Giacomo ... It sounds great! Couldn't I do something too?'). Then, later in 1913, and in another letter to Martoglio, he went so far as to offer a serious proposition:

So che Lucio [D'Ambra] t'ha parlato della mia intenzione di proporti alcuni temi di cinematografia minutamente compiuti e sceneggiati. Ce ne ho già uno Nel segno[12] – bellissimo – quasi pronto; qualche altro potrei approntare fra qualche giorno, e sarei anche disposto ad impegnarmi per contratto, a un prezzo decente per ogni film.

Che mi rispondi? Dimmi dove e come ci possiamo vedere.[13]

I know that Lucio [D'Ambra] told you about my intention to propose to you some cinematographic subjects organized and scripted in detail. I already have one *In the Sign* – beautiful – almost ready; I could have some others ready in a few days, and I would be willing to sign a contract, at a decent price for each **film**.

What do you answer? Tell me where and how we can meet.

At this time, Pirandello wrote for Martoglio not just one but two scenarios that were never produced, since Morgana Film ceased to exist soon thereafter.

It must be admitted that, at least initially, Pirandello was attracted by the moving pictures mostly because of his precarious economic situation, especially following his family's bankruptcy in 1903, which was also the main cause of his wife's mental breakdown. In spite of the attention he later devoted to the cinema, he was generally contemptuous of the new medium in the years preceding 1913. In an article published in 1932, Enrico Roma writes about that period: 'Io lo ricordo ironico e sdegnoso verso la prima cinematografia'[14] ('I remember him being ironic and disdainful toward the early cinematography'). Pirandello was already living at no. 10 of Via Alessandro Torlonia, when, not too far from his house, the studios of the Film d'Arte Italiana were established. Ugo Falena, a friend of both Lucio D'Ambra and Pirandello, was its artistic director, while Gerolamo Lo Savio was the administrator[15] of the new studio. Orio Vergani remembers that from Pirandello's windows 'si vedevano nei capannoni vetrati gli attori e le attrici gestire innanzi all'obiettivo della macchina da presa. E il grido d'avvertimento dell'operatore: "Si gira!," giungeva sino all'osservatorio dello scrittore'[16] ('Inside the glass buildings one could see the male and female actors move in front of the camera lens. And the cameraman's warning cry: "Shoot!" would reach the writer's observing post'). Given the physical proximity of these studios and his friends' involvement in film projects, Pirandello could hardly ignore the existence of the cinema.

Pirandello was introduced to the still-mysterious world of the moving pictures by Lucio D'Ambra, who took him inside studios he could otherwise only see from a distance – studios that made those peculiar sounds that were at first only unwelcomed intrusions into his quiet, studious life. In his article, Enrico Roma also characterizes Pirandello's reactions to the view of the studios before his actual entrance into them.

He writes that each time Pirandello's glance was caught by their shining windows,

si lisciava la barbetta, abbozzava di que' suoi sorrisi strani, indulgenti e quasi fanciulleschi se gli state di fronte, ma ironici, beffardi, se gli state di lato. Si sarebbe detto ch'egli non s'interessava alla cinematografia, che aveva a portata di mano, se non per procurarsi pensieri allegri.[17]

he used to smooth his short beard, to give a ghost of his strange, indulgent and almost childish smiles if you stand in front of him, but ironic and scornful if you stand beside him. One would have thought that he wasn't interested in the cinematography he had at hand if not just to afford himself cheerful thoughts.

After that first visit, there were to be quite a few others, for Pirandello became more and more curious about the mechanics behind the new world of celluloid, in particular about what was actually taking place 'behind the screen.' In his 1932 article, Enrico Roma aptly describes Pirandello's fascination with the new medium:

Una mattina, invece, non senza stupore apprendemmo che il poeta s'era lasciato vincere dalla curiosità di osservar da vicino un teatro di posa. Lucio D'Ambra gli aveva fatto conoscere Soava e Carmine Gallone, cineasti di singolari meriti. E con essi aveva messo piede nell'inferno. Volle conoscere tutto, saper tutto, rendersi conto in brevi ore di quel che avvenisse là dentro, fin dei risibili misteri della tecnica ancora primitiva. E vi tornò, altre volte, non molte, staccandosene quindi per un passo. Di lì a qualche mese fece la sua prima apparizione in libreria il *Si gira*, romanzo di costumi cinematografici, che svelò per primo al pubblico, non già i segreti d'un ambiente strano, ma la significazione intima di tutto quel travaglio, un'interpretazione filosofica del cinema, non soltanto nuovo mezzo artistico, ma novissimo aspetto della vita.[18]

One morning, instead, not without surprise we learned that the poet had allowed curiosity to win him over and had gone to get a close look at a studio. Lucio D'Ambra had introduced him to Soava and Carmine Gallone, two gifted cineastes. And with them he set foot in that inferno. He wanted to know everything and everybody; in a few hours he aimed at gaining a full grasp of everything that took place inside that place and even of the most insignificant mysteries of the still-primitive technique. And he went back a few other times, and later slightly stepped away from it. In a few months *Shoot!*, a novel about the world of cinematography, first appeared in the bookstores. That book was the first to unveil to the audience not just the secrets of a strange environment, but the intimate meaning of all that labour, a philosophical interpretation of the cinema, considered not only a new artistic medium but also a novel aspect of life.

Pirandello's early encounters with the moving pictures produced an immediate response: in 1914 he wrote that novel which, as Roma points out, represents both a philosophical and a phenomenological statement on cinema as an art form and as a new means of communication in a new society. *Shoot!* first appeared as a serial in the *Nuova Antologia* (June–August 1915). It was then published in book form in 1916 and subsequently reprinted in 1925 with a new title, *Quaderni di Serafino Gubbio operatore (Notebooks of Serafino Gubbio, Cameraman)*. The novel constitutes a pessimistic statement on the condition of man in the machine age; it is similarly doubtful about the nature of the new medium. Nevertheless, as Franca Angelini points out, 'Il romanzo critica ... il cinema ma appropriandosi, e spesso ironicamente, degli stessi elementi del cinema del suo tempo'[19] ('The novel criticizes ... cinema and yet appropriates, often ironically, some of the very elements of the cinema of his own times') – that is, Pirandello consciously exploits in this novel the language of cinema, and he often does so ironically, to the point of later proposing a film version of the novel to Anton Giulio Bragaglia. In a letter written in 1918, he went as far as to hint at the formula of 'film within the film' which much later became one of the main features of the French *nouvelle vague*.[20]

On 19 March 1915, the Compagnia Stabile Milanese, directed by Mario Praga, whose leading actress, Irma Grammatica, was soon to become one of the most luminous figures in the early years of Italian cinema, staged Pirandello's first three-act play, *Se non così (If Not So,* 1899).[21] Thus, cinematic and theatrical experiences seemed to parallel each other in Pirandello's progression toward artistic maturity.

Whatever his motives, Pirandello certainly lent his works and his name to a number of film projects in the years to follow. Beginning in 1918 with Lucio D'Ambra and Amleto Palermi's *Papà mio, mi piaccion tutte (Dad, I Like Them All)*, for which Pirandello suggested scenes and episodes, there appeared (and still do) a number of Italian films that were either adaptations of his works, or for which he wrote scenarios. In 1919, Mario Gargiulo directed *Il crollo (The Downfall)*, adapted from one of Pirandello's short stories, 'Lights in Sicily,' written in 1900.[22] In 1920, Ugo Gracci directed *Il lume dell'altra casa (The Light of the Other*

House), and Pirandello himself collaborated with Arnaldo Frateili on the screenplay for the film *Pantera nera (Black Panther)*. In the same year, Augusto Camerini directed *Ma non è una cosa seria (But It Is Not Something Serious)*, with a screenplay by Frateili himself. In 1921, three films were adapted from Pirandello's short stories: *Il viaggio (The Journey)* directed by Gennaro Righelli; *La rosa (The Rose)*, directed by Arnaldo Frateili; and *Lo scaldino (The Hand-Warmer)*, directed by Augusto Genina. Unfortunately, prints of these works are no longer available, except *The Hand-Warmer*, which has only recently been retrieved at the National Cinémathèque in Moscow.[23] Although these films might have proved useful in understanding Pirandello's collaboration with and contribution to early Italian cinema, it is quite certain that Pirandello played little or no role in the actual production of these films, or in the production of many to follow.

The first French film adaptation of a Pirandello work, Marcel L'Herbier's *Feu Mathias Pascal* (1925), can be considered an exception to what seemed to be habitual disposition as the director succeeded in translating the original literary text into another medium while preserving the author's intentions. While Pirandello remained for many years a relatively unknown author in his native Italy, his theatrical works achieved instantaneous success in France thanks to the support of Dullin, the Pitoëffs, and his excellent and influential translator, Benjamin Crémieux. It was in France that the term 'Pirandellism' was first coined to define a general sense of insecurity running through French society in the aftermath of World War I. A similar phenomenon was happening in Germany, where the Kafkian mythology seemed to be a latchkey to the expression and interpretation of the feeling of displacement observed in German society at the end of that disastrous war. As a consequence of the immense critical and popular recognition Pirandello gained in France, the French film industry became quite observant of his works. Although he had consistently refused to sell the rights for film adaptations of his works up to that time, Pirandello was quite happy to concede them to L'Herbier, as a letter cited by Jaque Catelain, L'Herbier's biographer, clearly shows:

Una grande società americana si è letteralmente gettata su un mio libro; mi ha offerto una notevole quantità di dollari se avessi accettato di lasciar filmare la mia storia modificandone il finale. Quest'ultima era condizione indispensabile per la conclusione dell'affare. Ho rifiutato perché avevo anch'io una condizione indispensabile nei confronti di questa richiesta: la mia dignità di scrittore che

mi vietava assolutamente, e mi vieterà sempre, di sacrificare i miei interessi morali, le mie idee filosofiche e la mia coscienza per fini commerciali.[24]
Oggi concedo con entusiasmo *Il fu Mattia Pascal* a Marcel L'Herbier del quale apprezzo infinitamente il carattere e il talento. Il realizzatore di *Don Juan et Faust* saprà inserire nel suo film ciò che non c'è nel romanzo, pur conservando l'assoluta originalità del soggetto. *Per la prima volta ho fiducia nell'arte muta.*[25]

A big American firm literally jumped on my book; they offered me a considerable sum to let them shoot my story with a different finale. This was an indispensable condition for the pulling together of the deal. I refused because I also had an essential condition toward this request: my dignity as a writer, something that absolutely prevented, and will always prevent me from sacrificing my moral interests, my philosophical ideas, and my conscience, for economic reasons.

Today I give *The Late Mattia Pascal* to Marcel L'Herbier with enthusiasm since I appreciate his character and talent highly. The director of *Don Juan et Faust* will be able to insert in his film what cannot be found in the novel and yet preserve the absolute originality of the subject. For the first time I trust the silent art.

Pirandello's conflict with the Hollywood film industry stands in sharp contrast to his enthusiastic reception of L'Herbier's avant-garde filmmaking, especially after having seen his 'cubist' film, *Don Juan et Faust* (1923). L'Herbier belonged to a group of rebellious impressionist filmmakers who fiercely reacted against their precursors' slavish imitation of the Hollywood code. This code was primarily one of narrative continuity, mostly interior action, seamless dialogues, and an unobtrusive montage. In one of her many insightful articles devoted to Pirandello and the cinema, Jennifer Stone analyses the numerous factors that made Pirandello's modernist text appealing to such an avant-garde group. I make special reference here to 'Cineastes' Textes,' in which Stone maintains that *The Late Mattia Pascal* (*Il fu Mattia Pascal*, 1904) was particularly suitable for adaptation by an impressionist filmmaker 'because of its resistance to narrative closure, of the mutability of images, and of its deconstruction of "real" facts.' Furthermore, as Stone observes, 'Pirandello's novel offered the challenge of non-chronological and overlapping experiences, flashback returns of the past, and the obviousness of the narrative devices.'[26] The text was, therefore, extremely suitable to cinematic adaptation by a director such as L'Herbier because of its basic consistency with the platform of the French impressionist *cinéastes.* The satisfactory result of this adaptation resulted from the many parallels between Pirandello's text and impressionist theory. It also demonstrates the fact that Pirandello stands as a precursor to the new directions the modernist movement was to take, since the film was made twenty-one years after he wrote his novel. Pirandello's expectations were fulfilled, for *Feu Mathias Pascal* certainly is the best film L'Herbier ever made and is equally one of the best film adaptations of Pirandello's works. L'Herbier himself was so enamoured of Pascal's doublings and rebirths that he identified with him to the point of calling the film his transposed biography.[27]

The movie was a co-production by Cinématographic (the studio founded by the director himself, together with some friends and collaborators, in the early twenties after his break with Gaumont) and Albatros, a film company founded in Paris by a group of Russian refugees and directed by Aleksandr Kamenka. The on-location shooting was done in Italy at San Gimignano and Rome, particularly at the Excelsior Palace and by the Spanish Steps. Alberto Cavalcanti designed the sets in collaboration with Lazare Meerson, a young Pole and recent arrival in France who was to revolutionize the entire concept of cinematic set design and décor. Meerson worked with such directors as L'Herbier, René Clair, and Jacques Feyder. The expressive Russian actor Ivan Mosjoukine played the leading role. Most importantly, however, the movie witnessed the film début of a twenty-nine-year-old actor, Michel Simon. Born in Geneva, Simon met Sacha and Ludmilla Pitoëff there during the war. He joined their theatrical company and went to Paris with them. By the time of the film's shooting, he had already gained fame for his interpretation of the role of the director in the Pitoëffs' production of *Six Characters in Search of an Author* in Paris in 1923. In *Feu Mathias Pascal,* Simon offered an impressive performance as the 'aiutobibliotecario' ('librarian hand'), while Mosjoukine reached the peak of his French career as Mathias Pascal. The film also marked the début of Pierre Batcheff, who was to become one of the greatest French actors during the years 1925 to 1929.

In September 1925, the film was shown twice at the Cinéma Marivaux in Paris, and with it L'Herbier obtained his greatest commercial and critical success. Its triumph was not limited to France but drifted abroad; the film was appreciated by London and New York critics, although it apparently received only private screenings in the United States. This film represents one of the most stimulating examples of cinematic adaptation of a Pirandellian text. Despite minor changes in plot development, the main difference between the novel and the film lies in the fact that while the novel contains Pirandello's biting satire of Italian society, in the film L'Herbier emphasizes the fantastic elements implicit in the tale, the mutability of personality, and the capacity of the characters to modify themselves according to the disparate situations in which they happen to fall.

In the first decade of the silent era, the Italian film industry had been predominant even over American cinema. By the end of World War I, in 1918, Italian film was still extremely active, but its influence on other national cinemas had declined. The freer expressive techniques of Russian, French, and German filmmakers began to surpass those of Italian film, while American directors began to develop original cinematic techniques of their own. By 1921, the Italian film industry was in a full-scale crisis, since its language had become prosaic, and its films incapable of competing with foreign movies invading the domestic Italian market. Unemployment became an urgent problem, and many studios had to close. Studio personnel began to emigrate, especially to Germany and France, two countries that subsequently fed the American film industry.

One of the directors who ultimately left the country to pursue a career abroad was Amleto Palermi, with whom Pirandello had collaborated in 1918. In 1926, Palermi directed, for the studios Nero-Film in Berlin, a film version of Pirandello's *Enrico IV* (*Henry IV*, a play first staged on 24 February 1922 at the Teatro Manzoni in Milan) entitled *Die Lebende Maske* (*The Living Mask*). In this film, Conrad Veidt, although an extraordinary Henry IV, brought forth an overtly theatrical quality which did not meet the paradigms of a new and original cinematic language.

The year 1929 marks another significant moment in Pirandello's venture into the world of the motion pictures. In this year, in collaboration with Adolph Lantz, the artist conceived a scenario inspired by his play *Six Characters in Search of an Author* and published it in a ninety-three-page volume with the title *Sechs Personen suchen einen Autor: Film-novelle ... nach dem gleichnamigen Theaterstück von Pirandello*.[28] The scenario was published together with the preface to the original play. Pirandello wished to make a film adaptation of his most famous and controversial play for a long time and attempted to produce the film on several occasions up to his death in 1936. During that year, he was again planning a production of the film, which was to be directed by Max Reinhardt and to star Pirandello himself in the leading role of the author, who is present in the film's script though absent in the original play.

While in Germany, Pirandello became involved in several important projects. In the fall of 1928, he supervised the German translation of *La nuova colonia (The New Colony)*, one of the three late plays he called 'myths.' In Berlin, he was probably involved in production plans for a filmed version of the same play. *Die Neue Kolonie* was to be directed by Gennaro Righelli and produced by Lothar Stark.[29] Since the German venture did not materialize, Pirandello turned elsewhere, and in 1935, while in New York, he proposed the film project to Max Reinhardt. Unfortunately this film, like so many others, was never made, and the typescript remained buried among Reinhardt's papers for a long time.

In a letter dated May 1929, Pirandello mentioned his intention to leave for the United States, where he was to sign a contract with Paramount. That year also witnessed Pirandello's first programmatic statement on the cinema and his attempt to untangle the threads of an intense polemical debate that occupied the literary world both within and outside of Italy. In these years, cinema was perfecting its technique, and the first experiments with sound film were emerging. Certain Italian literary figures, especially those in the theatre, were repudiating the idea of sound in film and defending theatre in an argument centred on a non-dialectical conception of the opposition of art versus non-art, theatre versus cinema. In an article appearing in the *Corriere della sera* titled 'Se il film parlante abolirà il teatro' ('If the Talkies Will Abolish the Theatre'), Pirandello entered this debate. But his essay is far from being a mere rant against cinema, as Gaspare Giudice and a few other critics maintain. On the one hand, Pirandello aligns himself with famous opponents of the talkies – Chaplin, Murnau, King Vidor, René Clair, and others; on the other, he also tries to suggest a definition for an aesthetic of the cinema, predicting the birth of *cinemelografia*, that is, a cinema of pure music and pure vision, finally and completely freed from literature. I shall return to this important article in Chapter 2. For the moment, it should be remembered that Pirandello's intervention in the debate was not simply meant to attack cinema in a conservative attempt to preserve theatre; on the contrary, Pirandello clearly hoped to provide an effective defence of film as an independent art form.

As fate would have it, the first Italian talking film ('film parlante') was actually adapted from one of Pirandello's short stories, curiously titled 'In silenzio' ('In Silence'). As is immediately suggested by its title, *La canzone dell'amore (Love Song, 1930)*, the film retained few similarities with the original literary text, but its appearance did mark the birth of another formula in Italian cinema: a love story with catchy songs and a moralizing finale. *Love Song* represents the prototype of a certain kind of sentimental comedy that constitutes a major element in Italian film production from about 1933 on, one that the Italians themselves defined as the 'cinema of the white telephones' ('telefoni bianchi'). Notwithstanding the technical deficiencies of the Italian industry of the day in terms of the new demands of sound film, the movie was finally made – directed by Gennaro Righelli – at the Cines studios in Rome. Since the film did fairly well at the box office, it was also adapted into French and German versions for foreign markets.

In spite of the film's success, Pirandello could not have been completely satisfied with the content of the film, for it transformed his short story. But it should also be remembered that his judgment of the final product was far less harsh and much more engaging than critics such as Giudice have argued. Pirandello commented on the film as follows:

Si è già parlato della mia insoddisfazione d'autore nei riguardi di quest'opera. Ma, in parte, si è falsato il mio pensiero. Bisogna tener conto, anzitutto, di due fatti incontestabili. Il primo, che *La canzone* era il film inaugurale dei nuovi stabilimenti Cines[30] e, credo per giunta che il Righelli, il quale è un esperto e bravo *régisseur*, non si fosse mai misurato precedentemente col 'parlato-sonoro.' Perciò, tecnicamente fu un tentativo, quasi un lavoro di collaudo degl'impianti e delle capacità artistiche degli artefici. E sarebbe ingiusto non riconoscere che, osservato con questi occhi, il film è quasi un miracolo. Il secondo fatto, che ha la sua grande importanza in un giudizio sereno, è l'esito finanziario ottenuto dalla *Canzone*. Dov'è largo consenso di pubblico, gli strali della critica si spuntano. Come negare, in fin dei conti, che come rappresentazione il film del Righelli fosse piacevole e interessante? Ciò stabilito, è logico però ch'io non potessi approvare i mutamenti che erano stati fatti alla mia novella, fino a svisarla del tutto. E sono convinto che se la si fosse realizzata com'è nel testo originale, si sarebbe fatto non soltanto un'opera d'arte cinematografica, ma il successo sarebbe stato di gran lunga superiore.[31]

People have already spoken about my dissatisfaction as an author toward this work. Yet, in part, my thoughts have been misrepresented. One ought to bear in mind two indisputable facts. First of all, *Love Song* was the inaugural film of the new Cines studios, and furthermore I believe that Righelli, who is a skilled and good *régisseur*, had never before worked with 'spoken-sound' film. Thus, technically the movie was an attempt, almost a trying-out work on the part of the machines and the very artistic capacities of the creators. And it would be unfair not to recognize that if one looks at it from this perspective the film is almost a miracle. The second issue that plays a major role in the formulation of a serene judgment is the economic outcome of the *Song*. Where the audience's consensus is large, the critics' darts get blunt. How can we deny ultimately that Righelli's film was pleasant and interesting as a spectacle? Taking this for granted, it is quite logical though that I could not approve of some changes brought to my short story – changes that almost altered it completely. And I am convinced that if they had realized it as it is in the original text, not only would they have made a work of cinematographic art, but its success would have been even greater.

Although Pirandello was disappointed with the film's basic betrayal of his original text, he was also aware of the importance of this first Italian venture into the realm of sound, and conscious of the true status of film as a popular art form.

In 1930, Pirandello travelled to the United States to supervise the shooting of the film adaptation of *Come tu mi vuoi* (*As You Desire Me*, a play written in 1930). The movie was directed by George Fitzmaurice, a French director then working in Hollywood, after a screenplay written by Gene Markey. The film soon became famous, and remains relatively well known to this day, essentially because of its outstanding cast: Greta Garbo, Erich von Stroheim, and Melvyn Douglas. Notwithstanding the enormous fame Pirandello gained from this film, it is hard to imagine his being happy with the final product, since the film is far from being 'faithful' to or, at least, 'respectful' of the Pirandellian text. Metro-Goldwyn-Mayer paid Pirandello $40,000, but afterwards he lamented that he had only been able to retain a tenth of the sum after paying all the intermediaries.

Because of the film's success, Pirandello received several other offers from Hollywood. However, *As You Desire Me* was the only American film adaptation of one of Pirandello's works produced during his lifetime. At a certain point, he was to return to the United States to pursue the production of a film adaptation of *Six Characters in Search of an Author*, since the 1929 project conceived in collaboration with Adolph Lantz in Germany had never materialized. The American version would have been directed by Irving Thalberg, but was never actually realized. A few years earlier, *Henry IV* had gone into planning but remained unmade because the producers wanted the film to end on a note of happiness, with the marriage of Henry IV and Matilde Spina.[32] As Giudice maintains, Pirandello apparently conceived another project that would have starred the Barrymore brothers, but this, too, was never produced, since, by the early thirties, these actors were no longer marketable at the box office.[33]

Most likely prompted by his disillusionment over both *Love Song* and *As You Desire Me*, in 1932 Pirandello decided to turn to a project for a true art film. In collaboration with his son, Stefano, he wrote a text specifically designed for the cinema, a true film scenario entitled *Gioca Pietro! (Play, Peter!)*. Pirandello had enormous expectations for this film project; in fact, when asked during an interview who would direct the film, he decisively replied: 'Un grande direttore di fama mondiale; con molta probabilità Pabst o, s'egli non potesse svincolarsi a tempo, Eisenstein'[34] ('A world-famous director; very likely Pabst or, if he cannot disengage himself in time, Eisenstein'). And when asked which actors would be starring in it, he answered: 'Ancora non sono stati fissati, perchè questo è facoltà del regista. Quasi certamente, però, la prima attrice sarà la mia grande interprete del teatro: la signorina Marta Abba, cui ho pensato ideando il personaggio femminile'[35] ('They have not yet been chosen, since this is the director's responsibility. Almost undoubtedly, though, the leading actress will be my great interpreter in theatre: Miss Marta Abba, whom I had in mind while creating the female character'). In the end, the German experimental filmmaker Walter Ruttmann directed the film for the Italian Cines studios and titled it *Acciaio (Steel)*. Furthermore, the cast was not the one Pirandello had envisioned: the film starred Piero Pastore and Vittorio Bellaccini, with Isa Pola replacing Marta Abba. With a sound score written by G.F. Malipiero, the script was eventually transformed into a documentary on the steel industry near Terni. Thanks to the ability of Emilio Cecchi, who supervised its production, and to Ruttmann's own peculiar style, the film nevertheless maintained the rhythmic elements Pirandello discussed when interviewed before the shooting of the film:

Ho promesso il silenzio. Ho composto uno scenario che è un vero e proprio spartito. In molte scene, ho tenuto conto degli effetti da ottenersi coi suoni, proprio come un musicista nello strumentale di un'opera lirica. La parte sonora avrà nel film una grande importanza. A un dato punto il ritmo delle macchine si umanizza; si raggiunge così un perfetto sincronismo tra il movimento meccanico e il pulsare della vita umana.[36]

I promised silence. I composed a script that is a true musical score. In many scenes I took into account the effects to be obtained with sounds, just like a musician does in the instrumental part of an opera. The sound will have a great importance in the film. At a certain point the rhythm of the machines becomes human; a perfect synchronism between the mechanical movement and the pounding of human life is achieved.

Pirandello conceived the film project as a harmonic synthesis of sounds and images, an example of that 'cinemelografia' he had discussed as early as 1929 in his article 'If the Talkies Will Abolish the Theatre.' Ruttmann's theoretical intent was much closer to the Italian artist's hypothesis than one might at first imagine. Remember, for instance, the beautiful editing Ruttmannn achieved in *Berlin, die Symphonie einer Grosstadt* (*Berlin, the Symphony of a Big City,* 1927). Carl Mayer, who conceived the original idea for *Berlin,* envisioned it as 'a melody of images' whose script was to be like a 'partitura' ('score'), as he called it.[37] Ruttmann edited the enormous amount of material collected by Karl Freund and other photographers and worked in collaboration with Edmund Meisel, the composer of the famous sound score for Sergei Eisenstein's *Potemkin* in 1925. Meisel intended to achieve a total synchronization of Ruttmann's visual symphony with his own music. The musical score was conceived in such a way that it could eventually be played alone, independently from the film. As is immediately apparent, the idea behind this film project was not too far removed from Pirandello's intention of shooting a visual score to a Beethoven sonata. Interestingly enough, the last sequence of *Berlin* is nothing but a roundabout in nocturnal Berlin, while, among other things, an orchestra plays Beethoven.

It should be noted that Ruttmann's conception of montage shows the strong influence of Dziga Vertov. Notwithstanding their ideological differences, both directors were geared toward the documentary, though Vertov intended not simply to divulge news but to compose 'optical music.' His *Man with the Movie Camera* (1929) can be considered, according to Kracauer, 'un documentario lirico'[38] ('a lyrical documentary'). Needless to say, Vertov's film bears strong affinities to Pirandello's novel *Shoot!,* and his concept of 'optical music' parallels Pirandello's idea of 'cinemelografia.'

What matters here, though, is to note the affinity between Pirandello's and Ruttmann's interest in experimentation with music and images. Ruttmann pursued this interest both in his 'montaggio ritmico' in *Steel* and in earlier works, such as *Die Melodie der Welt* (*The Melody of the World,* 1930). Eventually, Ruttmann moved more and more into abstraction with such films as *In der Nacht* (*In the Night,* 1931), in which he simply translated into abstract, visual forms the musical piece of the same title composed by Schumann. In many ways, Ruttmann's avant-garde position reflected similarities with Pirandello's conception of film as an art form composed primarily of images and music, where the images were meant to constitute a visual commentary for the soundtrack.

In 1934, Pirandello was awarded the Nobel Prize for literature. In the following year, he seemed willing to return to his earlier dreams about American film ventures. During an interview, he maintained that Edward G. Robinson, 'uno dei più grandi attori che oggi possiede l'America'[39] ('one of the greatest actors America possesses nowadays'), had been given the leading role in the projected film version of *Il piacere dell'onestà* (*The Pleasure of Honesty*, 1917). In 1935, Pirandello visited the United States for a few months, apparently in order to supervise the production of this film. It was never made.

In spite of Pirandello's genuine interest in the new medium, Gaspare Giudice is correct when he maintains that 'una provvidenza, si vede, vigilava sul teatro di Pirandello'[40] ('it is clear that a providential force was vigilant over Pirandello's theatre'), for ultimately the complexity of any Pirandellian text might well have been unsuitable to the prevailing Hollywood film code. In 1935, Mario Camerini directed the Italian and German film version of *But It Is Not Something Serious*. The play was adapted for the screen by Camerini himself in collaboration with Mario Soldati and Ercole Patti. The leading actors were Elisa Cegani and Vittorio De Sica, who was to become one of the most prominent directors of Italian neorealism.

In 1936 Pirandello once again worked on film projects as energetically as he had on the script *Play, Peter!* He collaborated with Guglielmo Giannini on the film adaptation of his play *Pensaci, Giacomino!* (*Think About It, Giacomino!*, 1916). The film was directed by Gennaro Righelli and produced by the Capitani-Icar Studios in Rome. Pirandello also gave constant assistance and supervision to his son Stefano and to Corrado Alvaro, who were adapting 'Romolo' and 'Requiem aeternam dona eis, Domine' – two of his short stories – for the screen. Corrado Alvaro declared that Pirandello could hardly bear the functional requirements of a film script, and that he primarily thought of a film's scenes in purely literary terms.[41] For instance, he insisted upon having a young lady offer her feudal lord a tiny olive instead of an egg or an apple, which are more plastic and, thus, more filmable objects. Moreover, he curiously wished to have not simply one but three fully detailed funerals in the film. Because of numerous problems in the production phase, the film was completed, by Mario Baffico, only in 1939.

Pirandello's greatest aspirations for revolutionizing the language of film were expressed in his constant return to a film project based on his play *Six Characters in Search of an Author*, whose screenplay he had written as early as 1929 in collaboration with Adolfo Lantz. In the last year of his life, Pirandello intended to initiate a film venture in the United States. He had been invited there by Max Reinhardt, who had plans to film a version of the play, but the project was left unrealized because of Pirandello's death. Even though Gaspare Giudice believes that the production would have been an artistic tragedy,[42] the film might have provided us with a good example of the artistic potentialities of the cinema as Pirandello envisioned them, potentialities which, according to him, were 'without limitation.' If the film had been produced, it would have deepened our knowledge of Pirandello's concept of film as an art form.

When Pirandello died, a new French adaptation of *The Late Mattia Pascal*, directed by Pierre Chenal, was in production. The director wrote the screenplay with the help of Armand Salacrou and Christian Stengel, while Pirandello himself, in collaboration with Roger Vitrac, worked on the dialogue.[43] This time, Pirandello was given the freedom to supervise the shooting, for the film was shot at the Cinecittà studios in Rome. Just before the film's completion, Pirandello caught pneumonia, and died on the morning of 10 December 1936.

As I have outlined in this brief discussion, Pirandello's relationship with the moving pictures was complex and controversial, revealing the dramatist's rather original attitude toward the new medium. First, Pirandello (contrary to what such critics as Giudice and, more recently, Giuseppe Petronio,[44] have maintained) was convinced of the artistic potentialities of the new medium, and repeatedly attempted to contribute to the debate focusing on the definition of a film aesthetics. Pirandello must have been aware of the filmic experimentation avant-garde movements were pursuing during the first decades of the century. By the time Pirandello's interest in the cinema developed, the new medium was perfecting its language and rapidly moving toward maturity. If film was at first influenced by literature and theatre, it soon began to have a strong impact on all modern forms of fiction and drama.

Second, Pirandello's narrative and dramatic techniques were eventually to be influenced by cinematic language. It is interesting to note that Pirandello's interest in the cinema paralleled his growing involvement in the theatre. He was not simply interested in participating in the debate centring around the differences and similarities between theatre and cinema; he was also concerned both with making films and clarifying the theoretical issues raised by cinematic expression for older artistic forms as well as those intrinsic in the new medium itself. It should be remembered that film adaptations of Pirandello's works during his lifetime constituted betrayals of the ethical and aesthetic intentions contained in his original texts, with the exception of the works by L'Herbier and Ruttmann. After Pirandello's death, film adaptations of his works multiplied, realized by such directors as Pàstina, Dieterle, Blasetti, Soldati, and many others, up to quite recent adaptations by the Taviani brothers and Marco Bellocchio.[45] A study of Pirandello's influence on contemporary film, however, must concentrate on the analysis of the work of those directors whose films come closer to the structure and the 'spirit' of Pirandello's revolutionary narrative and dramatic works, rather than upon the various film adaptations of his original texts.

2 Pirandello and the Theory of the Cinema

Luigi Pirandello's controversial interest in the moving pictures began as early as 1913 and lasted for over twenty years. As several scholars have repeatedly observed, Pirandello never actually developed an organic or coherent theory of the cinema. But he did formulate critical and theoretical statements constituting original and overlooked contributions to film theory and practice; he recognized the pivotal place cinema held in the development of twentieth-century poetics, and its inevitability as an immense instrument of human intellect.

A study of Pirandello's relationship with the motion pictures, however, cannot be diluted either to an analysis of his collaborations in film productions or to a discussion of his scholarly and journalistic writings on cinema. To understand fully and thoroughly Pirandello's attitude and the contours of his eventual influence over subsequent forms of cinematic discourse, one must also consider Pirandello's narrative and dramatic writings. His artistic works should be recognized as the true foundation for a novel approach to narrative and dramatic techniques and strategies, an approach that eventually led Pirandello to assume a critical yet progressive disposition toward cinema itself.

In his artistic works, Pirandello not only aimed at achieving new narrative and dramatic strategies; he also addressed several issues central to modernist discourse, such as the nature of the novel 'Subject' in his or her relationship with reality; the rapport between illusion – that is, fiction – and reality; the diverse roles that author, character, and audience perform in the artistic process; and the complex nature of both 'narrativity' and 'theatrality.'[1] These issues were also to become central to the period's debates over the true nature of what was then termed the Seventh Art, specifically in its relation to more traditional art forms, the novel and drama. Pirandello soon became aware of the radical revolution in human perception, and naturally in man's relationship to reality and art, which the mechanical reproduction of the natural world provoked. In particular, Pirandello immediately comprehended how movement and sound in cinema, ingenious outgrowths of earlier static and silent forms of mechanical reproduction of the world produced by photography, contributed to this revolution.

Although early cinema was highly influenced by pre-existing literary forms, it began, in turn, to modify the expression of traditional art forms as well. Where Pirandello was conscious of the borrowings and imitations occurring between the new and the older narrative and dramatic forms, he nevertheless repeatedly saw the necessity for cinema to found its own *specific* language. Further, Pirandello voiced the need to treat the new medium as a true art form, one that was changing constantly and hence could never be taken as a 'given,' or described in a definitive and fixed set of rules: 'Occorre considerare il cinema come problema artistico perpetuamente da risolvere e non fidarsi delle soluzioni già date che nel migliore dei casi servono soltanto a chi le ha trovate e per una breve stagione'[2] ('It is compulsory to consider the cinema as an artistic problem endlessly in the process of being resolved, and not to trust ready solutions that in most occasions can only help those who found them and only for a brief span of time'). Thus, for Pirandello, cinema was not to be considered as a static, technical device never to be submitted to change and development. Instead, film was a phenomenon of some complexity and a true art form; as such, it had to endure constant mutation and growth.

Pirandello opened his first essay on cinema[3] by comparing America and Europe, using the two continents as metaphors for cinema and theatre.

Ciò che sopra tutto in America mi interessa è la nascita di nuove forme di vita. La vita, premuta da necessità naturali e sociali vi cerca e vi trova queste nuove forme. Vederle nascere è un'incomparabile gioja per lo spirito.

In Europa la vita seguitano a farla i morti, schiacciando quella dei vivi col peso della storia, delle tradizioni e dei costumi. Il consistere delle vecchie forme ostacola, impedisce, arresta ogni movimento vitale.

In America la vita è dei vivi.

Senonché la vita, che da un canto ha bisogno di muoversi sempre, ha pure dall'altro canto bisogno di consistere in qualche forma. Sono due necessità che, essendo opposte tra loro, non le consentono né un perpetuo movimento né un'eterna consistenza.[4]

What interests me more in America is the birth of new forms of life. Pressured by natural and social needs, life looks for and finds there these new forms. To see them grow is an incomparable joy for the spirit.

   In Europe life is made by dead people, overwhelming the life of the living with the weight of history, tradition, and habits. The permanence of the old forms obstructs, impedes, and stops every vital movement.

   In America life belongs to the living.

   But life needs, on the one hand, to flow constantly, and, on the other, to consist in one form. They are two needs that, opposed to one another, do not allow life either a perpetual movement or an eternal consistency.

As he states it, cinema constantly needs to find new forms through which to express itself. But simultaneously, like any other true artistic expression, the cinema has to negate those very forms to remain 'alive,' for if life is pure 'flux,' a form is merely a static construction impeding life's flow. The word 'flux' constitutes one of the most important and recurrent signifiers in Pirandello's complex system of signification. It also represents one of the fundamental theoretical concepts expressed in his most famous essay, *On Humor*,[5] which can be considered the clearest manifesto of Pirandello's poetics. In this essay, one can detect the source of his revolutionary conception of narrative and drama and the foundations of his progressive attitude toward cinema.

   The concept of 'specificità cinematografica' or 'specifico filmico' ('cinematographic specificity' or 'filmic specificity'),[6] which was germane to Pirandello's critical investigation of the new medium, was also central to the debates on cinema taking place during Pirandello's life, but also to much later developments in film theory. Quite succinctly, this concept can be characterized as the catalyst of the opposition 'cinema versus literature,' which was then and for a long time after remained central to any theoretical approach to the new medium. As Emilio Garroni points out,[7] the concept of 'specifico filmico' should be rejected, as it offers nothing but a confusing myth. Eisenstein himself conceived montage as a notion not specifically linked only to the cinema; on the contrary, he maintained that the technique appears in virtually all artistic forms, in different degrees. Garroni further asserts that the specificity of cinematic language simply results from the particular combinations in which the various codes employed in such discourse enter. According to Garroni, codes that are specific to one and only one language do not exist.

In his book *Langage et cinéma*,[8] Christian Metz warns his reader against the concept of 'pre-cinema,' or that complex of devices or con-figurations – such as Tito Livio's trackings, Tacito's shot/reverse shot constructions, and Faulkner's alternating montage – that appeared be-fore the birth of the cinema and mirrored future cinematographic tech-niques. Thus, on the one hand, Metz warns us against seeing those con-figurations in a causal or anticipatory light. On the other hand, he also maintains that if it is important to establish specific cinematic codes, it is also true that once these codes are established, they may no longer appear so radically specific. Metz's complex theory moves from the as-sumption that cinema is a language and film a message. Since a code can manifest itself in more than one language, it follows (as Garroni states) that it is possible for a code to move from one means of expres-sion to another – that is, from one language to another – without modi-fying its own internal relational structure, or what Louis Hjemslev de-fined as the 'form of the expression.' Nowadays, we know the important role literary and dramatic techniques played and still play in the construction of a film. This sort of migration signifies nothing but the movement of a form through several means of expression. In each case, we note the presence of similar codes that are more or less com-mon to different languages. The various borrowings, imitations, and adaptations of the diverse signifiers constitute the vast domain of the so-called 'interferenze semiologiche'[9] ('semiological interferences').

It soon becomes apparent to any student of Pirandello's work that he anticipated many later critical and theoretical statements on the cinema – and in twentieth-century aesthetics. Pirandello understood the lin-guistic foundations of the various artistic media and therefore was also very likely conscious of this migration of forms from one medium to another. I also suggest that Pirandello practised and theorized the inter-changeability and the transposability of different forms from one means of expression to another. My purpose here is not simply to provide a criticism of Pirandello's theoretical positions toward the cinema in rela-tion to the period's theories or to discuss them in relation to the entire body of his own critical and theoretical remarks. On the contrary, a criti-cal review of Pirandello's theoretical statements on the Seventh Art is useful because of their relevance for contemporary theory. Therefore, I shall develop my analysis from the standpoint of the present and through a close study of Pirandello's observations, with the intention of reaching a consensus in the interpretation of contemporary cinematic discourses and eventually preparing the ground for new theoretical work.

Pirandello's attitudes toward cinema are clearly exemplified in both the narrative form and the content of the novel *Shoot!*, which, although written as early as 1915, can still qualify as an example, or rather as an anticipation, of his critical approach to film. Since the form and the ideology of Pirandello's entire opus correspond to such an extent that there are no changes in the one without immediate response in the other, an understanding of the novel's content implies a full comprehension of its form. Most of Pirandello's work can also qualify as an experiment in communication, since he constantly aimed at involving the reader in the text's production so as to bring that reader to a better understanding of his or her own true being. In the very opening of *Shoot!*, Pirandello's narrator clarifies this point:

Studio la gente nelle sue più ordinarie occupazioni, se mi riesca di scoprire negli altri quello che manca a me per ogni cosa che io faccia: la certezza che capiscano ciò che fanno ... Ma poi, se mi fermo a guardarli un po' addentro negli occhi con questi miei occhi intenti e silenziosi, ecco che subito s'aombrano ... No, via, tranquilli. Mi basta questo: sapere, signori, che non è chiaro né certo neanche a voi neppur quel poco che vi viene a mano a mano determinato dalle consuetissime condizioni in cui vivete. C'è un *oltre* in tutto. Voi non volete o non sapete vederlo.[10]

I study people in their most ordinary occupations, to see if I can succeed in discovering in others what I feel that I myself lack in everything that I do: the certainty that they understand what they are doing ... But afterwards, if I stop and gaze for a moment in their eyes with my own intent and silent eyes, at once they begin to take offence ... No, go your ways in peace. This is enough for me: to know, gentlemen, that there is nothing clear or certain to you either, not even the little that is determined for you from time to time by the absolutely familiar conditions in which you are living. There is a *beyond* in everything. You do not wish or do not know how to see it.[11]

As I argued in the first chapter, *Shoot!* can be interpreted as a philosophical and phenomenological statement on film as both an art form and as a *new* means of communication in a *new* society. This novel also qualifies as a pessimistic utterance on the alienation of the machine age, a period characterized by man's loss of control over his work and a dramatic increase in human distance from the products of that work. Furthermore, this period witnessed the proliferation of mechanical reproductions of artistic works and hence the commodification of culture. Pirandello's approach to this dilemma was twofold. On the one hand, he criticized the alienating power of the machine; on the other, he recognized the machine's manifest power to reproduce things, people, and events *objectively*.

The diary form he chose for *Shoot!* derived from his deep comprehension of the machine's true nature, for as Franca Angelini maintains: 'Il diario funziona qui da omologo narrativo del cinema: registra impassibile (o almeno ci prova), ingrandisce, isola, dispone il tempo nella linea della sequenza, anticipa con un'immagine lo svolgimento dell'azione, usa il *flash-back*'[12] ('The diary functions here as a narrative strategy homologous to cinema: it records with impassibility (or at least it tries to), enlarges, isolates, organizes time along the line of the sequence, anticipates the unfolding of the action with an image, uses the *flashback*'). In fact, the novel is a diary or at least a series of notebooks written in the first person by a movie cameraman. Serafino Gubbio is a character lacking distinctive physical and psychological features as well as any apparent emotional relationship: he is passive and absent to the point of becoming, at the end of the novel, completely dumb, or rather, just a gaze close to an impassive camera lens. However, the dramatic close of the novel simply constitutes a ratification of a condition existing before and beyond the novel itself, for the narrative text is an effect of, or rather results from, that very condition, as the protagonist explains in its opening: 'Sono operatore. Ma veramente, essere operatore, nel mondo in cui vivo e di cui vivo, non vuol mica dire operare. Io non opero nulla'[13] ('I am an operator. But, as a matter of fact, being an operator, in the world in which I live and upon which I live, does not in the least mean operating. I operate nothing').[14] And again, 'Soddisfo, scrivendo, a un bisogno di sfogo, prepotente. Scarico la mia professionale impassibilità e mi vendico, anche; e con me vendico tanti, condannati come me a non essere altro, che *una mano che gira una manovella*'[15] ('I satisfy, by writing, a need to let off steam which is overpowering. I get rid of my professional impassivity, and avenge myself as well; and with myself avenge ever so many others, condemned like myself to be nothing more than *a hand that turns a handle*').[16]

The analogy that immediately establishes itself is that of the impassivity of the movie cameraman as a reflection of the objectivity of the realist narrator. Therefore, the novel ought to be studied 'in questa sua struttura cinematografica, anch'essa in anticipo e all'inizio di un lungo processo di dissoluzione dei moduli narrativi di tipo verista operata dalla narrativa del Novecento'[17] ('in its cinematographic structure, ahead of time and at the beginning of a long process of dissolution of the narrative strategies pursued by verism, a process enacted by twentieth-century narrative'). The diary form (the dissemination of the narration into fragments that do not follow a sequential chronological order) is homologous to the cinematic technique. Narrative segments are constantly manipulated, juxtaposed, and edited; the narration moves back and forth from present to past. At times, the narrator evaluates events and occurrences, while at other times he simply narrates them. Pirandello exploits this technique over and over in many of his narratives through personality doublings, and he does the same in several of his dramatic works through exploitation of a device such as that of the 'raisonneur,' as in the case of Laudisi in Così è (se vi pare) (Right You Are [If You Think So], 1917). Yet, Pirandello's narrator travels the considerable distance that separates Serafino, a still-neurotic Subject filled with melancholy, and Laudisi, a psychotic Subject virtually void of empathy.

Montage is present in both the form and content of the novel Shoot! as well as in many of Pirandello's works, for his entire opus, strongly oriented toward both reader and audience, is characterized by a search for new communicative means. The technique of montage holds distinct ideological power and is directed toward the receiver of either the literary or cinematic text. Furthermore, as Eichenbaum and Eisenstein observed, the questions posed by montage are closely linked with those regarding nature, for this technique allows the artist to illustrate the objective state of nature with the minimum of interference. Montage also permits the artist to go beyond real events and understand that oltre ('the beyond') in which, according to Pirandello, the truth about things and humanity resides.

In many ways, Shoot! is essentially an experimental novel, for by inverting the diary form of story-telling – that is, by shifting his emphasis from subjective to objective description – Pirandello allows himself to use a new approach to narrative point of view. As Frank Nulf pointedly observes, Pirandello, because of his growing interest in the cinema and his previous experiences in writing film scripts, wrote a text 'which goes considerably beyond its genre limits without, in any way, losing its poetic impact. It may be possible to say that Si gira is not really a novel at all.'[18] I agree with Nulf when he maintains that in many ways Shoot!

is already 'a film at the scenario stage; pregnant with potential and with its crucial filmic structure.'[19]

Several examples of film technique appear in the novel, which is divided into notebooks loosely corresponding both to a personal diary and to a true scenario.[20] The transitions between one book and the next are often obvious, as in the case of the passage from Notebook I (which ends with the narrator announcing his visit to the Kosmograph studios a few days after he has encountered his old friend Cocò Polacco) to Notebook II (which begins with a flashback that obviously works as a cinematic dissolve). At other times, however, the transitions are not so obvious. But a common trait can be found in most transitional techniques employed by Pirandello in this narrative text; they all share a basic cinematic quality. See, for example, the transition between Notebook II and Notebook III, which represents the equivalent of a cinematic jump-cut. After some considerations of the strange relationship between the Russian actress Varia Nestoroff and the Italian painter Giorgio Mirelli, a desperate love story that ultimately leads to the man's suicide, Notebook II concludes with Gubbio's observations about his own destiny: 'Non so perché, mi dice il cuore che, girando la manovella di questa macchinetta di presa, io sono destinato a fare anche la vostra vendetta e del vostro povero Giorgio, cara Duccella, cara nonna Rosa!'[21] ('I do not know why, my heart tells me that as I turn the handle of this photographic machine, I am destined to carry out both your revenge and your poor Giorgio's, dear Duccella, dear Granny Rosa!').[22] Without any evident transition, Pirandello opens Notebook III with the following description, clearly homologous to a cinematic jump-cut:

Un lieve sterzo. C'è una carrozzella che corre davanti.
– Pò, pòpòòò, pòòò.
Che? La tromba dell'automobile la tira indietro? Ma sì! Ecco pare che la faccia proprio andare indietro, comicamente.

Le tre signore dell'automobile ridono, si voltano, alzano le braccia a salutare con molta vivacità, tra un confuso e gajo svolazzìo di veli variopinti; e la povera carrozzella avvolta in una nuvola alida, nauseante, di fumo e di polvere, per quanto il cavalluccio sfiancato si sforzi di tirarla col suo trotterello stracco, séguita a dar indietro, indietro, con le case, gli alberi, i rari passanti, finché non scompare in fondo al lungo viale fuor di porta. Scompare? No: che! E' scomparsa l'automobile. La carrozzella, invece, eccola qua, che va avanti ancora, pian piano, col trotterello stracco, uguale, del suo cavalluccio sfiancato. E tutto il viale par che rivenga avanti, pian piano, con essa.[23]

A slight swerve. There is a one-horse carriage in front.

– '*Peu, pepeeeu, peeeu.*'

What? The horn of the motor-car is pulling it back? Why, yes! It does really seem to be making it run backwards, with the most comic effect.

The three ladies in the motor-car laugh, turn round, wave their arms in greeting with great vivacity, amid a gay, confused flutter of many-coloured veils; and the poor little carriage, hidden in an arid, sickening cloud of smoke and dust, however hard the exhausted little horse may try to pull it along with his weary trot, continues to fall behind, far behind, with the houses, the trees, the occasional pedestrians, until it vanishes down the long straight vista of the suburban avenue. Vanishes? Not at all! The motor-car has vanished. The carriage, meanwhile, is still here, still slowly advancing, at the weary, level trot of its worn-out horse. And the whole avenue seems to come forward again, slowly, with it.[24]

The reader is immediately forced to participate rather than simply contemplate the action. The concise, relevant, present-tense description of the action constitutes an example of scenario style and establishes the mood of the various shots we detect in the scene. Through a description packed with details that nevertheless leaves room for interpretation, an entire sequence unfurls, one in which at least five shots are explicitly presented and many others are implied, as Frank Nulf perceptively points out.[25] If a scenario style is used here, it is certainly not a traditional one. Although he employs literary devices, Pirandello clearly aims at constructing a text that could transcend the formula of the diary. When facing this scene, the reader is no longer conscious of reading a diary; instead, he or she participates in an action, or rather, in the viewing of a filmic scene. The senses that Pirandello intended to stimulate – sight and hearing – are united in an emotional orchestration.

Later in the novel, we learn that Gubbio was on the carriage and that the scene we have just read and 'viewed' was written as if from his vantage point. This multiplicity of viewpoints, a characteristic feature of many of Pirandello's narrative works, is emphasized in this scene: Pirandello wrote, in a scenario-like style, a description of a scene as it would appear to the eyes of Gubbio, who is a participant in the events (for he is on the carriage), a voyeur (for he sees those events as if he were looking through the lenses of his movie camera), and the narrator of the story (for he describes the scene in his diary). Thus, for the reader, the text is a multi-levelled experience. On the other hand, if the narrative truly works as a metaphor for cinematic discourse, then Gubbio can be taken also as the primeval audience. He certainly is one of Pirandello's many character-spectators. Yet Gubbio is not simply a character in and an active spectator of the story, but also the author of that story. He *writes* the diary, even if that diary, more than the nostalgic recollection of past events, assumes the form of a work in progress – almost as if both the novel and his life were 'in the making.' *Shoot!* then is 'un romanzo da fare' ('a novel in the making') as well as 'un film da fare' ('a film in the making') and ultimately also 'una vita da fare' ('a life in the making').

When one discusses the 'scenario form' or the 'cinematic treatment' of a given literary passage, one does not merely refer to the organization of the words; the meaning of such a treatment within the total context of the novel is also investigated. In this light, the use of multiple points of view in the opening scene of Notebook III, and in the whole text, stands for the cinematic nature of the work as well as pointing toward its meaning. That is to say, Gubbio is a misplaced, alienated, fragmented Subject whose diverse perspectives on life and events are recorded by the text.

Fluctuation of point of view is a device much more natural to the cinema than to any other artistic medium. Walter Benjamin, in his influential study *Das Kunstwerk im Zeitalter seiner technischen Reproduzierbarkeit*, points out that the multiplicity of points of view constitutes the foundation of cinematic discourse. He then draws a parallel between cinema and Freudian psychoanalysis, stressing how they both isolate and analyse aspects of human perception that would otherwise flow unnoticed. 'Der Film hat in der ganzen Breite der optischen Merkwelt, und nun auch der akustischen, eine ähnliche Vertiefung der Apperzeption zur Folge gehabt.'[26] ('For the entire spectrum of optical, and now also acoustical, perception the film has brought about a similar deepening of apperception.')[27] Benjamin, then, makes a comparison between cinema and painting, and between cinema and theatre, and continues as follows:

Indem der Film durch Grossaufnahmen aus dem Inventar, durch Betonung versteckter Details an den uns geläufigen Requisiten, durch Erforschung banaler Milieus unter der genialen Führung des Objektivs auf der einen Seite die Einsicht in die Zwangsläufigkeiten vermehrt, von denes unser Dasein regiert wird, kommt er auf der andern Seite dazu, eines ungeheuren und ungeahnten Spielraums uns zu versichern! ... Unter der Grossaufnahme dehnt sich der Raum, unter der Zeitlupe die Bewegung.'[28]

By close-ups of the things around us, by focusing on hidden details of familiar objects, by exploring commonplace milieus under the ingenious guidance of the camera, the film, on the one hand, extends our comprehension of the necessities which rule our lives; on the other hand, it manages to assure us of an immense and unexpected field of action ... With the close-up, space expands; with slow motion, movement is extended.[29]

As the enlargement of a detail does not simply show it bigger, but also shows totally new structures in the matter of things, so the slowing down of motion allows us to detect aspects of those movements that would otherwise remain unknown. Benjamin, as well as Eisenstein, stresses the fact that the nature which talks to and through the camera differs from the nature which addresses and is addressed by the eye – 'Anders vor allem dadurch, dass an die Stelle eines vom Menschen mit Bewusstsein durchwirkten Raums ein unbewusst durchwirkter tritt'[30] ('If only because an unconsciously penetrated space is substituted for a space consciously explored by man').[31] He concludes by saying: 'Vom Optisch-Unbewussten erfahren wir erst durch sie, wie von dem Trieb-haft-Unbewussten durch die Psychoanalyse'[32] ('The camera introduces us to unconscious optics as does psychoanalysis to unconscious impulses').[33]

It is immediately evident to any student of Pirandello how Benjamin's pronouncements show clear affinities with the dramatist's positions, for Pirandello was also quite conscious of the psychological foundation of any artistic process. Moreover, in his narrative as well as in his dramatic works, Pirandello repeatedly gave artistic status to the dissemination of points of view that stands for the multiplicity of interior voices present within the new Subject. Since the novel Subject is fragmented and disjointed, any true modern art form ought to give voice to its fragmentation and alienation. Pirandello attempted to express this new status of the Subject in both his narrative and dramatic works, as is exemplified in the novel *Uno, nessuno e centomila* (*One, Nobody, and One Hundred Thousand*, 1926), and in his most famous play, *Six Characters in Search of an Author*.

In *Shoot!*, Pirandello occasionally effaces the narrator Gubbio, as in the scene quoted above. Whenever he does so, his purpose is to immerse the reader into the scene first, and then into the character. Since Gubbio is a character-spectator, Pirandello manages to pull off this dramatic effect by substituting Gubbio's eye with the camera's eye. But the camera's viewpoint may also be assimilated into the cinematic equivalent of first-person narration. In reading the novel, we are often lured into trying to distinguish between *real* reality and *film* reality, or rather between what Gubbio sees and what the camera sees. As the novel progresses, the reader is led to realize that ultimately there is no difference at all between these two visions.

The previously quoted passage, which opens Notebook III, as well as many others in this novel, could be diagrammed so as to become a true scenario sequence divided into at least five shots. However, this characteristic is quite common to most modern narrative texts, especially the novels of Steinbeck, Hemingway, and Virginia Woolf. It is well known that Dickens's narrative style was an influence on Griffith and Eisenstein, the latter maintaining that the principles of montage were to be found in the English writer's narrative technique.[34] What makes *Shoot!* such a striking example of the employment of film techniques in a literary text is that Pirandello repeatedly switches to a writing style that is both cinematic and scenario-like. Because of the total correspondence between form and content, both the scope and the finality of Gubbio's alienation are demonstrated beyond any doubt. The perfect impassivity with which he views events – even those in which he himself is immersed – parallels the dispassioned recording of the camera lens.

One ought to note that this scenario-like style of writing normally avoids those linguistic tropes that are commonly recognized as the novel's most effective tools. This does not mean that films do not use metaphor, irony, and symbolism, but that a necessary distinction needs to be made: a trope appears in the film, not in the scenario. That is, it becomes a visual, not a literary trope, and it is thus only accessible to the filmmaker through editing. Since filmic metaphor can only be constructed through the juxtaposition of shots, 'film ... has, through the process of editing, discovered a metaphoric quality of its own.'[35] As Bluestone has observed, then, 'the two strips, joined together, become a *tertium quid*, a third thing which neither of the strips has been independently.'[36]

Quite early in cinema's life, film directors and theorists comprehended the 'creative' nature of editing, based on the discovery that when two shots are joined together the spectator may infer a variety of contrasts and comparisons between two sets of information. In his *Theory of the Film*, Béla Balázs observes that each single shot is 'saturated with the tension of a latent meaning which is released like an electric spark when the next shot is joined to it.'[37] Eisenstein goes even further: 'Two film pieces of any kind, placed together, inevitably combine into a new concept, a new quality, arising out of that juxtaposition.'[38] And in the same essay, Eisenstein states:

The juxtaposition of two separate shots by splicing them together resembles not so much a simple sum of one shot plus another shot – as it does a *creation*. It resembles a creation – rather than the sum of its parts – from the circumstance that in every such juxtaposition *the result is qualitatively* distinguishable from each component element viewed separately.[39]

The idea that unity lies in the relation between parts, and that by juxtaposing two images a totally new image is born, is already present in Pirandello's conception of artistic creation. He expressed these concepts throughout his life and work, but we find them most directly stated in the fragments collected and published by Corrado Alvaro in 1934 in the journal *Nuova Antologia* with the title 'Taccuini di Bonn e di Coazze' ('Notebooks from Bonn and Coazze'). In one of these fragments, Pirandello maintains that 'ogni unità è nelle relazioni degli elementi tra loro; il che significa che variando anche minimamente le relazioni, varia per forza l'unità'[40] ('any unit depends on the relationship of the various elements; this means that if one slightly varies the relations, the unit necessarily changes as well'). In another, he goes even further: 'Fenomeno d'associazione: si presentano le immagini in contrasto, anziché associate. Ogni immagine, ogni gruppo d'immagini desta e richiama le contrarie – che dividono lo spirito perché lo spirito non riesce a fonderle'[41] ('A phenomenon of association: images are presented by contrast not by similarity. Every image, every group of images awakens and recalls its contraries – which divide the spirit since it does not manage to harmonize them').

As I argued earlier in this study, as soon as Pirandello became interested in the moving pictures, he also felt compelled to address the critical and technical issues raised by the new medium. However, he did not address these questions in any formalized way until 1929, although he did start considering them as early as 1914 and gradually became more preoccupied with them in the years to follow. Whenever he confronted the moving pictures, however, Pirandello was primarily concerned with two major questions that became increasingly relevant to the debates on the true nature of the cinema. First and foremost, Pirandello addressed the question 'What is cinema? What is its status?' This problem obviously connects with both aesthetic and sociological issues. An example of the former appears in the question of the constitution of film into an art form and its relationship with the more traditional artistic expressions – novel and theatre – which were immediately associated with cinema even in its early days.

Quite soon Pirandello faced another important issue, one with sociological connotations: the question of the audience's diverse response to the filmic event. In fact, Pirandello soon understood that film is, first of all, an 'event,' a fact:

Non più di tempo in tempo ... o per le grandi feste o per le grandi ricorrenze religiose, il popolo è attratto agli spettacoli, ma ormai cotidianamente per una abitudine divenuta bisogno, che è frutto d'incivilimento ... Il problema di soddisfare questa cotidiana sete di spettacolo, che ormai ha il popolo, è riuscito per ora a risolverlo soltanto il cinematografo.[42]

No more from time to time ... or on occasion of major celebrations or important religious events, people are attracted by spectacles, but now it happens daily as habit has become a need that is the product of civilization ... Only the cinematograph has managed for now to satisfy this daily thirst for spectacle that people lately have.

Quite early in the history of the cinema, although within the context of the controversy between theatre and moving pictures, the Italian artist detected one of cinema's most relevant traits, its actuality as an event. As Christian Metz was to write much later: 'Pris dans son ensemble, le cinéma est d'abord un *fait*, et comme tel pose des problèmes à la psychologie de la perception et de l'intellection, à l'esthétique théorique, à la sociologie des publics, à la sémiologie générale'[43] ('Taken in its entirety, the cinema is first of all a *fact*, and as such it poses problems to the psychology of perception and interpretation, to theoretical aesthetics, to the sociology of the audience, to general semiology').

Pirandello perceptively understood the second important question that had to be answered if film were to achieve the status of a true art form: What is film theory? That is, what are its necessary features? What does or should it seek to explain? Pirandello began inquiring into these issues as early as 1914 in the novel *Shoot!*, which also explored new narrative strategies by exploiting the device of having a film in the novel, a narrative within a narrative. As Franca Angelini observes, 'Il romanzo critica dunque il cinema ma appropriandosi, e spesso ironicamente, degli stessi elementi del cinema del suo tempo'[44] ('The novel then criticizes the cinema but by appropriating, and often ironically, the very elements of the cinema of its times'). Pirandello must have been conscious of this peculiarity of his novel since, in a letter written to Anton Giulio Bragaglia in 1918, he proposed a film version of it based on the formula of the film within the film – a formula that was to be the foundation of the much later *nouvelle vague* in French cinema as well as of the narrative device Federico Fellini so thoroughly exploited in his idiosyncratic film style. The same formula also appears in the novel as 'romanzo cinematografico sul cinema romanzesco'[45] ('a cinematographic novel on narrative cinema'). Pirandello's letter to Bragaglia goes as follows:

Tutto considerato mi pare che un film adatto per la Menichelli si possa trovare nel mio romanzo *Si gira* ... la cui protagonista è una russa: *La Nestoroff*, donna fatale ecc. Verrebbe anche un film originalissimo. Il cinematografo nel cinematografo. Il dramma infatti si svolge durante la confezione di una pellicola.[46]

All things considered, it seems to me that a film for Miss Menichelli can be found in my novel *Shoot* ... whose protagonist is a Russian woman: *Miss Nestoroff*, femme fatale etc. It would also be an extremely original film. The cinematograph in the cinematograph. In fact, the drama unfolds during the making of a film.

The issues that attracted Pirandello's attention as soon as he became concerned with film were the same pressing questions faced by everyone who grew interested in the cinema. Pirandello's numerous utterances on the cinema raised some important considerations that were explored in some film theories of the period. These theories, which developed in the early days of the moving pictures, were to have a great influence on many subsequent film theories, and so constituted working models for film critics and theorists for a long time.

The principal film theories that have developed can be classified into two types: part–whole theories and theories of relation to the real.[47] Examples of the first are the theories developed by Eisenstein and Pudovkin concerning the relation between cinematic parts and wholes. Examples of the second are those of Kracauer and Bazin, which concern the relation of cinema to reality; these can be considered as one-stage theories. Eisenstein's and Bazin's theories are the most influential and complete film theories. They can also be considered as being close to actual films as well as being based on a full knowledge of cinema history. Although closeness to the subject might not seem a guarantee of a good film theory, in the case of both Eisenstein and Bazin it ensured that the theoretical concerns of each nearly always matched the questions implicitly contained in the cinematic apparatus.

Although Pirandello participated in the theoretical debates of the period, he also understood that a comprehensive theory of cinema could only be achieved by detecting the linguistic and psychological aspects of the cinematic apparatus. Even when attempting to formulate a theoretical model for both theatre and novel, Pirandello emphasized the psycholinguistic foundation of his revolutionary approach.

Much time passed before a theory in film studies appeared that would fully account for the psychological and linguistic bases of filmic discourse. In fact, it is only with the application to film of the Lacanian re-reading of Saussurean linguistics performed by Christian Metz that we obtain a theory close to what Pirandello seemed to foreshadow for cinema as well as for both novel and drama, if not organically, then certainly quite insistently.

Pirandello's statements on the cinema consist of a plethora of diversified texts, including his narrative work written in 1914, *Shoot!* (partly analysed earlier), and two major essays: 'Se il film parlante abolirà il teatro,' written in 1929,[48] and 'Il dramma e il cinematografo parlato,' ('The Drama and the Spoken Cinematograph') which appeared in print in *La Nacion*, a newspaper in Buenos Aires, on 7 July 1929.[49] In addition, Pirandello left us a speech with which he opened a convention on theatre held by the Fondazione Alessandro Volta in Rome, 8–14 October 1934. This speech was published by the Italian Royal Academy in 1935. Pirandello's discourse constitutes, first, a documentation of his constant concern with theatre, and, second, an attempt to define the role of film and theatre in society and culture. That is, Pirandello attempted to provide a global redefinition of the status these diverse forms of spectacle held in society after the introduction of new technologies.

In addition to these formal remarks on cinema and on the theatre–cinema controversy, we also find frequent and intriguing comments in articles and interviews. The most frequently cited are those contained in the previously mentioned article by Enrico Roma (1932) and in the interview printed in the newspaper *La stampa*, in Turin, on 9 December 1932, signed 'Testor' and titled 'Per il film italiano. Intervista con Luigi Pirandello' ('For Italian Cinema. Interview with Luigi Pirandello').

Although he probably began writing film scripts for financial reasons, Pirandello repeatedly sought opportunities to put his theories into practice as both a producer and a writer of screenplays. At that time, virtually everyone felt compelled to write on or for the cinema, even those who did not have the faintest idea what film was or ought to be. Pirandello often complained about the trite literary formulas that characterized Italian cinema. As a writer, but as one who had a far-seeing concept of the true nature of film, he believed that filmmakers did not give enough attention to the scenario, which, as a consequence, turned more and more into a particularly weak form of narrative, especially after the introduction of sound in film. Pirandello's theorical position in relation to this issue was thoroughly illustrated in his presentation of the scenario for *Steel*, the film that Walter Ruttmann later directed:

Una delle più gravi colpe del cinema industriale è di non dare agli scenari l'importanza che meritano. A che servono grandiosità di messinscena, bravura d'interpreti, mezzi finanziari, se non siano messi al servizio di un'idea originale, di un soggetto appassionante, umano, logico, inattaccabile?[50] ... lo scenario che ho consegnato in questi giorni alla *Cines* e che s'intitola: *Giuoca, Pietro!*, superando gli equivoci delle deleterie esperienze, vuol essere uno dei primi saggi di cinematografia parlata e sonora, secondo le mie conclusioni. Com'è stato detto, ho ambientato il dramma nelle acciaierie di Terni. La scelta, naturalmente, non è stata fatta a casaccio, con la sola intenzione di trovare una messinscena interessante e di poca spesa, ma *subordinatamente alla ideazione del soggetto*,[51] che richiede appunto una ambientazione simile. Le macchine, le maestranze, il clima di quell'industria, non entreranno nel mio film come motivi decorativi, col carattere di pezzi documentari, inseriti, secondo l'uso corrente, per dar cornice, colore, movimento esteriore al dramma; ma assolveranno un còmpito di capitale importanza, giuocheranno nella rappresentazione né più né meno che come personaggi di primo piano. *L'artista non deve servirsi delle cose, ma esprimere lo spirito delle cose.*[52]

One of the greatest faults industrial cinema has is that of not giving screenplays the importance they deserve. What are grandeur in the mise en scène, expertise of the actors, economic means there for if they are not in service of an original idea, and of thrilling, human, logical, and unreprehensible treatment? ... the script I just sent to Cines and whose title is *Play, Peter!*, in overcoming the misunderstandings created by previous negative experiences, intends to be one of the first experiments of talking and sound film, according to my conclusions. As it has been said, I staged the drama in the steel plants in Terni. Obviously the choice was not made randomly, with the only intention of finding an interesting and cheap landscape, but on the contrary *the choice was subordinated to the creation of the treatment*, which requires such an environment. The machineries, the workers, the climate of a factory will not enter my film as decorative motifs, with the character of documentaristic pieces, only inserted, according to the current habit, to provide a proper framework, colour, exterior movement to the drama; on the contrary, they will fulfil a crucial function; they will play in the representation no less than true protagonists. *The artist should not use things, but express their spirit.*

However, it was with the scenario for the film adaptation of *Six Characters in Search of an Author*, written in collaboration with Adolph Lantz, that Pirandello expected to make an effective contribution to the founding of a new poetics as well as to a new aesthetics of sound film.

Ho idea di mettermi a lavorare con il compito di creare un'opera d'arte per cinema, un'opera d'arte che sia di pura visione, completamente distinta dal linguaggio che ho impiegato finora come mezzo di esprimere la mia esperienza della vita. Il dialogo ha sempre avuto nei miei drammi una parte più importante dell'azione ... cerco di risolvere in maniera puramente ottica il problema che s'incontra nella stessa radice del mio dramma *[Sei personaggi in cerca d'autore]* ... Mi sto sforzando di rendere intelleggibile, attraverso questo senso visivo, come i *Sei personaggi* e i loro destini furono concepiti nella mente dell'autore, e imbevutisi di vita si resero indipendenti da lui. Naturalmente, questa proiezione del problema su un nuovo piano, è solo una sostituzione, una creatura ibrida ... Esso sarà perciò sperimentato dall'autore fin dal principio come una pura visione, e che può per conseguenza essere riprodotto ... Voglio indicare nuove strade al cinema. Come sarà tecnicamente possibile che queste strade risultino transitabili è ancora il mio segreto, il quale però sarà presto rivelato dal mio lavoro che daró al pubblico.[53]

I intend to labour with the goal of creating a work of art for the cinema, a work of art that is pure vision, completely different from the language I used until now as a means to express my experience of life. In my plays dialogue has always had a more important role than action ... I try to resolve in a purely optical way the problem one finds at the very heart of my drama *[Six Characters in Search of an Author]* ... Through this visual means, I am trying to make intelligible how the *Six Characters* and their destinies were conceived in the author's mind, and once infused with life they made themselves independent from him. Naturally, this projection of the problem on a new level is only a substitution, an hybrid creation ... it will be experienced by the author, from the very beginning, as pure vision, and thus can be reproduced ... I intend to indicate new avenues for the cinema. How these new avenues will be technically practicable, this is still my secret, which though will be soon revealed by the work I will give to the audience.

Several important issues need to be underlined here, for they shed light on Pirandello's complex and far-seeing view of cinema. First of all, by subtitling his scenario a 'Film-novelle,' Pirandello both highlights the brevity and concentration of the subject, and implicitly makes the receiver aware of the 'tentativo, in parte riuscito, di elaborare il soggetto in modo che il testo rimanesse fruibile anche come narrazione'[54] ('attempt, partly successful, to elaborate the treatment in a way that would allow the text to be also enjoyable as narration'). In creating a text that could still be enjoyed as narration, Pirandello entered a debate that still exists today – a debate focused on the nature of the scenario as literary text. The artist was also clearly shifting the focus of his earlier, more severe statements on cinema. At the time of his first essay on the new medium, dated 1929, he strongly opposed the tendency motion pictures had manifested up to that point to imitate previous narrative and dramatic forms. Pirandello maintained that, particularly after the introduction of sound, cinema had primarily and persistently imitated literature. He was convinced that cinema was not going to hurt theatre, but also that film was ultimately destined to die. In 'Se il film parlante abolirà il teatro' ('If the Talkies Will Abolish the Theatre'), Pirandello stated that if a future existed for cinema, it would become 'il linguaggio visibile della musica'[55] ('the visible language of music'), that is, an art of pure vision and pure sound, for which he coined the term 'cinemelografia.'[56]

In the essay 'Dramma e sonoro' ('Theatre and Talkies'), quoted above, the Italian artist slightly modified his initially orthodox position and clearly attempted to define a cinematic form of narrativity. Significantly, Pirandello underlined the fact that what needed to be explored and made visible was the process by which the characters and their respective destinies were conceived in the author's mind, and the way in which these characters finally moved away from him once they had been imbued with new life. Thus Pirandello was pointing out that since cinema is primarily a visual form, or at least has the visual element as one of its central features, what needs to be stressed first of all is the visionary quality of the event, and then its internal processes of construction and deconstruction.

In any form of modern narrative, the critical issue is not so much *not* to tell a story, but how to denounce the 'fictionality' of the narrative construct. By defining the final product, in this case the scenario, as 'hybrid,' an experience that is multidimensional and precise at the same time, Pirandello obviously comprehended that what needed to be solved was the 'very broad historical and social collusion of cinema and narrative,'[57] as Christian Metz much later defined it. I maintain that, although he first addressed the aesthetic and technical problems posed by cinema within the context of the theatre–film debate, and thus attempted to define the specific field in which each medium does or ought to operate, Pirandello quite soon detected the primary role played by the theoretical questions posed to the new medium by literary 'narrative,' that is, by the novel. He foresaw the relation that exists between the two modern forms of narrative discourse, and the migration of techniques from one to the other and back. Pirandello very likely realized that the encounter between cinema and narrativity was certainly not fortuitous, but, on the contrary, that, as Metz stated, it constituted a historical and social event, 'un fatto di civiltà' ('a fact of civilization') that could and should not be avoided. In fact, if it is true that film did not have a 'specific' language from the very beginning, but was primarily a mechanical means of registration and reproduction of visual, mobile spectacles, it is equally true that 'c'est *justement dans la mesure où le film a affronté les problèmes du récit* qu'il a été amené ... à se constituer un ensemble de procédés signifiants spécifiques'[58] ('it is *exactly in the extent to which film has dealt with problems of narrative* that it was forced to ... build a series of specific procedures of signification').

In the essay 'Dramma e sonoro,' Pirandello strengthened his previous statements on sound in film while again shifting the focus of his earlier, more rigid positions in an effort to illustrate the new avenues that had opened for cinema. Frank Nulf devotes ample space in his study of Pirandello and the cinema to the analysis of Pirandello's first essay on the motion pictures, which, even though written for different purposes, nevertheless shows his progressive, theoretical approach to the new medium. As Nulf states in the chapter 'Pirandello as Film Critic,' Pirandello's positions were quite advanced compared with opinions expressed by many of his contemporaries. Although he at first concerned himself primarily with the economic threat film posed to theatre, he was one of the few 'able to see the film as an art form'[59] and 'able to isolate those qualities which were very uniquely cinematic.'[60] While virtually everybody felt compelled to write about cinema with the appearance of the first talking movie, *The Jazz Singer* (1927), only a few intellectuals and/or directors truly worked toward creating a reasoned theory of film that would account for the technologies that had recently developed in the cinema. Pirandello soon perceived that the new cinematic techniques constituted the foundation for a novel form of narrative discourse.

Whereas Pirandello could detect some problems inherent in and provoked by the use of sound in the cinema of the period, he also promptly understood, now that moving pictures were talking, that they would never be silent again: 'Ora che il film ha parlato ... Quel silenzio è stato rotto. Non si rifà piú. Bisognerà dare adesso ad ogni costo una voce alla cinematografia'[61] ('Now that film has spoken ... That silence has been broken. It can no longer be reproduced. Now it is compulsory to give a voice to cinematography'). Unlike those purists who insisted that the only true cinema was silent cinema, Pirandello realized that it would be necessary to provide film with its proper voice. He believed that if film had at first been so foolish as to look for that voice in literature, the time had come for it to leave narration to the novel and drama to the theatre. He felt at the time that cinema should immerse itself in music: not vocal music, but music that expresses itself purely with sound. Defining sight and hearing as the two most important senses, he suggested an art of pure vision and sound, which he called *cinemelografia*, or the visible language of music.

During those lively years, many other intellectuals were expressing their ideas about film. An interesting comparison can again be established between Pirandello and Eisenstein, whose pronoucements on sound were equally original. Eisenstein maintained that the future of sound in film lay only in non-realistic uses, and that synchronized dialogue contradicted all principles, or at least all his own principles, of what good cinema should be.[62] The affinity between Eisenstein's and Pirandello's positions becomes apparent if one reads the latter's declaration of intent – which I quoted earlier – in relation to the film adaptation of *Six Characters* written in 1929. Three years later, Pirandello came back to the issue of sound in film in the interview published in *La stampa*:

Il problema del sonoro non è risolto; il cinematografo, tanto audace nella sua meccanica, divenne timidissimo davanti al sonoro e si contentò di essere una contraffazione del teatro, rinunziando così alla sua natura. Simultaneità e sintesi, che erano il suo privilegio, cedettero il posto a un'arte statica, in aperto contrasto con le leggi che esso porta dentro di sè. *Il suono è per il cinema un mezzo di suggestione, un simbolo, l'accento di tutta una orchestrazione fusa e totale, e non ha nulla a che fare con quello che noi chiamiamo dialogo.*[63]

The problem of sound is yet to be resolved; the cinematograph, so audacious in its mechanics, became extremely shy when facing sound and was satisfied with being a counterfeit of theatre, thus renouncing its own nature. Simultaneity and synthesis, which were its own privilege, gave way to a static art, in open conflict with the laws inherent in cinema. *Sound is for cinema a means of suggestiveness, a symbol*, the accent of a whole, tight and total orchestration, *and it has nothing to do with what we call dialogue.*

In 1923, the Hungarian film theorist Béla Balázs had eloquently defended the purely visual by saying: 'The gestures of visual man are not intended to convey concepts which can be expressed in words, but such inner experiences, such non-rational emotions, which would still remain unexpressed when everything that can be told has been told.'[64] This resistance to sound found a much more orthodox voice in Herbert Read, who in 1932 wrote, 'The talk interrupts the continuity of the movement, or at least delays it. We begin to listen, instead of looking. But once we consciously listen in the cinema, we might as well be in the theatre. It is difficult to see any art-form evolving from the talkie.'[65]

From Pirandello's various utterances on this subject, we can conclude that he never held such an extreme position. If he saw no future for theatrical sound in film, he also saw clearly enough that since sound had become technically possible, it was inevitable. Were film to have a voice of some kind, he would first look for it in music, and he was not alone in holding this theoretical standpoint. The affinities between film and music, from their simple content to the rhythms of their montage structure, were recognized in the early days of cinema and continue to be relevant today. Pirandello, in the good company of Béla Balázs and many others, saw these similarities in the 1920s, just as many contemporary directors, such as Ingmar Bergman,[66] still see them today. Severe, though, were the limitations that Pirandello apparently wished to impose on the cinema, since in his early essay, 'Se il film parlante abolirà il teatro,' he defined cinema as the visible language of music.

The attempts made to reflect music's moods and meanings visually in film have been and are still numerous. Nevertheless, Pirandello's dictum seems to be mirrored primarily in the cinematic forms generally considered as 'experimental' cinema. In the 1920s Europe witnessed an incredible flourishing of these experiments, such as Hans Richter's *Rhythms 21*, Viking Eggeling's *Diagonal Symphony*, and Walter Ruttman's abstract films such as *Opus 1*. In France, Germaine Dulac, with her *Disque 957*, transposed Chopin's Prelude No. 6 into visual form, and

Marcel Duchamp and Fernand Léger made films based on pure rhythm.

From a close reading of Pirandello's comments on the use of sound in film, one can detect the parallel between his attitudes and the theoretical positions expressed by the French avant-garde of the twenties. The aesthetic values he progressively applied to film in his search for a proper cinematic discourse, or rather the complex of elements that would have made film a unique art form, bear strong affinities to the values advocated by Eggeling, Duchamp, Léger, Picabia, Cocteau, Richter, Ruttman, and many others. In like manner, Pirandello conceived film as an art form into which most of the primary problems and tendencies of modern art inevitably lead. In fact, cubism, futurism, and surrealism, with their respective concern for simultaneity, form, motion, and the orchestration of dream, illusion, and reality, find logical extension in film. It is certainly no coincidence that Pirandello selected Ruttman to direct *Steel*, since, as one of the representatives of the avant-garde, Ruttman was a director whose ideas were compatible with his own.

As I mentioned earlier, however, one ought to remember that, while Pirandello was sympathetic to the experiments of the avant-garde, and presumably felt quite close to it on an ideological plane, he certainly would not have advocated, as some of them did, the complete severing of all ties to story and narrative. Pirandello had a far-seeing concept of cinema as well as of all other artistic expressions, and thus he expected film form to undergo a total renovation that would account for and make use of all the techniques available from the other arts in a synthesized, uniquely *cinematic* structure. However, he still concludes his 1929 essay by stating that only by rejecting traditional narrative and dramatic forms would filmmakers find that unique mode of discourse that can be defined as 'cinematic.'

In his 1929 essay Pirandello also presented contradictory ideas; on the one hand, he advocated that film achieve an autonomous language, while on the other, he suggested that the actors and directors of the talking films come from theatre, which seems a narrow and unrealistic requirement. Certainly others could see alternative solutions. In his *Reflections on the Cinema*, for instance, René Clair maintains that 'film actors who have never spoken before may prove more suitable for sound films than stage actors.'[67]

A major issue Pirandello addresses in 'Se il film parlante abolirà il teatro' revolves around the mechanical introduction of speech into film, by means of which, according to him, cinema more and more aims at becoming like theatre, or rather a stereotyped copy of theatre.

Se io al cinematografo non devo piú vedere il cinematografo ma una brutta copia del teatro, e devo sentir parlare incongruamente le immagini fotografate degli attori, con una voce di macchina trasmessa meccanicamente, io preferirò andarmene al teatro, dove almeno ci sono gli attori veri che parlano con la loro voce naturale. Un film parlante, che volesse aver l'ambizione di voler sostituire in tutto il teatro, non potrebbe ottenere altro effetto che quello di far rimpiangere di non aver davanti vivi e veri quegli attori che rappresentano quel tale dramma o quella tale commedia, ma la loro riproduzione fotografica e meccanica.[68]

If at the movie theatre I should no longer watch the cinematograph but a poor copy of theatre, and should listen to the incongruous talking of the photographed images of the actors, with the voice of a machine mechanically transmitted, I'd rather go to the theatre, where at least one finds true actors who speak with their natural voice. A talkie with the ambition of substituting theatre completely, would have no other effect than that of making one miss the true and living actors who represent that particular drama or that specific comedy, in face of their photographic and mechanical reproduction.

First of all, Pirandello emphasizes a few fundamental contradictions: a voice must come from a living body; images obviously cannot talk; therefore, there is a basic contrast between the events taking place outside the showing room – that is, on the screen – and those happening within it. Pirandello's early critical remarks on cinema echo those of Serafino Gubbio, the protagonist of *Shoot!*, when he comments on the film actors' painful condition. Pirandello was already observing how, in silent films, the actor plays in front of and for a machine, not for a living audience. The only difference is that in sound film, he plays for two machines instead of one. But the substance of the problem does not change. In the novel, Pirandello describes, through Gubbio's self-conscious words, the film actors' condition:

Ma non odiano la macchina soltanto per l'avvilimento del lavoro stupido e muto a cui essa li condanna; la odiano sopra tutto perché si vedono allontanati, si sentono strappati dalla comunione diretta col pubblico, da cui prima traevano il miglior compenso e la maggiore soddisfazione: quella di vedere, di sentire dal palcoscenico, in un teatro, una moltitudine intenta e sospesa seguire la loro azione *viva*, commuoversi, fremere, ridere, accendersi, prorompere in applausi.

Qua si sentono come in esilio. In esilio, non soltanto dal palcoscenico, ma quasi anche da se stessi. Perché la loro azione, l'azione viva del loro corpo *vivo*, là, sulla tela dei cinematografi, non c'è più: c'è *la loro immagine* soltanto, colta in un momento, in un gesto, in una espressione, che guizza e scompare. Avvertono confusamente, con un senso smanioso, indefinibile di vuoto, anzi di vôtamento, che il loro corpo è quasi sottratto, soppresso, privato della sua realtà, del suo respiro, della sua voce, del rumore ch'esso produce movendosi, per diventare soltanto un'immagine muta, che trèmola per un momento su lo schermo scompare in silenzio, d'un tratto, come un'ombra inconsistente, giuoco d'illusione su uno squallido pezzo di tela ... Pensa la macchinetta alla rappresentazione davanti al pubblico, con le loro ombre; ed essi debbono contentarsi di rappresentare solo davanti a lei. Quando hanno rappresentato, la loro rappresentazione è pellicola.[69]

But they do not hate the machine merely for the degradation of the stupid and silent work to which it condemns them; they hate it, first and foremost, because they see themselves withdrawn, feel themselves torn from that direct communion with the public from which in the past they derived their richest reward, their greatest satisfaction: that of seeing, of hearing from the stage, in a theatre, an eager, anxious multitude follow their *live* action, stirred with emotion, tremble, laugh, become excited, break out in applause.

Here they feel as though they were in exile. In exile not only from the stage, but also in a sense from themselves. Because their action, the *live* action of their *live* bodies, there, on the screen of the cinematograph, no longer exists: it is *their image* alone, caught in a moment, in a gesture, an expression, that flickers and disappears. They are confusedly aware, with a maddening, indefinable sense of emptiness, that their bodies are so to speak subtracted, suppressed, deprived of their reality, of breath, of voice, of the sound that they make in moving about, to become only a dumb image which quivers for a moment on the screen and disappears, in silence, in an instant, like an unsubstantial phantom, the play of illusion upon a dingy sheet of cloth. ... The machine is responsible for the performance before the public, with their phantoms; and they have to be content with performing only before it. When they have performed their parts, their performance is film.[70]

As this important quotation proves, as early as 1914 Pirandello already recognized at least two basic problems any student of film must face. He questioned the issues revolving around the so-called 'illusion of reality' which the film event eventually does or does not produce, and he also addressed the problem of the 'image–viewer relationship.'

Pirandello eventually understood that the 'illusion of reality' and the peculiar relationship the viewer enjoys with the film image constitute the two basic problems film theory has to address in its attempt to define the 'specifico filmico.' In this sense, Pirandello unconsciously anticipated future developments in other disciplines, notably in a psychoanalytic approach to art, where the focus of inquiry shifted from reality–image interaction to image–viewer interaction.

In his essay *Das Kunstwerk im Zeitalter seiner technischen Reproduzierbarkeit*, Walter Benjamin meticulously studies the loss of 'aura' that, in his opinion, characterizes any modern form of artistic expression. According to Benjamin, the loss of the aura represents one of the most relevant effects resulting from the invention of photography and, later, of cinema. The condition of loss, though, does not simply apply to the work of art. Benjamin states that, because mechanical reproduction naturally constitutes a basic feature of the filmic event, the actors themselves experience a loss – the loss of their unique *hic et nunc*, which traditional aesthetics considered as the true foundation of a work of art.

Noch bei der höchst vollendeten Reproduktion fällt eines aus: das Hier und Jetz des Kunstwerks – sein einmaliges Dasein an dem Orte, an dem es sich befindet ... Das Hier und Jetz des Originals macht den Begriff seiner Echtheit aus ... Der gesamte Bereich der Echtheit entzieht sich der technischen – und natürlich nicht nur technischen – Reproduzierbarkeit.[71]

Even the most perfect reproduction of a work of art is lacking in one element: its presence in time and space, its unique existence at the place where it happens to be ... The presence of the original is the prerequisite to the concept of authenticity ... The whole sphere of authenticity is outside technical – and, of course, not only technical – reproducibility.[72]

Benjamin adds that this is also true for landscapes and for any other natural object. He concludes by stating that 'was aber dergestalt ins Wanken gerät, das ist die Autorität der Sache ... Man kann, was hier ausfällt, im Begriff der Aura zusammenfassen un sagen: was im Zeitalter der technischen Reproduzierbarkeit des Kunstwerks verkümmert, das ist seine Aura'[73] ('what is really jeopardized ... is the authority of the object ... One might subsume the eliminated element in the term 'aura' and go on to say: that which withers in the age of mechanical reproduction is the aura of the work of art').[74]

It is interesting to note that in analysing the alienating experience film actors undergo, Benjamin used Pirandello and his novel *Shoot!* to support his position, notwithstanding the ideological distance that separates the German from the Italian intellectual. Benjamin observes that although Pirandello primarily emphasizes the negative aspects that the film experience presents for actors and for virtually everybody else involved in it (director, audience, and more importantly in *Shoot!*, the operator), his observations are nevertheless valuable:

Es beeinträchtigt die Bemerkungen, die er [Pirandello] in seinem Roman *Es wird gefilmt* darüber macht, nur wenig, dass sie sich darauf beschränken, die negative Seite der Sache hervorzuheben. Noch weniger, dass sie an den stummen Film anschliessen. Denn der Tonfilm hat an dieser Sache nichts Grundsätzliches geändert. Entscheiden bleibt, dass für eine Apparatur – oder, im Fall des Tonfilms, für zwei – gespielt wird.[75]

Though his remarks on the subject [the loss of the aura for the actor who has to play in front of one or two machines instead of in front of a real audience, an audience that is instead given just an optic test, the performance of a machine] in his novel *Si gira* ... were limited to the negative aspects of the question and to the silent film only, this hardly impairs their validity. For in this respect, the sound film did not change anything essential. What matters is that the part is acted not for an audience but for a mechanical contrivance – in the case of the sound film, for two of them.[76]

Since the introduction of sound did not basically change the condition of the actor within the filmic event, as Benjamin notes, Pirandello's remarks preserve their value and relevance in relation to the embarrassing condition the actor experiences in the process of filmmaking. In sound as well as in silent films, actors face only a machine instead of confronting a living audience and eventually interacting with it.

Almost twenty years before Benjamin wrote his influential essay, Pirandello, in his artistic and critical writings, expressed a concept that qualifies the condition of the modern Subject. Because of film, humans found themselves acting with their entire, living body, and yet were compelled to renounce their 'aura.' For if the 'aura' results from a unique *hic et nunc*, the mechanical reproduction of humans' moving and speaking body presents only an image which, by being reproduced over and over in different places and at different times but in the same way, has necessarily lost its original uniqueness. Furthermore, as Benjamin, and Pirandello before him, understood, because of the devastating presence of the machine in place of the audience within the film studio, what ultimately gets lost is not simply the aura of the actor but also that of the character. It should be remembered that Pirandello inquired into this complex problem of the character's loss of aura in his revolutionary theatre, especially in *Six Characters in Search of an Author*, for which he so strongly pursued the translation into film.

In his metatheatrical works, from *Six Characters* to *I giganti della montagna* (*The Giants of the Mountain*, 1930–3), Pirandello proposed that the character exit his own being, enter the Other, and recognize the Other as Subject, or, in Lacanian terms, as the true place of subjectivity. In the last phase of his theatrical career, Pirandello hoped for the character to experience an intimate regression from the symbolic scene to the imaginary scene, or to the completely private space of his or her own unconscious. In *The Giants of the Mountain*, the Scalognati's villa perfectly represents that isolated place in which, thanks to the vanishing of the reality principle, it is possible to bring the total liberation of the Imaginary to completion. Those figures bustling in and out of that strange place are simply phantasmatic presences – puppets suddenly moving, shadows projected from the unconscious onto the wall of the villa, which obviously works as a huge screen. In other words, they are 'mere iniziative audiovisive' ('mere audiovisual events'), as Paolo Puppa defines them in his book *Fantasmi contro giganti*. Puppa also maintains that Pirandello's theatre, like all modern theatre, has undergone 'un processo inarrestabile di erosione e di corruzione del proprio statuto logico-ontologico' ('an unstoppable process of erosion and corruption of its own logical and ontological condition'). He continues by suggesting that theatre has given way to another expressive medium, the cinema, which is culturally and socially more suitable for sustaining the contradiction existing 'tra personaggio disgregato nei propri fantasmi e la necessità ultima di uno spazio comunicativo'[77] ('between the character disintegrated in its own phantoms and the profound necessity of a communicative space').

In his essay, Walter Benjamin also states: 'Das Befremden des Darstellers vor der Apparatur, wie Pirandello es schildert, ist von Haus aus von der gleichen Art wie das Befremden des Menschen vor seiner Erscheinung im Spiegel'[78] ('The feeling of strangeness that overcomes the actor before the camera, as Pirandello describes it, is basically of the same kind as the estrangement felt before one's own image in the mirror').[79] Thus Benjamin recognizes Pirandello's fundamental understanding of the psychological basis of the discomfort the actor experiences in front of the camera. It is the same kind of uneasiness man experiences whenever confronted with his image in a mirror. The mirror, in turn, becomes one of the objects most obsessively used by Pirandello's characters in their processes of self-analysis and self-recognition.[80] The particular sense of unease Benjamin talks about, however, was most specifically and thoroughly analysed by Pirandello in a narrative work, *One, Nobody, and One Hundred Thousand*, which, although it preceded the 1929 essay on sound film, can nevertheless be extremely helpful in understanding his attitude toward the new medium.

From a close analysis of his artistic and critical writings, then, we realize that through an almost obsessive inquiry into the true nature of narrative and dramatic discourses, Pirandello actually attempted to provide an artistic form and a theoretical response to the loss of aura in art that, on a psychological and sociological level, corresponds to the loss of a unified identity that modern man experienced and still experiences. This loss stands as the true foundation of the cinematic experience, a fact that explains Pirandello's concern with a definition of the specific contours of the new medium.

In the nineteenth century, profound mutations in our perception of the world and our place in the 'order of things' occurred. Revolutionary discoveries forever modified our relationship to nature as well as the rapport between reality and its artistic representation. In the mid-1800s, artists grew deeply aware of the unrecoverable fracture which had occurred in the perfect synthesis between object and subject that had stood as a foundation of earlier dramatic and narrative forms. In his study of modern drama,[81] Peter Szondi maintains that such a fundamental crisis was due to the introduction of an epic element, 'die Episierung des Dramas'[82] ('the tendency toward the epic in Drama'),[83] in a still-traditional form to produce the relativization of the absolute. With the apparition of the narrator on stage, an epic relationship substitutes the traditional dramatic conventions, one of the characters becomes a reflection and a true projection of the author, and the others become his or her objects. Szondi maintains that this 'epic relativization' is due to the split of the synthesis between subject and object that was typical of drama: the two terms enter into an oppositional relationship;[84] one of the characters becomes a reflection, or rather a true projection of the author's 'I,' and the others become its object. With the appearance of the figure of the narrator or the Pirandellian 'raisonneur' on the stage, an epic relationship is then substituted for the traditional dramatic one.[85]

Da die Entwicklung in der modernen Dramatik vom Drama selber wegführt, ist bei ihrer Betrachtung ohne einen Gegenbegriff nicht auszukommen. Als solcher stellt sich 'episch' ein: es bezeichnet einen gemeinsamen strukturellen Zug von Epos, Erzählung, Roman und anderen Gattungen, nämlich das Vorhandensein dessen, was man das 'Subjekt der epischen Form' oder das 'epische Ich' genannt hat.[86]

Since modern theatrical works develop out of and away from the Drama itself, this development must be considered with the help of a contrasting concept. 'Epic' will serve here. It designates a common structural characteristic of the epos, the story, the novel, and other genres – namely, the presence of that which has been referred to as the 'subject of the epic form' or the 'epic I.'[87]

The crisis of drama, which, according to Szondi, begins around 1860, is precisely the result, then, of the appearance of an epic theme within a still-traditional form. Several attempts to solve this crisis occurred from Ibsen to Chekhov, and from Strindberg to Maeterlinck and Hauptmann. However, it was only with Pirandello and, later, Bertolt Brecht, that the European theatrical scene found two of its most original and influential protagonists. In many ways, as Wladimir Krysinski remarks in his latest study on Pirandello, *Le paradigme inquiet. Pirandello et le champ de la modernité,*

Pirandello est un vecteur significatif en amont et en aval de ces differentes modélisations narratives ou théâtrales du réel et de l'oeuvre dans la mesure où son discours, plus qu'aucun autre, fait éclater les codes thématiques et formels.[88]

Pirandello is a significant vector at the beginning and at the end of the diverse narrative and theatrical modalities of reality and of the work of art insofar as his discourse, more than any other's, makes formal and thematic codes explode.

In Pirandello's theory and praxis, it is thus possible to trace a typical series of problematic categories such as 'l'humorisme, le perspectivisme, l'ironie, la fragmentation, l'autoréflexivité, l'autothématisme, le centomilisme'[89] ('humor, perspectivity, irony, fragmentation, self-reflexivity, self-thematism, proliferation'), which shed light on the role and place of the author's work in a general history of the theatre. Krysinski continues by suggesting that Pirandello's theatrical theory and praxis are historically identified both in the long-term perspectives of Cervantes and Shakespeare and the romantic irony, and in the short-term perspective of 'modern' theatre – expressionism, dadaism, and surrealism, futurism, the theatre of the absurd, Antonin Artaud's theatre of cruelty, and even the theatre of Bertolt Brecht.[90] If it is true that the main antinomy inherent in dramatic art is that between text and performance, it is also true that this paradox has haunted and to a certain extent still troubles most of the dramatists in our century. As a matter of fact, Krysinski remarks, the development of twentieth-century theatre records various attempts either to accentuate the irreconcilable nature of the antinomy, or to harmonize it.

Pirandello's theory and practice actually centre around the conflict between drama and theatre – that is, text and performance/mise en scène – without ever solving it. Brecht's work focuses primarily on dramaturgy; that is, it centres around the many problems of the mise en scène. These distinct solutions are primarily due to different views of the relationship between theatre and society, and ultimately to dissimilar concepts of History. Notwithstanding these many differences, it is, however, possible to maintain that Pirandello's metatheatre – or, better, the peculiar meeting of theatre and metatheatre at work in his famous trilogy, but especially in *Questa sera si recita a soggetto (Tonight We Improvise)* – certainly opened the way to the theatre of the absurd,[91] but also, and more importantly, to political theatre, and thus to the theatre of Brecht.

The apparently arbitrary operation of placing Pirandello and Brecht next to each other seems less arbitrary now that a number of critics have opened the way for and sustained a discussion that is still to be thoroughly developed, the implications of which doubtless aid our understanding of twentieth-century dramatic and narrative art forms.[92] A comparative study of Pirandello's and Brecht's theoretical positions on theatre must have seemed a deflection, to say the least, for the audience in Venice that listened to Paolo Chiarini presenting his now well-known essay 'Brecht and Pirandello' at the International Congress of Pirandellian Studies in 1961.

Chiarini's opening remark on the one-sidedness of the search for influence and symmetry in Pirandello and Brecht is still substantial. Obviously, to talk about Brecht's influence on Pirandello would not be a strongly rooted discourse. Yet, as Chiarini points out, Brecht's name was already known in Italy by virtue of special mentions in various studies of German contemporary theatre published between 1925 and 1930 (Vincenti 1925; Mazzucchetti 1926; Rocca 1932; Spaini 1930). Moreover, Brecht's *Dreigroschenoper* was brought to the Italian stage in 1929 and 1930 by Anton Giulio Bragaglia at the Teatro degli Indipendenti in Rome and the Teatro dei Filodrammatici in Milan.

It seems, however, that Pirandello was not affected by all this, although he *was* influenced by the classics of German literature and, in particular, by Lessing and Goethe. We also know that Pirandello was well acquainted with the most prominent figures of German romanticism, such as Friederick Schlegel and Ludwig Tieck.[93] As Chiarini observes, even in Pirandello's well-known essay, 'Teatro nuovo e teatro vecchio' ('New and Old Theater'), a revised version of a lecture that he delivered in Venice in July 1922, there was no shift in perspective. Instead of commenting on the new currents in German theatre, Pirandello made references to 'classic' European authors such as Sardou and Becque, Bataille, Bernstein, and Ibsen. Chiarini closes the opening section of his study by stating that Brecht's influence on Pirandello could hardly have had any foundation, and this would be corroborated by the fact that interest in Brecht's work is a quite recent phenomenon in Italy.

Chiarini, however, failed to notice that in those years, and precisely in 1926, Pirandello did comment on the new tendencies in German theatre in an interview he gave to the *Neue Zürcher Zeitung*, as André Bouissy rightly remarks in his essay 'Pirandello et le théâtre de son temps (notes de lecture)' published in 1978 in *Lectures Pirandelliennes*. After stating his aversion toward the new trends in German theatre as they were developing at that time, a time also characterized by the final decline of expressionism, Pirandello remarked, 'si je peut me permettre une critique: la nouvelle orientation de l'art dramatique ne me plaît guère. Je veux dire l'orientation suivie par les *tendenzstück* – pièces engagées et autres *lehrstück*, pièces didactiques'[94] ('if you allow me a criticism: I totally dislike the new orientation of dramatic art. I mean the direction taken by the *tendenzstück* – committed plays and by the other *lehrstück*, didactic plays'). If not influenced by the new German theatre, Pirandello must at least have been acquainted with some of the new authors.

While Bouissy agrees with Chiarini on the improbability of an influence of Brecht's theoretical and dramatic writings on Pirandello, he dismisses the possibility of an influence of the Italian on the German, which, according to Bouissy, may only be found in one of Brecht's plays, *Mann ist Mann*, written in 1924–5 and first staged in 1926. Bouissy's assertion is, unfortunately, born out of the historic prejudice that pervades so large a section of the scholarship on Brecht's work and that recognizes two separate moments in it: the lyric and the Marxist.

Conversely, there is no discontinuity between the two moments, and Brecht's work is characterized by a progression toward a thoroughly materialistic vision of both historical processes and artistic production.

I share Chiarini's opinion that the question of the Italian's influence on the German is complex and intriguing. The domain of influence is slippery and one that I do not want to address directly. But the presence of a common background, the existence of a precise cultural context in which Pirandello's work and its *fortuna* can be considered as a basic and fundamental element, is unquestionable. Pirandello's work found in Germany a most suitable terrain, partly due to the intellectual links he established during his university years in Bonn, partly to his knowledge of German culture and literature, and partly because his theatre was centred on issues that were mostly congenial to German theatre. His plays were staged in Germany immediately after their premières in Italy. In the mid-twenties, Max Reinhardt staged three of the most famous of Pirandello's plays in Berlin: *Six Characters in Search of an Author* (1924), *The Pleasure of Honesty* (1925), and *Vestire gli ignudi* (*To Dress the Naked*, 1926). It is also well known that Brecht was then a collaborator, although not a very attentive one, with Reinhardt. It must be remembered that even the German tournée of the Pirandellian 'Teatro d'Arte,' with its performance of *Six Characters in Search of an Author* in Italian at the Berlin 'Staatstheater,' was an incredible success. Such success continued, and soon reached even Austria, thanks to Max Reinhardt's staging of *Six Characters* in Vienna in 1924 and 1934.[95]

Quite interestingly, this is loosely the decade that would be most inspiring to a discussion of Pirandello's and Brecht's dramatic texts and theoretical writings on the theatre. The fact that this decade was a uniquely fertile period in the friendship between Bertolt Brecht and Walter Benjamin is of particular interest. In his essay on the work of art in the age of technical reproduction, and in discussing the loss of the aura produced in an actor's performance in the passage from theatre to cinema, Benjamin cites Pirandello and his novel *Shoot!* as the first examples of an awareness of the alienating nature of mechanical reproduction, disregarding the obvious ideological differences between Pirandello's position and his own as quite irrelevant for his analysis. Benjamin further comments:

Da gerade ein Dramatiker, wie Pirandello, in der Charakteristik des Films unwillkürlich den Grund der Krise berührt, von der wir das Theater befallen sehen, ist nicht erstaunlich.[96]

It is not surprising that it should be a dramatist such as Pirandello who, in characterizing the film, inadvertently touches on the very crisis in which we see the theatre.[97]

It is interesting to remember that, within their similar progression from poetry to narrative writings and to theatre, Pirandello and Brecht also developed a growing interest in the Seventh Art both as an autonomous form of expression and means of communication, and as an integral part of their dramatic constructions.

It is irrelevant at this time to establish a sort of genetic descendance of Brecht from Pirandello and vice versa based on real chronology, no matter how intriguing and inspirational such a study would be, as it would unquestionably open up new avenues for a critical investigation of twentieth-century theatre. It seems vital instead to contribute to a discussion on the differences and similarities of intents between Pirandello and Brecht, the protagonists of the two major revolutions in modern and contemporary theatre. Such an investigation should include their dramatic, narrative, and theoretical writings, since Pirandello and Brecht were strongly committed to both theory and practice, and both were decisively interested in defining a new *koiné*, linguistic as well as cultural. As dramatists, they were both engaged in revolutionizing the Aristotelian dramatic unities and the illusionistic stage; as theorists they were both occupied with looking for a solution to the dichotomy between art and life, and with defining the role of art in society.

To comment on a platitude in the evaluation of Pirandello's complex *Weltanschauung* becomes a necessary step. The position of those who remark on Pirandello's lack of historical awareness appears to be problematic. More than lacking an awareness of the historical period, Pirandello did not have a clearly defined and stated political ideology or an understanding of the division in classes within society and of the necessity to overcome class differences. He was perhaps lacking that awareness of the need for social change and progress that was a constant concern for Brecht. In many ways, then, Pirandello is the poet of the crisis of the bourgeois subject, but not of the bourgeois ideology. However, one ought to remember that he eventually came to make important statements on the alienating power of the age of mechanical reproduction, and these statements are strikingly parallel to some of Brecht's most famous arguments. For instance, both Pirandello and Brecht start with 'void' characters – that is, characters without interior motivation (for example, Mattia Pascal in Pirandello's *The Late Mattia Pascal*, and

Galy Gay in Brecht's *Mann ist Mann*) – but while Brecht fills his character(s) through a positive process of historicization, Pirandello records the negativity of the character's coming to an awareness of the historical processes.

If the major working dichotomy in Pirandello's *Weltanschauung* is that between life and form, History can be considered 'pirandellianamente,' the supreme type of Form, and thus a form of Death; if the 'word' becomes the sign of an achieved awareness of the historical condition of modern man, then no choice is left to the Pirandellian subject but silence and even aphasia. Thus, with painful awareness, the Father in *Six Characters in Search of an Author* states:

Ma se é tutto qui il male! Nelle parole! Abbiamo tutti dentro un mondo di cose; ciascuno un suo mondo di cose! E come possiamo intenderci, signore, se nelle parole ch'io dico metto il senso e il valore delle cose come sono dentro di me; mentre chi le ascolta, inevitabilmente le assume col senso e col valore che hanno per sé, del mondo com'egli l'ha dentro? Crediamo d'intenderci; non c'intendiamo mai![98]

But don't you see that the whole trouble lies here! In words, words! Each one of us has within him a whole world of things, each man of us his own special world! And how can we ever come to an understanding if I put in the words I utter the sense and value of things as I see them; while you who listen to me must inevitably translate them according to the conception of things each one of you has within himself? We think we understand each other, but we never really do![99]

Soon afterwards, he arrives at his desperate cry born out of an achieved awareness of the alienating and alienated condition of modern man,

Il dramma per me è tutto qui, signore: nella coscienza che ho, che ciascuno di noi – veda – si crede 'uno' ma non è vero: è 'tanti', signore, 'tanti', secondo tutte le possibilità d'essere che sono in noi: 'uno' con questo, 'uno' con quello – diversissimi![100]

For the drama lies all in this – in the conscience that I have, that each one of us has. We believe this conscience to be a single thing, but it is many-sided. There is one for this person, and another for that. Diverse consciences. So we have this illusion of being one person for all, of having a personality that is unique in all our acts. But it isn't true.[101]

Such examples abound in Pirandello's narrative writings as well, and one need only remember the alienation of the cameraman as soon as he realizes he is only a hand turning a handle – Serafino Gubbio, the protagonist of Pirandello's *Notebooks of Serafino Gubbio, Cameraman*, eventually decides *to become* just a hand turning a handle. This, I believe, is an act of social revolt, like Moscarda's decision to retreat from social life in *One, Nobody and One Hundred Thousand*; moreover, by the time Pirandello arrives at the *miti*, that is, his so-called 'theatre of the myths,' he has already perfected his social and political critique and moved progressively toward the idea of a utopian society.[102]

At this point, it is useful to remember that parallel discussions of Pirandello and Brecht truly began in the early 1960s when an interest in Brecht's work developed in Europe, particularly in Italy and France. At the time, the European stage experienced a crisis that in France, for instance, was due to a rapidly growing interest in the avant-garde cinema of the *nouvelle vague*, an artistic expression that seemed to represent the needs and desires of the bourgeoisie more effectively than theatre.[103] This leads us to consider the relationship between theatre and society in the twentieth century. Regardless of what the intentions of its authors were, in our times theatre was and is a form of entertainment for a cultivated audience, for the audience Pirandello wished to have for his 'Teatro d'Arte.' One must not forget that Brecht's theatrical theory and practice do contain an intrinsic contradiction – that is, Brecht staged a proletarian subject and addressed, whether consciously or not, a bourgeois one (while Pirandello overtly staged and addressed the bourgeois subject). Such contradiction between form and message, between a provocative thesis and its aesthetic fruition by a bourgeois audience, is particularly at work in one of Brecht's most famous plays, *Die Dreigroschenoper*. The summa of Brecht's paradigms on the relationship between art and society often registers the impossibility of reaching the audience he set himself out to address. Also, it must be noted that Brecht's historicism was a 'problematic' one because of his historical pessimism. Brecht's position was somehow different from that of Erwin Piscator, for instance, who was the most sincere and in many ways the most outstanding among the German disciples of the Proletkult, the Soviet Cultural and Educational Organization, and the only dramatist who perhaps nearly accomplished the Marxist dream of a political theatre.[104]

In the sixties, the European theatrical scene was faced with obsolete dramatic forms and the impossibility of recomposing the rapport between theatre and society. Thus, at a time in which European society was undergoing a general politicization, so did the theatre also participate in this, and, in need of an intellectual Father, sought to find one in Bertolt Brecht. Unfortunately, the most exterior aspects of Brechtian dramatic theory were often embraced (for example, acting techniques and stage directions); by pursuing merely a political reading of Brecht's propositions, contemporary theatre fundamentally betrayed, and eventually 'killed,' the newlyfound Father. As a matter of fact, one of the major points of Brecht's dramatic theory and practice – the deliberate unseating of the supremacy of tragedy and tragic inevitability – was often forgotten. On the contrary, it is in this awareness of the impossibility of tragedy that Pirandello and Brecht can be most profitably compared. As Giorgio Barberi Squarotti has rightly observed, 'Il discorso di Pirandello ... è anzitutto la dichiarazione della morte della tragedia come genere'[105] ('Pirandello's discourse is first of all the declaration of the death of tragedy as genre'). Since tragedy exists only outside the bourgeois dimension of theatrical fiction, in Pirandello's trilogy one is faced not simply with a formulaic 'theatre in the theatre,' but with the refusal to reduce the tragic to the pure spectacle of the mise en scène in the symbolic and abstract space of the theatre. Pirandello goes even further by proving that, since tragedy is no longer possible as genre, then it cannot even have an author, or be rehearsed on stage. Thus, the tragic destiny of the six characters, for instance, is not repeatable. What is repeatable is only theatre, the norm, the rite. As Barberi Squarotti remarks, 'Pirandello risponde così alle rinascite e alle riscritture delle tragedie classiche quali il primo novecento offre, soprattutto a opera di D'Annunzio'[106] ('This is Pirandello's answer to the rebirths and rewritings of classical tragedies offered by the early twentieth century, mostly thanks to D'Annunzio').

As Paolo Chiarini has outlined on more than one occasion, but especially in his previously mentioned essay on Pirandello and Brecht, another interesting field of investigation concerns Brecht's renowned *Verfremdungseffekt* and Pirandello's search for aesthetic distance, which is immediately linked to his discussion of 'humour.' Pirandello intended to represent man in his incongruence and internal division – to portray the tragic inevitability of the impossibility of recomposing the unity, and thus the aura, of the tragic hero. In Pirandello's world, the sky has been irreparably torn apart, and Orestes will forever be Hamlet. Thus, Pirandello's narrative and dramatic works become the place in which the awareness of the rupture between man and nature, and of the interior division of man, produces infinite reflections and mirrorings until a polyphony of voices finally prevails. On the contrary, Brecht attempts to retrieve what, in Pirandello's vision, is no longer recoverable, that is, the unity of the epic hero. Such a unity is not searched for and then realized via the purging of emotions through empathy with the stirring fate of the hero. As Walter Benjamin has observed,[107] Brecht's drama eliminated the Aristotelian catharsis that was at the very basis of old theatrical forms such as naturalist drama. On the contrary, the art of Brecht's 'epic theatre' consists of producing astonishment rather than empathy. The task of epic theatre is not the development of actions but the representation – or, better, the discovery – of the conditions of life through what has been problematically translated in English as 'alienation,' and instead finds in both French ('distanciation') and Italian ('straniamento') a much better, if not completely satisfactory, translation. Thus, Brechtian alienation uses didactic interruption,[108] obtained in diverse ways, such as acting techniques, stage directions, and an effective use of multimediality as a means of recomposing the unity of the epic hero.

Pirandello's stage, on the contrary, is the locus of an unresolved conflict between modernist interruption and postmodernist 'jouissance de répétition,'[109] since, in his conception, the co-existence of contraries destroys the very unity of the Subject that is no longer the place of true identity and integrity. Brecht attempts to recompose such a unity, giving back to the character its integrity via a process of social recognition and self-reflection. As Romano Luperini has pointed out in his discussion of the birth of the character in Pirandello's narrative works, particularly in *The Late Mattia Pascal*, in Pirandello *acronia* prevails – that is, the condition of the *personaggio* who has renounced being or becoming *persona*.[110] I would like to suggest that, on the contrary, in Brecht, synchronicity prevails – that is, the condition of the *personaggio* who is or becomes *persona*. Brecht's characters live, while Pirandello's see themselves live (Mattia Pascal vs. Galy Gay; Mother vs. Mother Courage). While Brecht's stage is a historical place where 'reality' reigns, Pirandello's characters move at the *borders* – or, better, as Cotrone puts it in *The Giants of the Mountains*, 'Siamo qua come agli orli della vita, Contessa. Gli orli, a un comando, si distaccano; entra l'invisibile: vaporano i fantasmi'[111] ('We stand here as though at borders of life, Countess. At a command, the borders pull away, the invisible enters: the phantoms evaporate'). It is from the Pirandellian *oltre*, an area of penumbra between life and death, that his characters un/rest.

Brecht's work shows from the outset the intention of shattering the illusion and stopping the spectator from being swept away by the story, the characters, the actors who represent them on the stage, 'and/or the naturalistic devices with which that stage set out to make their representation truly life-like.'[112] But it is not until 1937 that Brecht starts talking about the *Verfremdungseffekt* in a long essay entitled 'Verfremdungseffekte in der chinesischen Schauspielkunst.'[113] Here the expression *Verfremdungseffekt* appears to be a literal translation of Victor Shklovsky's term *Priëm Ostraneniya*, that is, 'the device (or trick, theatrical effect) of making strange' that is part of the Russian formalist literary theory. Thus, Brecht's *Verfremdungseffekt* did not have much to do with the political-philosophical-psychological aspects of *Entfremdung* or 'Alienation' as used by perhaps too many writers. As John Willett points out in his *Brecht in Context*, 'For Brecht it was a matter rather of perception and understanding: or gaining new insights into the world around us by glimpsing it in a different and previously unfamiliar light.'[114] Obviously, this is a concept that can be traced back long before the Russian formalists, and its basic idea is of art as a means of productive reorientation, making 'familiar objects to be as if they were not familiar,' or 'to make the strange familiar and the familiar strange.'[115] By doing so, Brecht wished to restore the audience's capacity to act in society, and thus in history, and in this effort he looked to Marxist ideology.

Nothing is more useful to a discussion of the differences between Brecht's *Verfremdungseffekt* and Pirandello's concept of 'humour' than one of Brecht's most familiar examples: 'To see one's mother as a man's wife one needs an A-effect; this is provided, for instance, when one acquires a stepfather.' The parallel here is all too obviously established with Pirandello's *Six Characters in Search of an Author*, but while in the German author one faces a merely theatrical effect meant to make the familiar strange, for Pirandello the familiar is, in fact, strange, and moreover it is the very subject matter of the play. In most of his dramatic as well as narrative works, Pirandello aimed at expressing what Freud defined as *Unheimlichkeit*, the *dépaysement* provoked in the Subject by the awareness of belonging to the Chaos and actually producing the liberation of difference instead of a process of identification.

According to Pirandello, estrangement, thus, is both necessary and functional. The paper sky has been torn apart, and his characters live in a universe of arbitrary signs, a universe in which the Subject is lonely, unbound, and raving. On the one hand, for Pirandello, alienation is a necessary, or better, a basic condition of the Subject who can no longer make sense of reality, and through continuous mirrorings, reflections, and doublings records the impossibility of closing the hermeneutic circle. On the other hand, Pirandello also proposes the so-called humoristic division ('divisione umoristica') as a functional element of the artistic creation that produces a number of real and true *Verfremdungseffekten* in both his narrative and dramatic works.[116] An analysis of the various kinds of A-effects in Pirandello's dramatic as well as narrative works would be challenging and quite beneficial. Such an investigation may show how Pirandello in many ways anticipated Brecht, and perhaps even inspired him, since it is certainly in that overturning of the tragic, in that pulling away the spectator from the illusion and out of the 'magic ring' which centuries of tradition had made him/her used to, that Pirandello's main objective ought to be found. It is easy to see, then, parallels with that *Verfremdungseffekt* the young Brecht was at the time elaborating, perhaps even inspired by Pirandello's example. As Michele Cometa suggests in his *Il teatro di Pirandello in Germania*, 'Brecht avrebbe strappato gli spettatori alla loro letargica illusione con la riflessione, mentre Pirandello ... riuscirà con la violenza'[117] ('Brecht would pull away spectators from their lethargic illusion with reflection, while Pirandello ... will manage with violence').

Another significant aspect that one ought to remember is that the overcoming of the fourth wall, which in Brecht's case is primarily achieved through stage directions, acting techniques, and various forms of interference, is accomplished by Pirandello, particularly in his trilogy, via the invasion of the orchestra, the involvement of the spectator in the event, the 'theatralization' of life itself. In his insightful analysis of *Tonight We Improvise*, Lucio Lugnani maintains that in this play 'l'*apparire*[118] e l'*essere*[119] si scambiano continuamente le parti, la scena e il retroscena debordano nella sala e nel ridotto e viceversa, si parla indebitamente nella sala e nel retroscena mentre si tace sulla scena, ossia nell'unico luogo da cui possa levarsi legittimamente una voce durante lo spettacolo'[120] ('*appearing* and *being* exchange roles continuously, stage and backstage invade the orchestra and the foyer and vice versa, people talk unlawfully in the orchestra and in the backstage while silence prevails on the stage, that is in the only place where a voice can legitimately arise during a performance'). It is true that we also have glimpses of this in Brecht's work – see, for example, *Mann ist Mann*, where the stage directions include suggested behaviours for the audience, such as the indication that between tableaux spectators should go to the bar and order cocktails. But while Brecht's stage directions are often restricted to the status of devices, in Pirandello's vision they are necessary elements of his complex theatrical as well as philosophical and cultural disquieting paradigm.

Both Pirandello's and Brecht's theatrical revolutions aimed at reintroducing narrativity in the theatre, not at the level of the fabula but at the level of the plot, of the *action*. Pirandello, however, went further than Brecht, since, by drawing the audience back into the theatrical event, not only does Pirandello reintroduce it inside the narrative but he also recaptures and reinstates the ritualistic aspect of the theatre, this time, though, deprived of its aura, of its unicity. One of the major differences between the two authors seems to be that, unlike Pirandello, Brecht still believed in the possibility of a direct rapport between theatre and society, and thus in the continuity between the stage and the *platea*, a continuity achieved through a process of self-reflection and self-recognition that would necessarily bring about social revolution. Both authors aimed at creating 'allegorical' discourses; however, in Brecht the allegory seems to be 'full' since the 'other-talk' is identified with a strong idea – that is, Marxism and a message of social revolution – and thus predicates the reacquisition of centrality by the Subject.[121] In Pirandello, instead, one can decisively detect a 'void' allegorical discourse, since the 'other-talk' is the 'void' itself, the uncanny, the chaos in which it is impossible for the Subject to recover a centrality lost forever. Pirandello is the conscious witness of this loss of meaning, this loss of a unified paradigm, but certainly not, as many have maintained, its passive and nihilistic poet. Brecht is the equally conscious witness of such a loss but is also an 'actor' in the recovery of the Subject's centrality, since his vision of History was, if not linear, certainly progressive.

In modernity, both the theatrical stage and the written text become the forum for an irreparable conflict of the significations and, thus, of the interpretations. The history of twentieth-century theatralogy becomes nothing more than a series of attempts to redefine the somewhat paradoxical relationship between text and performance. Two diverse approaches develop in relation to the artistic representation of reality but more precisely two dissimilar interpretations of History and subjectivity. In one instance, one envisions the possibility of a 'mimetic' and thus harmonious relationship between art and nature. In the other, one records the impossibility of such rapport; one verifies the fundamental division of the Subject, and the search for meaning becomes not only the objective and the true content of the artistic production, but also its form. Within the second perspective, there develops Pirandello's complex discourse as he becomes, according to Wladimir Krysinsky, 'un vecteur significatif en amont et en aval de ces différentes modélisations narratives ou théâtrales du réel et de l'oeuvre'[122] ('an important vector at the origin and at the end of these diverse narrative and theatrical models of reality and of the work of art') when his disquieting paradigm provokes the true *explosion* of pre-existent thematic and formal codes. It is well known that Pirandello's discourse is organized according to the paradigms outlined in his essay *On Humor*. It is relevant here to keep in mind that humour, in opposition to both comedy and tragedy, and as a result of the juxtaposition of them both, is profoundly transgressive, as Mikhail Bakhtin observed in his study of Dostoevsky's poetics.[123] Umberto Eco reminds us that humour is more transgressive than comedy and tragedy precisely because it works within the interstices between narrative and discoursive structures,[124] and thus necessarily redefines the roles of the various participants in the production of meaning. This is why, since romanticism, so much attention has been given to that particular mode of discourse that was variously defined as irony or humour. As previously observed, the fracture between Subject and Object takes place in the romantic and post-romantic period, and Charles Baudelaire was the artist who initiated the investigation that inevitably led to the particular discourse on humour that was to characterize most twentieth-century poetics.

One of Baudelaire's often-forgotten essays, *De l'essence du rire*,[125] is of particular use here. Written in July 1855 – in the heart of the nineteenth century, when, according to Peter Szondi, the crisis of traditional theatrical forms began and led to twentieth-century avant-gardes – the essay's comments on the nature of laughter are extremely pertinent to our discussion of Pirandello's concept of humour. Baudelaire first states that laughter is profoundly human and essentially contradictory, a sign of an infinite grandeur and an infinite misery.[126] Baudelaire then states that 'c'est du choc perpétuel de ces deux infinis que se dégage le rire'[127] ('it is from the perpetual shock between these two infinites that laughter bursts out'), and underlines that the 'puissance du rire' ('the power to laugh') resides in the one who laughs not in the object of laughter.[128] It is quite impossible here to forget the moment of reflection that seizes the Pirandellian humorist, in the essay *On Humor*, when he looks at the old woman's 'masked' and, thus, disfigured face as she attempts to preserve the favours of her much younger husband. For both Pirandello and Baudelaire, thus, the process of the humoristic dissociation takes place significantly in the one who laughs, that is, in the one who 'looks,' the spectator. Baudelaire continues by saying that only 'le philosophe

... ait acquis ... la force de se dedoubler et d'assister comme spectateur désintéressé aux phénomènes de son moi'[129] ('the philosopher ... has acquired ... the capacity to double himself and to witness as an uninterested spectator to the manifestations of his own self'). Yet, the *raisonneur*, the typical Pirandellian humorist, is nothing but an exasperated form of the Baudelairian philosopher since, in the complex Pirandellian paradigm, he is the one who is not only able to split in two, but he is internally divided, unrestrained, unable to live, but totally absorbed in seeing himself live. Numerous are the examples one could draw from Pirandello's dramatic and literary works since such condition of division and estrangement is the very nature of the typical Pirandellian character.[130] In establishing parallelisms between Baudelaire's study of laughter and Pirandello's interpretation of humour, it is relevant to remember that Baudelaire subsequently maintains that laughter is nothing but a symptom, the expression of an internally doubled and contradictory feeling[131] – a statement that leads one directly to Pirandello's essay on humour, in which he states that the difference between comedy and humour resides in that *feeling of the opposite* that is the result of the act of reflection following the *perception of the opposite* that instead characterizes comedy.[132]

In *De l'essence du rire*, Baudelaire then makes a necessary distinction between comedy and the grotesque in a work of art, and states that while the former is *imitation*, the latter, the grotesque or 'absolute comedy,' is *creation*.[133] The 'absolute comedy,' according to Baudelaire, is one of those artistic phenomena that denote the coexistence of two beings, that is, 'l'existence d'une dualité permanente, la puissance d'être à la fois soi et un autre'[134] ('the existence of a permanent duality, the possibility of being oneself and another at the same time') in every human being. This is clearly a Pirandellian theme as well, since there are many internally divided beings (including the humorists) in Pirandello's world. In closing his essay, Baudelaire states that an artist is such only provided that he or she is doubled (that is, divided and replicated) and does not ignore any of the characteristics of his or her divided nature.[135] The very fact of not ignoring this doubled and irreconcilable nature of his being – his existing and his becoming – introduces a tragic note in Pirandello's humorist, as is testified by Pascal, Serafino, and Moscarda in the narrative works, but also by Henry IV and many other characters in Pirandello's plays; because they are internally divided, all these characters are fundamentally unable to recompose a harmonic relationship with the world of experience.

Umberto Artioli is correct when he maintains that 'il passaggio dall'ironia allo humor segnerebbe, così, l'introduzione di una nota tragica, largamente testimoniata, del resto, dalle poetiche novecentesche che, da Jarry a Pirandello a Beckett, hanno assegnato all'umorismo un ruolo centrale'[136] ('the passage from irony to humour would mark the introduction of a tragic note, largely testified by twentieth-century poetics that, from Jarry to Pirandello and Beckett, have assigned a central role to humour'). Within this particular perspective, then, Pirandello's entire opus – especially his famous trilogy of the 'theatre in the theatre' as well as his narrative writings beginning with *The Late Mattia Pascal* – constitute not simply a breaking away from naturalism and the *mimetic* tradition, but also *self-reflexive* stages of theatre on theatrical representation and of narrative on the very nature of narration itself. Within this particular perspective, then, *Six Characters in Search of an Author* becomes the moment of the unveiling of such a fracture – a split that is only possible by employing the specific type of estrangement that is defined by applying humour not merely to the text but to the wholeness of the dramatic representation. The humoristic dissociation is here considered not only as an instance of poetics, but as a true structuring principle of the mise en scène, a dramatic strategy that produces dislocation of space and time, but also of the character and of the fabula itself; that is, it produces not 'effects' but 'cases of estrangement,' which are cause and effect of the continuous and incessant sliding of meaning and of the very act of signification. As previously discussed, 'estrangement' does not refer here to the Brechtian tension toward the recomposition of a narrative and epic, and thus historical continuity between the stage and the orchestra; on the contrary, 'estrangement' here means the attentive recording of a reciprocal, contingent, and thus historical extraneity – an unrecoverable hiatus between the *being* (the world of author and director, of actors and spectators), the *appearing* (the world of the characters),[137] and the *becoming* itself of the production of meaning. The same hiatus can also be found between the Self and the Other contemporarily present in the Subject of enuciation, but also between the 'I' and the others, between the stage and the audience, between the theatrical event – that is, art – and life.

If in his search for aesthetic distance Pirandello aimed at representing human beings in their incongruence and internal division, he thus intended to portray that tragic inevitability of the impossibility of recomposing the unity and thus the aura of the tragic hero Walter Benjamin so thoroughly discussed,[138] now that '[è] finito il tempo degli eroi'[139] ('the time of heroes is over'). Now that Orestes will forever be Hamlet, Pirandello's narrative and dramatic works become the locus where the awareness of the fracture between humans and nature, and the understanding of human beings' internal division produce infinite reflections and mirrorings so that in the end a polyphony of voices ultimately prevails. So thoroughly redefined, Pirandello's discourse then is no longer the product of an isolated voice in the chaos, but 'regains' its place as an integral part of a countertradition of a *critical*, if not negative, thought that had so much relevance in modernity, and eventually paved the way to postmodernity.[140] Pirandello, unlike Brecht, thus belongs to Baudelaire's 'constellation,' that 'constellation' Walter Benjamin talked about,[141] where estrangement is not simply the effect of a psychological condition, but a true and unavoidable element of the 'allegorical signification.'[142] Estrangement becomes form and content, and thus a true strategy of the mise en scène and of theatrical discourse in its entirety. Because of this particular discursive and signifying strategy, in Pirandello's triology, the stage, the orchestra, the foyer, the hallways leading to the theatrical event, and ultimately even the space outside the theatre become the forum for the conflict of 'meanings.' In this progressive spatial dislocation from inside to outside and back, in this constant temporal sliding, in the incessant alluding to the 'past' of the 'drama' – the 'other' time in which it was still feasible 'to imitate an action,' to represent 'romantically,' or, more generally, in which tragedy was still possible – that is, in the time of modernity, emphasis is necessarily placed on that 'existence d'une dualité permanente, la puissance d'être à la fois soi et un autre.'[143] After the shock produced by, first, the perception and then the understanding of this unrecoverable hiatus, nothing remains but the vertigo of the grotesque, the 'absolute comedy,' which, as Baudelaire remarked, is *creation*, in constrast with 'comedy,' which is mere *imitation*. A sort of 'intertextual magnetism,' then, links Pirandello and Baudelaire, but also Beckett, Artaud, and ultimately Carmelo Bene, in theatre, but also, and more importantly for us here, a large segment of European and, in particular, Italian, cinema as it developed from the early 1960s onward. The 'genetic trace' is that critical and/or negative discourse that finds form and content in the humoristic division; through true estranging strategies, such discourse produces a constant 'contamination,' and certainly not a parthenogenesis, between comedy and tragedy, allegory and symbolism, but also and significantly, between the various genres.

Conclusion

After this long and necessary detour, a conclusion is in demand. A re-evaluation of Luigi Pirandello's wealth of comments on the cinema becomes critically relevant only insofar as it provides film scholars with new interpretative tools. Similarly, an in-depth discussion of Pirandello's contribution to the founding of a true aesthetic and poetics of the cinema becomes meaningful only to the extent that it contributes to a re-evaluation of subsequent forms of cinematic discourse. In order to understand thoroughly Pirandello's contribution to film studies, it is not enough to examine a film director's work merely in the light of Pirandello's theory of the theatre. Nor is it satisfactory to limit one's critical work either to the study of Pirandello's collaborations in film productions or to the discussion of his various critical remarks on the cinema simply in light of the debates revolving around the polemic on cinema versus theatre that took place during the first few decades of the twentieth century.

It would also be unsatisfactory to describe Pirandello's controversial attitude toward the new medium as expressed in his artistic writings without relating his critical position to the various debates on film taking place at the time, or to those that were eventually to develop much later in the twentieth century. I am referring specifically to the major shift in film theory and practice that took place in the 1950s. Although there has been an avant-garde movement in film since the 1920s, it was not until the 1950s that this movement reached a critical point. It was only at that time that film managed to challenge the critical establishment on its own terms.

Even though some scholars have been successful in partially defining Pirandello's contribution to the founding, or rather the development, of an aesthetic of the cinema,[144] a comprehensive study of Pirandello's influence on contemporary forms of filmmaking has yet to be successfully undertaken. Some works need to be remembered here, however, such as Maurizio Del Ministro's enlightening study of some of Ingmar Bergman's films in his *Pirandello: Scena personaggio e film*, and Pietro Ferrua's article 'Incontri di Pirandello col cinema,' in which an influence of Pirandello's relativistic theatre on the cinema of Michelangelo Antonioni, Akira Kurosawa, and Hugo Santiago is certainly suggested, although not thoroughly discussed.[145]

On 15 November 1924, the French journal *Les Nouvelles Littéraires* published an article-interview signed by René Jeanne titled 'Cinq minutes avec Pirandello.' The occasion for the journalistic piece was the public announcement of Marcel L'Herbier's forthcoming film adaptation of Pirandello's novel, *The Late Mattia Pascal*. Paradoxically, this five-minute conversation with the Italian writer constitutes an unprecedented and irreplaceable document in the often contradictory and complex history of Pirandello's commentaries on the cinema. In that article, a close collaboration between Pirandello and L'Herbier on the script is said to be for the Italian artist the necessary premise for the creation of 'une oeuvre *nouvelle* à côté du titre de laquelle son nom pourra *légitimement* figurer'[146] ('a *new* work next to whose title his name can *legitimately* appear'). Pirandello expanded on this remark by saying that the reason for his long-lasting avoidance of working for the movie industry was his unwillingness to permit drastic changes to be forced upon his works by directors who behaved merely as salespeople:

Il est inadmissible ... qu' un directeur de firme cinématographique, un commerçant, vienne sans nous consulter modifier le cours des événements que nous avons imaginés ou la vie, superficielle ou profonde, des êtres que nous avons créés et cela sous prétexte que le public a ses raisons ... C'est pour cela que je restai si longtemps éloigné du Cinéma.[147]

It is quite inadmissable ... that the director of a film company, a businessman, without consulting with us, comes to modify the arrangement of the events that we have imagined or the life, superficial or profound, of the beings that we have created, and as an excuse maintains that the audience has its reasons ... This is the reason why I have stayed away from the cinema for such a long time.

Pirandello then expressed his confidence in the quality of L'Herbier's adaptation of his novel, given the fact that, first and foremost, the scenario was to result from a close collaboration between the French filmmaker and the Italian author himself. He also eventually questioned the possibility of changing the original text which, according to him, was 'cinematographic' in nature, and stated: '*Feu Mathias Pascal* est l'histoire d'un homme qui vit avec, constamment, près de lui, l'ètre qu'il a été dans une existence antérieure. N'est-ce pas cinématographique?'[148] ('*The Late Mattia Pascal* is the story of a man who constantly lives together with the being he was in a previous existence. Isn't this cinematographic?'). Pirandello, then, identifies personality doubling as a specifically cinematographic feature, and therefore he maintains that his novel *is* cinematographic insofar as it deals with a character that experiences such a doubling. This statement is the premise for some of Pirandello's most important remarks on the cinema, which reveal his exceptionally insightful approach to the new means of artistic expression. The Italian writer concluded the interview as follows:

Je crois que *le Cinéma*, plus facilement, plus complètement que n'importe quel autre moyen d'expression artistique, *veut nous donner la vision de la pensée* ... Je connais mal le Cinéma ... C'est un film russe, *Le Père Serge*, qui m'a, pendant la guerre, laissé entrevoir les possibilités de cet art jeune: *le Rêve, le Souvenir, l'Hallucination, la Follie, le Dédoublement de la personnalité!* Si les cinégraphistes voulaient, il y aurait de si grandes choses à faire![149]

I believe that *cinema*, more easily, more completely than any other means of artistic expression, *will give us the vision of thought* ... I don't know cinema well ... There is a Russian film, *Father Serge*, that during the war made me see the possibilities of this young art form: *dream, memory, hallucination, madness, personality doubling!* If the cinematographers want, they'll have grand things to do!

In 1948, the young novelist, critic, and filmmaker Alexandre Astruc wrote a landmark essay entitled 'The Birth of a New Avant-Garde: La Caméra-Stylo,' in which he observed that 'the fundamental problem of cinema is how to express thought. The creation of this language has preoccupied all the theoreticians and writers in the history of cinema.'[150] Pirandello addressed a similar critical and theoretical question twenty years before the same issue became the focal point for a new approach to film studies. Far ahead of his times, Pirandello stated that film not only *is* a means of artistic expression, but also that cinema better than any other means of artistic expression can represent thought. Moreover, it is quite apparent that he also anticipated other and subsequent developments in film theory. In the same essay, Astruc also remarked:

The cinema is quite simply becoming a means of expression ... After having been successfully a fairground attraction, an amusement analogous to boulevard theatre, or a means of preserving the images of an era, it is gradually becoming a language. By language, I mean a form in which and by which an artist can express his thoughts, however abstract they may be, or to translate his obsessions.[151]

Pirandello's and Astruc's comments on the status of cinema are remarkably similar, even though separated by twenty years' time. It is interesting to note, however, that quite a few years had yet to pass before even Astruc's dream for what can be defined without doubt as 'free cinema' could be fulfilled. A movement toward a truly freer cinema developed only in the late fifties, and continued to grow, reaching full maturity in the sixties and seventies. The most authoritative representatives of this movement as it developed in Europe were Ingmar Bergman, the directors of the English 'Free Cinema' movement, the French New Wave filmmakers, Michelangelo Antonioni, and, perhaps most importantly, Federico Fellini.

The first two chapters of this work offer a comprehensive discussion of Pirandello's interest in the cinema as his attitude moved from initial refusal to ultimate acceptance and praise of the new artistic medium. It is no surprise that in 1932, when asked by Enrico Roma about the future of the cinema, Pirandello would answer with no hesitation: 'Without limitations.'[152] Some of the theoretical issues raised by the birth and development of film theory, which Pirandello addressed directly and/or indirectly in his critical and artistic writings, were also analysed. His observations and remarks on the use of sound in film, on montage, on the relationship between moving image and viewer, and on the necessity for cinema to found its own specific language constitute original, important, and overlooked contributions to film theory and practice.

My study, then, proceeds by employing Pirandello's concept of the cinema as the means of expression that, better than any other, can represent thought, dream, memory, and split personality in a work of art. A quite similar concern seems to be central to Federico Fellini's idea of cinema. Better than any other director, Fellini brings to completion Pirandello's dream of a cinema that is free and without limitations. Through a comparative analysis of these two authors and their works, it has been possible to assess the existence of a 'legacy' passing from Pirandello to Fellini. If such a legacy does not always allow us to speak of a direct influence of Pirandello upon Fellini, it nevertheless permits us to demonstrate the existence of an aesthetic and ideological 'affinity,' or a proximity between the two artists that is theoretically interesting and useful. The value of such a study resides in its capacity to provide a viable interpretation of the theoretical and existential foundations of Fellini's cinema of freedom and poetry. The Italian director – in the good company of a few others, such as Ingmar Bergman and Luis

Buñuel – perfectly meets Pirandello's expectations insofar as his cinema results from the interplay of reality and fantasy, dream life, and hallucinatory states. Moreover, Fellini's cinema, particularly from the 1960s with *8½* and its multiplicity of points of view, visually records the existential and psychological condition of modern man. During that period, Fellini felt the need to provide a linguistic, or, rather, psycholinguistic, response to the state of extreme alienation modern man experienced in an age of mechanical reproduction.

Fellini never admitted to having been significantly influenced by Pirandello or even to having read Pirandello's works, since he made a point of proclaiming himself an 'anti-intellectual' who neither read too much nor went to movies. In *Fare un film*, a collection of essays written by Fellini himself, the director maintains: 'Non conosco i classici del cinema: Murnau, Dreyer, Eisenstein, vergognosamente non li ho mai visti'[153] ('I don't know film classics: Murnau, Dreyer, Eisenstein, shamefully I never saw them'). Thus, in order to prove any sort of relationship between the two artists' works, one has to untangle the knots of their respective discourses and to capture the visible and invisible threads that link Fellini's artistic and existential statements to Pirandello's.

In the third chapter of this study, I postulate the existence of a common poetics in the two artists' respective works. Initially, I define this poetics as a 'poetics of islanders.' Pirandello and Fellini at times experienced in their lives and careers a distance from the 'centre' of life and culture, while at other times they perceived themselves as being right in the 'centre,' in the place where things happen. In both circumstances, however, they constantly recognized their distance from their various objects of desire, and thus experienced alienation. This peculiar sense of alienation progressively became the informing principle of their works and, especially, of their characters' existences.

Subsequently, I trace the contours of Pirandello's and Fellini's internal geography or mental topology. To do so, I shall analyse the processes underlying the formation and subsequent disintegration of their respective but quite similar myths and metaphors. Initially, I use the image of the 'island' as a metaphor for security and refuge, but then to refine this definition, I discuss how the 'island' eventually came to stand as a metaphor for separateness and 'peripherality' in their works as they reached full maturity.

I then discuss the myth of the City as it develops in the two artists' work. Since the City is the geographical locus of modernism, I examine how the myth of Rome progressively dissolves into the myth of the

nameless City, the locus of the labyrinth in both authors' artistic statements. Pirandello and Fellini are thoroughly conscious of the linguistic
and psychoanalytic foundation of the artistic experience. In their respective artistic statements, cities, like dreams, possess a rebus-like
structure. In this complex configuration, they ultimately reflect the fundamental alienation born in the Subject out of the impossibility of
reaching the center, of regaining a sense of unity.

Moreover, both Pirandello's and Fellini's artistic productions can be
metaphorically described as journeys. Their informing principle is the
quest of the author, of the characters, of the text itself. What is searched
for may vary, but it is always located somewhere else. Therefore, both
Pirandello's and Fellini's works can be described as allegorical discourses. Allegory in a modern text differs from allegory in a medieval
text, for in the former there is no universally accepted set of values (i.e.,
Christianity) to which they can refer. The outside referent of a modern
allegory varies constantly, since modern man has no certainties. Thus a
modern allegory is basically 'void.' As I discuss later in the present
study, the archetypal biography of modern man can first be defined as a
search for a centre, subsequently as a continuous denial of access to that
centre, and finally as the progressive fragmentation of the centre itself.
Through their fluctuating allegorical discourses, both Pirandello and
Fellini participate in developing a new ontology of the modern Subject.

In light of Chapter 3's analysis of the parallel processes of construction and deconstruction of the two artists' metaphorical and mythical
worlds, I then postulate the presence of a common genre tradition in
both artists' works. We can acknowledge the progressive lowering,
degradation, and disintegration of a myth – that of Rome – which is
initially powerful for both Pirandello and Fellini, but which is gradually dismantled in their respective artistic visions. This development,
so impressively common to both authors' works, happens to be a qualifying characteristic of the genre of the serio-comical as it has been clas-
sically defined by Mikhail Bakhtin, the famous Russian critic and literary theorist.

In the fourth chapter, I argue that Fellini's artistic statements can be
included within the genre Pirandello defined as 'umoristico,' a genre
that bears striking similarities to the one Bakhtin defined as 'carnivalistic.' In particular, I explain how Pirandello's definition of the Subject as
'umorista' – a subject that is constitutionally ambivalent, eccentric and,
at times, even grotesque – also provides a perfect definition of Fellini's
typical protagonist. In fact, Fellini's archetypical protagonist is an ex-

tremely ambivalent Subject sharing with his creator a condition of 'non-being-thereness,' an incapacity to assume any responsibility in life, and who might also be accurately described as the 'perennial traveller.'

Modern forms of metadiscourse provide a linguistic response to this specific psychological and existential condition, a condition defined by fragmentation, division, and thus alienation. An initial sense of alienation develops in modern man from the recognition of his basically discordant relationship with the natural world and with other human beings. Later on, with the recognition of a more fundamental division within himself – the division between the Self and the Other inside the Self, a division discovered through both Freudian and post-Freudian, namely Lacanian, psychoanalysis – a new kind of reflexivity comes into existence. This new reflexivity offers the linguistic response to the needs expressed by a new Subject, and produces a different perception of the Real and of the relationship between the Real and the Imaginary worlds as it is reworked through the activity of the unconscious. If this development of the Subject and its relationship with reality is correct, it implies that the whole concept of traditional artistic mimesis necessarily needs to be re-examined and reinterpreted. Such a thorough reinterpretation of the concept of mimesis is a crucial feature of the 'umoristico' or 'carnivalistic' genre. It is within this very genre that Fellini's cinema develops along lines parallel to the development of the literary works of the first modern Italian exponent of this genre, Luigi Pirandello.

Federico Fellini

Federico Fellini

A grotesque party scene in Federico Fellini's *Variety Lights* (1950)

The romantic Wanda staring at the White Sheik (Alberto Sordi) in Federico Fellini's *The White Sheik* (1952)

Alberto, one of the loafers, gazing at his sister Olga in the foreground as his friends stare at the scene in the background, in Federico Fellini's *I Vitelloni* (1953)

At a carnival party, Alberto (Alberto Sordi) holds a huge mask in Federico
Fellini's *I Vitelloni* (1953)

Gelsomina (Giulietta Masina) and Zampanò (Anthony Quinn) in one of their
routines in a town square in Federico Fellini's *La Strada* (1954)

Juxtaposition of opposites – the sacred and the profane – in Federico Fellini's
La Dolce Vita (1959)

Lowering and debasement in a grotesque party scene with journalist Marcello (Marcello Mastroianni) at the closing of Federico Fellini's *La Dolce Vita* (1959)

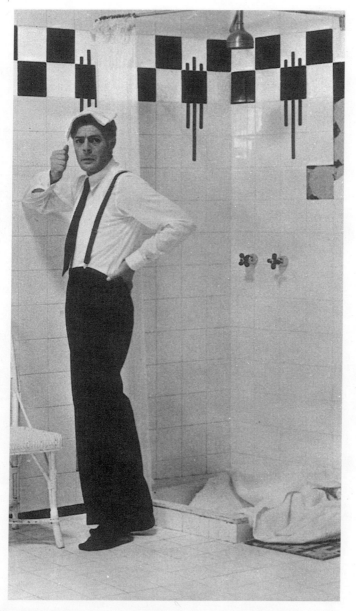

Guido Anselmi (Marcello Mastroianni) in the opening section of Federico
Fellini's *8½* (1963)

Guido Anselmi wearing a Pinocchio nose in the nightclub sequence in Federico Fellini's *8½* (1963)

The joyful circus parade that closes Federico Fellini's *8½* (1963)

Self-reflexivity and subversion in Fellini's *Satyricon* (1969)

Giacomo Casanova played by Donald Sutherland in Fellini's *Casanova* (1976)

The White Clown and the Augusto in Federico Fellini's *The Clowns* (1970)

Federico Fellini on the set of *The Clowns* (1970)

A humorous moment between Titta and the tobacconist in Federico Fellini's
Amarcord (1974)

Ciccio's fantasy of his fascist marriage to Aldina in Federico Fellini's *Amarcord* (1974)

Amelia (Giulietta Masina) helps Pippo (Marcello Mastroianni) after his dramatic fall during their tap dance routine in the grotesque TV show 'We Proudly Present' in Federico Fellini's *Ginger and Fred* (1985)

Roberto Benigni and Federico Fellini on the set of *The Voice of the Moon* (1990),
Fellini's last film before his death on 31 October 1993

3 The Origins of the Myths: From Pirandello to Fellini

COTRONE ... Siamo qua come agli orli della vita, Contessa. Gli orli, a un comando, si distaccano; entra l'invisibile: vaporano i fantasmi.

Pirandello, *I giganti della montagna*

A Necessary Preface

I don't like: parties, festivals, tripe, interviews, round tables, requests for autographs, escargots, traveling, standing in line, mountains, ships, the radio turned on, music in restaurants (when I have to put up with it), wire broadcasting, jokes, soccer fans, the ballet, creches, gorgonzola, awards, oysters, hearing people talk about Brecht over and over, official dinners, toasts, speeches, being invited, requests for advice, Humphrey Bogart, quizzes, Magritte, being invited to art shows, theatre rehearsals, stenotype machines, tea, camomile, caviar, the preview of anything, citations, he men, films for the young, theatricality, temperament, questions, *Pirandello*,[1] crepes suzettes, beautiful countrysides, subscriptions, political films, psychological films, historical films, obligation and release from obligation, ketchup.[2]

In a long interview with Giovanni Grazzini, Federico Fellini thus lists Luigi Pirandello among his many dislikes. And yet we know that few directors have given as many interviews as Fellini himself has; we also understand that he did not refrain from participating in film festivals whose many prizes he graciously accepted, even though at times with subtle irony. In short, we may believe him on the 'ketchup affair,' and perhaps we will give him credit for his opinion on the nonsensical and vacuous chattering over Brecht, but we find it hard to accept the rest, since Fellini himself has thrown some light this way:

I'm a liar, but an honest one. People reproach me for not always telling the same story in the same way. But this happens because I've invented the whole tale from the start and it seems boring to me and unkind to other people to repeat myself.[3]

Over the years, Fellini has been 'labelled' in many ways, mostly in an attempt to make sense of his peculiar mode of filmic discourse. But earlier in his career, he defied this, and made a statement that curiously encourages us in pursuing our line of investigation, no matter how hazardous it may seem: 'I'm not a man who approves of definitions. Labels belong to luggage as far as I'm concerned; they don't mean anything in art.'[4] Undoubtedly, we are not looking for cheap labels and easy definitions; on the contrary, we are moved to escape facile solutions, to pay homage to two of the most influential artists of modern Italian times, and to eventually open new avenues for a critical investigation that can at last lead us to a true understanding of contemporary Italian cinematic production.

At times, Fellini has been defined a 'neorealist,' a 'realist,' or a 'surrealist'; his work has been described as extravagant, baroque, flamboyant, and excessive. An overall consensus, however, can be found in one particular label, that of Fellini as an *auteur*. This definition is only apparently flattering; on the contrary, it hides a quite misleading and restrictive interpretation. It elevates Fellini and places him in the good company of artists – those 'lucky few' who live in ivory towers, who are allowed to be extravagant, and who have 'full control' over their work. Their dreams, delusions, and revelations have found some fixed orbit, and their fortune will travel virtually intact through the centuries. As soon as Fellini gained public and critical recognition in the 1950s and early 1960s, as Peter Bondanella observes in the opening remarks of his recent study of Fellini's life and career,

perhaps more than any other director of the postwar period, Fellini's public persona has projected the myth of the director as creative superstar, as imaginative magician. His name has become synonymous with fantasy and exuberant creativity.[5]

While we certainly agree with Bondanella's remarks, we question that line of interpretation that places Fellini among the *auteurs*, the few directors whose work cannot be fully described and does not fit well-established critical categories. To label Fellini an *auteur* may be extremely flattering to the director and evocative to the critics, but it also implies a limited possibility for influence on others' work and a narrow space within the historical evolution of cinema in general, and of Italian film in particular. Profound parallelisms can be established in the destinies of Fellini and Pirandello, two of the major figures of Italy's modern and contemporary cultural history. At different times, both Pirandello and Fellini provided a similar critique of existing interpretations of realism, and then participated in the creation of self-reflexive and metadiscoursive artistic statements. Both artists then experienced controversial critical response, as they constantly stood 'at the borders,' that is, both at the edge and outside of mainstream artistic and cultural discourse. While Pirandello's relation with contemporary dramatic and cinematic theory has been discussed in the previous chapters, it is necessary here to outline briefly Fellini's place and role in the development of Italian film.

Abundant critical investigation has been devoted to *auteur* film theory and practice, and Fellini has always been numbered among the most prominent figures of this trend in filmmaking, together with Ingmar Bergman, Louis Buñuel, François Truffaut, and others. Yet, the classification of *auteurism* itself is quite evanescent and fundamentally unsatisfactory. By following it, one could easily argue that Italian cinema, as it developed from 1945 to the present, can be entirely described as *auteur cinema*. Beginning with neorealism, this national cinema, perhaps more than any other, was and to a certain extent still is, a cinema that bears the powerful signature of its makers, of its 'authors.' However, we should not be content with a definition that does not truly account for the social, political, historical, and economic critiques that Italian cinema persistently expressed in the works of its so-called 'masters,' including Fellini, of course, as well as in mainstream fiction film all the way up to the directors of the new generation. Through this 'politics of the authors,' Italian cinema has always refrained from expressing itself via codifiable genres, and has instead constantly pursued a progressive contamination of the various genres to produce an ever-changing and fluid cinematic form. This tendency can be detected even in the works that film historians have labelled as the 'masterpieces' of Italian neorealism, for example, Roberto Rossellini's *Roma città aperta* (*Rome Open City*, 1945) and *Paisá* (*Paisan*, 1946). Even these classical works abundantly use different genres such as war film and documentary, the 'lower' genres of Hollywood western and slapstick, and, more generally, an original combination of comedy and melodrama. This freefall of language from one genre to another became a persistent and pervasive feature of Italian cinema; the development of this national cinema would then record the predominance of comedy or melodrama alternatively, or a successful and balanced combination of both, depending on the historical and social content and the films' peculiar politics.

In an Italian context, the prevalence of comedy will correspond with extradiegetic concerns revolving around social and political issues;[6] the supremacy of melodrama will generally reflect a higher tension in investigating film as artefact. The term melodrama is used here with no reference to the rhetorical and sentimental cinematic melodramas of the 1930s and 1950s, but to a new style that pursues a different rapport between word and image, as well as between music and image, and that 'states' the impossibility for cinema to express such a relationship. Rossellini's *Viaggio in Italia* (*Voyage to Italy*, 1953) can be considered the 'ideal' beginning of this new 'melodramatic imagination' in Italian cinema. Complex and increasingly abstract cinematic narratives began to develop in Italy, narratives whose first goal was to investigate and express the increasingly difficult relationships between people and environment, people and objects, but also and more importantly, between reality and its artistic representation. These filmic narratives pursued such investigations by constantly redefining and often undermining their own status as mechanical representations of those relationships, and can thus be described as self-reflexive and 'metacinematic.'

According to Gianni Rondolino, 4,416 films were produced in Italy between 1945 and 1974. In his study of Italian cinematic comedies, Masolino D'Amico maintains that 1,150 of these works were comic films. Italian comedy, as it developed in the cinema, was quite different from French and English humour, and can be generally described as

la commistione di comicitá e di dramma, la predilezione di eroi tutto sommato negativi, una viva attenzione al presente se non addirittura all'attualitá, e l'intreccio spesso ambiguo di satira, denuncia morale e irridente caricatura priva di un autentico spessore etico.[7]

the mixture of comedy and drama, the preference for mostly negative heroes, a vivid attention to the present time, if not even to actuality, and the often ambiguous intertwining of satire, moral denunciation, and scornful caricature deprived of an authentic ethical dimension.

Although film comedy is an international genre, there are significant differences, for instance, between American and Italian comic film. If one agrees with most theoretical studies of comedy, according to which two of its qualifying elements are imitation and serenity, then in American comedies serenity predominates, and, thus, the restoration of the original order of things, while in Italian comic film the principle of imitation, and thus realism, generally prevails.[8] Italian film comedy has constantly reflected upon contemporary economic and political issues, and has mostly avoided daring flights into fantasy worlds with consoling happy endings. Comedy 'Italian style' as we know it today was a pervasive feature of Italian film production for nearly thirty years after World War II. A conspicuous symptom of a society that was experiencing rapid growth, Italian film comedy often bordered on satire and on the grotesque; it produced episodic and inconclusive narratives that did not allow its audience to sit back comfortably as the films constantly reflected and commented upon Italian contemporary life.

As stated earlier, comedic elements were already present in such neo-realist masterpieces as *Rome Open City*, and even Vittorio De Sica's *Ladri di biciclette* (*Bicycle Thieves*, 1948). It is with neorealism, therefore, that a melodramatic imagination and a contemporary comic sensibility developed in Italian cinema. While the melodramatic mode was primarily responsible for the birth and growth of *auteur cinema*, as with the works of directors such as Rossellini, Antonioni, and Pasolini, comedy became the Italian popular 'genre' par excellence, where *popular* has to be interpreted as a mode of production (and not of reception) as described by Maurizio Grande in his study *Il cinema di Saturno*. Yet the melodramatic and the comic often contaminated each other, and from such contamination a diverse 'mode of discourse' developed, a mode that we will define as 'umoristico,' that is humoristic and, more generally, serio-comic.

Additional comments are appropriate here since our investigation implies a revisitation of another important category in film history and criticism – that of *genre*. The fortune and influence of Italian cinema in the silent period were immense, and, to a certain extent, this national film contributed to the birth of the Hollywood film industry. Once born, American cinema expressed itself prevailingly through formalized genres that came to be recognized as 'classical,' were exported everywhere, and became extremely popular in Italy starting roughly in the 1930s. American cinema has nourished the imaginary world of so many of our great directors, and it is sufficient and pertinent here to mention Fellini, who has repeatedly and openly declared his debt, at least an 'ideal' one, toward this cinema and its many mythical figures.

Notwithstanding its thorough penetration of the Italian market, over the years American cinema has not produced a 'visible' phenomenon of imitation in the Italian film industry. This is certainly odd, and it urges one to reconsider a number of important issues. Italian cinema has developed through a progressive contamination of the various 'classical' genres. Furthermore, these genres eventually underwent a gradual 'lowering,' almost a Bakhtinian 'carnivalization.' The gradual contamination of the genres has been mostly activated and carried out by melodrama, which in the Italian context has become a genre that crosses all genres, and is almost a *hypergenre*. Melodrama is here interpreted as a mode of discourse that pursues a renewed rapport between word and image, and 'states' the impossibility for cinema to express such a relationship. In this way, this peculiar 'genre' prefigures an expressive dimension that ascribes to the image 'un quoziente informativo per difetto' ('an informative quotient by defect'), as Franco La Polla stated.9 Following this line of critical investigation, it would, thus, be simple to understand how Italian cinema in its entirety from neorealism to the present can be described as being 'metacinematic,' at least *in potentia*.

The lowering – or, better, progressive carnivalization (as Bakhtin would define it) – of the various genres has also been activated by humour, which stands here openly juxtaposed to comedy. According to Maurizio Casadei in his essay 'Momenti dell'umorismo' ('Moments of Humour'), included in the volume *Ipotesi sul cinema*, humour is a fundamental aspect of contemporary aesthetics as well as of the filmic event, and is here considered primarily because of one of its intrinsic qualities, one that is 'ipercritica, riflessiva, o quantomeno espressiva di un sottofondo tematico che ne scalza o rilancia perennemente la ragion d'essere, al di lá di ogni senso unilaterale e precostituito'10 ('hypercritical, self-reflexive, or at least expressive of a thematic foundation that undermines or restates its essence, beyond any given, unilateral and pre-existing meaning').

In his book *Rabelais and His World*, Mikhail Bakhtin points to the revolutionary nature of medieval carnival. According to Bakhtin, carnival is a revolution where kings are decapitated and crowds are crowned. However, more than simply formulating an ideological reading of carnival as actual liberation, in the sum of his writings Bakhtin gives us a model of interpretation for a mode of discourse, in society and in literature, meant to subvert the monologism of authoritarian discourse. Thus, Bakhtin's renowned study of Dostoevsky's poetics,11 for instance, can be inspirational in a reading and interpretation of a countertradition in narrative as well as dramatic art that, I believe, started in Italy with Pirandello and then developed in contrast to, or rather in critical dialogue with, more traditionally accepted modes of discourse such as tragedy and comedy. It is by reason of this countertradition that parallelisms and similarities between Pirandello and Fellini can be legitimately assessed.

The close relationship between carnival and comedy is discussed accurately by Umberto Eco in his article 'The Frames of Comic *Freedom*.'[12] He states that 'comedy and carnival are not instances of real transgression; on the contrary, they represent paramount examples of law reinforcement. They remind us of the existence of the rule.'[13] Eco reminds us that since the romantic period, however, many scholars and artists have dealt with and spoken about a mode of discourse that differs from comedy, one variously defined as irony, or humour. According to him, such discourse varies from comedy primarily because of the differently balanced relationship between rule and violation.[14] In his essay *On Humor*, Pirandello defines the comic as the perception of the opposite, while humour is the *feeling of the opposite* produced by the 'special' activity of reflection. Pirandello gives as example an extravagant old woman smearing her face with make-up and wearing flashy clothes. In comedy, one would simply understand that she is not, in this shorthand of communication, what a respectable old 'lady' ought to be (and 'we' are), and one would laugh at her. In humour, we would 'see' why the woman masks herself: that is, that she strives to regain the desired and forfeited youth in order not to lose her younger husband. Thus, humour lies halfway between tragedy and comedy. The laughter of comedy merges with the pity of tragedy and becomes a smile. We still feel a sense of hauteur as an audience, but this soon becomes mixed with a shade of tenderness.

As Eco remarks, in comedy we laugh at the character who breaks the rule, the set of social values, or in other words, the frame. In tragedy, we sympathize with the character who has broken the frame but we enjoy the reaffirmation of the rule. In humour, instead, we smile because of the contradiction between the character and the frame that the character cannot comply with. But we are no longer so certain that the character is at fault. It may be that the frame is wrong. By restoring the binary opposition between the character and the rule in a dialectic and open-ended fashion, humour acts as a form of social criticism and, thus, is truly transgressive, while comedy is not. Moreover, since humour, as Eco maintains, 'works in the interstices between narrative and discoursive structures,'[15] it necessarily redefines the roles of the various elements involved in the textual production: the author, the audience or the reader, the text itself, and, obviously, the character. Humour, then, is always metalinguistic and/or metasemiotic.

With these theoretical premises in mind, an apparently abstract and merely academic operation such as that of instituting a parallel between Pirandello and Fellini may prove helpful and revealing if performed against the background of the serio-comical genre. Within this theoretical and cultural frame, to verify similarities and affinities between Pirandello and Fellini, and particularly between the two authors' poetics and aesthetics, their respective conceptions of character, as well as their privileged forms of discourse will prove a challenging, but ultimately revealing journey.

In his recent study of Fellini's filmography, Peter Bondanella suggests that

Pirandello's revolt against realism in the theatre provided Fellini with a model for his move away from neorealism and its socially derived concept of film character. The example of Pirandello's metadramatic revolution would be even more important as inspiration for Fellini's own metacinematic examination of the cinema as an art form.[16]

Bondanella also emphasizes the unreliability of Fellini's declarations of dislike for Pirandello. He underlines the dramatist's importance to Italian theatre in the 1950s and Giulietta Masina's[17] early dramatic training, and thus the likelihood of Fellini's knowing Pirandello's work quite well.[18] At any rate, a case of 'direct' influence can hardly be proven, for on the one hand we do not possess examples of 'true' adaptation, and on the other Fellini would very unlikely admit a specific source to his fertile and unrestrained imagination. It is compulsory, then, to assume a broader perspective rather than that provided by a positivistic juxtaposition of a literary and a cinematic text. As a matter of fact, a relationship between Pirandello's and Fellini's works can be legitimately and fruitfully discussed only against the background of the cultural and artistic countertradition of the serio-comical, as it has been variously defined by Bakhtin and by Pirandello himself. This particular genre finds its privileged linguistic expression in metadiscourse, a discourse that is, by its very nature, self-reflexive and self-referential as well as extremely ambivalent. On a linguistic level, metadiscourses both postulate the destruction of traditional narrative and dramatic strategies, and encourage the search for the 'new' in art. In their dismantlement of traditionally accepted artistic conventions and social hierarchies, these discourses participate in what Bakhtin has defined as the 'carnival sense of the world,'[19] that is, a forceful drive toward transgression, or rather subversion, of the rule, of the Law, and, last but not least, of the frame.

A Poetics of 'Islanders'

As Giovanni Macchia once noted,[20] there are essentially two environments in which Pirandello's narrative works spring into existence: Sicily and Rome. The same can be said of Fellini's cinematic narratives, which repeatedly focus on Rome and on Rimini and the Romagna. Both Pirandello and Fellini, then, chose Rome as their 'city of election,' the city where they lived their adult life and reached artistic plenitude, and this urban 'centre' is frequently juxtaposed to another type of existence in the provinces. While the relevance of this choice to each author's life and work will be studied in the second section of the present chapter, I shall first establish similarities in the formation and development of Pirandello's and Fellini's mythical worlds. At first, both authors begin by turning Rome, a traditionally accepted centre of culture and society, into their own 'centre.' Later on, in their lives and works, they proceed to dissolve that ideal centre, for they not only recognize but also understand the condition of total de-centredness[21] in which the modern Subject finds himself or herself living.

If the city of election becomes extremely important for the Subject's progression toward maturity, so does the place of birth and childhood, which strongly influences the Subject's relationship with the world during adult life. Pirandello was born and grew up in Sicily. Fellini was born in Rimini, and lived there until his early twenties. Thus, if not in terms of 'real' geography, then on an existential and artistic plane, and in terms of their respective poetics, both Pirandello and Fellini can be considered 'islanders.' Quite early in their lives and artistic careers, both Pirandello and Fellini experienced a feeling of distance from the 'centre' of life and culture. At times they felt a deep sense of alienation born out of the recognition of that geographical and ideal distance. At other times, because of the all-enclosing nature of their 'islands,' they felt right in the centre, but still experienced alienation, now born out of the recognition of the division within themselves and from others. Once they eventually reached the 'centre,' Rome, they experienced the vacuity of that centre, and therefore still felt misplaced and de-centred, and thus alienated.

If the signifier 'island' were to be given the meaning of 'province' – that is, if it were charged with the connotations of a decentred, peripheral place in terms of both real geography and intellectual history – then it would become evident that Fellini's Rimini is an island as much as is Pirandello's Sicily. Pirandello always preserved a sense of being a Sicilian, even when in his later life and career he tried to make more universal statements. Similarly, Fellini's past in Rimini is constantly present in his entire cinematic production. Quite curiously, both authors had to suffer accusations of 'provincialism' or 'regionalism' for a long time. For both Pirandello and Fellini, however, the issue does not seem to be so much one of defining a cultural identity as one of transforming either Sicily or Rimini into metaphors for a specific existential and artistic condition. At one point, for instance, in answering Rossellini's accusations of provincialism regarding *La dolce vita* (*La Dolce Vita*, 1959), Fellini maintained:

To call an artist provincial is the best way of defining him. For an artist's position in the face of reality must be exactly that of a provincial, he must be attracted by what he sees and at the same time have the detachment of a provincial. What is an artist, in fact? He is merely a provincial who finds himself standing between a physical and a metaphysical reality. Faced with a metaphysical reality, we are all provincials.[22]

Therefore, being a provincial for the artist implies a certain way of looking at life. It is a way of 'seeing' that immediately defines a way of 'being' and of existing, and not the contrary.[23]

In fact, the artistic statements of Pirandello and Fellini constitute tremendously fertile 'islands' in their respective intellectual and artistic times. What Macchia stated for Pirandello – 'Non sarà difficile contemplare da molto lontano, nella geografia letteraria contemporanea, l'estensione e la ricchezza dell' *isola Pirandello*'[24] ('It will not be difficult to contemplate from far away, in contemporary literary geography, the extension and richness of *Pirandello's island*') – can be easily applied to Fellini's cinema. After decades of conspicuous lack of critical attention and even contempt toward Fellini's work, it is possible now to evaluate fully its impact on the history of Italian cinema from neorealism to the present. Only today can we thoroughly assess the extension and richness of *Fellini's island*.

Furthermore, both Sicily and Rimini can be considered as psychic as well as intellectual and existential 'islands' in terms of an imaginary geography that has far more important intellectual consequences than their actual locations have. Sicily and Rimini were for Pirandello and Fellini, respectively, points of departure for existential and artistic journeys. The symbolist theme of the journey, in fact, assumes extreme importance in both artists' work. While for the symbolists the point of arrival is the most important element in their voyage toward the light, what truly counts in Pirandello's and Fellini's narratives is the journey itself. In addition, these journeys constitute dimensions of the Subject's – the artist's and the character's – memory, and therefore become the structuring principles of their artistic and existential statements. Sicily and Rimini also become perfect stages for the private as well as the public trials the individual undergoes, for with both artists the Subject is also the product of particular social conditions. Furthermore, an island – real or imaginary – considered as a decentred place becomes the perfect metaphor for the modern Subject, who is more and more defined as a divided Self – divided within itself and from others.

The island also becomes a working metaphor for that Pirandellian 'cannocchiale rovesciato' ('reversed telescope'), which affords the Subject diverse perspectives. On the one hand, it allows an obsessively analytical study of the object, almost a deforming glance that often culminates in the grotesque. On the other hand, that peculiar telescope allows the Subject to assume a distancing perspective over his object, an attitude that finds its rationalization in that 'filosofia del lontano' ('philosophy of the faraway') which Dr. Fileno – one of Pirandello's many 'umoristi' ('humorists') – talks about.[25] For both Pirandello and Fellini, the distance from one's object – the object being either the Self or the Other – is always painful, even when ironic or, more likely, 'umoristica' ('humoristic'). Consequently, in both authors, one finds a stratification of meanings within the extreme fragmentation of discourse. The imperfection of their seemingly circular discourses grants their works an incredible openness. They both, nevertheless, create their 'islands' by exploiting the potentialities of repetition, for each of their works constitutes an extremely fertile ground for future developments. Situations and characters return over and over in Pirandello's and Fellini's works; Macchia has remarked that Pirandello built his island 'con una monotonia nella diversità, insistendo sui luoghi fissi, su certe stramberie di un paesaggio che non ammette nella sua insularità scampo e liberazione, su temi, modi, che si trasmettono come per creare un clima ed un'ossessione'[26] ('with a monotony in the diversity, insisting on fixed places, on certain eccentricities of a landscape that in its insularity does not allow for escape and liberation, on themes and modes that are transmitted as to create an atmosphere and an obsession'). Fellini's artistic works certainly reveal a similar disposition; his world is built around the same places and metaphors, and Rimini itself plays a peculiarly obsessive role in his personal evolution as well as in the development of his peculiar cinematic discourse:

Non riesco a considerare Rimini come un fatto oggettivo. E' piuttosto, e soltanto, una dimensione della memoria ... Rimini: cos'è. E' una dimensione della memoria (una memoria, tra l'altro, inventata, adulterata, manomessa) su cui ho speculato tanto che è nato in me una sorta d'imbarazzo.[27]

I cannot consider Rimini as an objective fact. It is rather, and only, a dimension of my memory ... What is Rimini? It is a dimension of memory (a memory that in any case has been invented, adulterated, violated) on which I have speculated so much that I developed a kind of embarrassment.

Rimini, thus, is not to Fellini an objective fact, but primarily a facet of his memory, however adulterated in his constant reinvention of that locale.[28] In Fellini's idiosyncratic recreation of Rimini, the town truly becomes an island, insofar as an island represents a private place, protected by the sea, where the individual can freely nourish his or her own most secret dreams. Rimini, then, becomes for Fellini a secluded site, totally isolated since it is surrounded by both the sea and complete darkness. It is a place apparently removed from history, where life seems to be eternally still. Movement of any sort appears to be extremely difficult in Fellini's Rimini, as if it truly were an island distant from the mainland (that is, the city of Rome), which is also defined in metaphoric terms. To Fellini, then, Rimini is simply a 'dimensione della memoria' ('a dimension of memory'). To us, the image of the island becomes the ideal metaphor providing Rimini with the quality of a far-off, distant land, almost a foreign country in Proustian terms, which can nevertheless be reinvented and, therefore, changed as much as one pleases. What counts, ultimately, is the present; in order to live in, understand, and make sense of the present, the Subject has somehow to be able to rejoin his or her past. The way Fellini chooses to come to terms with his present is by recreating his own autobiography over and over through a constant violation of the sacredness of the past.

Vivevo una vita appartata, solitaria: cercavo modelli illustri, Leopardi, per giustificare quel timore del costume, quell'incapacità di godermela come gli altri, che andavano a guazzare nell'acqua (per questo, forse, *il mare* è così affascinante per me, come una cosa mai conquistata: la zona dalla quale provengono i mostri e i fantasmi).[29]

I lived a secluded and solitary life: I looked for illustrious models, Leopardi, to justify that fear of the bathing suit, that inability to enjoy life like the others, who would go and splash about in the water (this is perhaps why *the sea* is so fascinating to me, as a never conquered thing: the zone from which monsters and phantoms come).

Nature is not necessarily a comforting element in Fellini's personal mythology. In his films, the sea, as well as other 'natural' objects, must be transformed into elements of a personal mythology, for 'reality' constantly has to become fabulous, almost magical. The sea is the carrier of mysterious threats to the individual: in *Giulietta degli spiriti* (*Juliet of the Spirits*, 1965), the monstrous boat in Juliet's nightmare comes from the sea. This narrative segment constitutes the moment of unmasking of Juliet's interior sexual repressions and fears. Moreover, from the sea the flare of distant countries comes to the 'islanders' and makes them dream. In *Amarcord* (*Amarcord*, 1973), in the depth of night, out of the open sea appears the *Rex*, the ocean liner of the Italian royal navy and the symbol of a golden and glamorous life. It embodies the life everyone dreams of in that magic country where everybody is beautiful and rich, the land of plenty, as well as an artificial and cardboard embodiment of the Fascist regime's projections of power.

In Fellini's films, the seashore is where people often have to face the inconsistency and the emptiness of their lives. In *Lo sceicco bianco* (*The White Sheik*, 1952), Wanda's illusions conflict with a more banal reality at the beach when, after having played the role of a harem girl with the hero of her dreams, the actor of the 'fotoromanzi' ('popular picture stories'), she sails out onto the ocean with him. As his clumsy attempt to seduce her terminates in tragicomic fashion, she has to face the crude reality of the profound deceitfulness that characterizes the people who work in the world of the 'fotoromanzi.' They are people who can no longer distinguish between illusion and reality or, rather, people who, through the illusions they provide, cheat on life and on other people. Wanda realizes that she can no longer live the dream she has nourished for so long, that she cannot escape her daily life by flying into her dream world. Thus, she understands that she has to make her own world into an illusion, for if she went back to life as it was before her escape, she would be crushed by disillusionment. As Peter Bondanella argues, both Wanda and her husband will eventually decide to live a lie, since they are 'frozen in their respective roles' and in the end 'both [will] ultimately reject an awareness of the truth and take refuge in another illusion.'[30]

In *La strada* (*La Strada*, 1954), we first see Gelsomina, the main female character, at the beach, and she is obviously associated with the sea from the opening sequence of the film. At the shore, later on, she dares assert herself for the first time with Zampanò. After the famous pebble sequence, during which the Fool teaches her that everything has meaning (including herself), Gelsomina waits for Zampanò to leave the police barracks, where he has spent the night. They drive away, but eventually stop to take a stroll on the beach. It is at this point that Gelsomina confronts Zampanò with a clear demand for love and commitment, a demand which he ultimately fails to satisfy, although he is overtly disturbed by her assertiveness. It is also at the seashore, at the conclusion of the film, that Zampanò finally has to confront his own need for love. Now that Gelsomina has died, he recognizes his own hopeless solitude. At the shore, he is able to weep, and probably for the first time in his entire life and in the film, he finally becomes capable of revealing and expressing his primitive feelings.

In *E la nave va* (*And the Ship Sails On*, 1983), the sea actually stands as the background against which the entire film takes place. The story unfolds on an ocean liner, a ship of fools embarked on a voyage of farewell for an opera singer whose ashes are on board and whom everyone on the vessel either knew or has heard of. While they are at sea, a group of Serbian refugees comes to subvert the social order established on the ship. Also, from the sea a belligerent warship eventually comes to put an end to the journey, and to the film itself, by sinking the ocean liner.

It is at night by the seashore where, in *I vitelloni* (*I Vitelloni*, 1953), Leopoldo, the would-be playwright, has to face his ultimate disillusionment. After a music-hall show, he finally meets the great actor Sergio Natali, the man he has always cherished as the symbol of dramatic art and as the focus of his own most intimate dreams – the man to whom he had sent his first complete play. At the end of the show, all five *vitelloni* go to meet the actor in his dressing room. The Pirandellian 'sentimento del contrario' is clearly at work in this sequence, as dreamed-of grandeur brutally confronts a far more squalid reality. The actor flatters Leopoldo by telling him that his play contains both mind and heart, both intellect and sentiment.[31] However, it soon becomes quite obvious that Natali's declarations are empty compliments intended to hide the fact he has not read the play. In the end, he suggests that they go to a trattoria[32] where Leopoldo will be able to read the play to him while he has dinner. Once they are at the trattoria, however, Leopoldo's inspired reading is dramatically counterpointed by the sexual advances and erotic verbal exchanges between the other *vitelloni* and the variety dancers. After a while, Natali claims that he is disgusted by Leopoldo's friends and asks him to go out for a walk. Now Leopoldo releases all of his frustration: he lets out the long-repressed humiliation of living in a provincial town populated by narrow-minded individuals without ideals whose only interests are money and sex. But unconsciously he gradually falls into Natali's snare: the actor's sexual intentions eventually become explicit when he asks Leopoldo to follow him in the dark by the sea and read the play there. Overcome by disgust, Leopoldo runs away, underscoring his farewell to his illusions. Our examples could continue, since in Fellini's films there are as many 'seas' as there are dreams, personal fears, and individual fantasies.

An island, real or imaginary, serves as a perfect stage, or at least a metaphoric backdrop, for the public, social trials of the individual – the typical Pirandellian 'stanza della tortura' ('torture chamber'). At the end of these real trials, the Subject has to face his or her own isolation and alienation. This situation characterizes several of Pirandello's works as early as *L'esclusa* (*The Outcast*, 1901),[33] where the main protagonist is progressively expelled from collective life. A similar situation exists in a later work such as *Right You Are (If You Think So)*, where a whole family has to undergo a painful social trial during which each individual's existence and the reciprocal relationships of the family members are exposed to public examination on the haunting stage of Pirandello's revolutionary theatre.

The trial-like situation that characterizes so many of Pirandello's works is also central to many of Fellini's films, such as the early *I Vitelloni*. In this movie, Rimini truly becomes an island, that is, a 'total' universe where each one of the five protagonists progressively undergoes gradual unmasking so as to expose his empty inner life, which is metaphorically paralleled by a vacuous social existence.

Pensare a Rimini. Rimini: una parola fatta di aste, di soldatini in fila. Non riesco ad oggettivare. Rimini è un pastrocchio, confuso, pauroso, tenero, con questo grande respiro, questo vuoto aperto del mare. Lí la nostalgia si fa piú limpida, specie il mare d'inverno, le creste bianche, il gran vento, come l'ho visto la prima volta.[34]

To think about Rimini. Rimini: a word made of pot-hooks, little toy-soldiers in a line.[35] I'm not able to objectify it. Rimini is a hotchpotch, yet confused, scary, and tender with this profound breath, this open void represented by the sea. There nostalgia becomes more limpid, especially the sea in winter, the white crests, the forceful wind, as I saw it the first time.

The sea in winter as the director envisioned it that first 'magic' time recurs throughout Fellini's films. When considering *I Vitelloni* and *Amarcord* in reverse chronology, one realizes that the image of the winter sea retains the same immediate metaphoric meaning. Although it always stands for a world of dynamism, it necessarily implies different connotations at the various stages in the *vitelloni*'s lives. In *Amarcord*, the young *vitelloni* ecstatically watch the turbulent winter sea, since to them it represents a world of movement that immediately signifies change and possibility. They are not adults yet; hence they can still hope to escape, to fly away from reality into the world of their fantasies and dreams – a world that is not yet well defined.

Although the five protagonists in *I Vitelloni* are no longer so young, they still go to the shore and stare at a sea that is always the same on an ontological plane, still symbolizing change and possibility. If Fellini's image of the sea is characterized by repetition, it is also qualified by difference and change because of the incessant movement that is its most relevant, structural characteristic. The sea thus serves as a cruel counterpoint to the condition of stasis and changelessness of the *vitelloni*'s lives. The sea also serves as a transparent metaphor for their isolation, and becomes the symbol of an increasingly unattainable object of desire: it represents a way out of their now apparently frozen forms.

The island is also the perfect metaphor for an isolation that, far from being merely geographic, is in fact more existential and linguistic. Such a decentred place constitutes both the perfect refuge and the perfect point of departure for the typical Pirandellian and/or Fellinian Subject. For both artists, the character embodies the new modern Subject no longer unified, but instead divided and fragmented. He or she is an anti-hero who constantly tries to fly away from the highly metaphoric island, aiming at the 'centre,' while at the same time continuously flying back to it once realizing that there is no 'centre' any more, either in real or in imaginary terms, or rather that many 'centres' actually exist.

In both artists' narratives, the flight to and from the mostly 'ideal' island takes the form of a journey. This journey does not necessarily take place within a literal geographical environment; it can also be a journey in an imaginary geography, or in an individual's unconscious. While the literal journey can be either completed, interrupted, or merely suggested, what really counts is the process of undergoing a journey, as Fellini once noted while speaking about *And the Ship Sails On*: 'La verità é che la vera meta di questo viaggio sta nel viaggio stesso'[36] ('The truth is that the real end of this journey is the journey itself'). In any case, movement in place and time has an immediate parallel in movement back and forth between identification and alienation, a movement that becomes more and more dramatic as both Pirandello and Fellini approach a later stage in their artistic lives and works.

While travelling, Fellini's characters identify squares, normally at night, as ideal resting places. Squares become a sort of leitmotiv in Fellini's works, and they seem to echo the square in the central section of *The Late Mattia Pascal*. In both artists' works, however, squares also serve as the locus of the unmasking: in *The Late Mattia Pascal*, of the character's inconsistent identity as both Pascal and Adriano; in Fellini's movies, of the *vitelloni*'s lack of in-depth self-knowledge and, thus, of meaning in social as well as in existential terms, of Gelsomina's diversity in *La Strada*, and of Cabiria's loneliness in *Le notti di Cabiria* (*Nights of Cabiria*, 1957).

It must be noted that in Italy, moreover, squares often lie at the *literal* centre of the city and certainly embody the heart of social life. Insofar as the city can serve as a perfect metaphor for the realm of the Norm, or in other words the Law, squares can also be double-coded: they are simultaneously the stages of public trials imposed upon the individual (and thus the places where the dominant culture celebrates itself), and the locations of the 'carnival' – that is, the place of transgression of socially codified behaviours, in other words, of the Law.

Rome, or the Dismemberment of the Myth

The place of birth and childhood can be extremely important to an individual's formation as a public persona as well a private being. There lies the source of both our earliest and most important dreams, and our most persistent psychological disturbances. However, the city of election – the city chosen as the place for adult life – also becomes extremely relevant in the Subject's progression toward maturity. That city will supposedly represent for the Subject, and particularly for the artist, the place where dreams can come true, where psychological traumas can find resolution, and where he or she can achieve artistic plenitude. The archetypal biography of the modern Subject can be defined first of all as a search for a centre, then as a continuous denial of access to that centre, and therefore as the gradual fragmentation of the centre itself. At the very basis of the new ontology of the modern Subject, one finds, on the one hand, the desire to achieve an unattainable *unity*, and on the other, the drive toward *dissolution* and *decentredness*. Furthermore, the development of the new Subject becomes a movement from homogeneity to difference through repetition.

If one analyses Pirandello's entire work from a synchronic perspective, it soon becomes apparent that, in terms of real or imaginary geography, his whole opus represents the story of an erratic movement from the province, Girgenti, to the city, Agrigento, and back; then, from Agrigento to Palermo, and back; and, finally, from the periphery, Sicily, to the centre, Rome, and back. The same can be said for Fellini, for his entire production consists of an equally erratic movement from Gambettola to Rimini, from Rimini to Bologna, from Rimini to Rome, and then back again from Rome to Ostia, from Rome to Viterbo, from everywhere to Cinecittà, and back again to Rome. This time, though, the city becomes his own personal Rome as he recreates it in the city of cinema, his very own 'city,' the place of many different 'centres,' actually all the 'centres' one might want or need. Fellini once made the following revealing statement while speaking about Rimini:

Ages ago I bought a house ... I thought I had found a centre, a fixed point: or rather, I thought I would take up the simple life. But it must have been a phony idea because I never even saw the house; in fact I felt annoyed at the thought of a house that was shut up with no-one living in it, and that it was there, pointlessly waiting.[37]

While Pirandello and Fellini both display a remarkably similar desire for the acquisition of a 'fixed point,' they also recognize the impossibility of achieving that single 'centre.' As a result, in both authors' works, the real city progressively dissolves into a more private, less frightening, and much more comfortable place: the stage of a revolutionary theatre in Pirandello, or Cinecittà with its magic studios in Fellini. Both artists eventually found their own ideal 'centre,' which became the locus of many possible 'centres,' and in which they could freely stage their own peculiar and similar interplay of illusion and reality with a fascinating mixture of reveries and dreams.

For both Pirandello and Fellini, the city of election can be identified with Rome. In their representations, the Eternal City first of all embodies their fascination with its myth. Although each artist was obviously grounded in totally different historical and political situations, the myth is still extremely powerful in their works. Second, both artists associate Rome with an evasion of the claustrophobic condition the Subject is forced into when living on a real or metaphoric island. As a consequence, in the beginning of Pirandello's and Fellini's careers, Rome becomes an alluring object of desire, or rather the place where desire can be fulfilled and dreams realized. Even though their approaches differ, both authors' works eventually disclose the dissolution, or rather dismemberment, of the official myth of Rome. The difference in interpretation stems from the fact that Pirandello was essentially a nineteenth-century man who personally experienced the rapid evolution of modern society that led to the metropolitan era. Pirandello instinctively understood from the outset what could result from hectic progress, and he recoiled from it to the point of developing a sense of nostalgia for a past which he very early identified with Rome. In *The Late Mattia Pascal*, Pirandello states, through Mr. Paleari's words to Pascal, that Rome cannot become a modern city and therefore is as dead as the past.[38] In his later work, the image of the mythic city dissolves into a threatening metaphor for the modern metropolis, the realm of machines. A similar progression can be easily detected in Fellini's filmography as it moves from the devastating images of Rome in *La Dolce Vita* and *Fellini Satyricon* (*Fellini's Satyricon*, 1969), to the dismal representation of contemporary Rome in *Ginger e Fred* (*Ginger and Fred*, 1985) and *Intervista* (*Interview*, 1988).

Although he certainly understood the incredible new possibilities offered to modern man, Pirandello developed a tragic sense of his times, which he expressed through many of his characters. Mattia Pascal, for example, ends up in Milan after his long journey. While observing the continuous turmoil of the city, he wonders:

Oh perché gli uomini si affannano così a rendere man mano più complicato il congegno della loro vita? Perché tutto questo stordimento di macchine? E che farà l'uomo quando le macchine faranno tutto? Si accorgerà allora che il così detto progresso non ha nulla a che fare con la felicità? Di tutte le invenzioni, con cui la scienza crede onestamente d'arricchire l'umanità (e la impoverisce, perché costano tanto care), che gioia in fondo proviamo noi, anche ammirandole?[39]

Oh why ... I asked myself desperately ... does mankind toil so to make the apparatus of its living more and more complicated? Why this clatter of machines? And what will man do when machines do everything for him? Will he then realize that what is called progress has nothing to do with happiness? Even if we admire all the inventions that science sincerely believes will enrich our lives (instead they make it poorer, because their price is so high), what joy do they bring us, after all?[40]

Pascal's words are echoed by another Pirandellian character, as Serafino Gubbio, the cameraman who is both the subject-narrator and the protagonist of the novel *Shoot!*, responds to someone who asks him if he is really *necessary* after all, or if he could be replaced by a mechanism capable of turning the handle of the 'macchinetta' ('little machine'):

Non dubito però, che col tempo – sissignore – si arriverà a sopprimermi. La macchinetta – anche questa macchinetta, come tante altre macchinette – girerà da sè. Ma che cosa poi farà l'uomo quando tutte le macchinette gireranno da sè, questo, caro signore, resta ancora da vedere.[41]

I have no doubt, however, that in time, Sir, they will succeed in eliminating me. The machine – this machine too, like all the other machines – will go by itself. But what mankind will do then, after all the machines have been taught to go by themselves, that, my dear Sir, still remains to be seen.[42]

The ideal 'centre,' however, of Pirandello's as well as of Fellini's autobiography and artistic production remains Rome. The Eternal City[43] thus appears to them as a wide and intriguing metaphor for different things at different times. To both Fellini and Pirandello, Rome is not 'one,' but 'una, nessuna e centomila' ('one, nobody, and one hundred thousand'). The 'centre,' then, for both these Italian artists is ineffable, frightening, and, after all, unattainable. Ultimately, Rome turns into a perfect metaphor for artistic creation, as becomes evident in works such as Pirandello's *The Late Mattia Pascal* and *Shoot!*, or *Roma* (*Fellini's Roma*, 1972) and *Fellini's Satyricon*.

As the myth of the Eternal City progressively dissolves and the two artists search for a more private place that can embody countless 'centres,' their works gradually choose different artistic solutions. Pirandello expresses himself in the illusion of the theatre, however ambiguous. He then proceeds to the dramatic dissolution of that very illusion as well, particularly in the famous trilogy of the 'theatre in the theatre,' producing a theatrical form that has been defined as 'metatheatre.' After his 'Lumière' stage, Fellini eventually turns to his 'Méliès' phase, to use Barthélemy Amengual's terminology,[44] moving 'du spectacle au spectaculair'[45] ('from spectacle to spectacular'), that is, decisively turning to a cinema of fantasy and illusion that, nevertheless, constantly discusses the validity of its own discourse and therefore can be defined as 'metacinema.' Later in this study, I shall discuss the similarities between these two paths to artistic maturity, and the obvious influences of Pirandello's theory of the theatre in the theatre upon Fellini's enticing metacinema.

Pirandello and Fellini, then, chose Rome as their city of election for quite similar reasons. 'Perché a Roma e non altrove?' ('Why Rome and not somewhere else?') wonders Mattia Pascal while looking back at his past and reconsidering the events of his peculiar life. At that point in the novel, he decides not to unveil the true reason for his choice, or rather, he decides to reveal only part of the truth, 'Scelsi allora Roma, prima di tutto perché mi piacque sopra ogni altra città, e poi perché mi parve più adatta a ospitar con indifferenza, tra tanti forestieri, un forestiere come me'[46] ('I chose Rome first of all because I liked it more than any other city, and also because it seemed more suited to receive with indifference, among all the other foreigners, a foreigner like myself').[47]

As will become apparent through the novel, Rome is the city where, according to the statements Pirandello has Mattia Pascal make, one can be 'forestiere della vita' ('a stranger in life'), and then really 'live,' or rather see oneself live and 'crearSi' ('to create Oneself'). Similarly, Rome is the city where, according to Fellini, 'non sei nessuno, quindi puoi anche essere tutto'[48] ('you are nobody, thus you can be anything'). The ideal affinity present in the two artists' points of departure and in their relationship with Rome thus becomes immediately evident. Although their subsequent artistic statements will produce a slightly different picture of the Eternal City as they individually experienced it, they somehow maintain close points of contact and strong similarities. Rome, after all, is a place where one can be anything one wants to be; in Rome it is always possible to start afresh. By being the place where different times and places meet, Rome also becomes the city where the individual can be a 'nobody' and, thus, also be anybody and/or anything he or she wants to be.

Both Fellini and Pirandello went to Rome in their early twenties. To both of them, Rome symbolized an escape from the claustrophobic provinces as well as an avenue to the realization of their dreams. Pirandello hoped to become a writer and a dramatist, while Fellini desired to become a journalist. At the time of his arrival in Rome as a young man, Fellini was not yet thinking about the cinema, although most of his imagery was imbued with the allusiveness and the magic of the moving pictures.

That longed-for escape from the provinces is cinematically portrayed in Fellini's *Amarcord* as well as in *I Vitelloni*, where the five *vitelloni* seem to stand for different facets of the same individual – an archetypal Mattia Pascal. In Pirandello's *The Late Mattia Pascal*, in fact, Mattia describes both his brother and himself as *vitelloni*: young idlers, oblivious to their true identity, unwilling to take on either emotional or social responsibility. Pirandello's *vitelloni* thus provide a literary precedent for Fellini's youngsters. Both authors regard their characters with tender complacency, although they constantly unmask their emptiness and idleness.

As Mattia's departure from his home town is partially fortuitous, so is the parting of Moraldo in *I Vitelloni*. Neither Pascal nor Moraldo really decides his future; life decides for them. Moraldo leaves Rimini early one morning, when everyone else is still asleep. At the station, when he is about to get on the train, a young boy named Guido, who has served as his questioning alter ego throughout the entire movie, asks him why he is leaving. The only answer Moraldo manages to provide is, 'Non lo so. Parto' ('I don't know. I'm leaving'). As Guido pressures him for further details about where he is going, Moraldo can only reply with the same answer: 'Non lo so' ('I don't know'). The last sequence of the film presents a series of subjective travelling shots from Moraldo's point of view which constitute a lengthy and caressing gaze from the train onto the other *vitelloni* who are still sleeping at home. The other *vitelloni*, on the other hand, are nothing but various facets of Moraldo himself that he leaves behind, or tries to leave behind, even though he is oblivious to the true motives underlying his departure.

Pascal leaves his home town by chance as well. Thanks to the money his brother sent him for their mother's funeral – which he did not have to spend since the city paid for it – Pascal goes to Montecarlo to seek his fortune at the casino. When, later on, he is about to return to his unhappy family situation with the money he has won at the roulette table, he can avoid returning because of a fortuitous and rather unbelievable circumstance. He reads in a local paper that his family has identified the body of a suicide as his own.

It becomes apparent in both artists' narratives that the Subject does not truly decide his own fate. Life, with its strange and unpredictable occurrences, somehow brings each character to take one particular path rather than another. At this point, the Subject is no longer able to assume any true responsibility for his destiny: he does not really live, but sees himself living, as Pirandello repeatedly observed. At first, then, in both Pirandello and Fellini, the Subject's journey toward self-understanding and self-recognition parallels the mythic process that leads to the very roots of the foundation of a city that is the well-established centre of society, culture, and religion. The foundation of Rome as a psychic centre for the Subject assumes the same mythic dimension that the foundation of Rome as a centre of civilization had reflected.[49] In the end, however, both Pirandello and Fellini eventually realize that there is no longer one 'valid' centre for the new Subject. They seem to postulate that the solution relies on the acceptance of psychological as well as social *decentredness* as a constitutional, structural element of the Subject, which becomes even more apparent in such works as *Shoot!* and in Pirandello's trilogy of the theatre in the theatre, as well as in Fellini's *Otto e mezzo* (*8½*, 1963) and, in such later films as *Fellini's Satyricon, Fellini's Roma, Prova d'orchestra* (*Orchestra Rehearsal*, 1979), and *And the Ship Sails On*. Even in his two last artistic efforts, *Intervista* (*Interview*, 1988) and *La voce della luna* (*The Voice of the Moon*, 1990), Fellini brings that quite early existential and philosophical intuition to extreme fruition.

As the narrator informs us over the opening credits, *Fellini's Roma* is the story of a city, a story filtered through the director's own subjective recollections. The film juxtaposes flashbacks from Fellini's childhood and his youth with present-day filmmaking. The narration proceeds at a slow tempo in scenes of the distant past, but progressively accelerates as the film approaches the present. Then there is the 'time' of Rome, apparently 'objective' but instead remarkably deceitful. After all, this film is *not* the story of a city, but the story of Fellini's Rome as the director's voice-over informs us as the opening credits roll across the screen: 'When I was a young boy, Rome for me was only a mixture of strange and contradictory images.'[50]

The film opens with a pretension of historical validity, and hence masks the narration with a semi-real sequential progression. Although the movie starts by presenting apparently objective scenes from Fellini's youth in Rimini organized in chronological progression, the sense of actuality is defeated by the narrator's voice-over, which serves as a distancing factor to remind us, the audience, that we are witnessing only a flashback, a memory. Leaving aside for the moment the intriguing question of the narrator's identity, the ontological 'validity' of that memory, and therefore the important problem of subjective discourse in Fellini's work, I shall for the moment accept that memory as a piece, however fictionalized, of Fellini's past. But the quality of the images and the tempo of the cinematic narration give that memory the character of a fairy-tale: the past is a magic place; things are different there, almost awe-inspiring. This narrative segment, like so many other nostalgic recollections from the past in Fellini's cinema, bears the epiphanic quality of Proust's 'intermittences du coeur' ('intermittences of the heart'). Yet, while for Proust the past is a foreign country where people do things differently, to Fellini's mind the past is both a comforting and a magic place. It is certainly not a far-away or foreign country, since the director constantly reinvents it through his own imagination and therefore makes it familiar to himself and to us as well.

'The first Roman image I can recall is that of a mysterious stone eaten up by time.' This opening comment of the voice-over is joined to a fantastic landscape where an ancient street sign marked 'Roma km.340' stands out in the moonlight. A group of *contadine* ('women fieldhands') walk by, holding their bicycles and talking about someone who just wrote from 'America.' Assuming a childlike perspective, Fellini exploits one of the major traits of traditional fairy-tale narration[51] by turning the street sign into a charm-object with magic powers to evoke the time when Rome was to him a distant and enchanted place, the ancient parallel of what America stands for today – a new world, a land of dreams. The dreamlike quality of that first nocturnal image of Rome eventually reverberates in many subsequent nocturnal images of the Eternal City in Fellini's films.

This same dreamlike quality can be detected in many of Pirandello's nocturnal images of Rome, such as the one provided by Mattia Pascal in one of his many nocturnal wanderings:

Ricordo una notte, in Piazza San Pietro, l'impressione di sogno, d'un sogno quasi lontano, ch'io m'ebbi da quel mondo secolare, racchiuso lí tra le braccia del portico maestoso, nel silenzio che pareva accresciuto dal continuo fragore delle due fontane. M'accostai ad una di esse, e allora quell'acqua soltanto mi sembrò viva, lí, e tutto il resto quasi spettrale e profondamente malinconico nella silenziosa, immota solennità.[52]

I remember one night, in St Peter's Square, I felt I was in a dream, an almost distant dream, which came to me in that past world, gathered there in the arms of the majestic colonnade, in the silence that the constant sound of the two fountains seemed only to increase. I went over to one of them, and then that water seemed alive to me, and all the rest seemed ghostly and profoundly melancholy in the motionless solemnity.[53]

At first, then, Mattia's impression of nocturnal Rome is one of a dream as well – until the silence is interrupted, and even emphasized, by the noise of the fountains in St Peter's Square. As Mattia approaches one of the fountains, the living water stands in sharp contrast to the ghostlike stillness of the monumental surroundings.

This Pirandellian picture of the Eternal City finds a curious parallel in the next-to-last narrative segment of *Fellini's Roma*. After the open-air trattoria sequence, in which we witness the metaphorical contamination of the day by the night, the director's 'mechanical eye,' the camera, wanders around a silent and mysterious Rome where everything is still but the fountains, which incessantly pour water and thus constitute the only *living* image in that sepulchral atmosphere. In these two narratives, a negative analogy obviously connects the night with the past, and with stasis and death, while the incessant cycle of the water in the fountains stands for continuous flux, and therefore for life escaping from form.

On the other hand, Rome soon becomes associated with the impossibility of connecting the time of myth (and its impossible reappropriation by the Subject) with the new, historical time produced by the invasion of the bourgeoisie in Pirandello and of the *new barbarians* in Fellini. The Pirandellian protagonist is caught between two conflicting Romes. First, one finds a diurnal Rome, a hectic and yet sterile world whose incessant movement does not lead to any meaningful thing or place since it has lost any sense of its own meaning and purpose (for example, the analogy between Rome and the ashtray made by Mr Paleari in *The Late Mattia Pascal*). One also confronts a nocturnal Rome, a realm of stasis and void embodied by a frozen monumentality. This dichotomy between day and night, movement and stasis is perfectly portrayed in many of Fellini's films. Pirandello's and Fellini's mythological worlds grow through self-reflection and self-reproduction, and hence these early analogies soon develop into others, such as the dichotomy of upper/lower: the lower world, or rather the underworld, is for Pirandello a place where dreamers and artists live (i.e., *Shoot!*), while the 'upper world' constitutes the realm of mechanized man – of man reduced to being merely a hand turning a handle. Since the juxtaposition of city and countryside seemingly parallels, by negative analogy, the juxtaposition of form – and, therefore, death – and life, in both Pirandello's and Fellini's artistic statements, the Subject is progressively expelled from the city and from the scene, as becomes evident in the pessimistic endings of such later works of Pirandello as *The Giants of the Mountains* and of those of Fellini, such as *Ginger and Fred* and *Interview*.

The seemingly elegiac beginning of *Fellini's Roma* is constantly contaminated by the ironic juxtaposition of images and words, a narrative technique that is characterized by the deceitful retelling by an older and more mature Fellini (now a director) of his first encounters with Rome. This artful recounting of his past obviously works toward the creation of a humorous effect. Young Fellini encountered Rome through different social institutions – school, church, family – as well as through various artistic media (the theatre and, of course, the cinema). Dominant images were, then, those of papal Rome, Mussolini's Rome, and, above all, the glamorous portrayals of the imperial Rome of Julius Caesar, as represented on the screen in the epics of Italian silent cinema. Every piece of this filmic autobiography is, however, 'contaminated' by Fellini's irreverent humour, which undermines any possible ceremonial and commemorative tone: from the outset, *Fellini's Roma* does not appear to be a celebration of the official myth, for Rome was not, to Fellini's mind, nor to Pirandello's, a 'bella totalità'[54] ('a beautiful totality').

The same irreverent tone one finds in Fellini's early pictures of Rome also characterizes Pirandello's first impressions of the city, as becomes apparent in a letter he wrote to his sister on 9 March 1888. In it he describes a visit to the Colosseum at night, and then continues:

Salii al Campidoglio, ed ammirai il *deretano* del cavallo di Marco Aurelio e: te beato, gridai, che l'hai di bronzo antico, di bronzo antico che si scopre in oro!. ... *Mi ridussi* in via Vittorio Emanuele, e poi, gironzando, in via Ripetta, e dall'alto del Ponte di Ripetta guardai il Tevere, e pensai: Se mi vi gettassi dentro, morirei da proconsole! Ma *mi acchetai* a vivere da 'homo novus.'[55]

I went up to the Campidoglio, and admired the buttocks of Marco Aurelio's horse and: you lucky one, I shouted, who have it made of antique bronze that looks like gold! ... I ended up in Via Vittorio Emanuele, and then, wandering about, in Via Ripetta, and high from the Ripetta Bridge I gazed down to the Tiber, and thought: If I jumped in, I would die like a proconsul! But I settled down to living as a 'homus novus.'

A signifier such as 'deretano' in reference to the rump of Marco Aurelio's horse obviously implies a derogatory judgment, which is, nevertheless, modified by the fact that the horse's rump is at least made of bronze. The reflexive verb 'mi ridussi,' which describes his heading toward 'via Vittorio Emanuele,' displays an irreverent attitude toward the new monarchy, and clearly signifies the contempt in which Pirandello held the Rome of the present and which painfully reminds the night wanderer of the disintegration of the earlier, nobler imperial myth. The phrase 'mi acchetai a vivere da 'homo novus" reinforces the sense of a possible nostalgia present in the artist, who has to resign himself to live as an ordinary, middle-class individual, being denied even the possibility of dying in heroic fashion. This irreverent perspective clearly finds an echo in all of Fellini's various portrayals of the Eternal City's mythical dimensions.

In Fellini's Rome, as in Pirandello's, the present is a time of confusion, the time of the ultimate contamination of the past. This past is no longer the heroic past of imperial Rome, however, but the past of one's youth. But for the director, it is also a magic time in which he could dream of Rome through the movies, through the myth of the music halls; the Rome of beautiful and ineffable women, the Rome of his sweetest illusions. When that mythical Rome was to be compared with the real Rome of the war, the postwar years, and the new democracy, the earlier illusions were shaken and remained almost completely unrealized.

For Pirandello, the past is immediately connected to the dream of the Italian Risorgimento – the re-establishment of a new, modern republican Rome on the ruins of its ancient republican and imperial ancestors – which would eventually prove illusory. The myth of Rome had developed in his mind since childhood through the stories of both his mother and her family – all of whom were actively engaged in the fight against the Borbons – and of his father, who fought with Garibaldi in 1860 in Milazzo, Reggio, and by the Volturno River. The young Pirandello's fascination with the Rome of the Risorgimento eventually ran up against the far cruder reality of Humbertine Rome, characterized by political scandals, general corruption, and uncontrolled urban development. Such a depressing situation finds a parallel in Fellini's Rome of the 1950s, when the country was experiencing a so-called 'economic boom' during the first decade of its newly born Republic. To both authors, the *illusione* became *fatale* once it confronted reality, and therefore produced complete disillusionment in them. This historical process, however, plays a far more dramatic role in Pirandello's existential and artistic experience than it does in Fellini's.

After his early films, which constitute the basic steps in Fellini's definition of an ideal 'centre' for existential as well as artistic growth, the director definitively recognized and chose Rome as his city of election. The archetypal Fellinian Subject, therefore, also chose Rome as the place in which to experience adult life, to fulfil his dreams, and to achieve maturity: Rome became the city of the ultimate illusion. In *Fellini's Roma*, after the flashbacks into his childhood, we find young Federico – possibly Moraldo, Fellini's alter ego in *I Vitelloni* – getting off the train in Rome almost twenty years later. Only at the time of the making of *Roma* could Fellini look back at himself as a young man, now that his dream had come true and he was finally able to revisit that past and then recreate it in order to make it part of his mythical world through his artistic creations. The situation parallels Mattia Pascal's attempt to explain the motivation for his move to Rome as Adriano Meis, and ultimately for his act of writing the novel. What counts is not a faithful retelling of past events, for reality does not interest either Fellini or Pirandello: for both of them, art is, in any case, truer than life. Furthermore, in Fellini's vision, reality has to become 'fabulous' to be viable for the Subject, who otherwise constantly tries to escape from it.

The sequence of the young man's arrival at the station in Rome constitutes one of the many flashbacks in *Fellini's Roma*. As he gets off the train, the camera assumes his point of view and subjectively records the extreme confusion in the station, in order to charge the images with the puzzlement young Federico – or, at least, the voice-over narrator – is experiencing. The station itself represents Rome in microcosm – simply a metaphor for the city. Although Fellini's picture of Rome is more benign than Pirandello's, the sequence at the station and the scenes that follow, which provide a vivid description of the city, parallel Pirandello's more moralistic and severe works. For example, in 'Triste,' a poem he wrote as a young man, Pirandello describes his first impressions of the Eternal City and its inhabitants:

Ecco la folla. – Chierici e beoni,
giovani e vecchi, femine ed ostieri,
soldati, rivenduglioli, acattoni,

voi nati d'ozio e di lascivia, seri
uomini no, ma pance, lieti amanti,
bottegaj, vetturini, gazzettieri,
voi vagheggini, anzi stoffe ambulanti,
donne vendute da l'inceder franco,
goffe nutrici, e voi dame eleganti,
quale strano spettacolo a lo stanco
di rimirar, non sazio, occhio offerite
cosí male accozzate in largo branco.
Oh vïaggio curioso de le vite
sciocche d'innumerabili mortali!
Oh per le vie de la città spedite,

che retata di drammi originali![56]

Here is the crowd – Clergymen and drunkards,
youth and elderly, women and innkeepers,
soldiers, peddlers, tramps,
you born of idleness and lust, serious
men certainly not, but only bellies, merry lovers,
shopkeepers, coachmen, hack reporters,
you young gallants, or better wandering clothes,
lost women with a frank gait,
clumsy wet-nurses, and you elegant ladies,
what strange spectacle to the tired
to gaze, not satisfied, eye you offer
so poorly jumbled up together in a large flock.
Oh curious journey of the silly
lives of innumerable mortals!
Oh you dispersed along the streets of the city,

what a catch of original dramas!

That the Romans are truly 'seri uomini no, ma pance' to Fellini, too,
becomes immediately apparent in the sequence at the open-air trattoria
on the night of the young man's arrival in Rome. For Fellini, women are
likewise 'donne vendute da l'inceder franco,' which becomes evident
from the way they are portrayed in this movie and in many other
Fellini films. Few female characters in the director's entire oeuvre es-

cape this inclement description, although it must be said that in Fellini's peculiar imaginary world, this is not necessarily a negative description, while it certainly is derogatory in Pirandello's poem. In conclusion, Rome certainly appears as a 'retata di drammi originali' in both authors' representations of it.

In his short but enlightening study of Pirandello's relationship with Rome, Giovanni Marchi describes the artist's first impression of the city as one of 'trista allegria' ('sad cheerfulness').[57] This definition also seems applicable to Fellini who, while not failing to be attracted by the vivacity and colourfulness of Rome and the Romans, nevertheless provides an irreverent portrayal of both the city and its inhabitants. By contrast, Pirandello himself was deeply fascinated by the grandiose live spectacle performed on that unique stage, since in his poem he defined Rome as an amazing network of original dramas.

Following the station sequence, Fellini affords us a series of travelling shots of Rome from young Federico's point of view as he travels by bus. The celebratory tone is progressively deflated by the desecrating editing, which contrasts the glamòrous picture of monumental Rome with the vulgarity of the Romans and reaches its peak at the end of the bus ride in a short interlude in front of a butcher shop. Fellini continues this narrative segment with a medium shot of himself as a young man, his back to the camera, as he stands at the front door of a building looking upward. He then climbs the first flight of stairs, stops on the stairway, and asks a man (shown back to the camera in medium close-up) where the Palletta family lives. This is the boarding house where he will eventually settle in Rome, and this is the point of departure for his long-awaited and dreamed-of Roman adventure.

Whether or not this constitutes a fragment of authentic autobiography, the story is similar to that of one of Pirandello's characters in the short story, 'Un'altra allodola' ('Another Skylark,' 1928). In this work, Luca Pelletta – whose last name is clearly echoed in the family name in Fellini's film – is the one who arrives in Rome as young Federico does, with a suitcase full of dreams. Although the surface structure of the two works might be slightly different, the names 'Palletta' and 'Pelletta,' besides sounding alike, reveal a similar and implicit authorial intention: they are both diminutives with derogative meaning, and therefore show a similarity in the two narratives' deep structures.

Luca Pelletta non avrebbe riconosciuto alla stazione di Roma Santi Currao, se questi non gli si fosse fatto avanti chiamandolo ripetutamente:

– Amico Pelletta! Amico Pelletta!
Intontito dal viaggio, tra la ressa e il rimescolio dei passeggeri che gli davano la
vertigine, restò a mirarlo sbalordito.[58]

At the railway station in Rome, Luca Pelletta wouldn't have recognized Santi
Currao, if he did not come forward calling him repeatedly:
– Pelletta, my friend! Pelletta, my friend!
In a daze from the journey, in the throng and the excitement of the passengers
that gave him dizziness, he remained looking at him in bewilderment.

Luca Pelletta is only one of the two protagonists of Pirandello's short
story. Both men are artists, but the friend who meets him at the station,
'un gran maestro di musica'[59] ('a great music teacher'), has come to the
capital before him, and now lives in poverty. However, not only has he
failed to discover what he went there to find – an opportunity to exer-
cise his art and a recognition of his artistic value – but also in the big
city, pressured by economic needs, his family has disintegrated, and his
wife has left him to become a prostitute. In Pirandello's world poverty
not only destroys people's dreams but also contaminates their moral
standards. When Currao asks him how long he intends to remain in
Rome, Luca expresses his intention of staying there forever, since after
all, he adds ironically, Rome is the city he always dreamed of: 'E' la mia
città! L'ho sempre sognata'[60] ('It is my city! I always dreamt of it'). The
last words of the short story – 'Santi, risorgeremo! lascia fare a me!'[61]
('Santi, we'll be resurrected! leave it to me!') – unmask the underlying
irony contained in the previous assertion and reveal the typical attitude
of the Pirandellian 'umorista' who is constantly conscious of the clash
between illusion and reality. The figure of the 'umorista,' normally associated with individualistic concerns, here connects to a more collective condition, and hence is charged with political connotations, for
Luca's words stand in sharp contrast to his dismal reality. In Pirandello's vision, then, the city also becomes the place where the individual undergoes deep corruption. Yet in this particular short story, and
through a metaphoric process, in most of his novels, Pirandello's discourse seems to take on the characteristics of a message to the collectiv-
ity, or at least to one specific social group – the artists and the dreamers
– instead of being simply charged with his usual, merely individualistic
concerns. Similarly, in Fellini's Roma, the director appears for once engaged in a discourse that does not simply affect the individual as artist,

but addresses the collective consciousness (the malaise running through the entire social organization) and the unconscious (each individual's secret fears of an approaching end of the world).

Thus, to Fellini and Pirandello, the Rome of their youth stood for the place where dreams could be realized, the locus of their fondest illusions. In the next-to-last sequence of *Fellini's Roma*, there is no longer any ambiguity over the identity of the narrating voice, for now the artistic and existential experience clearly declares itself as Fellini's. The director's crew is filming the yearly summer event in which the Romans celebrate themselves, the 'Festa de noiantri.' After the camera has restlessly moved around a piazza in an increasingly erratic carousel, it finally comes to a halt and begins recording the central section of the sequence and perhaps of the whole film. This is the narrative segment that will provide the intellectual justification for the entire work. The crew spots the famous American writer, Gore Vidal, who just happens to be part of that group of wild revellers coarsely consummating a celebration of 'themselves.' As soon as the crew approaches the writer to interview him, and even before they begin questioning him, Vidal starts speaking:

Well, I suppose you are about to ask me that inevitable question: Why do I live in Rome? You could say I live here because it's so ... CENTRAL *(turning to one of his table-mates, obviously Italian)* CENTRALE!! ... But most of all, I like the Romans. They don't care if you lived or died ... They're like cats. And, of course, it is *the city of illusions*. The city, after all, of the Church, of government, of the movies. They are all makers of illusion. I am one, too. And so are you ... and now that the world dies through over-population ... *(The Italian interrupts him)* Yes, by Americans! *(Vidal smiles and continues)* ... the last illusion is at hand. And what better place than a city which has died so many times, and was resurrected so many times, to watch the real end through pollution, over-population. It seems to me the perfect place to watch if we end or not. *(The other at the table proposes a toast)* Well, to the end![62]

As the echo of Vidal's words dies out, on the other side of the hedge that divides the tables of the trattoria from the rest of the little square, a large group of youngsters sitting on the stairs singing is suddenly and forcefully charged by the police. This scene receives an ironic parallel in the scene of a boxing match that follows immediately. The message relies on the juxtaposition of the two displays of violence – both gratuitous, but of a substantially different nature. Such a juxtaposition ultimately meets Fellini's usual need to ridicule each event's substance, that is, collective celebrations of power and violence.

A literary antecedent of this cinematic narrative can be found in one of Pirandello's early novels, *Suo marito* (*Her Husband*, 1911), where in the beginning of the narration Attilio Raceni, on his way to the house of Dora Barmis, finds himself in the midst of a violent riot in Rome's Piazza Venezia. In order to understand what will follow in the story, one has to bear in mind Raceni's features: he is a kind of pseudo-intellectual (his mother had been a famous poet), a representative of the literary salons in the Italy of the Risorgimento. In the novel, the intellectual milieu of the time is described as being vacuous and idle, the literary counterpart of the society's political 'entourage.' Raceni is a perfect member of that society, and is in fact the chief editor of a magazine for women, which he defines as 'femminile' and, of course, not 'femminista.' As the wealthy descendant of a famous American family, Gore Vidal is strikingly similar to Raceni in both temperament and social standing, quite aside from his role as a passively observant intellectual in the Eternal City.

In Fellini's film, after the boxing match scene, two things occur. First of all, at a table (and therefore in a place set apart from what is taking place in the square) a man – possibly a politician – criticizes the new Romans for being permissive, and then praises the police for suppressing any form of dissent expressed by the younger generation, which he defines as the 'dregs of society.' Then, another old man not only reacts to what is happening, but actually sides with the youngsters and is consequently attacked by the police.

In Pirandello's novel, Raceni also gets charged by the police, although not because of his sympathetic attitude toward the protesters or his identification with the issues they express. Raceni constitutes a literary parallel and a historical antecedent to both Vidal and the 'politician' who criticizes the Romans. Unable to go his own way because of the riot, Raceni begins to resent the rioters: 'Ora ci voleva anche la canaglia che reclamava per le vie di Roma qualche nuovo diritto; e, santo Dio, s'era d'aprile e faceva un tempo stupendo: il fervido tepore del primo sole inebriava!'[63] ('Now the only thing we needed was indeed that rabble claiming some new rights in the streets of Rome; and, for God's sake, it was April and the weather was splendid: the lively warmth of the first sun was intoxicating'). And again, soon after, 'nel dispetto rabbioso contro tutta *quella feccia dell'umanità* che non voleva starsi quieta'[64] ('in the angry annoyance against all those dregs of humanity who wouldn't remain quiet'), he tries to get help from the police but is violently pushed away with the others, with the 'mob.' Pirandello's attitude here, far from being simply 'umoristica,' clearly falls into harsh sarcasm: 'Via, via con gli altri, via a gambe levate, lui, Attilio Raceni, inseguito dalla cavalleria, Attilio Raceni direttore della rassegna femminile (non femminista) Le muse ... – Vigliacchi! Canaglia! Farabutti! – gridava'[65] ('Away, away with the others, away in flight, he, Attilio Raceni sought after by the cavalry, Attilio Raceni the editor-in-chief of the female [not feminist] journal The Muses ... – Cowards! Scoundrels! Rascals! – he shouted').

Contrary to what one might imagine, the abusive names are not addressed to the police but are intended for the rioters. Raceni does not learn, for he does not wish to. He belongs to a class that does not wish to know, for that would mean becoming contaminated and then, inevitably, changing and losing one's privileges. His reaction, therefore, is to show outraged contempt: 'Avrebbe voluto, per riacquistare il sentimento della propria dignità mortificata, riandar lì, ricacciarsi nella mischia, afferrare per il petto a uno a uno quei mascalzoni e pestarseli sotto i piedi'[66] ('He would have liked to go back there, to regain the feeling of his mortified dignity, and, upon delving into the fray, to grab one by one those rascals by the lapels and stamp his feet on them').

Although enraged for having been associated with and dirtied by the mob, he ends up transposing what happens to him into an image; that is, he translates the event into an aesthetic experience that becomes just another way of reaffirming his separation and superiority: 'Ah bestie, bestie, bestie! come si rizzavano trionfanti su le zampe posteriori, urlando e annaspando, per ghermire l'offa dei ciarlatani! Quest'immagine gli piacque, e si confortò alquanto'[67] ('Ah animals, animals, animals! how triumphantly would they rise on their hind legs, screaming and groping blindly to seize the charlatans' sop! He liked this image, and took courage considerably').

Pirandello is here clearly mocking those pseudo-intellectuals who crowded the Rome of the Risorgimento, and who were more interested in turning the artist and his or her work into a commodity and in quantifying them both rather than in considering the quality of the work itself. His Raceni clearly epitomizes the Dannunzian artist, who interprets everything in life in aesthetic terms. This fact is underscored later when Raceni does not hesitate to expose Silvia Roncella, the writer who is the main female character of the story, to an equally, if not more, violent expropriation during the banquet Raceni himself has organized to introduce her into the Roman literary salons. The narrative segment of the banquet stands in the same relation to the previous one of the riot as the sequence of police aggression stands to the boxing match in Fellini's movie. Each unit in both narrative pairs works together with the other toward one single meaning through ironic or, rather, humoristic juxtaposition.

As the Rome of the literary salons progressively dissolves into the Rome of the film studios, Pirandello's narrative works testify to the negative analogy linking the city to the machine, which becomes an obvious threat in the author's imagination and consciousness. As Franca Angelini pointed out, the image of the city portrayed in Pirandello's later works is nothing but 'una sintesi antifuturista perchè condotta con la stessa percezione spazio-temporale dei futuristi ma in termini valutativi rovesciati'[68] ('an anti-futurist synthesis since it was conducted with the spatio-temporal perception of the futurists but with reversed evaluational terms'). The ideological overturning of the futurist ideology becomes particularly evident in Pirandello's novel on the cinema, *Shoot!*, as is exempified in Serafino Gubbio's most quoted statement, which is almost a manifesto of Pirandello's late existential and artistic visions:

Avanti! Avanti perchè non s'abbia tempo né modo d'avvertire il peso della tristezza, l'avvilimento della vergogna, che restano dentro, in fondo. Fuori, è un balenio continuo, uno sbarbaglio incessante: tutto guizza e scompare.

Che cos'è? Niente, è passato! Era forse una cosa triste; ma niente, ora è passata.

C'è una molestia, però, che non passa. La sentite? Un calabrone che ronza sempre, cupo, fosco, brusco, sotto sotto, sempre. Che è? Il ronzio dei pali telegrafici? lo striscio continuo della carrucola lungo il filo dei tram elettrici? il fremito incalzante di tante macchine, vicine, lontane? quello del motore dell'automobile? quello dell'apparecchio cinematografico?

Il battito del cuore però non s'avverte, non s'avverte il pulsar delle arterie. Guaj, se s'avvertisse! ma questo ronzio, questo ticchettio perpetuo, sì, e dice che non è naturale tutta questa furia turbinosa, tutto questo guizzare e scomparire d'immagini; ma c'è sotto un meccanismo, il quale pare lo insegua, stridendo precipitosamente.

Si spezzerà?[69]

On! On, that we may not have time nor power to heed the burden of sorrow, the degradation of shame which remain with us, in our hearts. Outside, there is a continuous glare, an incessant giddiness: everything flickers and disappears.

'What was that?' Nothing, it has passed! Perhaps it was something sad; but no matter, it has passed now.

There is one nuisance, however, that does not pass away. Do you hear it? A hornet that is always buzzing, forbidding, grim, surly, diffused, and never stops. What is it? The hum of telegraph poles? The endless scream of the trolley along the overhead wire of the electric trams? The urgent throb of all those countless machines, near and far? That of the engine of the motor-car? of the cinematograph?

The beating of the heart is not felt, nor do we feel the pulsing of the arteries. The worse for us if we did! But this buzzing, this perpetual ticking we do notice, and I say that all this furious haste is not natural, all this flickering and vanishing of images; but that there lies beneath it a machine which seems to pursue it frantically screaming.

Will it break down?[70]

Within the perspective assumed in the present study, Serafino Gubbio's words in Pirandello's *Shoot!* find an echo in a number of Fellini's images – for example, in *Fellini's Roma*, but also in a number of other films, such as *Ginger and Fred* and *Interview*. After the sequence at the open-air trattoria on the night of young Fellini's arrival in Rome, *Fellini's Roma* continues with a frenetic roundabout along the circular highway that surrounds Rome. This Saturnian ring becomes a surrealistic place, a semi-hellish and completely recreated reality where humanity is portrayed in its wholeness, both present and past, through Fellini's indiscrete and merciless camera eye.

In both Pirandello's words (through Serafino's reasoning) and Fellini's images, then, reality becomes reduced to flickering reflections of self-replicating cars caught in a terrifying traffic jam, of faceless people packed in automobiles and buses with virtually no way out, of ever-changing landscapes where real and unreal follow each other without solution or continuity. Over this Babel-like confusion there reigns a perpetual and haunting screeching sound, the sound of an all-devouring mechanism that, in Pirandello's words, hastily chases after the ever-changing and darting images of life caught on this blind path. This gripping representation is the apocalyptic prophecy of the approaching end of the world, an end that will occur while the sky is crying. Will everything collapse? Will we witness the end of the world? In Pirandello's pessimistic statement, in the machine age one can no longer hear the heart beating. In Fellini's apocalyptic vision, a white horse, appearing out of nowhere (a direct citation from *La Strada*, where the animal's appearance served the same surrealistic and poetic purpose), eventually finds its way out of the apparently suffocating reality. The white horse clearly symbolizes the creative mind, and creativity is Fellini's answer to a world that seems to have lost its sense of true meaning in life, a world where man is trapped or victimized by automatization, dehumanization, and alienation.

Pirandello provides a similar answer to an almost identical existential and artistic problem at the end of his last novel, *One, Nobody, and One Hundred Thousand*, in which the city, now at last the perfect metaphor for a world of social conditioning and alienation, is far away. At a certain point in both Pirandello's and Fellini's artistic works, then, the myth of the Eternal City as a centre of culture and as a symbol of rebirth – either of the Risorgimento or of the fascist regime – gives way to the image of a nameless metropolis, the perfect locus for futurist and positivist mythology. As a consequence, the Subject is now called upon to acknowledge first of all his or her alienation (once he or she finally recognizes the fact of being the locus of the clash between social mask and interior face), and, second, to acknowledge the frustrating reality of being restricted inside closed boundaries within the social organization—which is one of the main structuring principles not only of the modern city, but of human life itself. In order to escape the fatal impoverishment produced in the Subject by being reduced to a mere function within a society based primarily upon economic values, the individual in general, and the creative mind in particular, is obliged to leave the city, which now symbolizes the norm or, as defined by Jacques Lacan, the Law. At the conclusion of Pirandello's last novel, his protagonist is freed from the all-enclosing conditionings of a society where man no longer attains any freedom or is granted merely an illusory liberty. The ultimate response to such a situation in the vision of both Pirandello and Fellini expresses itself as a fantastic, free play of the imagination.

At the end of *Fellini's Roma*, the director's camera is at first caught up in recording the frenetic roundabout that the new barbarians perform on their motorcycles around the city and its heart, the Colosseum. Once it reaches the centre, however, Fellini's camera, and therefore Fellini's eye, is freed and can 'lead' the barbarians – and, more importantly, his viewers – out of the circle. In the same way, the ending of *8½* shows Guido as a young boy leading the clowns out of the circus ring, thus avoiding a restricting and confining sense of closure. In a later and somewhat more pessimistic conclusion, two old musichall dancers, the main protagonists of *Ginger and Fred*, not only leave Rome, but are also literally expelled from the scene, together with Fellini's camera. The Rome depicted in this film has been invaded by newer barbarians symbolized by the heartless world of television. This new medium brings the Subject back to a cruder sense of reality. At the end of the film, Ginger and Fred not only leave the city, but actually renounce their own fantasies and memories. Now that the new, all-devouring machine has adulterated everything, it is no longer possible to escape from a disturbing reality by finding refuge in past memories. Unfortunately, in fact, even this ultimate dream proves to be illusory for the two protagonists, since in a world that is ruled by the ever-changing and hectic present, past recollections are rendered vain and devoid of meaning and function in the Subject's search for a viable identity.

In his last years, Fellini seemed to be experiencing a sort of regression in which he nurtured a nostalgia for a now at last truly impossible 'centredness.' When Rome turned out to be no longer credible as a maker of illusions and myths, Fellini found refuge in his own city, Cinecittà. When even that recreated and invented 'centre' lost its magic powers, the creative mind's only choice seemed to be to disappear from the scene. Consequently, the dominant images in Fellini's later films are suggestive of death: dying becomes a way to escape disintegration, for in and beyond death man finds an ultimate and everlasting form. Similarly, as Paolo Puppa maintains, in Pirandello's later works the funeral scene becomes an alternative to the precarious nature of life. Yet the theatrical stage offers a life after death to characters, who thus obtain a social compensation. In Fellini's late, pessimistic visions of a world invaded by television, the creative Subject no longer receives any form of compensation and necessarily can only and truly disappear from the scene, and from life. In the recognition of the need for the Subject to vanish from the artistic and existential scene, to disintegrate as a unifying element of the work of art, a true affinity between Pirandello's and Fellini's visions can be inferred at last.

4 Character and Discourse from Pirandello to Fellini: Defining a Countertradition in an Italian Context

Mais les ténèbres sont elles-mêmes des toiles
Où vivent, jaillissant de mon oeil par milliers,
Des êtres disparus aux regards familiers.

Charles Baudelaire, 'Obsession' in *Les Fleurs du mal*

The description of the parallelisms in the destinies of Federico Fellini and Luigi Pirandello is a necessary and yet merely a prefatory stage leading to the discussion of their respective roles in the creation and evolution of that countertradition in narrative and dramatic art variously defined as serio-comic, carnivalistic, and most importantly, 'umoristica.' As previously stated, at different times in Italian modern and contemporary history, both Pirandello and Fellini provided a thorough critique of existing interpretations of realism, and worked toward the creation of self-reflexive, ambivalent, and metadiscoursive artistic statements. Both artists worked in an area of penumbra between tragedy and comedy in which it was possible to develop their own idiosyncratic conception of the dramatic and cinematic character, as well as their own revolutionary discoursive strategies. In an Italian context, Pirandello and Fellini occupy two central positions in the passage from modernity to postmodernity, as they both address the questions raised by the interruption of the pacified relationship between Man and Nature, and by the fracture in the synthesis between Subject and Object that characterized former artistic expressions.[1]

In modernity, two diverse approaches to artistic discourse develop, and specifically two divergent interpretations of History and Subjectivity. In one case, the possibility of a mimetic and, thus, harmonious relationship between art and nature is foreseen; in the other, one records the impossibility of such rapport, verifying the fundamental division of the Subject, and the search for meaning becomes form and content of the artistic representation. It is within the latter and much richer perspective that Pirandello's work develops, and he thus becomes 'un vecteur significatif en amont et en aval de ces différents modélisations narratives ou théâtrales du réel et de l'oeuvre dans la mesure où son discours, plus qu'aucun autre, fait éclater les codes thématiques et formels.'[2]

Luigi Pirandello's discursive strategies are organized according to the paradigms defined in his essay *On Humor*. It is relevant here to remember that humour differs from comedy and tragedy, and is characterized by the juxtaposition of both. As such, humour is profoundly transgressive, as Mikhail Bakhtin stressed in his famous study of Dostoevsky's poetics, and it is so because it operates in the interstices between narrative and discursive strategies.[3] Humour, then, redefines the roles of the various elements involved in the production of meaning. This is why since romanticism much attention has been given to the particular mode of discourse that has been variously defined as 'irony' or 'humour.' In the romantic and post-romantic periods, a fundamental break occurred, which became the focus of many artists' works. In particular, Charles Baudelaire initiated an investigation that led to the elaboration of that particular concept of humour that was to have so much relevance in twentieth-century poetics.[4] Baudelaire is one of the protagonists of that movement from romantic irony to humour. As Umberto Artioli maintains in his study of Antonin Artaud's theatre, 'il passaggio dall'ironia allo humor segnerebbe, cosí, l'introduzione di una nota tragica, largamente testimoniata, del resto, dalle poetiche novecentesche che, da Jarry a Pirandello a Beckett, hanno assegnato all'umorismo un ruolo centrale'[5] ('The passage from irony to humour would, thus, mark the introduction of a tragic note, largely attested, for instance, by twentieth-century poetics that, from Jarry to Pirandello and Beckett, has assigned humour a central role'). Thus, for instance, Pirandello's trilogy of the so-called 'theatre in the theatre' constitutes not only a move away from naturalism and the mimetic tradition but also a self-reflexive stage in the theatrical representation.

Fellini's cinematic production, particularly beginning with *8½*, stands in a quite similar position in relation to former interpretations of the filmic experience, specifically, to neorealism. Born in January 1920 of middle-class parents at Rimini in the province of Emilia Romagna, Fellini soon drifted away from his home town and landed in Rome, his 'city of election' to the day of his death. For a few years, he supported himself by sketching caricature portraits in Roman restaurants and writing for *Marc'Aurelio*, an Italian humour magazine for which a number of other soon-to-be directors also worked. His apprenticeship in the world of caricature and cartoon would be extremely significant to the development of Fellini's cinematic world. In the aftermath of World War II, he eked out a living of sorts by making caricature sketches of American soldiers in the Eternal City. Yet, because of a fortunate friendship with Roman actor Aldo Fabrizi, Fellini was soon introduced to the world of cinema, and began a career as a scriptwriter, which lasted up to his directorial debut with *Variety Lights*, a film that he co-directed with Alberto Lattuada in 1950. Fabrizi paved the way for one of the most important meetings in Fellini's life, that with Roberto Rossellini, the soon-to-be-famous neorealist director for whom he co-scripted *Rome Open City*, one of the masterpieces of Italian film history. Besides his work with Rossellini on *Rome Open City*, Fellini embarked on a series of associations that led him from minor gag writing to major scriptwriting. He was responsible for the enigmatic monastery sequence in Rossellini's *Paisan*; he co-authored the screenplays for Alberto Lattuada's *Il delitto di Giovanni Episcopo* (*The Crime of Giovanni Episcopo*, 1946) and *Senza pietá* (*Without Pity*, 1948). Fellini not only wrote the script for Rossellini's *Il miracolo* (*The Miracle*, 1948), but he also played the male lead in this controversial film in which a simple-minded village woman (Anna Magnani) is seduced by a stranger (Fellini), whom she identifies as St Joseph, and by whom she is to become a second Virgin Mary. Fellini then contributed to several other neorealist films such as Pietro Germi's *Nel nome della legge* (*In the Name of the Law*, 1948) and *Il cammino della speranza* (*The Path of Hope*, 1950); Roberto Rossellini's *I fiori di San Francesco* (*The Flowers of St Francis*, 1949) and *Europa '51* (*Europe '51*, 1951); and Lattuada's *Il mulino del Po* (*The Mill on the Po*, 1949).

Even though Fellini came of age in filmmaking under the auspices of neorealism, from the outset his cinema was marked by a decisive move away from the political and socioeconomic concerns typical of neorealist cinema. Focusing on character at first, and then on discourse, especially from *8½* onward, Fellini developed his own personal interpretation of cinematic realism. We now know that neorealism was not a homogeneous phenomenon, much less a movement, as Peter Bondanella has pointedly remarked,[6] or a genre. It was characterized by a polyphony of voices. It did not start in that magic and almost mythical

1945, nor end in 1951 or 1953.[7] In brief, we know that the neorealistic mode was not canonical, and could not be reduced to a single ethical and aesthetic vision. We know that there were many differences among the so-called 'masters' of neorealism, and that between Rossellini's gaze and that of De Sica, Visconti, De Santis and the others, there existed cultural, moral, and stylistic differences so profound as to raise doubts about any arguments favouring a shared poetics and orientation.

Notwithstanding these differences, it is, possible to trace a common denominator that undeniably links films as diverse as De Sica's *Sciusciá* (*Shoeshine*, 1946), and Rossellini's *Paisan* and Visconti's *La terra trema* (*The Earth Trembles*, 1948). What these films shared, if nothing else, was the same ethical and stylistic tension in which *to see* or rather *to look* meant *to understand*, or at least the effort to understand. Emphasis, thus, was placed on the ability to interpret, and the Zavattinian *pedinamento* – that is, the tailing of the character with the camera in his or her daily chores would necessarily lead to an understanding of the character as part of or, rather, as a product of the environment. Fellini's cinematic vision is born exactly from the interruption of this pacified relationship between the director and reality; his cinema develops from the persuasion that between facts, between visible and invisible worlds, a hiatus exists. Other directors obviously participated in this awareness of the irreparable fracture between reality and its artistic representation, and yet in some cases such awareness was profoundly painful, as in Michelangelo Antonioni's cinema, while Fellini's work constantly expressed a playful sense of the relativity of the human experience. Right from its very start, with *Variety Lights* but especially beginning with *La Strada*, Fellini's cinema virtually closes the neorealistic 'parenthesis' by exposing the entire set of paradigms that built the neorealistic 'lie' – that is, the conviction that it is possible to provide an unambiguous and reliable representation of reality, a reality that, according to Cesare Zavattini's 'orthodox' interpretation of neorealism, was unequivocal and thus thoroughly interpretable. The characters living in that reality were equally representable, as they were fully determined by their environments, and had no ears or words for their internal motivations, or as Fellini would put it, their inner 'voices.' Such a monolithic view of the world was doomed to be dismissed, and so it was by many, including Antonioni, Visconti, and even Rossellini and De Sica, but perhaps most of all by Fellini himself, who significantly claimed, 'Neorealism means looking at reality with an honest eye – but any kind of reality: not just social reality, but also spiritual reality, anything man has inside him.'[8]

Most of Fellini's early films up to *La Dolce Vita* were primarily dedicated to the investigation of the nature of the cinematic character, which, in Pirandellian terms, was defined by the clash between public mask and interior face, as exemplified by films such as *The White Sheik* and *I Vitelloni*. Later on in his career, particularly beginning with *8½* in 1963, Fellini became more and more involved in the exploration of a character's discourse, which was becoming increasingly fragmented and discontinuous. From the naked masks to the myths, Pirandello and Fellini explored the boundaries of previous interpretations of realism in art, and both occupy two landmark positions in the evolution of that particular mode of discourse variously called 'serio-comic' or 'humoristic,' almost a hypergenre that occupies a large segment of Italian modern and contemporary artistic production.

Pirandello's and Fellini's artistic productions may be described as 'artistic journeys,' for one of their basic features is their status as works-in-progress. The theme of the journey itself frequently appears in their respective works, and represents a proper metaphor for the Subject's coming to knowledge and self-knowledge. In a recent study of Pirandello, Paolo Puppa remarks:

Gli sbocchi che si offrono quindi, per uscire dalla disperazione, sono il *viaggio per treno* (sequenza cardinale in tutti i testi pirandelliani che hanno per centro *l'iniziazione alla metamorfosi conoscitiva*, come s'è già visto per *La carriola*),[9] lo spostarsi cioè nello spazio quale spia per uno spostarsi nel tempo, là dove emergono relitti d'un'altra condizione, quasi di *rimosso* culturale d'un'altra *mens*, e dove il tempo passato si coniuga febbrilmente col tempo futuro.[10]

The way-outs offered to escape from despair are the *journey by train* (a central sequence in all Pirandellian texts that centre on *the initiation to the cognitive metamorphosis*, as we have already seen in *La carriola*), the movement in space as evidence of a movement in time, there where the wreckages of another condition emerge, almost the cultural repression of another *mens*, and where the time past feverishly conjugates with the future.

The journey, particularly the journey by train, constitutes the central sequence in the Subject's initiation into the cognitive process in many of Fellini's films as well. In *I Vitelloni*, all of the characters long to take a journey throughout the entire movie. Moraldo's departure by train ultimately ends the film on an inconclusive note, since the character's progress toward self-knowledge only begins as the end-titles run across the screen. In a film such as *Fellini's Roma*, the train clearly serves as a mediator in the protagonist's progression toward initiation into adult life and creative maturity, and therefore toward self-discovery. In *Block-notes di un regista* (*Fellini: A Director's Notebook*, 1969), Fellini's cinematic diary about the making of *Satyricon*, one of the central sequences consists of a journey on a subway train. During this quite peculiar train ride, the normal dialectical relationship between time and space becomes reversed: time moves backward as the train goes forward. The director clearly attempts to join past and future metaphorically in a desperate attempt to force the remains of another, and probably better, *mens* to re-emerge, and to unmask the corruption and decadence of the present. A journey by train also becomes central in one of Fellini's later films, *Ginger and Fred*, where movement in space is obviously matched by a movement in time. In this case, the two motions are in accord. Ginger moves forward to meet Fred, and together they attempt to unite past and future. Their effort results in a dramatic failure because of the destructive power of the present, and in the end her journey needs to be re-travelled backward, and forever. The journey is re-proposed as a theme but also as an efficient narrative strategy in Fellini's last two films, *Interview* and *The Voice of the Moon*.

For both Pirandello and Fellini, however, the real 'end' of a journey is the journey itself, and the various stops are sometimes more important than the actual destination. The sojourn 'somewhere else,' even for a limited amount of time, ensures the Subject the possibility of escaping from his or her own Self, of evading a suffocating reality through death and finding a consequent rebirth with a new name and, thus, a constantly new identity. Pirandello's Mattia Pascal is the perfect traveller and is also an archetypical 'vitellone,' a literary antecedent to so many of Fellini's real or metaphorical travellers. The condition of the traveller – the Subject who is always somewhere else, and who therefore is condemned to finding it impossible to make any true statement, in existential as well as in social terms – is also characteristic of Fellini himself. Even though Fellini hated to travel, he once declared:

Per dire una cosa vera bisognerebbe togliere 'io'; e invece non si può farne a meno. Anche per dire 'io non c'ero.' Che è la mia condizione perpetua, quella in cui mi riconosco totalmente. Io non posso testimoniare su niente perché almeno il 99 per cento delle volte non c'ero, ero altrove. *Sono sempre stato un latitante,* dalla nascita ai nostri giorni. E come si fa a raccontare la storia di uno che non c'è?[11]

In order to make a truthful statement, one would have to remove the 'I,' and on the contrary it is not possible to avoid it. Even just to say 'I wasn't there.' Which is my perpetual condition, the one in which I recognize myself entirely. I cannot testify on anything because at least 99 per cent of the times I wasn't there, I was elsewhere. *I have always been a fugitive*, from birth to this day. And how can you tell the story of someone who isn't there?

Yet the impossibility of omitting the 'I,' even if just to say 'I was not there,' and the basic condition of being someone who is never 'there' where and when things happen – that is, the condition of 'non-being-thereness' – constitute the main features of the Pirandellian traveller par excellence, Mattia Pascal.[12] The novel *The Late Mattia Pascal* opens with a revealing statement: 'Una delle poche cose che sapevo, anzi forse la sola ch'io sapessi di certo era questa: che mi chiamavo Mattia Pascal. E me ne approffittavo'[13] ('one of the few things – perhaps the only one that I know for certain is that my name is Mattia Pascal. I used to take advantage of this').[14] Moreover, the closing words of the novel emphasize the Subject's condition of non-beingness as it was introduced at the opening of the narration. Answering an onlooker who has inquired about his identity, Pascal states: 'Eh, caro mio ... Io sono il fu Mattia Pascal'[15] ('Ah, my dear friend ... I am the late Mattia Pascal').[16] The 'I,' then, refers to a dead man. With this statement, the narrator emphasizes his condition as a fugitive, his state of 'non-being-thereness.' The novel's end seems to tell us that we have just finished the story of a living dead man, a Subject caught up in the clash between the fatality of 'being' and the desire of 'being there' (in life and in the text). Such a character is a Subject who has to experience what Roland Barthes calls the *stéréotype*: 'la fausse mort, la mort atroce, c'est ce qui n'est pas un terme, c'est l'interminable ... Le stéréotype, c'est cette impossibilité nauséeuse de mourir'[17] ('the false death, the atrocious death, is what has no end, the interminable ... The stereotype is this nauseating impossibility of dying').[18] Mattia Pascal represents a Subject who is condemned 'to be' but cannot really 'be there';[19] he embodies a Subject who ultimately has to realize his fictionalized nature, since he is condemned to live within the present of fiction forever and to experience only fictive 'deaths' but never be capable of dying.

The same sense of nausea and void that seems to lie in the deep structure of a character such as Mattia – a figure unable to assume any kind of responsibility, a man incapable of truly being somewhere at a specific time, a stereotype more than a living image – supplies the constitutional feature of the protagonist in *Il Casanova* (*Fellini's Casanova*, 1976). Yet, Fellini's interpretation of this archetypal Latin lover represents quite an extreme extension of the Pirandellian *vitellone*, as the director himself defined the film as 'anticinematografia: un film dove non c'è racconto ... un film astratto e informale su *una non vita'*[20] ('anticinematography: a film where there is no narration ... an abstract and non-figurative film on *a non-life'*). Fellini defined his Casanova much more negatively than Pirandello ever depicted Pascal, therefore bringing to an extreme some of the personality traits that are most disturbing in Mattia Pascal:

Casanova è soltanto il recinto anagrafico di una massa di episodi, azioni, persone, materia vorticosa, ma inerte, spesso muta; Casanova è un uomo tutto esteriore, senza segreti e senza pudori ... Ha girato tutto il mondo, ed è come se non si fosse mai mosso dal letto ... una totale mancanza di individualità, l'indistinto, ecco.[21]

Casanova is only an enclosure of personal data represented by a heap of episodes, actions, people, a vorticous but inert and often silent matter. Casanova is a merely exterior man, without secrets or shame ... He has travelled all over the world, but it is as if he never left his bed ... a total lack of individuality, the indistinct, that's it.

Fellini's Casanova, a peculiar traveller quite indifferent to space and time, is a Subject who learns nothing in life, who has no real motivations, who can only lead a mechanical life and face a similarly mechanical death. Therefore, he cannot truly either live or die. By repeating 'I' over and over again in a nauseating refrain, Casanova ultimately nullifies his various attempts to affirm his own Self and reduces it to the 'degree zero' of signification. On the one hand, since Casanova goes through life without learning anything, his journey involves no progression toward a different dimension of knowledge. On the other hand, Casanova is not at all interested in any other knowledge except that which relates to his own exterior Self. The character of Casanova brings to an extreme one of the main features of Fellini's many journeys. As the director once remarked, in fact, what really counts in both the character's development and the Subject's progress to self-knowledge is the journey itself.[22]

To verify similarities between Pirandello and Fellini and to trace the influence of the dramatist's theory and practice on those of the director may in itself be a revealing journey. Ultimately, though, even this peculiar journey, like that of so many of Pirandello's and Fellini's characters, may become a process of initiation leading to a dimension of knowledge that can provide the attentive student with a better understanding of each author and of the visible and invisible threads linking the two artists. My study aims at defining that countertradition that began in Italy at the turn of the century and developed thereafter, and which I describe as 'carnivalistic,' or, adopting a Pirandellian term, 'humoristic.' Both Pirandello and Fellini belong to this 'countertradition,' which stands in contrast to the traditionally accepted modes of tragedy and comedy. In modern Italian cultural history, moreover, these two artists stand in the good company of many others, such as Italo Svevo and, later on, Italo Calvino.

To this point, an analysis of the processes underlying the construction and deconstruction of Pirandello's and Fellini's myths and most recurrent metaphors has been presented. This investigation has revealed the existence of several parallels between their individual poetics, as well as a similarity in the processes they use in the formation and disintegration of their respective mythical and metaphorical worlds. These parallels may permit us to postulate the presence of a common, generic tradition underlying both men's artistic expressions. The progressive lowering, degradation, and disintegration of myth in their work is not simply the result of certain historical and existential conditions, but is also a qualifying feature of the serio-comical or 'humoristic' genre within which both authors clearly develop their respective artistic discourses.

Both Pirandello and Fellini must, therefore, be understood against the background of the generic tradition of the serio-comical. This tradition, or rather, countertradition, finds its privileged linguistic expression in metadiscourse, a discourse that is, by its very nature, self-reflexive and self-referential as well as extremely ambivalent. On a linguistic level, metadiscourses postulate the destruction of both traditional narrative and dramatic strategies, and encourage the search for the 'new' in art. In their dismantlement of traditionally accepted artistic conventions and social hierarchies, these discourses participate in what Mikhail Bakhtin has defined as the 'carnival sense of the world.'[23] Therefore, they align themselves with that tradition in Western culture which Bakhtin defined as 'carnivalistic.'

In particular, Pirandello and Fellini share the same joyful sense of the relativity of everything in life and express this sentiment in their artistic and existential predicaments. In his famous study of Dostoevsky's poetics, Bakhtin maintained:

Carnival is a pageant without footlights and without division into performers and spectators ... Carnival is not contemplated and strictly speaking, not even performed; its participants *live* in it, they live by its laws as long as those laws are in effect; that is, they live a *carnivalistic life*. Because carnivalistic life is life drawn out of its *usual* rut, it is to some extent 'life turned inside out,' 'the reverse side of the world' (*'monde à l'envers'*).[24]

Although legitimately focusing on linguistic concerns at first, a study of the influences of Pirandello's metatheatre on Fellini's intriguing metacinema would have to conclude with the discovery of a common psychoanalytic basis to those artistic solutions that mirror such a vision of the world in reverse. Employing psychoanalysis in a study of Pirandello and Fellini is legitimate, since the two artists repeatedly underline the importance of the symbolic apparatus of dream life to their work and the psychological foundation of artistic creation. My analysis here will unveil the mechanics behind the passage from the symbolic scene to the imaginary scene – that is, the realm of the unconscious – which occurs in both authors' progression toward artistic maturity.

At the very foundation of a psychoanalytic approach to Pirandello's and Fellini's works lies the need to define the true nature of the Pirandellian and Fellinian character and to establish the true identity of that character, as well as that of each author himself. In Pirandello's and Fellini's artistic and existential Subject, we may detect a similar psychological and linguistic substratum that directly connects to their use of the serio-comical mode in their respective artistic discourses.

Pirandello defines his concept of 'umorismo' as the 'sentimento del contrario, provocato dalla speciale attività della riflessione'[25] ('feeling of the opposite produced by the special activity of reflection'),[26] and as 'un fenomeno di sdoppiamento nell'atto della concezione'[27] ('a phenomenon of doubling in the act of artistic conception').[28] 'Umorismo' – a particular point of view in life, a certain way of looking at or, rather, 'seeing' things – represents the central tenet of the Sicilian author's artistic and critical corpus and the peculiar metadiscourses he chooses. Pirandello's notion of 'umorismo,' closely related to Bakhtin's concept of a 'carnival sense of the world,' provides the perfect heuristic tool for understanding the psychological and linguistic basis of the modern Subject. This emergent Subject finds its germinative seeds in the romantic period, matures and develops in the modern age, and later reaches fullest expression in the postmodern period.

In many ways, Pirandello stands at the gateway between modernity and postmodernity. Understanding Pirandello may not completely resolve the debate about a proper definition of the difference between modernism and postmodernism; nor can Pirandello merely serve as a key for opening the gates of these often still mysterious worlds. However, an understanding of him can offer a peep-hole through which we may glance at what lies beyond. Pirandello's vision may also provide a useful springboard to a fuller understanding of Fellini's world, which is certainly closer to postmodernity than Pirandello's world ever was.[29]

In a sense, then, Pirandello was to nineteenth-century realism and naturalism what Fellini and Calvino have been to neorealism in cinema and literature. In early works such as *Il turno* (*The Shift*, published in 1902 but written in 1895), which were superficially indebted to the naturalistic tradition, Pirandello already intentionally undermined the canons of that very tradition. He was openly searching for an appropriate artistic expression for a new Subject who was pressuring bourgeois society and conscience from both the outside and the inside.

Something quite similar occurs in Fellini's early films. Not only in works such as *Luci del varietà* (*Variety Lights*, 1950) and *The White Sheik* (1952), but even much earlier, in the convent episode which he scripted for Roberto Rossellini's *Paisan* (1946), Fellini was already searching for an escape from orthodox neorealism (if such a thing ever existed). The director soon aimed at achieving a cinematic form with which to provide a proper expression for the new Subject emerging from the Second World War. It was immediately clear to Fellini that this Man needed something different from an emphatic portrayal of an unfortunately squalid reality. Fellini, in fact, stated that neorealism was to him a new way of looking at, of 'seeing,' things with sincerity and, certainly, without ideology: 'Neorealism means looking at reality with an honest eye – but any kind of reality: not just social reality, but also spiritual reality, anything man has inside him.'[30] Interestingly enough, both artists' statements seem to centre on the search for a new way of looking at or seeing the world: by emphasizing vision, then, both Pirandello and Fellini posit the centrality of the Subject, although, quite interestingly, the Subject to whom they both refer no longer possesses any certainty about his or her own psychological and existential centre.

One of the keys for understanding Pirandello's conception of art and life, and hence his influence on Fellini, is his notion of the nature of the new Subject in its multifaceted roles within and outside the text. The problem of defining this nature of the new Subject connects closely to the question of language and communication. In passing from realism and naturalism to modernism, language loses its capacity to convey true communication, and increasingly becomes the locus of alienation. Reality itself no longer seems comforting and linear but becomes increasingly discontinuous, and therefore both alienates and is alienated from the new Subject. Both author and character therefore assume the form of neurotic Subjects, expressing themselves through linguistic repetition as they try to recover from their loss of comforting identities. Of all of Pirandello's narrative works, this is particularly true in both *The Late Mattia Pascal* and *One, Nobody, and One Hundred Thousand*, although in the latter work, the author proposes a different solution to the pressing problems of identity and alienation.

In postmodernism, language is still no longer a unified and comforting apparatus; we actually witness its complete dissemination into diverse linguistic messages, a dissemination that produces a Babelic disorder of discourses. Nevertheless, such disordered proliferation of linguistic utterances makes it possible for the Subject to overcome alienation. In postmodernist texts such as John Fowles' *The French Lieutenant's Woman* (1969), Resnais' *Hiroshima mon amour* (*Hiroshima My Love*, 1959) and *L'année dernière à Marienbad* (*Last Year at Marienbad*, 1961), and in Fellini's *8½*, the artist constantly finds himself in the midst of the action, which now overtly takes place both inside and outside the text. In both loci, the Subject as author is nothing but a divided Self: within the text, he is character and author; outside the text, he is author and also at least one potential reader or spectator. The role of the reader or spectator also seems schizophrenic, for he or she is part of the process that takes place both inside and outside the text, but is always denied one role when given the other. In most twentieth-century literary discourses, then, the Subject, in the diverse roles of author, character, or receiver, becomes an increasingly divided Self who initially searches neurotically for an identity that is either lost or missing, but then progressively accepts his or her own division and fragmentation.

Although in works such as *The Outcast* and *The Shift*, Pirandello concerned himself primarily with the decomposition of earlier literary conventions, even then he was searching for a narrative form that could give full artistic expression to the new social and existential condition the modern Subject experienced. Beginning with *The Late Mattia Pascal*, but especially in the later works such as *Shoot!* and *One, Nobody, and*

One Hundred Thousand, Pirandello certainly moved beyond modernism by attempting to resolve certain dilemmas inherent in a modernist perspective. With much of his theatre and these last narrative works, Pirandello made a forceful impact upon the European scene in the postmodernist period, insofar as his works reflected the disintegration of traditional character as well as a revolutionary shift in the author's function and in the reader's or audience's relationship to the text. In short, Pirandello became central to the movement toward the acquisition and definition of a postmodernist poetics and aesthetics that eventually proved to be crucial to Fellini's cinematic narrative.

The typical Pirandellian Subject, defined by his author as 'humorist,' is constitutionally ambivalent, eccentric, and fully self-conscious. In the essay on Dostoevsky's poetics cited earlier, Bakhtin maintains that the Russian author conceived the hero 'as a *particular point of view on the world and on oneself*':

The hero as a point of view, as an opinion on the world and on himself, requires utterly special methods of discovery and artistic characterization. And this is so because what must be discovered and characterized here is not the specific existence of the hero, not his fixed image, but the *sum total of his consciousness and self-consciousness*, ultimately *the hero's final word on himself and on the world*.[31]

The Pirandellian character as 'humorist' bears a certain resemblance to the Dostoevskian hero as defined by Bakhtin, since he is characterized as a way of 'seeing' himself and the world. Moreover, the hero no longer has a given, fixed image but is defined by the abstract of his consciousness and self-consciousness, by his conscious and subconscious life; as a consequence, he constantly seems to be searching for an identity that is either lost or lacking.

Ambivalence is a basic feature of the Pirandellian concept of subjectivity, for the Subject is constantly both 'persona' and 'personaggio,' both creator and creature. At first, the Subject performs an obsessively neurotic search for unity which finds in repetition the perfect metaphor for the Subject's basic lack of definition. In the end, however, the solution appears to lie, first, in the recognition of the loss of a unified identity, and second, in the acceptance of the fundamental disunity of an ultimately schizophrenic Subject. Therefore, the integrity of the monologic-autobiographical discourse, typical of so-called 'serious' genres and expressive of a fully rounded Subjectivity, soon gets replaced by the discontinuity and incongruity of the 'humorist's' dialogic discourse. This form of discourse is typical of many of Pirandello's narrative works as well as of most of Fellini's films; in addition, I believe, it is possible to trace a legacy running from Pirandello to Fellini, a legacy that finds its foundation in the genre of the serio-comical.

In his early novels, Pirandello uses third-person narration, but already with *The Late Mattia Pascal*, and then in such narrative works as *Shoot!* and *One, Nobody, and One Hundred Thousand*, the author as 'humorist' chooses the first-person narration to exploit one of its basic features: ambiguity and ambivalence. Pirandello tries to make the most of the possibility of being both author and character, creator and created. As a result, the walls of mimetic representation are finally torn down. The same thing happens in Fellini's work after such early movies as *Variety Lights*, *The White Sheik*, and even in *I Vitelloni*, *La Strada*, and *Il bidone* (*The Swindle*, 1955), although only to a certain extent. Whenever Fellini maintains that all his work is autobiographical, but then slyly adds that his autobiography has been adulterated in the process of remembering and therefore constantly reinvented, he subtly warns us against expecting a comforting monologic-autobiographical discourse. What we must expect to receive from him is a multi-voiced interior dialogue, a form of discourse particularly evident in such films as *8½* and *Juliet of the Spirits*.

In both films, the protagonists undergo something quite similar to what Vitangelo Moscarda, the main character of Pirandello's *One, Nobody, and One Hundred Thousand*, experiences. In these three instances, the Subject is forced to face his or her fictionalized existence; he or she is compelled to experience a fundamental alienation born out of repression of the desire to be the one element that would complete the Other. Such a sense of alienation relates closely to the Subject's realization of his or her condition of division. Assuming the perspective of the Lacanian re-reading of Saussurean linguistics, one can state that, in linguistic terms, the Subject understands the fact of being nothing else but the place of opposition between enunciation and statement. In both film and novel, the Subject's image is constantly scattered as if in a room full of mirrors (as are reality and truth). The Subject repeatedly fails to locate the unified Self for which he or she searches. But again, as when, in a room full of mirrors, it is necessary to look constantly at all the images since they change continuously, in like manner, it is necessary for the Subject to look constantly at all the diverse enunciations and statements in his or her effort to locate and unite the Self. Since, as Jacques Lacan maintains, the Subject is actually born 'divided,' he or she can achieve existential and artistic completion only by accepting the fact of his or her division and by listening to the multiple voices within and outside himself or herself.

Mirrors constitute almost obsessive objects for both Pirandello and Fellini. They serve as the perfect metaphor for the fragmentation of the Subject as well as provide a means by which he or she proceeds toward self-knowledge. While analysing the nature of the Dostoevskian hero, Bakhtin maintains:

Dostoevsky forces the hero to contemplate in the mirror. And thanks to this fact all concrete features of the hero, while remaining fundamentally unchanged, are transferred from one plane to another ... they can no longer finalize and close off a character, can no longer construct an integral image of him or provide an artistic answer to the question, 'Who is he?' We see not who he is, but *how* he is conscious of himself; our act of artistic visualization occurs not before the reality of the hero, but before a pure function of his awareness of that reality ... Dostoevsky literally introduces the author into the hero's field of vision.[32]

I agree with Bakhtin that the introduction of the author within the hero's field of vision is one of the main features of modern narrative strategies, for it embodies the linguistic response to a new type of re-flexivity which becomes especially influential in the postmodern pe-riod. Nonmonologic discourse responds to new psychological condi-tions of man, to the knowledge modern man has of his incapacity to achieve an integral image of himself. Interior dialogic discourse offers the linguistic answer to a psychological condition characterized by the division and fragmentation contemporary man experiences.

In the case of Pirandello and Fellini, first-person narration rarely as-sumes the form of a comforting 'monologue intérior' typical of a Prous-tian form of recollecting past autobiographical memories. As Paolo Puppa also notes:

I vari Mattia Pascal, Serafino Gubbio, Vitangelo Moscarda ... si fanno soggetti di enunciazione, procedendo con una compenetrazione argomentativa sempre più autorevole verso *l'autonarrazione*. Ovviamente non siamo più alla prima persona del romanzo settecentesco ... Non siamo neppure, però, con un ulte-riore scarto, nelle vicinanze del *monologo interiore*, nel flusso di coscienza, nel-l'area della *lingua notturna desimbolizzata*, vale a dire nel senso di rinuncia alla *langue* sociale, alla legge del padre.[33]

The various Mattia Pascals, Serafino Gubbios, Vitangelo Moscardas ... turn themselves into subjects of the enunciation, proceeding with an argumentative compenetration that becomes increasingly authoritative toward *self-narration*. Obviously this is no longer the first person of the eighteenth-century novel ... Nor, though, do we find ourselves, with a further gap, in the vicinities of the *interior monologue*, in the flux of consciousness, in the area of *nocturnal and desymbolized language*, that is, in a sense of renunciation to social *langue*, to the law of the father.

Moreover, Puppa argues, the return of the past in Pirandello – and, I would maintain, in Fellini as well – is characterized by a loss of the 'aura' that permeates the 'memoria involontaria' of Proust's *À la Recherche du temps perdu* (*Remembrance of Things Past*, 1913–27). What emerges from an image long before experienced by the Subject is a stratified construction strewn with non-homogeneous series of images: 'Ricordare è un po' sognare, produce iati tra le sequenze che si elidono a vicenda'[34] ('to remember is a little like dreaming; it produces hiatuses between the sequences that annul one another'). Nevertheless, for Pirandello's anti-heroes the act of writing becomes central, since through the written word they try desperately to narrate their painful distance from the world. As Puppa goes on to argue, 'Inevitabilmente, il *personaggio dello scrittore* è metaforicamente richiesto, dentro la *fabula*, per giustificare la caduta di contatto col reale'[35] ('Inevitably, the *character of the writer* is metaphorically required, inside the *fabula*, to justify the loss of contact with reality'). A quite similar process takes place in many of Fellini's films, where the presence of the director as a character in the story does not simply serve as a narrative device; instead, together with the very act of film-making, it seems to compensate the Subject partially for his loss of contact with reality, as is clearly the case in such films as *8½* and *Fellini's Roma*, but also in *Fellini: A Director's Notebook* and *Interview*.

In Pirandello's mature narrative works, then, monologic discourse is replaced by dialogic discourse – that is, the dialogue of the Self with the Other – which, according to Bakhtin, is a feature of both early and later forms of 'carnivalized' literature. In Pirandello's narratives, the Other is initially represented by the 'you' outside the Self, as in the instance of Mattia Pascal. The narrative thus becomes an obsessive recounting of the neurotic search for identity, for unity, and for centredness performed by the Subject when confronted by others. The Subject, on the one hand, verifies the impossibility of achieving a unified identity through others' eyes, since socialized life mostly grounds itself on mendacity: 'Sembra, in somma, che la menzogna debba ritenersi più vantaggiosa della veracità, in quanto quella può unire, laddove questa divide'[36] ('In other words, it seems that lying is to be considered more advantageous than telling the truth, insofar as the former can unite where the latter divides').[37] On the other hand, Pirandello continues, 'si mentisce psicologicamente come si mentisce socialmente. E il mentire a noi stessi, vivendo coscientemente solo la superficie del nostro essere psichico, è un effetto del mentire sociale'[38] ('we lie psychologically just as we lie socially. And, since conscious life extends only to the surface of our psychic being, lying to ourselves is a result of social lying').[39] Thus, socialized life is ruled by simulation and dissimulation. Furthermore, according to Pirandello, the solitary Subject reflecting upon himself is forcefully influenced by all other members of society. Then each individual performs the same act of simulation or dissimulation toward himself so as to double and, quite often, multiply his image when confronting other people or facing his own conscience.

If simulation is one of the informing principles of socialized life, two matters become central to the artist's concern: the problem of identity, both in linguistic and in social terms, and the question of 'learning,' of achieving a 'valid' truth. These two issues are central to both Moscarda, the protagonist of Pirandello's One, Nobody, and One Hundred Thousand, and Guido Anselmi, the main character of Fellini's 8½, as they progress toward existential and artistic maturity. The two narratives furthermore display points of contact in their respective progressions. As the novel opens, the Subject-narrator is addressed by his wife while he is looking at himself in the mirror. Moscarda's first gaze into the looking-glass constitutes the beginning of both his process of self-analysis and the textual production.[40] Through subsequent gazes, both into the mirror and into the eyes of others, the Subject will undergo a process of self-analysis that will lead him to a constant movement from identification to alienation and back again. The Subject progressively acknowledges the existence of the unknown Other inside himself ('l'estraneo inseparabile da me'), and ultimately admits his fragmentation in relationship to the others – his wife, his neighbours, and the entire town. Initially, the text unfolds as a witnessing of the repetitious and neurotic reasoning of the Subject as Moscarda tries to recover the original sense of unity and harmony, both inside and outside the text, that is here defined in linguistic, psychological, and social terms. However, as the Subject comes to realize his extremely precarious nature both in personal and social terms, the text becomes 'the narration of the impossibility of achieving a believable narration,' and the locus of an equally impossible communication.

The opening sequence of *8½* represents a somewhat different situation, since the existence of 'everyday' reality is immediately denied. Fellini's protagonist is identified as a dreaming Subject, and, as such, is not offered to us as a full body. We only see his back in the nightmare. Even when he is awakened by the entrance of the doctor and his crew, we do not 'see' his full, corporeal image until he finally recovers his own image as a reflection in the mirror, and thus, like Moscarda, recognizes himself as a divided Self. The dreaming Subject, once reawakened, is immediately questioned by others in a purely mechanical manner. They ask him how he feels, how old he is, if this is the first time he has visited the spa, and, finally, if he is once again about to make another of his movies 'without hope.' At first, Guido's condition appears similar to that of Mattia Pascal, who is likewise defined in external terms at the beginning of *The Late Mattia Pascal*, when Pascal himself declares that the only thing he knew about himself was his own name. In addition, if Guido is about to make a movie, Mattia is about to write a novel. Mattia, however, represents an example of great simulation or deception, for he first of all maintains that he never wrote a novel, and later asserts that he no longer believes in the use of writing more novels. Just born in the narrative, the Subject seems unwilling to recognize his condition of indefiniteness as an alienating condition, and pretends to have total control over both his narrative and his life. In Fellini's film, after the opening sequence of the nightmare, the Subject is viewed as a dummy, shot from behind, covered with sheets, or in almost total darkness. We immediately have to face one of the underlying concerns of the whole movie: subjects, as well as movies, are nothing but illusions and lies.

Interestingly enough, the main role for both Pirandello's 'humorist' and Fellini's artist must be to unmask the lie that rests at the very core of public and private life. In his essay *On Humor*, in fact, Pirandello states: 'L'umorista coglie subito queste varie simulazioni per la lotta della vita ... L'umorista rivela come le apparenze siano profondamente diverse dall'essere intimo della coscienza degli associati'[41] ('The humorist readily perceives the various simulations used in the struggle for life ... the humorist ... reveals how profoundly different the outer appearances are from what takes place in the inner consciousness').[42] He also notes that the humorist can thus take up the task of unmasking all vanities and fictions, and of depicting society.[43] In an interview on the character of Casanova, the archetype of his many *vitelloni*, Fellini declared to Aldo Tassone: '*smascherare la bugia, identificare l'inautentico, smantellare l'approssimativo o falsi assoluti*, continua ad essere per ora l'unica risorsa correttiva – un'irridente inesausta salvaguardia – della nostra storia fallimentare'[44] ('*unmasking the lie, identifying the inauthentic, and taking apart the indefinite and false absolutes* continues to be, for now, the only corrective resource – a mocking, inexhaustible safeguard – against our bankrupt history').[45] The primary goal for Pirandello and Fellini is to unmask the lie, to identify the inauthentic, and finally to represent and express the multiple and diverse voices the Subject assumes within society as well as within his own conscience.

Narrative becomes the witnessing of the progressive acceptance of the schizoid condition[46] by the Subject, who comes to experience the innumerable creative possibilities provided by his new, profoundly anarchist condition. I thus agree with Elio Gioanola when he maintains that

la forma delle opere non monologiche, a partire almeno dal polifonismo di Dostoevsky, risponda ad una condizione profonda di 'io-diviso,' cioé sia una risposta nella creatività della scrittura ad una sofferenza di tipo schizoide. In questo senso pensiamo che si possa risolvere il problema, altrimenti irrisolvibile, dell'assurda 'mancanza di un'unitaria coscienza poetica' corrispondente, come la situazione pirandelliana dichiara, ad una vera e propria 'mancanza d'autore.'[47]

the form of nonmonologic works, at least beginning with Dostoevsky's polyphonism, corresponds to the profound condition of a 'divided Self,' and thus finds in the creativity of writing an answer to schizoid suffering. This is the way in which, we think, it is possible to resolve the otherwise unsolvable problem of the absurd 'lack of a unifying poetic conscience' corresponding, as the Pirandellian condition declares, in the true 'lack of an author.'

Nonmonologism in art thus provides the creative answer to the painful condition of the divided Self and resolves the otherwise vexing problem of the lack of a unified poetic consciousness, which in the Pirandellian text corresponds to the true lack of an author.

The dialogic approach toward oneself obviously breaks the ingenuous integrity of self-representation lying at the very basis of a lyric, epic, or tragic image of man, and leads to the discovery of the Other within oneself. Therefore, according to Bakhtin, the monologue typical of 'serious' genres gives way to the dialogic discourse of the carnival-ized genre, which is born out of the contrast between the two Selves lo-cated within the Subject. This dialogic approach may be associated with the dualistic conception of truth which Bakhtin traces back to the So-cratic dialogue. Pirandello, who would certainly agree with Bakhtin, once stated: 'Umorista non è Aristofane, ma Socrate'[48] ('Aristophanes is not a humorist, but Socrates is').[49]

Within the framework of a genre without qualifying adjectives, or rather, 'humoristic' – a genre that pursues the break with monologic discourse that started with the Socratic dialogue via the nonhierarchic dissemination of truth in multiple voices – the hero becomes not simply the object of the author's discourse, but also is the subject of his own discourse, which becomes immediately meaningful. This is the condi-tion of Pirandello's characters without an author and Fellini's obsessive images (his 'fantasmi'). The fundamental problem these two authors face seems to lie, in fact, in the 'independence' of their characters. Es-sentially because of this peculiar condition of their characters, both artists ultimately lack the possibility of creating an *authentic* autobiog-raphy.

In both Pirandello's and Fellini's artistic visions, this condition of in-dependence of the character becomes clear in numerous instances. Their characters are almost like obsessive phantoms appearing from some other life – the famous Pirandellian 'oltre,' which finds a clear echo in Fellini's 'subconscious' – who pressure the author into giving them true artistic expression and, thus, new life. According to Piran-dello, humour is a sort of doubling in the act of creation. No single form can actually fulfil these shadows' thirst for life; therefore, they re-main in the darkness of the artist's imagination, returning obsessively over and over again. This may explain the apparent monotony that characterizes both authors' conspicuous galleries of characters. It should be remembered, though, that this is a monotony in diversity, for in a text defined as 'humoristic' no single-faced character and no sin-gle-toned truth exists.

In his analysis of Pirandello's many-faceted production, Giovanni Macchia has maintained:

I personaggi, a volte gli stessi, altre volte lievemente alterati, con qualche pic-colo rilievo fisionomico, vanno e vengono: escono da una novella ed entrano in un romanzo, escono da un romanzo e vanno a finire in un saggio, e, ancora scontenti, dalle silenziose pagine di un romanzo affrontano, nelle alterne vicende della loro vita di condannati, le scricchiolanti tavole di un palcoscenico.[50]

The characters, at times the same, at times slightly altered with an unsubstantial physiognomic feature, come and go: they exit a short story and enter a novel, they get out of the novel and end up in an essay, and then, still unhappy, from the silent pages of a novel, within the shifting chances of their life of condemned beings, they face the screeching wood of the stage.

In Pirandello's entire artistic work, characters come and go – from short story to novel, from novel to essay, from everywhere to the screeching stage of his theatre. Sometimes they arrive totally unchanged, sometimes they are slightly modified, although more in their physical than in their psychological substance. The same occurs in Fellini's cinema, where extremely similar characters appear over and over. Moraldo jumps from *I Vitelloni* to *La Dolce Vita* and becomes Marcello; from *La Dolce Vita*, Marcello then jumps to *8½* and becomes Guido, the character-director, who eventually becomes Fellini himself in the trilogy of the cinema in the cinema: *Fellini: A Director's Notebook*, *I clowns* (*The Clowns*, 1970), and *Fellini's Roma*. Ultimately, all these characters, together with their various sympathetic companions, jump into *Amarcord*, a film that develops through a choir of perspectives rather than through the experience of a single conscience (that of Fellini) that attempts to revisit its own past. Fellini, in fact, has insisted repeatedly on the ambivalence of the word 'amarcord.' Although this expression does mean 'I remember' in the Rimini dialect, the director has repeatedly pointed out the arbitrary and idiosyncratic qualities of the term:

Un giorno, al ristorante, mentre scribacchiavo disegnini sul tovagliolo è venuta fuori la parola *Amarcord*; ecco, mi sono detto, adesso verrà immediatamente identificata nel 'mi ricordo' in dialetto romagnolo, mentre ciò che bisognava accuratamente evitare era una lettura in chiave autobiografica del film. *Amarcord*: una paroletta bizzarra, un carillon, una capriola fonetica, un suono cabalistico, la marca di un aperitivo, anche, perché no? Qualunque cosa, tranne l'irritante associazione al 'je me souviens.' Una parola che nella sua stravaganza potesse diventare la sintesi, il punto di riferimento, quasi il riverbero sonoro di un sentimento, di uno stato d'animo, di un atteggiamento, di un modo di pensare duplice, controverso, contraddittorio, la convivenza di due opposti, la fusione di due estremi, come distacco e nostalgia, giudizio e complicità, rifiuto e adesione, tenerezza ed ironia, fastidio e strazio. Mi sembrava che il film che volevo fare rappresentasse proprio questo.[51]

One day, at the restaurant, while I was scribbling drawings on a napkin, the word *Amarcord* came out; that's it, I told myself, now it will be immediately identified with 'I remember' in the dialect from Romagna, while what should have been accurately avoided was an autobiographical reading of the film. *Amarcord* is a bizarre little word, a carillon, a phonetic capriole, a cabalistic sound, even the brand of an aperitif. Why not? Anything but the irritating association with 'je me souviens' ['I remember']. A word that in its extravagance could become the synthesis, the point of reference, almost the sound reverberation of a feeling, a mood, an attitude, *a way of thinking that is doubled, controversial, contradictory, and basically the coexistence of two opposites, the fusion of two extremes, such as detachment and nostalgia, judgment and complicity, refusal and assent, tenderness and irony, weariness and agony.* It seemed to me that the film I wanted to make represented all this.[52]

Fellini's statement here constitutes one of his many declarations of intention, which, besides supporting my assumption about the purely non-autobiographical nature of *Amarcord*, also unveils clear similarities to Pirandello's definition of the creative process he terms 'umorismo':

Nella concezione di ogni opera d'arte umoristica, la riflessione non si nasconde, non resta invisibile, non resta cioè quasi una forma del sentimento, quasi uno specchio in cui il sentimento si rimira; ma gli si pone innanzi, da giudice; lo analizza, spassionandosene; ne scompone l'immagine; da questa analisi però, da questa scomposizione, un altro sentimento sorge o spira: quello che potrebbe chiamarsi e che io difatti chiamo *il sentimento del contrario*.[53]

During the conception of all works of humor, reflection is not hidden, it does not remain invisible: it is not, that is, almost a form of feeling or almost a mirror in which feeling contemplates itself; rather, it places itself squarely before the feeling, in a judging attitude, and, detaching itself from it, analyzes it and disassembles its imagery; from this analysis and decomposition, however, there arises or emerges a new feeling which could be called and in fact I call the *feeling of the opposite*.[54]

It is precisely within this 'feeling of the opposite,' as opposed to the much simpler 'avvertimento del contrario' ('perception of the opposite'), that the main difference between the comic and the humoristic lies, according to Pirandello. The dramatist's definition finds immediate resonance in Fellini's critical and artistic statements. Fellini gives both verbal and especially visual form to a similar state of mind, a way of thinking that is ambivalent, controversial, contradictory, and representative of a cohabitation of two opposites, a fusion of two extremes: tragedy and comedy, tears and laughter. Moreover, Fellini has declared, in terms that both Pirandello and Bakhtin could accept, that 'humour is a type of view, of rapport, of feeling one has about things.'[55]

The primacy of the Subject is thus restated in the artistic and existential statements of both Pirandello and Fellini. This Subject, however, now represents the stage for an active opposition between two Selves. The only way to gain access to the 'interior Self' is through the dialogic approach toward oneself, an approach that breaks the ingenuous integrity of self-representation characteristic of the comic and tragic genres. This dialogic tradition, which Bakhtin defines as 'carnivalistic' and Pirandello as 'humoristic,' witnesses the representation of unusual and abnormal psychic states in art such as madness, split personality, unrestrained fantasizing, strange dreams, and wild passions bordering on madness or suicide. Bakhtin maintains that Dostoevsky is responsible for the invention of all contemporary narrative structures meant to convey the totality of the neurotic-psychotic opposition.[56] Whoever the inventor of the new narrative strategies may have been, it is certainly true that the modern period witnesses a clear tendency to provide narrative expression to a nervous suffering, which moves from a neurotic to a schizoid stance within the Subject. Both Pirandello and Fellini obviously participate in this countertradition, which expresses in negative terms the fundamental conflict between father and son, and which can be detected at the very basis of all the nervous sufferings troubling modern man.

In an essay entitled 'Pirandello e l'oltre,' included in the volume *Dalle parti di Pirandello*, Paolo Puppa makes an interesting parallel between the condition of the *avvocato* (lawyer) and that of the *auctor* (author), and maintains that, in the Pirandellian plot, continuous exchanges take place between the two. What allows the movement from one role to the other is the concept of 'soul,' which, according to Puppa, gives birth to the idea of character. What needs to be found is a door to the 'oltre,' to the 'al di là,' as Pirandello terms it, or to the 'subconscious,' if we were to define it in Fellini's terms. In Pirandello's short story 'La casa del Granella' ('Granella's House'), a lawyer named Zummo pleads the cause of the 'creature dell'*al di là*':

L'anima immortale, i signori spiriti che fanno? vengono a bussare alla porta del mio studio: 'Ehi, signor avvocato, ci siamo anche noi, sa? Vogliamo ficcare anche noi il naso nel suo codice civile! E noi, allegramente, dal regno della morte, veniamo a bussare alla porta dei vivi ... ad atterrir la povera gente e a mettere in imbarazzo, oggi, un avvocato che passa per dotto.'[57]

The immortal souls, the honourable spirits, what do they do? They come and knock at the door of my studio: 'Hey, mister lawyer, there is us too, d'you know? We also want to peek into your civil code! Thus, cheerfully we come from death's realm and we knock at the door of the living ... we come to scare the poor human beings and to embarass today a lawyer who is famous for his knowledge.'

Innumerable references to the 'spiriti' – that is, both the voices from 'beyond' and those from 'within,' which undermine the very ontology of the Subject – can easily be found in Fellini's cinema. The film 8½ is the cinematic narration of a director's total existential and artistic crisis: it is the story of an individual who, once facing the many different voices that pressure him from inside and outside himself, progressively loses contact with all of them and experiences a state of complete confusion. During a visit with some friends and a few production people to the spaceship built for the science fiction film he is supposed to shoot (but never will), Guido Anselmi first admits he has nothing to say but wants to say it anyway. He then turns to Rossella, his wife's best friend, and anxiously asks her what her 'spirits' think about him:

470. *Guido in MS, right foreground, turns in Rossella's direction:*
GUIDO: And your spirits, why don't they help me?
471. *CU: Rossella.*
GUIDO *(off)*: You always said that they were loaded down with messages for me. Well, they should get to work!
ROSSELLA: I already told you, Guido. *(She turns away.)* Your attitude about them is wrong. *(She walks and turns nervously, in MCU.)* You're curious ... childishly curious. And you have too many reservations ... you want too many guarantees.
GUIDO *(off)*: All right ... but what do they say to you?
ROSSELLA *(looking in Guido's direction)*: They always say the same things, even right now. They're very reasonable spirits. They know you very well. *Slow track in to CU of Rossella.*
GUIDO: Well?
ROSSELLA: They say that you're free. But you have to choose, and you haven't got much time left.[58]

In his quest for recognition of both his social and artistic identity, Guido constantly cries out for help. First of all, he seeks assistance from the multiplicity of socially constituted voices that surround him: the voices of his mother, father, wife, lover, critic, producer, and, last but not least, the overwhelming voice of the Church. Second, he asks help from the 'spirits,' the voices from within. In both instances, however, the Subject must choose; in fact, 'to choose' seems to equal 'to be,' in social as well as in existential terms. The quest for recognition and the recognition of loss become the central guidelines of Fellini's masterpiece. The loss that is recognized is a loss of identity on behalf of the author/Fellini, of the characters and of the text itself. What Pirandello expressed in his famous theatrical trilogy as the circular search for something lacking, Fellini's 8½ expresses in terms of a loss, the loss of the Other and/or the others produced by the act of choosing. Having lost his identity, the Subject tries to recover it in relationship both to the Other and to others.

The situation of loss the Subject experiences in Fellini's film finds a more adequate parallel in Pirandello's *One, Nobody, and One Hundred Thousand*. Both Guido and Moscarda are Subjects caught up in the terrifying reality of an irreparable loss, the loss of a comforting identity. Therefore, they both move from a neurotic search for lost unity, a search conducted mainly through a quest for recognition from others, to an acceptance of their acknowledged division and fragmentation – that is, their schizoid condition.

According to Jacques Lacan, true subjectivity is only possible in the Other through language, while the Self represents merely a narcissistic function. The continuously frustrated desire of the Self to complete the Other results in alienation.[59] In Pirandello's artistic works, this alienation expresses itself in a twofold manner. It is first of all linguistic, born in the Subject from its recognition of being the locus of the opposition between enunciation and statement. Second, alienation becomes a constant factor in social life, as the Subject recognizes its being the locus of opposition between mask and face, illusion and reality, form and life. Ultimately, then, for Pirandello, at the very core of social alienation there still lies a problem of language, precisely that of the clash between the language of the Imaginary and that of the Symbolic or the Law. To unmask the lie, to tear away the social mask, to free the Imaginary from the language of the Symbolic in Lacanian terms – that is, from the language of the Father – becomes the only way to overcome alienation.

However, 'truth,' or at least 'honesty,' becomes an extremely precarious concept, although it is certainly a necessary, if not sufficient, requirement in being absolved, and therefore in producing a work of art. The relationship between lawyer and client, judge and imploring defendants, is a useful aid in understanding the relationship between author and characters. The legal situation recalls the fantastic meeting between author and characters in Pirandello's work. Before becoming the subject matter of the 'theatre within the theatre' trilogy, this encounter found a first and preparatory treatment in several short stories centred on the nature of character: 'La tragedia di un personaggio' ('The Tragedy of a Character,' 1911); 'Colloqui coi personaggi' ('Colloquia with the Characters,' 1915); and 'I pensionati della memoria' ('The Pensioners of the Memory,' 1914).

Fellini's *A Director's Notebook* may be fruitfully compared with these short stories in at least two of its most significant sequences. First of all, close to the end of the film, Fellini has himself filmed in his office while he is receiving the many peculiar persons who knock at his door demanding to become characters – to find a place in his imaginary world and, thus, in his films. The situation recalls Pirandello's 'The Tragedy of a Character,' which begins as follows:

E' mia vecchia abitudine dare udienza, ogni domenica mattina, ai personaggi delle mie future novelle.

Cinque ore, dalle otto alle tredici.

M'accade quasi sempre di trovarmi in cattiva compagnia.

Non so perché, di solito accorre a queste mie udienze la gente piú scontenta del mondo, o afflitta da strani mali, o ingarbugliata in speciosissimi casi, con la quale è veramente una pena trattare.

Io li ascolto tutti con sopportazione; li interrogo con buona grazia; prendo nota de' nomi e delle condizioni di ciascuno; tengo conto de' loro sentimenti e delle loro aspirazioni ... E voglio penetrare in fondo al loro animo.

Ora avviene che a certe mie domande piú d'uno aombri ... perché forse gli sembra ch'io provi gusto a scomporlo ...

... si fa presto a volerci in un modo o in un altro; tutto sta poi se possiamo essere quali ci vogliamo. Ove quel potere manchi, per forza questa volontà deve apparire ridicola e vana.

Non se ne vogliono persuadere.

E allora io, che in fondo sono di buon cuore, li compatisco. Ma è mai possibile il compatimento di certe sventure, se non a patto che se ne rida?[60]

It is an old habit of mine to receive, every Sunday morning, the characters of my future short story.

Five hours, from eight to one in the afternoon.

I normally find myself in bad company.

I don't know why, but usually the unhappiest people in the world, or those plagued by the strangest illnesses, or saddened by the most unusual cases, all people with whom it is truly painful to deal, they all rush to my audience.

I listen to them all with patience; I interrogate them with kindness; I write down their names and problems; I take into consideration their feelings and aspirations ... And I aim at delving deep into their soul.

Now it happens that at some of my questions a few of them grow suspicious ... perhaps because they think I enjoy unsettling them ...

... it is quite easy to want oneself to be in one and specific way; the problem resides in verifying whether it is then possible to be what we would like to be. Whenever that power is lacking, then that will appears ridiculous and vain.

They refuse to acknowledge this.

And then I feel compassion for them because I am good-hearted. But is compassion for these strange cases possible without laughing at them?

The same situation recurs in 'Colloquia with the Characters,' where the author is besieged by a character, one of the cheekiest, even though that day the audiences have been suspended. The main parallel between the audition sequence in *A Director's Notebook* and the two short stories apparently lies in the fact that, in both cases, the author 'receives' his characters as if they were his clients. In both Pirandello's short stories and Fellini's film, then, the artists go through a ritual not unlike a legal procedure. The analogy lies much deeper, however, since in both Fellini's film and Pirandello's short stories, the author begins with a judgmental attitude but is soon moved to compassion. The grotesqueness and freakishness so often noted in Fellini's mature characters needs to be revisited in light of Pirandello's theory of 'umorismo,' as the Sicilian author argues that laughter is the necessary premise to reaching true compassion when man faces certain misfortune. In Fellini's film, we hardly see the director, although we hear his voice as a number of peculiar characters flow past us. We watch them from a special vantage point – from behind Fellini's desk and next to him. As these strange and, at times, grotesque people – 'la gente più scontenta del mondo' ('the unhappiest people in the world'), as Pirandello might call them – parade in front of him and us, Fellini's voice moves from affection to amusement, to condescension, to vexation, to laughter, and ultimately to compassion for them as well as for himself.

Yes, I know it must seem sinful, cruel, but no, I am very fond of these characters who are always chasing after me, following me from one film to another. They are a little mad, I know that. They say they need me, but the truth is that I need them more. Their human qualities are rich, comic, and sometimes very moving.[61]

While these words die out – as Joseph McBride reminds us in his essay 'The Director as Superstar' – the camera pans over a new group of characters, all talking at once and smiling, all waiting to be seen and heard by the director. 'It is a fresco of human absurdity and loveliness, and it is all Fellini has to say. At the end of *A Director's Notebook*, we see him back in action on the set, brash, jovial, and liberated.'[62] The typical Pirandellian 'sentimento del contrario' is clearly at work here, in that mixture of absurdity and loveliness, tragedy and comedy, tears and laughter, that constitutes the main requirement for the Pirandellian 'scrittura umoristica' ('humoristic writing').

Moreover, characters represent recurrently obsessive images, phantoms who stand in the Pirandellian *oltre* and/or in the Fellinian subconscious while waiting to be brought to light. An early sequence in *A Director's Notebook* bears a remarkable resemblance to an event in Pirandello's 'The Tragedy of a Character.' At a certain point in the short story, the author is confronted by a strange and unfortunate character, Dr Fileno. This figure is 'strange' because of the peculiar method he has invented to overcome pain and sorrow in life – by distancing the present and making it already part of the past. He calls his method the 'filosofia del lontano' ('philosophy of distance'). Dr Fileno is 'unfortunate,' since he has been treated by an author who has completely misunderstood the rich potential of his peculiar case and has thus impoverished his personality. After Pirandello's author reads the novel in which Dr Fileno appears and spends the entire night fantasizing about him, the character appears to him in the midst of all his other characters and tries to receive new life from him. The author refuses to grant him his wish, since the character's need for immortality cannot be satisfied in a written work:

Ella va cercando, oggi, tra noi, uno scrittore che la consacri all'immortalità? Ma guardi ... noi ... Siamo e non siamo, caro dottore! E sottoponga, insieme con noi, al suo famoso cannocchiale rivoltato i fatti piú notevoli, le questioni piú ardenti e le piú mirabili opere dei giorni nostri. Caro il mio dottore, ho gran paura ch'Ella non vedrà piú niente né nessuno.[63]

Today, among us, you are looking for a writer who can consecrate you to immortality? But look ... we ... We are and we are not, dear doctor! Please submit to your celebrated reversed telescope ourselves as well as the most important cases, the hottest issues and most beautiful works of our times. My dear doctor, I am afraid you'll see nothing and nobody.

Dr Fileno's story is that of a character who hopes to be given new life and immortality, a character refused a written form by an author who fears that if he expressed him in words, he would make him vanish. This peculiar character bears a striking similarity to Fellini's most famous but still unfilmed fictional character, G. Mastorna. In the opening sequence of *A Director's Notebook*, the camera wanders around outside an abandoned movie set whose only remnant is the skeleton of an airplane. Fellini's voice-over comments on the surreal setting: 'These strange, lonely shapes were built for a film I planned, but never made. It was called *Il viaggio di Mastorna [The Voyage of Mastorna]*. The settings have remained like this, useless and empty, in a studio near Rome.'[64] All of a sudden, the sound of an airplane can be heard, a snowy blizzard rages, and a figure materializes from nowhere, his back to the camera: 'This is Mastorna, the hero of my film, a cellist. His voyage would have begun like this. *An unexpected landing in a strange, dreamlike "piazza"* ... it is the story that I prefer the most ... because the character materializes himself.' Then Fellini, now in side-face close-up as he walks toward the right of the screen, continues: 'Some time I have had the feeling to have met *personally* Mastorna, but every time he slips away ... For the moment, Mastorna has not arrived yet, but every scene is ready to receive him.' Mastorna seems to embody the typically Pirandellian situation of a character in search of his author, and, moreover, of an author in search of his character, or rather, of an author who is almost unwilling to give aesthetic form to a character who desires to be given his very own form.

Later in the movie, we are shown the screen tests for *The Voyage of Mastorna*, with Marcello Mastroianni playing the role of the cellist. Fellini's voice-over informs us that 'Mastorna was not there, was still hiding his face from me.' Mastroianni, looking at the camera, adds: 'It is as if you were scared ... If you only believed that I was Mastorna, I would have automatically become Mastorna.' The author, then, has to believe in his phantoms in order for them to become alive and for the actors to be able to represent them. Mastorna was one of Fellini's most obsessive shadows, and this is probably why the director seemed almost terrified of the possibility of translating him into the flickering images of the cinema, and why he never represented Mastorna in a film.

Spirits, phantoms, and obsessive shadows pressure the author from beyond and from within. Legal procedures often trespass onto the realm of spiritualist séances, of magic rituals. When this occurs, the author is obviously forced into the ambivalent role of the 'medium.' However, an author actually *is* a medium, a translator into words and/or cinematic images of an image born in his imagination. According to Pirandello, a further and often fatal mediation takes place in theatre through the representation of the character by the actor. What is ultimately left of the creature, the living image that initially pressured the author into receiving new life, becomes simply 'un adattamento, una maschera, anziché una vera incarnazione'[65] ('an adaptation, a mask, rather than a true embodiment') when it achieves concrete form on the stage.

The problematic relationship between director and actors is likewise analysed in Fellini's *8½* when, near the end of the movie, the protagonist's artistic crisis reaches its peak during the viewing of the screen tests for the film to be made. The overwhelming distance between the original images and voices as they presented themselves in the director's imagination and the banal, mundane form of the *provini* (already parts of a symbolic apparatus) cannot be bridged by the feeble efforts of the actors, mere shadows on a screen within the screen. Fellini analyses and thematizes the intriguing question of the true nature of the character, as well as of the author, in many of his narrative films, but particularly in *8½*, a work that constitutes a cinematic parallel to Pirandello's trilogy of the 'theatre in the theatre.'

The nature of the character as humorist is central to most of Pirandello's works, and certainly is crucial to his 'novels of identity,' *The Late Mattia Pascal, Shoot!*, and *One, Nobody, and One Hundred Thousand*. In these narrative works, the main character bears strong similarities to the central figure in Dostoevsky's 'The Dream of a Ridiculous Man.' In this character, as Bakhtin points out, 'there are clear traces of the *ambivalent* – serio-comical – image of the "wise-fool" and "tragic clown" of carnivalized literature.'[66] One of Fellini's most important artistic statements on character is *The Clowns*; it is not by chance that in order to provide a full definition of his conception of character the director turns to the world of the circus. Fellini focuses on the ambivalent figure of the clown in its two variants, the 'Augusto' and the White Clown, contradictory embodiments of opposites.[67] The Pirandellian concept of humour – that 'feeling of the opposite' – thus seems to constitute the most obvious source of Fellini's conception of character. Fellini once declared, while speaking about the making of *La Strada*,

Gelsomina appeared to me in the guise of a clown, and immediately beside her, as a contrast, there appeared a massive and dark shadow, Zampanò. And, naturally, the road, the circus with its colorful rags, its menacing and heartbreaking music, its cruel fairy-tale atmosphere.[68]

Thus, it is Fellini's habitual practice to place his ambivalent and eccentric characters in the equally ambivalent and eccentric atmosphere of the circus, a social institution that reflects the carnival atmosphere better than any other art form can.

Eccentricity, a characteristic common to all of Dostoevsky's protagonists, typifies Pirandello's and Fellini's protagonists, or rather 'anti-heroes.' In fact, a character defined primarily by ambivalence necessarily becomes an anti-hero: 'L'umorista non riconosce eroi ... Il mondo, lui, se non propriamente nudo, lo vede, per così dire, in camicia'[69] ('The humorist does not recognize heroes ... The humorist sees the world, not exactly in the nude but, so to speak, in shirt sleeves').[70] Many of Fellini's characters are truly 'humorists' – that is, individuals caught up in the clash between public mask and interior face, people unable to take on any serious responsibility in life, who seem to parody an archetypal character by constantly reflecting doubles of themselves. Pirandello notes that 'l'umorista ... *scompone* il carattere nei suoi elementi ... si diverte a rappresentarlo nelle sue incongruenze'[71] ('the humorist ... will *decompose* the character into his elements and ... enjoys representing him in his incongruities').[72] In like manner, Fellini portrays his characters by emphasizing their many incongruities (both physical and psychological), often reaching the extremes of the grotesque.

As Elio Gioanola observes,[73] with Dostoevsky the protagonist of the novel first became an anti-hero, or in other words a madman without qualities, a ridiculous man. After the bourgeois revolution, the traditional Hegelian master–slave dialectic is replaced with the Freudian father–son opposition, which generates all modern forms of nervous suffering.[74] While it was formerly impossible to kill God and men could only laugh at Him by parodying His sacredness, today it has indeed become possible to kill God – that is, the Father – now that the father has taken His place. This fatal temptation leaves the Son full of remorse and pain, and possibly leads him to madness. In an essay entitled 'Arte e coscienza d'oggi,'[75] Pirandello defined modern man as 'slegato ... e che farnetica' ('unrestrained and raving'). This new raving Subject no longer appears as a romantic hero, but rather as an anti-hero for whom language as a social institution no longer serves as an adequate means of expression. Given this totally changed existential and social condition, both the role of art and of the artist in society have to change. Art no longer legitimates the order of things, and so for the artist nothing remains but unmasking the lie, expressing the disorder.

The freedom that bourgeois society reached through revolution marked the end of the joyful explosion of the carnival in the public squares and relocated it, together with all serious dogmatism, within the family group. By transferring dogmatism into the family, social liberation made that dogmatism itself far more overwhelming because of the blackmail and ambiguity hidden in the love-hate relationships people entertain with their family members. The joyful relativity Bakhtin analyses, which is typical of the carnival and of all carnivalized literature, 'scompare rapidamente in una letteratura ormai nevrotizzata'[76] ('rapidly disappears in a now neurotic literature'), giving way to what Bakhtin has characterized as 'Dostoevsky's restrained laughter,' and what Pirandello has defined as 'humour' in opposition to comedy, where 'oggetto del rovesciamento parodistico é lo stesso personaggio-protagonista, delegato a mostrare "umoristicamente" i segni della sconfitta di fronte all'assolutezza dei valori paterni'[77] ('the object of the parodic overturning is the character-protagonist, who is delegated to show "humoristically" the signs of defeat in the face of the Father's absolute values'). These are the characteristics of a rich gallery of humorists in the modern and contemporary history of Western culture, a gallery that includes Dostoevsky's 'underground man' or 'idiot,' Italo Svevo's 'inept,' the funny hero of Kafka's *America*[78] or Thomas Mann's Felix Krull, and Musil's 'man without qualities' as well as Pirandello's 'man without identity' and Fellini's 'vitellone.' The typical Subject of such modern narratives is thus literally 'dominated' by otherness, and by the irreversible division of madness, since 'la folie commence là où se trouble et s'obscurcit le rapport de l'homme à la vérité'[79] ('madness begins where man's relationship to truth becomes troubled and obscure').

Freud has provided us with the interpretative tools required to understand nervous suffering psychologically, and therefore culturally, and has opened the way to place neurotic-psychotic phenomena into a historical perspective – that is, to see them as pathological answers to the many and different pressures the environment exerts upon the Subject.[80] However, comedy is the genre in which conflict with the Father becomes accepted without neurotic effects, and which ultimately proposes a successful opposition for the Son. This is why, according to Bakhtin, the comic mode represents the exact opposite of the tragic mode. The serio-comic and the 'humoristic,' however, instead reflect the area of neurotic opposition, of joyful and anguishing compromise, of ambivalence, and of ambiguity.

Anyone seeking a satisfactory definition of the identity of the typical Pirandellian and Fellinian Subject ought to bear in mind that, on the one hand, with his essay *On Humor*, Pirandello moved toward acquiring an organic theory of the literary character's disintegration. On the other hand, both Pirandello's dialectical theatrical scene and his evolved narrative syntax produced an irreversible fracture between the *raisonneur* and the others. Serafino Gubbio, who in 1915 looked at the world with his insensitive eye 'dall'alto' ('from above'), in 1925 turns into Vitangelo Moscarda, the hero who seizes the real 'da vicino' ('from close') and therefore disintegrates into innumerable epiphanies that no word can explain or author represent upon the stage. As Paolo Puppa maintains: 'Si tratta, in questo caso, per esprimerci con categorie psichiche, d'un passaggio da un atteggiamento *paranoide* ad uno *schizoide*, intendendo per paranoia un tentativo di rallentare la dispersione dell'Io'[81] ('Using psychological categories, this is clearly the movement from a *paranoid* to a *schizoid* attitude, where paranoia here means an attempt to slow down the dispersion of the Self'). A movement from a neurotic to a psychotic state in the modern Subject parallels the passage from comforting monologic discourse to the discontinuous, disintegrated and disintegrating dialogic discourse of the serio-comic genre, whether it be called 'carnivalistic' or 'humoristic.'

The same passage can be discerned in Fellini's career. We observe characters such as Moraldo in *I Vitelloni*, who bears striking resemblances to Pirandello's Mattia Pascal: both are incapable of transformations, of 'epifanizzarsi'[82] ('having an epiphany'). There are also characters such as Casanova, the archetypical neurotic Subject who reaches the point of total mechanization and, as such, finds a literary parallel in Serafino Gubbio, the protagonist of Pirandello's *Shoot!*, since Serafino apparently reaches total mechanization, too, as he progressively becomes just a hand turning a handle. A synchronic analysis of Fellini's entire cinematic production thus allows us to detect the same passage from a neurotic to a schizoid Subject that we find in Pirandello's artistic works. Besides characters such as Moraldo and Casanova, however, Fellini produces the figure of Guido Anselmi, the protagonist of *8½*. This film can be considered a watershed in Fellini's entire production, for Guido embodies the neurotic-schizoid passage itself. He represents a consciousness in progress, almost a metaconsciousness, while the film *8½* is a work in progress, a metafilm. Metaphorically, Guido moves from the situation of Mattia Pascal to that of Serafino Gubbio, but ultimately becomes a Vitangelo Moscarda, the man of many epiphanies, the man who avoids mechanization by disintegrating his social and his private being. He is a character who finds in the dissolution of his given social and existential image and in his 'difference' the foundation for a new and fulfilling creative life.

Some parallels between Guido and Moscarda have already been mentioned, but more exist, especially in the ultimate message both characters embody. In both instances, the 'fabula' is the story of a wilful and accomplished social and linguistic suicide, a titanic effort to escape from frozen forms and to move toward life as pure movement, or rather 'flux,' as Pirandello would define it.[83] Significantly, both Moscarda's and Guido's fathers are dead. According to Lacan, the symbolic Father, insofar as he signifies the Law, is the dead Father.[84] In order to overcome the neurotic and obsessional state, the Subject has to kill the father and thus rejoin the mother by fulfilling her desire. In Pirandello's novel, the protagonist kills the Name-of-the-Father metaphorically by 'ex-nominating'[85] himself, and thus privileges his 'being' over his 'form,' both in social and in linguistic terms. He does so by undergoing a sort of schizophrenic process. At first he empties his narcissistic Self of meaning, then re-signifies himself in the Other – the unknown Other whose existence he has progressively acknowledged inside himself, since his very first gaze into the mirror. Entering the world of the ever-changing, multiple, and nameless Other, which in Lacanian psychoanalysis is the locus of true subjectivity, Moscarda can escape both social and artistic alienation.

As the film *8½* nears its conclusion, Guido experiences a progression toward self-dissemination quite similar to that experienced by Moscarda. The movie is characterized by the interdependent progression of three levels of discourse, which I loosely define here as imagination and fantasy, reality, and dream life. These three levels of discourse are strongly affected by two main driving forces: the 'quest for recognition' – of the Subject by the Other and by the others – and the 'recognition of a loss' – what is lost is the Subject's integral image of himself, or his unified identity. The last three sequences of *8½* can be considered a single narrative segment if one assumes them to represent the conclusion to the film, or rather, all the possible conclusions to it. These sequences may also be considered the ideal resolution of the interior discourse of the Self with the Other – which started in the very moment Guido looked at himself in the mirror, at the film's opening – as well as of the Self with the others and with its Object of desire. Each sequence corresponds loosely to the three levels of discourse, which I shall here define in terms of Lacanian psychoanalysis: The oneiric life can be identified with the Symbolic; the present of narration can be loosely associated with the Real; and the fantasy constitutes, within this particular narrative, the Imaginary in Lacanian terms.

The first of the three final sequences is a press conference during which the science-fiction film the production wants Guido to make is going to be presented to the public. This cinematic segment, however, represents nothing but a conclusion to the opening sequence of the entire movie – the nightmare. At the beginning of the film we see the hero, almost constantly with his back to the camera, escaping from a suffocating and claustrophobic tunnel, then flying away. He is finally and definitively pulled back to earth in a breathless fall by the agent of Claudia/the real woman (as opposed to Claudia/the ideal, the girl of the spring in the hero's fantasy). The nightmare continues in the last narrative segment, but here the Symbolic unfolds and finds its resolution. Drawn back to earth, the Subject abruptly has to face the demands of both the Real and the Imaginary, which press him to make clear choices. Unable to satisfy those demands, the hero ultimately kills himself.

At this point, the present of narration takes over. Solicited by the intellectual demands of Daumier (the French critic who has reflected Guido's false conscience during the entire movie) and faced with both his lack of a 'unifying idea' and his incapacity to make definitive aesthetic choices, Guido has to acknowledge his inability to create an honest and true work of art. Thus he has to kill the movie the others wanted him to make – the science-fiction film – and with it the movie he *really* wanted to make. With the demise of the film, he ultimately negates and thus destroys his own desire.

The actual film *8½*, however, could not possibly end in this way. The true dreaming Subject – Fellini himself – still stands behind the camera and wants to fulfil his own desire, that is, to achieve an honest and true creation. Must this film be another of Fellini's movies without hope?[86]

The Imaginary intervenes at this point to provide the only possible answer. Dressed in white, the characters of Guido's memory, fantasy, and so-called reality come back to him, now all smiling. Also with them comes Guido/the child, now the carrier of hope, who comes back to help Guido/the man fulfil his desire. At this point, Guido realizes that he is that confusion that has disturbed him all along; he is that plethora of voices and images that have pressured him from without and within. Guido comprehends that the only possible choice he has left is to accept such multiplicity. In so doing, he will finally achieve creation and overcome alienation. In both psychoanalytic and cinematic discourses, the Subject comes to realize that the identity for which he has been searching must necessarily be fragmentary. Guido/the man finally manages to direct his film, but leaves the concluding shot to Guido/the child, who is leading a group of clowns inside the circus ring. As the clowns leave the circle, the child at first remains alone in an illuminated spot in the centre of the circle, but then he himself exits the circle as darkness prevails.

At the conclusion of both Pirandello's novel and Fellini's film, then, there is no longer *one* 'valid' fictional construct, just as there is no longer only one 'valid' character or Subject. In both instances, though, recognizing this disunity and fragmentation is a joyful process. The last word is not one of nihilism. The Subject is 'new,' without haunting memories, not inside but outside, finally 'there' in the recreated reality of the Imaginary. Moscarda's incapacity to speak and Guido's fading into darkness do not represent the silence and absence characteristic of annihilation. On the contrary, these responses present the consequences of willful choice. The new Subject can no longer express himself in traditional linguistic and social ways. This new Subject is anarchic in his very spirit, and hence restless towards any given form. The text that is the expression of this new Subject has to become multi-meaningful and multi-levelled, hence metaphoric and poetic, not in romantic but in Aristotelian terms.

This was Pirandello's message at the conclusion of his last narrative work, a message that Fellini accepted completely, I believe, and carried to its furthest consequences. According to Roland Barthes, in the age of the death of the Father, literature has been deprived of its many pleasures:

La mort du Père enlèvera à la littérature beaucoup de ses plaisirs. S'il n'y a plus de Père, à quoi bon raconter des histoires? Tout récit ne se ramène-t-il pas à l'Oedipe? Raconter, n'est-ce pas toujours chercher son origine, dire ses démêlés avec la Loi, entrer dans la dialectique de l'attendrissement et de la Haine? Aujourd'hui on balance d'un même coup l'Oedipe et le recit: on n'aime plus, on ne craint plus, on ne raconte plus.'[87]

The death of the Father would deprive literature of many of its pleasures. If there is no longer a Father, why tell stories? Doesn't any narrative lead back to Oedipus? Isn't storytelling always a way of searching for one's origin, speaking one's conflicts with the Law, entering into the dialectic of tenderness and hatred? Today, we dismiss Oedipus and narrative at one and the same time: we no longer love, we no longer fear, we no longer narrate.[88]

To regain the 'pleasure principle,' Pirandello metaphorically suggests the Subject return to the period in which he or she is not yet aware of alienation – to the period of the child's 'jubilant assumption of his specular image,' as Jacques Lacan defines it in 'The Mirror Stage.'[89] In that pre-grammatical stage, the ego is not yet determined socially and can still situate its formation in a fictional direction. For both Pirandello and Fellini, such a realm lies in the world of the Imaginary.

As I have tried to outline here, the revolutionary impact Pirandello exerted on literary canons was linguistic at first, but soon became metalinguistic. Pirandello initiated a countertradition that can be defined in terms of a reaction against false concepts of 'normality' both in art and life, to which it opposes first 'abnormality,' and then 'transgression' beyond the given laws and norms. This countertradition progressively works toward the creation of a new artistic form that is extremely self-conscious and self-referential. According to Bakhtin, the appearance of a dialogic relationship to one's own Self, fraught with the possibility of split personality, needs to be traced back to the Menippean satire, while the exploration of the dialogic nature of truth first surfaces in the Socratic dialogue. I believe that both Pirandello's and Fellini's works participate in the *generic* tradition Bakhtin so accurately described. It must be understood, however, that any generic label applied to literature or any other form of modern narrative, such as cinema, is merely 'a means of designating the *essence of a genre*, and not a specific genre canon (as in antiquity).'[90]

Francesca and Fred in the Rome episode of Roberto Rossellini's *Paisan* (1946)

Partisans in the Po Valley episode of Roberto Rossellini's *Paisan* (1946)

The Joyces embrace in the miraculous ending of Roberto Rossellini's *Voyage to Italy* (1953).

The two girlfriends, dark-haired Anna (Lea Massari) and blonde Claudia (Monica Vitti), in Michelangelo Antonioni's *L'Avventura* (1959)

Sandro, the male protagonist played by Gabriele Ferzetti, in Michelangelo
Antonioni's *L'Avventura* (1959)

Vittorio De Sica

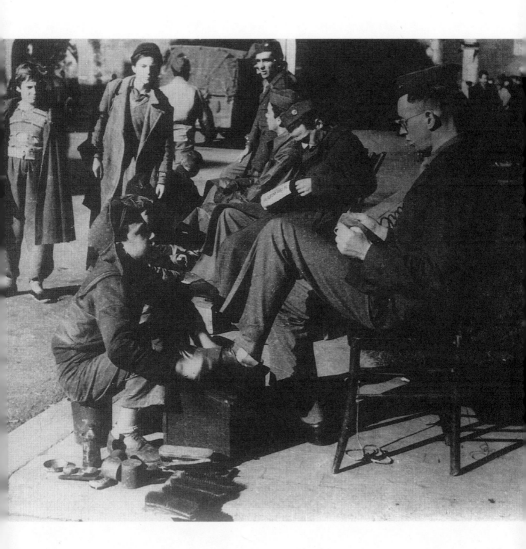

Shoeshine boys and American GIs in Vittorio De Sica's *Shoeshine* (1946)

Behind bars, the faces of Giuseppe (Rinaldo Smordoni) and Pasquale (Franco Interlenghi) mirror and express the despair and abandonment of youth in Vittorio De Sica's *Shoeshine* (1946)

Antonio, the father, and Bruno, the son, sitting on a curb in Vittorio De Sica's *Bicycle Thieves* (1948)

Antonio, the father; Bruno, the son; and their bike in Vittorio De Sica's *Bicycle Thieves* (1948)

Totò and his girlfriend flying over Milan in Vittorio De Sica's *Miracle in Milan* (1950)

The humorous thieves in Mario Monicelli's *Big Deal on Madonna Street* (1958)

Bruno Cortona (Vittorio Gassman) and Roberto Mariani (Jean-Louis
Trintignant) in Dino Risi's *The Easy Life* (1962)

Nicola (Stefano Satta Flores), Gianni (Vittorio Gassman), and Antonio (Nino Manfredi) at the Trattoria 'Half Portion' in Ettore Scola's *We All Loved Each Other So Much* (1974)

Antonio and Luciana (Stefania Sandrelli) at the end of Eugene O'Neill's *Strange Interlude* in Ettore Scola's *We All Loved Each Other So Much* (1974)

Vittoria (Monica Vitti) and Piero (Alain Delon) in Michelangelo Antonioni's *The Eclypse* (1962)

A tender moment in the 'strange interlude' between a homosexual journalist (Marcello Mastroianni) and a frustrated housewife (Sophia Loren) in Fascist Italy as portrayed in Ettore Scola's *A Special Day* (1977)

Enrico (Jean-Louis Trintignant), the modern artist and humorist, who, unable to write a new comic script, decides to chop his finger in an electric sharpener in Ettore Scola's *The Terrace* (1980)

A border-bound coach bearing the Countess de la Borde (Hana Schygulla, at window) stops to pick up two stranded travellers, Casanova (Marcello Mastroianni, second from right) and writer Restif de la Bretonne (Jean-Louis Barrault, extreme right) in Ettore Scola's *The New World* (1982)

The ballroom in Ettore Scola's *Le Bal* (1983)

A family portrait in Ettore Scola's *The Family* (1987)

Father (Marcello Mastroianni) and son (Massimo Troisi) in Ettore Scola's *What Time It Is* (1989)

5 Ettore Scola: A Cinematic and Social Metadiscourse

Le rire naît ainsi que cette écume.
Il signale, à l'extérieur de la vie sociale,
les révoltes superficielles. Il dessine instantanément
   la forme mobile de ces ébranlements.
Il est, lui aussi, une mousse à base de sel. Comme la mousse, il pétille.
C'est de la gaîté. Le philosophe qui en ramasse pour en goûter
y trouvera d'ailleurs quelquefois, pour ne petite quantité de matière,
une certaine dose d'amertume.

Henri Bergson, Le rire[1]

Laughter, then, is a flimsy substance, and shines like the meerschaum of the ocean in the sun. It signals the superficial revolutions in society and immediately reflects their fluid form. In Bergson's vision, nothing is left to the philosopher but a pervasive sense of bitterness as he tastes such an evanescent substance. Yet this is only one interpretation of laughter, or rather, only one type of laughter.

Generally speaking, in the nineteenth century several new interpretations of comedy evolved. Notwithstanding the many differences between Bergson and, say, Freud, a novel approach to the mechanisms of laughter developed, and became increasingly relevant to a delineation of contemporary poetics. As previously discussed, the passage from *irony* to *humour* as constitutive elements of artistic representation marked the introduction of a tragic note largely attested by twentieth-century poetics, which generally assigned humour an increasingly conspicuous role. Charles Baudelaire can be considered among the first artists and intellectuals who consciously addressed this issue in both their creative and theoretical writings.[2]

Almost a 'genetic trace' links Baudelaire with Pirandello, the author who is most responsible for the elaboration of a novel approach to narrative and dramatic discourse in an Italian context. Pirandello was the founder of that serio-comic or humoristic mode of discourse that would play a pivotal role in the development of twentieth-century Italian poetics. This mode of discourse is characterized by the contamination of comedy and tragedy, and produces diversified results reflecting different signifying and cognitive strategies. At times, one records the supremacy of comedy in works that are primarily concerned with extradiegetic issues and engage the reader/viewer in social and political commentary; at other times, one observes the predominance of melodrama, a genre that better serves an Italian sensibility, in works that are mostly preoccupied with reflecting on the status of the artistic representation of the Real, and thus become extremely self-reflexive and self-referential. In a few circumstances, one notes the fair balance between comedy and melodrama, or comedy and tragedy, and thus an equal tension in understanding the essence and status of the work of art as well as in investigating and criticizing the existing social and political establishment. Such works can be rightly inscribed in that mode of discourse that has been defined as 'serio-comic' or 'humoristic.' This particular discursive and narrative strategy becomes a *hypergenre*, a container within which a free contamination between comedy and tragedy, and between allegory and symbolism, significantly occurs.

In the history of Italian postwar cinema, Roberto Rossellini and Vittorio De Sica played a primary role in paving the way for future developments of Italian cinematic production after the 'golden age' of neorealism. Rossellini's *Voyage to Italy* initiated what I have termed 'a melodramatic imagination' in Italian film;[3] De Sica's *Miracle in Milan* opened the way to fantasy and utopia, and possibly to a new and diverse kind of 'comic imagination.'[4] As previously argued, even the masterpieces of cinematic neorealism, such as *Rome Open City* and *Bicycle Thieves*, contained elements of comedy and melodrama, and yet it was with *Miracle in Milan* and *Voyage to Italy*, significantly made in two consecutive years,[5] that Italian cinema consciously moved beyond neorealism and started exploring new avenues for the investigation and representation of Reality.

Federico Fellini greatly contributed to the overcoming of an orthodox interpretation of neorealism, and came to occupy a central position in the elaboration and definition of a new mode of cinematic discourse, a discourse that is thoroughly grounded in realism, and yet also pursues a constant contamination of the diverse approaches to the Real. As Gian Piero Brunetta maintains in his volume *Cent'anni di cinema italiano*, Fellini travelled the filmic scene of the last forty years 'più come un *unidentified object* che come un autore il cui universo fosse possibile esplorare e decifrare'[6] ('more like an *unidentified object* than like an author whose universe could be explored and deciphered'). While the 'island Fellini' appeared for a long time to be isolated and basically 'unidentified,' we can now attempt a revisitation of the territory he explored in the five decades that constitute the history of postwar Italian cinema. By placing Fellini's cinematic extravaganzas against the background of the serio-comic or the 'humoristic' mode of discourse, we can connect his cinema to other experiences in Italian film history.

Central to Fellini's revolutionary filmic inventions are certain narrative and discursive strategies as well as a specific notion of character. The narrative structure that Fellini developed over the years can be easily described as a progression toward nothingness, since it is mostly 'la storia di una ricerca che non approda a nulla, di una serie di interrogativi lanciati come sonde nello spazio circostante'[7] ('the story of a search that leads nowhere, of a series of questions launched like probes in the surrounding space'). The journey is thus not only a metaphor, but the structuring principle of Fellini's discontinuous and fragmented narratives, beginning with his very first cinematic *fatigue*, *Variety Lights*. As Brunetta states, the journey Fellini's characters travel is always one of discovery of the Self; it is a journey in which the foreign becomes familiar and helps one to decipher past, present, and future.[8]

After the war, it was through the mechanism of the journey that the films of neorealism allowed Italians to discover parts of the country they had never before seen and to gain a feeling of togetherness. In the late fifties, the era of the so-called 'economic boom,' Italians were shown, through cinematic journeys, the dramatic dissonance created by the juxtaposition of a rapidly industrializing North and a still rural and backward South. In the sixties, the cinematic journey moved inward, as Italian film began investigating the inner spaces, the private and interior geography of the character's world. From the seventies onward, this journey became a cognitive strategy that allowed Italian film to investigate the past, to revisit Italian history, and bring it to a reasonable distance, as in films like Ettore Scola's *C'eravamo tanto amati* (*We All Loved Each Other So Much*, 1974). In the late 1980s and early 1990s, the journey still remained a preferred narrative strategy as Italian cinema tried to rewrite the modern history of the country, as in Gabriele

Salvatores' *Mediterraneo* (*Mediterraneo*, 1991).

The history of postwar Italian cinema itself can be easily described as a journey of discovery and self-discovery. Travelling through time and space, Italian cinema progressively unveiled unknown territories in real or mental geography. Journeying within the domain of cinematic discourse, Italian film discovered unforeseen expressive possibilities for the medium itself. The theme of the journey soon became a fundamental structuring principle of the Italian cinematic experience, as it crossed genres and investigated the innumerable possibilities offered by the juxtaposition of opposites: the South and the North, the poor and the rich, low and high culture. As soon as all boundaries were erased, free contamination between genres, as well as between social, political, and geographic realities, occurred. The search for identity became an endless 'work in progress,' and Italian cinema assumed a fluid form, unmistakably and constantly reflecting and commenting upon the everchanging shape of its society. While Italian cinema before and during Fascism mostly expressed itself via formalized and codifiable genres, after the Second World War this national cinema constantly attempted to escape easy and formulaic solutions as it aimed at establishing not only the identity of a country but its own as well.

In cinema come in letteratura, il comico raccoglie le *scorie* degli altri generi e non desidera affermare la propria autonomia narrativa ed espressiva.[9]

In cinema as in literature, comedy collects the *drosses* of the other genres and does not wish to assert its own narrative and expressive autonomy.

With this statement, Brunetta again solicits our investigation by pointing at the mobile and fluid nature of comedy. Yet, such definition perfectly adheres to the spirit of Italian cinematic comedy as it progressively developed into a mode of discourse that can move freely between genres. By not aiming at establishing its narrative and expressive autonomy, and thus authority, such national interpretation of comedy was fundamentally subversive of established discoursive strategies and critical toward the existing social organization.

La struttura della commedia prevede un iniziale moto di disintegrazione dell' 'ambiente originario' ed una finale reintegrazione del corpo sociale, nel quale vengono ammessi con formula piena i personaggi che ne erano stati esclusi.[10]

The structure of comedy entails an initial movement of disintegration of the 'original environment' and a final reintegration of the social body, in which one fully admits the characters who had previously been excluded.

Generally speaking, then, comedy is grounded on the idea of *serenity* and results in the restoration of the original order of things. In postwar Italy, however, film comedy was firmly grounded in *realism;* it concerned itself with actuality, portrayed 'negative' heroes, and produced mostly episodic and inconclusive narratives. For quite some time, critics identified comic films produced the late 1950s and early 1960s as a 'national genre' bearing the label 'comedy Italian style.' This definition, coined by French critics when they 'discovered' Italian film comedy in the 1970s,[11] contains partially diminishing connotations that recent critical investigation has attempted to remove by inserting the comic production of the period of the 1950s to the 1960s in a continuum or, rather, in a constant progression of the 'genre.' Italian cinematic comedy has undergone an *unlimited semiosis* by reworking the codes, morphology, and syntax of the genre as it participated in and reflected the incessant change of Italian postwar society. By constantly involving itself with extradiegetic concerns, Italian film comedy has changed via its thorough permeability to the social and political transformations the whole country has experienced.

The diverse critical interpretations that have developed over the years all agree that Italian film comedy cannot be defined as a 'genre.' It has been defined as 'metagenre' in an attempt to explain its elasticity, its tendency to traverse and appropriate different genres;[12] it has also been called a 'supergenre' or 'infragenre,' since

del 'genere' la 'nostra commedia' ha qualche codice, ma li applica in modo imprevedibile: del 'genere' non ha le delimitazioni, le costanze, le iterazioni, i luoghi topici, le strutture permanenti.[13]

"our comedy' contains some of the codes of the 'genre,' but it applies them in an unpredictable way: of the 'genre' it does not possess the limitations, the constant elements, the reiterations, the topical loci, the permanent structures.

In his recent study *Il cinema di Saturno*, Maurizio Grande discusses Italian film comedy against the background of comedy as 'macrogenre,' while Gian Piero Brunetta, in his *Cent'anni di cinema italiano*, discussing the evolution of Italian cinematic comedy from 1945 to the 1960s, states that in the third stage of its development, comedy meets history and

in pratica, nel giro di poco tempo, la commedia diventa una sorta di grande container per il trasporto di tutti i tipi di materiali e l'assemblaggio di codici e motivi sempre più vasti e complessi.[14]

practically, within a short period of time, comedy becomes a kind of large container for the transfer of all types of material and the assembly of progressively larger and more complex codes and motifs.

Even Ettore Scola, the director who was eventually called on to collect and preserve the heritage and the memory of the 'genre,' at one point stated:

Per quanto riguarda la 'commedia all'italiana', essa è diventata un *super-genere* e troverà differenziazioni più chiare. Anche il critico dovrà ridefinire i nostri film inventando catalogazioni diverse.[15]

As far as 'comedy Italian style' is concerned, it has become a *super-genre* and will soon find clearer differentiations. Even the critic will have to redefine our films by inventing new classifications.

Scola then calls the critic to a thorough revision of Italian cinematic comedy, one that is possible only by employing different critical categories.

As early as 1939, Vittorio Metz declared in an interview:

In Italia, in meno di un decennio, si è creato un tipo di umorismo modernissimo, inconfondibile e interamente nostro, con caratteri di assoluta originalità. Noi umoristi italiani siamo fuori dal binario della comicità francese e da quello del cosiddetto humor inglese e avanziamo da anni su di un terreno del tutto diverso. Il nostro è un tipo di umorismo acceso, sconcertante, fulminante, un umorismo violento che possiede la rarissima qualità di arrivare facilmente sia all'intellettuale che al popolo.[16]

In Italy, in less than a decade, one has created a new kind of humour, extremely modern, unmistakable and entirely ours, with absolutely original characteristics. We Italian humorists are outside the path of French comicality as well as removed from the so-called English humour; for years, we have progressed within a totally different territory. Our humour is fervent, inflamed, disconcerting, and withering, a violent humour that possesses the extremely rare quality of easily reaching out for both the intellectuals and the populace.

Although Metz was referring to satiric magazines founded during Fascism, specifically to *Marc'Aurelio* in Rome (1931) and *Bertoldo* in Milan (1937), whose humour can hardly be defined as 'violent,' he raises two important issues. First is the fundamental difference between comedy and/or humour 'Italian style' and the French or English tradition. Second, Metz emphasizes the 'popularity' of this national type of humour, even though the populace he was referring to was the middle class – the traditionally privileged subject and recipient of Italian literary, dramatic, and cinematic comedy.

From its very outset, then, comic artistic expressions in an Italian context assumed the contours of a 'national' and 'popular' genre. *Popularity* and *nationality* soon became the basic characteristics of Italian film comedy; in fact, they were to constitute the qualifying traits of a much larger segment of Italian cinema as it developed from neorealism to the present. Neorealism promoted the 'stereoscopic' gaze that placed the diverse realities – first spatial, in the 1940s and 1950s, and then also temporal, in the 1960s – in a relationship of absolute continuity and interchangeability, with the primary intention of establishing direct communication between the screen and the orchestra, fiction and reality.[17] Because of neorealism, Italian cinema soon proceeded

alla disgregazione dell'idea di racconto unitario fondato sui processi di consequenzialità narrativa, di progressione temporale, alla dissoluzione dell'idea di intreccio, di costruzione a tutto tondo dei personaggi, di valorizzazione dei protagonisti.[18]

to the disintegration of the idea of a unified story grounded in narrative consequentiality and temporal progression, and to the dissolution of the idea of plot, of building fully rounded characters, of emphasis and exploitation of the protagonists.

In the late 1950s, then, within a thorough disintegration of the 'neorealistic body' into the complex and variegated system created by *genre film* and *auteur cinema*, a new mode of discourse developed through the crossing of all categories and the activation of their reciprocal contamination. This discursive strategy was the result of a collective effort and cannot be restricted to a 'genre canon,' since one of its fundamental characteristics is the subversion of traditional codes of expression and representation of the Real. Generally speaking, then, one must agree with Lorenzo Pellizzari when he states that the 'comedy Italian style' represents '*un certo cinema italiano*, fra comico e patetico, satirico e melodrammatico, indigesto e gastronomico'[19] ('*a certain Italian cinema*, between comic and pathetic, satiric and melodramatic, indigestible and gastronomic'). Pellizzari goes on to describe the two trends that developed in Italian cinematic production: 'quella "fredda" (di testa, di idee, di grigio, di serietà, di sguardi, di monologhi, di tecnica e di regia, tanto per fare una brutta elencazione)' ('the cold one – cerebral, ideological, greyish, serious, monologic, emphasizing technique and directing, just to give an arid enumeration') and the other, 'quella "calda" (di pancia, di trovate, di colore, di scherzo, di gesti, di riprese e di testo, tanto per fare un'elencazione parallela di comodo)' ('the warm one – visceral, witty, colourful, playful, expressive by gestures, emphasing shooting and script, just to come up with a convenient definition parallel to the previous one').[20] He pointedly observes that these two currents eventually intertwined and contaminated each other to produce that 'certain Italian cinema,' which could be described as a *school* with no teachers or pupils, only a vast laboratory of artisans. Directors as different as Rossellini and De Sica at first, and then Risi, Comencini, Fellini, Pasolini, and even Antonioni all contributed to the development of this distinctively 'national' and extremely 'popular' mode of filmmaking.

Fellini was one of the directors who most consciously moved toward the definition of that 'certain Italian filmmaking' that we want to define as serio-comic or *umoristico*. This mode of cinematic discourse is characterized by internal doublings and mirrorings; it practises citation and digression, unveils a constant tension toward nothingness and silence, and privileges the *mise en abîme* and self-reflexivity. The cinematic medium itself becomes 'humoristic' – that is, it turns into the locus of the doubling and of the fatal split that does not allow one to believe and identify. This new 'filmic imagination' thus participates in the general rethinking of the relationship between Reality and its artistic representation, a rapport that can no longer be fideistic and where no continuity can be found. In the 1960s, a time in which society was undergoing fundamental and rapid transformation, Italian cinema began investigating its own status as a means of artistic expression and provided its own 'delayed' participation in the so-called 'crisi dell'arte' ('crisis of art'). As the unpleasant French critic comments in *8½*, upon reading Guido's new script,

One wonders what the authors really intend. Do they want to make us think? Do they want to frighten us? Right from the start, the action displays an impoverished poetic inspiration. You'll have to excuse me for saying so, but this may be the most pathetic demonstration that the cinema is irremediably fifty years behind all the other arts.[21]

Comedy and melodrama are two ever-present tensions in the development of postwar Italian cinema as it attempted to untangle itself from formalized *genre film* and later from the so-called *auteur cinema*.[22] In the composite panorama Italian cinema offered as it developed from 1945 to the present, perhaps no director embodies the passage itself from *generic* to *auteuristic* cinema, and then the dissolution of both, like Ettore Scola. The body of his work more than that of any other director becomes the forum for the free contamination between tragedy and comedy, as well as between the many codified genres. Such free contamination unmistakably produces narratives that owe much to the countertradition of Baudelaire's *grotesque* or *absolute comic*, of Bakhtin's *seriocomic*, and of Pirandello's *umorismo*.[23]

The elaboration of this *certain Italian cinema* resulted from the collective efforts of many different personalities sharing a fairly similar background. A number of the soon-to-be directors of postwar Italian cinema began their career by working for satiric journals, then moved to scriptwriting, and eventually to directing, since, as Ennio Flaiano rightly observed, 'quello dello sceneggiatore nel cinema italiano non è una professione ma uno stato transitorio'[24] ('in Italian cinema screenwriting is not a profession but simply a transitory stage'). Scola worked on over forty screenplays before he made his directorial debut in 1964 with *Se permettete parliamo di donne (Allow Me to Talk about Women)*. Scola's career resembles that of many Italian directors, but especially that of Federico Fellini. In an article published in the French film journal *CinémAction* in 1987, Peter Bondanella provides a prefatory discussion of the similarities between Scola's and Fellini's creative development, and suggests the influence of Pirandello's 'metatheatrical works' on their unique 'metacinematic discourses.'[25]

Despite differences in age and cultural background,[26] both directors began by working for the satiric journal *Marc'Aurelio*, like many of their contemporaries, and then moved to scriptwriting in the good company of the best writers of their time. Fellini began with an unaccredited collaboration on the script of Mario Mattoli's *Imputato alzatevi! (Defendant Rise!*, 1939) with Vittorio Metz and Mattoli himself, and then collaborated on nearly thirty films, among these Rossellini's *Rome Open City* and *Paisan*, and Alberto Lattuada's *Senza pietà* (*Without Pity*, 1948), and Pietro Germi's *Il cammino della speranza* (*The Path of Hope*, 1950).[27] Fellini's apprenticeship in filmmaking was thus marked by the 'effetto Amidei,' as Brunetta would term it,[28] and then under the 'sign' of Rossellini's ethical and aesthetic vision.

Ettore Scola began scriptwriting when Fellini was entering filmmaking; in fact, Scola's first credited script is dated 1952, Domenico Paolella's *Canzoni di mezzo secolo* (*Songs of Half a Century*). From the outset, then, the distinctive path taken by Scola's contribution to the history of Italian cinema was that of comedy, and consequently an extremely complex panorama of tendencies and contaminations, since, as he once stated,

la commedia all'italiana è stata un ginepraio in cui è difficile districarsi, una specie di mercato delle pulci dove c'è stato di tutto. Perchè Fellini ha fatto commedia italiana; Pasolini l'ha fatta; Franchi e Ingrassia l'hanno fatta, Corbucci, Monicelli, Comencini, io e altri ancora.[29]

the 'comedy Italian style' was a maze in which it was quite difficult to untangle oneself, a sort of flea market with everything in it. Because Fellini has done Italian comedy; Pasolini has done it; Franchi and Ingrassia have done it, Corbucci, Monicelli, Comencini, myself and others too.

Together with Ruggero Maccari, Steno, Age, and Scarpelli, Scola formed the creative battalion of writers that gave life to the so-called 'comedy Italian style.' For a number of years after the beginning of his career as a director, Scola continued writing scripts, particularly with Dino Risi and Antonio Pietrangeli, two of the most influential presences in his progression as a filmmaker. After 1964, for Risi, he wrote the screenplays of *Il gaucho* (*The Gaucho*, 1964), *Il profeta* (*The Prophet*, 1968), and *Noi donne siamo fatte così* (*That's the Way We Women Are*, 1971); for Pietrangeli, he worked on the script for *Il magnifico cornuto* (*The Beautiful Cuckold*, 1964) and *Io la conoscevo bene* (*I Knew Her Well*, 1965). With Ruggero Maccari, who would eventually co-script many of his own films, Scola also wrote Nanny Loy's *Made in Italy* (*Made in Italy*, 1965). His latest collaboration as screenwriter was Enrico Oldoini's *Cuori nella tormenta* (*Hearts in the Storm*, 1984).[30]

Scola's 'apprenticeship' as one of the main representatives of Italian cinematic comedy in the years 1958–64, is significant to the study of his later films, especially starting with *We All Loved Each Other So Much*. This film can be considered a watershed in Scola's cinematic production inasmuch as it leads to *Brutti sporchi e cattivi* (*Down and Dirty*, 1976) and *La terrazza* (*The Terrace*, 1980) – two films that are unquestionably central to a discussion of a 'Pirandellian mode' in Italian cinema – but also to later works like *La famiglia* (*The Family*, 1987), *Splendor* (*Splendor*, 1989), and even *Il viaggio di Capitan Fracassa* (*The Journey of Captain Fracassa*, 1990). Scola's filmmaking is a necessary step in the evolution of that mode of cinematic discourse that one can comfortably define as 'Pirandellian,' that is, a mode in which discursive and narrative strategies owe much to Pirandello's interpretation of humour.

Italian cinematic comedy as it developed in the 1960s was the result of a collective effort, and was characterized by a slow and yet progressive transformation. The journey leading to the present began with the early comedies of Petrolini,[31] and then with Totò's surreal film comedy.[32] It is a journey in which film borrowed from all forms of spectacle: theatre, variety shows, musicals, and even the circus, going as far back as the traditional commedia dell'arte.[33] Yet, in the late fifties and early sixties, a fundamental transformation took place due to internal and external pressures, and with Mario Monicelli's *La grande guerra* (*The Great War*, 1959) Italian cinematic comedy 'entra a pieno titolo in terreni riservati alla produzione alta'[34] ('rightly enters areas normally reserved for high culture'). A genre that up to that point had unsympathetically represented the middle class took a decisive turn with the 'heroicomic narration' of Monicelli's *I soliti ignoti* (*Big Deal on Madonna Street*, 1958), but it is with *The Great War* that for the first time Italian film comedy tackled a difficult moment in the country's recent history and subverted the traditional comedic structure by providing a dramatic ending. It is the story of two soldiers, one from the North, played by Vittorio Gassman, and one from the South, played by Alberto Sordi, during the collective and absurd tragedy of the First World War:

Due soldati comuni, nella massa, un po' 'lavativi' e molto pacifici, che però alla fine rinunciano anche alla vita pur di non disonorarsi, di tradire, più di se stessi che non la patria, forse.[35]

Two common soldiers, in the mass, slightly lazy and extremely peaceful who though at the end give up life itself in order not to dishonour themselves, not to betray, more than themselves the motherland, perhaps.

From the outset, they are just two cowards who, with corrupt schemes and cheating, constantly attempt to avoid the war and any kind of human responsibility. At the close of the film, though, these two modern and extremely Italian 'anti-heroes' – the perfect Fellinian *vitelloni* – perish to save their fellow soldiers rather than betray, with them, their own country.

In Fellini's 1953 film, *I Vitelloni*, Sordi had already offered a disturbing potrayal of a 'negative hero' who undergoes a progressive unmasking, a process of disintegration of traditional character that had indeed begun with *The White Sheik*. Although in the early 1950s Fellini's seemed to be a solipsistic 'voice in the desert' (but certainly was not), by the end of the decade the dissolution of the neorealistic body allowed the progressive transformation of the character, the rhythm, and the syntax itself of traditional comedy. With the collapse of the optimism of the immediate postwar years, Italian film had to rethink its own status and to renegotiate the entire concept of 'nation' as it continued reflecting and commenting on Italian social and political reality. Different and apparently constrasting forces – the comic and the tragic, comedy and melodrama, realism and fantasy – began contaminating one another to perfect a particular and thoroughly Italian 'mode of filmmaking.'

Among the so-called 'masters' of Italian cinematic comedy, one who especially influenced Scola's early career is Dino Risi, a director who constantly worked within the genre in order to 'dilatarne le coordinate e modificarne morfologia, tipologie, ritmi e sintassi'[36] ('expand its coordinates and modify its morphology, typology, rhythms, and syntax'). From *Una vita difficile* (*A Difficult Life*, 1961) to *Il sorpasso* (*The Easy Life*, 1962) and *I mostri* (*The Monsters*, 1963), Risi's cinema progressively unveils the void behind the mask; the mask itself is familiar at first, and then becomes grotesque and ultimately funereal. In the early 1960s, Risi provided Italian cinema with a gallery of characters expressing the malaise of a society in all-too-rapid growth. Risi's cinema participates in a more generalized tendency toward the expression of fantasy and dream life; Italian cinematic comedy, even in the works of its so-called 'masters,' soon became coloured with melodrama, gruesomeness, and grotesquery. Furthermore, the fundamental loss of an ideal centre – political, geographic, and existential – not only provoked a sense of *dépaysement* in society, it also produced the disintegration of genres that could no longer adequately represent changed social and existential conditions.

Against this background of constant transformation Ettore Scola made his directorial début in 1964 with *Allow Me to Talk about Women*, a film that, on the one hand, refers back to Antonio Pietrangeli's gallery of sensitive women, and, on the other, bears the same narrative structure of Risi's *The Monsters*, since the episodic story revolves around Gassman's 'proteiform' male character. Scola's second work, *La congiuntura* (*The Recession*, 1964), has been described as a variation of *The Easy Life*,[37] and indeed, like Risi's film, is the chronicle of a journey, a *topos* that will recur in innumerable variations throughout Scola's entire production to the point of becoming a 'componente quasi imprescindibile'[38] ('almost an unavoidable componenent') of his cinema. As his subsequent works demonstrate, Scola's cinema is also characterized by an unmistakable tendency toward experimentation in the various genres, and the reciprocal lowering and contamination leading to the eventual dismantling of their codes, syntax, and morphology.

After a long apprenticeship as writer, scriptwriter, and then as director within the boundaries of a fairly conventional comedy, Scola eventually found his own original directorial 'voice,' and this progression toward artistic maturity led him to a personal interpretation of comedy. This original interpretation is thoroughly indebted to the teachings of neorealism even when Scola conducts a critical investigation of its ethical and aesthetic foundations. Aside from superficial similarities, this process constitutes a fundamental parallel between Fellini's and Scola's apparently diverse artistic statements. Moreover, their paths to maturity are characterized by the same tension toward circularity and continuity, so much so that, for instance, Gian Piero Brunetta's general assessment of Scola's narrative strategies can also apply to Fellini; that is, his journey,

partendo da situazioni molto comuni, progressivamente, grazie quasi a un gioco di specchi, o di obiettivi a profondità variabile, entra nelle dimensioni della memoria, della fantasia, dell'immaginzione, del sogno.[39]

starting from extremely common situations, progressively, almost thanks to an interplay of mirrors, or of lenses with different profundities, enters in the dimensions of memory, fantasy, imagination and dream.

As previously argued, Italian postwar cinema was first characterized by an urge to discover reality in its multiplicity and then to place it within a comprehensible visual field; later, in the early sixties, Italian cinema moved toward the free and simultaneous acquisition of time and space. It is fair to maintain that directors of different generations and diverse aesthetic and ethical convictions then seemed to aim for a collective retrieval of the past that had *memory* as a common denominator. Yet, in the case of Fellini and Scola, the issue was not simply that of retrieving the past to build a better future: memory and fantasy, dream and daydreaming offered them a diverse discoursive strategy, an avenue beyond the appearance of things, a thoroughly original and novel approach to the Real and its artistic representation.

In the progression toward the disintegration of traditional narrative strategies, both Fellini and Scola profited from the collaboration of Bernardino Zapponi, a scriptwriter who was particularly interested in the possibilities offered by the interaction of different levels of consciousness and the investigation of the inner spaces of the mind.[40] Zapponi co-scripted *I nuovi mostri* (*The New Monsters*, 1977), but Scola's meeting with this visionary writer was also made possible by Risi. Fellini's and Scola's careers were also affected by other writers who left distinctive marks on their works – for example, Sergio Amidei, Ruggero Maccari, Tullio Pinelli, and many others. As a matter of fact, an original history of Italian cinema could be written by focusing on the scriptwriters who so thoroughly affected the development of this national cinema, many of them eventually turning to filmmaking or becoming a trademark of some directors' entire production.

The sixties brought fundamental changes to both Scola's and Fellini's careers. In 1964, Scola directed his first film, and in 1963 Fellini initiated a novel approach to filmmaking with *8½*, in which 'l'orizzonte realistico è varcato ma non perso di vista, le coordinate spazio-temporali sono destrutturate, tutto un mondo immaginativo è convocato in scena simultaneamente per essere sistemato in un quadro grandioso'[41] ('the realistic horizon is exceeded but not lost sight of, the spatial and temporal coordinates are deconstructed, and an entire imaginative universe is called on stage simultaneously to be organized in a magnificent ensemble'). Not only is *8½* a watershed in Fellini's filmography, in many ways the film initiated a journey of no return for Italian cinema, marking the beginning of the acquisition of self-consciousness of that 'certain Italian cinema' that has been here defined as Pirandellian, or 'humoristic.' It was in the early sixties, particularly with Fellini's unprecedented and unparalleled contribution, that this extremely 'national' mode of filmmaking began to reach expressive maturity. Never losing sight of realism, Italian cinema became increasingly engaged in the effort of renewing the paradigms of neorealistic cinema.

Beginning with *Riusciranno i nostri eroi a ritrovare l'amico misteriosamente scomparso in Africa?* (*Will Our Heroes Manage to Find the Friend Mysteriously Disappeared in Africa?*, 1968), Scola's primary concern was to rework the *topoi* of neorealism, and to present them with a negative and/or paradoxical sign. He attempted to find a solution with a new kind of comedy characterized by an undercurrent of bitterness and grotesqueness, one that can be unmistakably defined as 'humoristic.' The film thoroughly exploits the theme and the structure of the journey, as a successful Roman publisher, Fausto Di Salvio, played by Alberto Sordi, sets out for Angola to look for his brother-in-law, Oreste Sabatini, nicknamed Titino, played by Nino Manfredi. Once he arrives in Africa accompanied by his reluctant accountant, Ubaldo Palmirani, he discovers that in the last three years Titino has held all sorts of jobs – mercenary, truckdriver, and even missionary – and then has disappeared. From Titino's supposed former lover, they learn he is dead, and are shown what is thought to be his grave. They are about to return to Italy when a Portuguese man, called Pedro, tells them Titino is still alive, and his death was merely a deception, designed to spare him punishment for his numerous swindles. The search thus continues in a series of misadventures as the two Italians are abandoned by their guide, spend a terrifying night in the jungle, and lose their jeep. They are 'saved' by a Portuguese couple who do not spare them a wealth of racist comments; they are robbed by the mercenary and then are seized by an indigenous tribe. At this point, the last and most important surprise awaits them: they realize that the tribe's sorcerer is Titino himself. At first he denies, but ultimately admits the truth and agrees to go back home. Once on the boat, though, Titino looks at the waving natives, turns around, gives his brother-in-law a last and pregnant gaze, then dives in the blue ocean and swims back to the virgin African land where the loving tribe is awaiting him.

The Zavattinian theory of the character's *pedinamento* is parodied in the paradoxical tailing of a character who is 'familiar' and becomes increasingly 'foreign'; the search takes places in an unfamiliar territory that progressively unveils its primordial 'familiarity.' Thus, the quest for an objective knowledge of the character's actions, which constituted an important tenet of the neorealistic mandate, is subverted in a tale where the collection of data does not result in an acquisition of knowledge or self-knowledge, but, on the contrary, equals a declaration of impotence in the face of reality. Offering no happy ending, this unpredictable and unconventional comedy ends with defeat. The audience is cruelly forced to stare at the reflection of its own fatal loss of innocence. Yet there is a place beyond official 'history,' where happiness comes to the character, who is now removed from daily, alienated, and alienating experience.[42] The issue is no longer that of providing an objective and faithful portrayal of a Reality that is possible to 'see' and thus describe, to understand and therefore represent. A mystery stands behind the surface of things, and it is equally and even more real than the visible side of human experience. A fundamental doubt, one that was both ethical and aesthetic, began undermining the neorealistic 'lie,' and initiated the conscious elaboration of a new mode of filmmaking that we have defined as 'humoristic,' serio-comic, or even grotesque.

Il cinema è dubitativo, non affermativo. Un film non deve dare soluzioni. Però porre interrogativi, sottolineare certi dubbi, avvertire domande che sono nell'aria, riproporle. Credo sia questo uno dei compiti del cinema. Ma non solo del cinema, di ogni altra forma d'arte.[43]

Cinema is dubitative, not affirmative. A film should not offer solutions. On the contrary, it must pose queries, underline doubts, perceive the questions that are floating around, identify and ask them. I believe this is one of cinema's duties. And not only of cinema, but of any other art form.

While Europe was shaken by social and political turmoil, and most directors were engaged in sombre commentaries on the new, troubled social and existential reality and were attempting to offer primarily ideological solutions, fierce criticism was directed at Scola's 1968 film, a work that was said to privilege easy and escapist solutions, or to offer none. Yet, with this film Scola began his relentless critique of Italian, and Western, contemporary history, leading him and others to an integral questioning of the neorealistic experience in order to regain access to its precious heritage, a legacy sought for after the questionable 'parenthesis' represented by the 'comedy Italian style.'

La commedia italiana è stata la figlia un po' degenere del neorealismo, una sorta di reazione un po' reazionaria, in quanto nata come pacificatoria, 'testimone' di un'Italia consolata, grassoccia e paesana, dai pochi riferimenti con la realtà. Un cinema di fantascienza (o di fantacoscienza). Poi la commedia italiana è cresciuta, è entrata in maggior contatto con la realtà, ha scavato di più, si è fatta più inquietante, da consolatoria che era è diventata spesso provocatoria. E' in questa direzione che credo di aver lavorato: verso una commedia italiana nella quale, dietro l'eredità del neorealismo e le 'magie' della satira, traspariva l'apologo civile.[44]

Italian comedy was the slightly degenerate daughter of neorealism, a kind of slightly reactionary reaction, since it was born as pacificatory 'witness' of a consoled, fatty, and provincial Italy that had little reference to reality – a science-fiction cinema (or conscience fiction). Then Italian comedy grew, better connected with reality, delved deeper, became more disquieting, and from being consolatory it turned into often being provocatory. I believe this is the direction I worked in, moving toward an Italian comedy in which, behind the heritage of neorealism and the 'magic' of satire, the civil apologue would shine.

In this important statement, Scola comments on the evolution of Italian cinematic comedy, but he also defines his own inherent role. He identifies himself as one of the protagonists of that unrestrained movement that brought comedy to grow closer to reality, to delve deeper into the matter of things, to become increasingly disquieting. Laughter no longer aimed at consoling and, thus, masking, but progressively unveiled the void and the uncanny and became a grimace; or else it exposed dissonance and 'otherness,' and turned into a smile, the characteristic outcome of Pirandello's 'procedimento umoristico' ('humoristic procedure'). Scola is one of those few directors who immediately understood and investigated the difference between a mechanical comedy based on the levelling of situations shown on the screen and a comedy that instead goes deep into the matter of things, to the point of undermining the syntax, morphology, and the codified structure of traditional comedy.[45]

Even though it consciously uses the medium of comedy, *Will Our Heroes ...?* offers no easy solutions, and on the contrary exposes the importance of social and existential *choice*. Here the journey to the primordial Eden is no longer a temporary escape from civilization; it is an occasion when one is confronted with the pressing awareness of the fact that it is no longer possible to be simultaneously *savage* and *civilized*. The existential indecision that haunted Antonioni's characters in *L'avventura* and led them to a static and desperate condition is exposed, and, as in Fellini's *8½*, the importance of choice in an existential, social, and even artistic plane is emphasized. Yet, like Guido, the protagonist of *8½*, who will forever leave behind the anguish of indecision in the acceptance of multiplicity, Scola's characters evolve in the same direction and become increasingly aware of their being just *characters*, realizations of innumerable narrative possibilities. This is unquestionably the condition of the typical Pirandellian character, who is caught in the condition of being 'one, nobody, and one hundred thousand.'

Il mio punto di partenza riguarda sempre la soluzione di un problema narrativo. Quello che mi interessa in un film è il racconto, ciò che si vuole esprimere, con quali sentimenti, con quali psicologie. Uso la macchina da presa come lo scrittore la matita o la penna ... E qui mi ricollego alla mia tendenza e predisposizione per un cinema teatrale, per il *Kammerspiel*, nel quale l'attenzione si appunta su quanto dicono i personaggi, su ciò che rappresentano, sui loro volti e gesti ... Come ispirazione, la natura ... mi lascia indifferente.[46]

My point of departure is always the solution of a narrative problem. What interests me in a film is the story, what one wants to express, with which feelings and psychologies. I use the camera in the same way a writer uses a pencil or a pen ... And I refer here to my tendency and predisposition toward a theatrical cinema, the *Kammerspiel*, in which emphasis is given to what the characters say, to what they represent, to their faces and gestures ... As a source of inspiration, nature ... leaves me quite indifferent.

Scola's cinema stages the characters and their stories, their psychologies and feelings, in progressively enclosed spaces as he perfects his original and personal interpretation of comedy and of the cinematic experience in its entirety. The movement toward an increasingly 'theatrical cinema,' for instance, is particularly highlighted in films such as *Una giornata particolare* (A Special Day, 1977), *Ballando, ballando* (Le Bal, 1983), *The Family*, and even *The Voyage of Captain Fracassa*. The story of *A Special Day* takes place on 6 May 1938, in a Rome apartment building where a housewife and a homosexual, two outcasts in an authoritarian Fascist society are forced to confront their own diversity in a strange interlude. In *Le Bal* fifty years of French history unfold in a *signifying* macrocosm – a ballroom – that allows History to confront Chronicle through the medium of popular culture. In fact, dance constitutes a *topos* of popular imagination: it stands for joy of life, friendship and communion, desire and seduction.[47] In *The Family*, the camera and, thus, the audience are never allowed out of the apartment as eighty years pass in the life of a family and of a country, Italy. Paradoxically, in his constant attempt to give History a sense of contemporaneity, Scola manages here to annul it, or, better, 'a scioglierla in un quotidiano che muta nelle apparenze ma non nella sostanza'[48] ('to dissolve it in a daily experience that changes in appearance but not in substance'). In previous films Scola attempted to show how individual lives chose specific avenues in the face of history, but in *The Family* he stages the impermeability of daily experience to historical events, and the difficulty History finds in penetrating the depth of life.[49] *The Voyage of Captain Fracassa* never leaves the theatre as it portrays the roundabouts of a company of actors from the Commedia dell'Arte. These are certainly extreme examples of Scola's preference for closed spaces and his interest in a confrontation between cinema and theatre. Yet one can comfortably maintain that most of his cinema displays an obsession with enclosed spaces, and can thus be described as *claustrophobic*.

After *Will Our Heroes ...?*, for a number of years Scola randomly exploited various genres in his search for a voice of his own. For instance, *Il commissario Pepe* (*Lieutenant Pepe*, 1969) uses the codes of the thriller in a 'comic' vein while providing a bitter depiction of a Northern Italian province that becomes the locus of a collective trial. According to Brunetta, it is only with *Dramma della gelosia – Tutti i particolari in cronaca* (*A Drama of Jealousy – All the Details in the Newspapers*, 1970) that 'la sua vena più originale emerge'[50] ('his most original vein emerges'). It is certainly true that in *A Drama of Jealousy* Scola perfuses comedy with melodrama, and the film ultimately possesses the grotesque tone of a tragicomedy. Here the director avoids falling into the pathetic and leaves the audience with a sense of melancholy. The film is far from being a true novelty in Scola's filmography; it is more the reaffirmation of a method.

Conversely, it is interesting to note that in *A Drama of Jealousy*, for the first time in his career, Scola depicts the lower class, and does so in a tragicomic way, therefore removing his text from traditional neorealism. The lower class, and more generally the segment of society normally excluded from wealth and power, is represented in several of his films. America, the land of plenty, is the backdrop for the story of an Italian emigrant in *Permette? Rocco Papaleo* (*May I? Rocco Papaleo*, 1971), and the shack-dwellers in the outskirts of Rome populate a grotesque subproletarian tale in *Brutti, sporchi e cattivi* (*Down and Dirty*, 1976). New also are the oneiric digressions that play such an important role in *May I? Rocco Papaleo* and, later, in *We All Loved Each Other So Much*, *The Terrace*, and *Splendor*. As he reached directorial maturity, Scola's cinematic discourse became increasingly fragmented as different planes of reality progressively contaminated one another.

There are two ever-present tensions within Ettore Scola's cinema: one leads him to a thorough reinterpretation of Italian comedy; the other guides him to a revisitation of the ethical and aesthetic foundations of

Italian cinematic neorealism. Scola soon understood that dealing with that glorious and yet extremely authoritarian past was instrumental to the creation of a new and forceful ethical and aesthetic discourse in Italian cinema. Scola's *We All Loved Each Other So Much* attempted to confront that heritage, so much so that Peter Bondanella felt that the film actually 'buried the myth of Italian Neorealism.'[51] Millicent Marcus, on the other hand, stated that Scola's film emphasized 'the urgency and appropriateness of the cinematic quest.'[52] Quite appropriately, Marcus chose to conclude her study of Italian cinema *in the light of neorealism* with an analysis of *We All Loved Each Other So Much*, a film whose major achievement was to bring the myth of neorealism to a reasonable distance, allowing for a fruitful reconsideration of the tradition and its final and irrevocable overcoming.

In a period of crisis in Italian cinematic production, Scola's 1974 film also attempted to suggest new avenues for Italian cinematic comedy, but one had to wait for his 1980 work, *The Terrace*, to get a comprehensive discussion of the aesthetic and ethical foundations of a thoroughly *national* and profoundly *popular* interpretation of humour. In many ways, these two films can be considered as companion pieces, as they revisit recent Italian cultural, social, and cinematic history.

We All Loved Each Other So Much is significantly dedicated to Vittorio De Sica, and at one point Scola stated:

Uno dei registi che più ho amato è Vittorio De Sica. Con Zavattini ha 'pedinato' l'uomo, schiacciato dalla tragica realtà degli anni del neorealismo anche nei momenti in cui nonostante tutto ride, quando è buffo e fantasioso: credo che *la dimensione umana somigli appunto a questo miracoloso miscuglio di tragedia e di favola, di mistero e di riso*.[53]

One of the directors that I have loved the most is Vittorio De Sica. With Zavattini, he "tailed" man as he was overwhelmed by the tragic reality of the neorealistic years; he tailed him even when he laughs after all, when he is funny and imaginative: I believe that *the human dimension resembles this miraculous medley of tragedy and fable, mystery and laughter.*

In our times, human reality is intrisically serio-comic and humoristic since it is characterized by the mixture of comedy and tragedy, laughter and tears, fairy tale and mystery. Scola pointedly identified De Sica as being the neorealist director who, more than any other, paved the way for the development of a specifically Italian 'comic imagination' in the cinema. This comedic countertradition – which, following Pirandello's teaching as exemplified in his essay *On Humor*, can be defined as 'humoristic' – transgresses given social, political, and aesthetic orderings, and prompts the search for the *new* in society and in art. This is De Sica's legacy to *We All Loved Each Other So Much*, a film that initiated Scola's most fertile season and a work that unquestionably constituted a milestone in the development of Italian cinematic comedy as well as the beginning of a new age in Italian filmmaking.

On the one hand, the film paints the vivid fresco of a generation; on the other, it leads the spectator to experience the journey that Italian cinema has travelled from neorealism to the the mid-seventies. The film is also Scola's first consciously autobiographical statement as he attempts to trace and make sense of a collective and yet also personal history in society and in the cinema. The plot of the film follows the lives of three friends who meet while fighting in the Italian Resistance, then fall in love with the same woman, take different paths in life, lose sight of each other, and eventually meet again at the end of the film. Significantly, the film has three beginnings, one for each of the three stories the audience has to witness. There are three main male characters, three points of view, and three narratives. Yet all three characters and their narratives develop around the same three fields of attraction: one is the woman, one is Italy, and one is the cinema. Three is the magic number that allows for internal mirrorings and transformations; paradoxically, through such a proliferation of subjective textual constructions a thorough retrieval of reality is enacted. The woman, Italy, and the cinema itself are awaiting to be mastered and conquered; they all become the fields of narration. Luciana, played by Stefania Sandrelli, together with Italy and the cinema, embody the world of possibility and provide the links between the three male characters. Because of Luciana, three worlds and three narratives unfold in front of our eyes, as well as three different interpretations of comedy and of the filmic event.

Initially, the film was only supposed to focus on Nicola, a professor whose life is transformed by the viewing of *Bicycle Thieves* and by De Sica's subsequent 'betrayal' of the ideals of neorealism in the 1950s. As Scola himself remembers,

il film doveva essere soltanto la storia di un lungo *pedinamento* che durava trent'anni: il personaggio seguiva De Sica e diventava per lui – naturalmente De Sica avrebbe dovuto interpretare se stesso nel film – una vera ossessione ... C'era dunque questo grillo parlante, questa coscienza che lo seguiva, lo rimproverava, lo perseguitava e il film terminava con la stessa frase che è rimasta nella versione definitiva: 'Noi pensiamo di cambiare il mondo, ma è il mondo che cambia noi.'[54]

The film was supposed to be only the story of a long *tailing*, which would last for thirty years: the character would follow De Sica and become for him – obviously De Sica was supposed to play himself in the film – a true obsession ... There was, thus, this talking cricket, this conscience who would follow him, reproach him, pester him, and the film ended with the same sentence that can be found in the final version: 'We think that we are going to change the world, and on the contrary it is the world that will modify us.'

Although the film was originally going to focus entirely on cinema, Scola later felt that a film with a single character would be somewhat limiting, and he wrote two other characters, emblematic of two different social classes: the bourgeoisie and the proletariat. Meeting during the Resistance, the three characters, all different from one another, shared the same ideals during the movement for the liberation of Italy from Nazi–Fascist occupation in the years 1943–5. The memory of the past is what connects them over three decades, as the story of their lives unfolds together with that of a country and its cinema.

From the initial optimistic vision for the future and a cinema informed by the belief in a faithful representation of reality, one then passes through disillusionment in the 1950s, a loss of ideals and subsequent alienation in the 1960s, and a frenzy of fragmentation in the 1970s with the reassessment of the past, the inevitable unmasking, and a pervasive sense of melancholy. Yet, paradoxically, an increase in realism is ultimately achieved through fragmentation and repetition with difference informed by a subjective recovery of the past and an equally subjective and thus unreliable mapping of the present.

Gianni, Antonio, and Nicola embody three geographical parts of Italy, three different social segments, and thus three diverse avenues for Italian cinema to take. Gianni, played by Vittorio Gassman, is a lawyer who comes from the industrialized North and who holds a preference for the Socialist party. He comes to symbolize the pessimistic and grim detour that traditional 'comedy Italian style,' and the country, took during Italy's economic boom.[55] Antonio, played by Nino Manfredi, comes from the centre of Italy, from Rome itself; he is a hospital worker and a communist. Antonio clearly symbolizes the optimism of the years of the reconstruction. He represents a hopeful version of De Sica's Antonio in

Bicycle Thieves, an Everyman no longer lost in the debris of the war but one who has found a way for his future in the Marxist ideal of a fairer and more equal society. In cinematic history, Antonio unquestionably stands for neorealism. Nicola, played by Stefano Satta Flores, comes from the South, from a small town in Campania, Nocera Inferiore; there he teaches at a high school, and attempts to heighten his fellow citizens' historical and cinematic awareness by showing them the masterpieces of neorealism, in particular, De Sica's *Bicycle Thieves*. He thus aspires to become a film critic, and to found a journal titled *Cinema e cultura (Cinema and Culture)*, as shown in a sequence where, having left his hometown and settled in a dismal apartment in Rome, he writes to his wife of the glamorous life he is supposedly leading in the capital. This celebratory vision stands in sharp contrast to his squalid and lonely reality; his wife's self-reflexive voice ironically contemplates whether or not he should be believed. This is one of the many examples of a typical Pirandellian 'processo umoristico' through which the character as 'humorist' becomes doubled in the act of reflection and, thus, forced to an understanding of his hopeless condition. Nicola represents the Italian leftist intelligentsia that, caught in rigid ideological paradigms, shows little understanding of the Italian reality in constant evolution and of the cinema that develops as a reflection of and as a comment on an increasingly unstable social organization.

In its journey through nearly thirty years of Italian film history, *We All Loved Each Other So Much* makes three direct quotations from such history, reflecting the three distinct cinematic visions the film confronts itself with. First, this story of a lost love affair refers back to De Sica's *Bicycle Thieves* and to his interpretation of neorealism. Interestingly enough, segments of the 1948 film are shown in relation to Nicola, and not to Antonio. Scola seems to be hinting at, and formulating, a critique of the questionable role critics played in the growth and development of cinematic neorealism. Thus, the authoritarian place given to the neorealistic masterpiece is emphasized, since Nicola's entire life is determined by his unconditional reliance on the ideals of neorealism. Because of this, he not only leaves his family and his home town, but he virtually ruins his professional and personal life. In the sixties, he participates in a television game show called *Lascia o raddoppia* (literally, 'quit or go for double,' a quiz patterned on the American 'The $64,000 Question') and hosted by Mike Bongiorno, a mythic figure of Italian popular culture who achieved fame in the age of television. Significantly, Bongiorno is here juxtaposed with Vittorio De Sica when Nicola must answer the jackpot question of why Enzo Staiola, the boy who plays the character of the child, Bruno, in *Bicycle Thieves*, weeps in De Sica's masterpiece. The heartless and superficial rules of television culture are exposed: Nicola's answer is declared wrong as he narrates the artifice by which De Sica managed to make Enzo Staiola weep. (De Sica placed cigarette butts in the boy's pocket and accused him of stealing them; the boy thus cried in shame for the unjust accusation.) Yet, in the world of television, fiction is reality – what you see is 'real,' and Bongiorno invalidates Nicola's answer with the 'correct' reply: Bruno (not Enzo) cries because he sees his father arrested for stealing a bike. Paradoxically, television's 'literal' interpretation of the neorealistic mandate operates a reversal of the ideals of verisimilitude fostered by neorealism itself. Later in the film, by evoking De Sica himself while he is giving an interview to a large crowd in Rome and explaining the 'truth' behind Bruno's weeping, Scola points to the fundamental 'lie' beneath the neorealists' strenuous attempt to provide a photographic portrayal of reality.

The same fundamental tension underlying the unambiguous verification of the truth in the surface of things constitutes the qualifying element of the second important citation in Scola's *We All Loved Each Other So Much*, that is, Michelangelo Antonioni's cinema, and specifically one of the films of the 'great tetralogy,' *L'eclisse* (*The Eclipse*, 1962).[56] This citation, relating to Gianni's wife, Elide, constitutes a digression from or a reversal of Gassman's traditional roles in the 'comedy Italian style.' Elide, like so many of Antonioni's female characters, is a direct and degenerate product of the economic boom. She is an alienated character who has lost contact with and is unable to communicate with nature and human beings, finding pleasure only in her contact with man-made objects. She hears voices coming from the human artefacts, as, in a similar and yet reversed situation, Gelsomina, the female protagonist of Fellini's *La Strada* heard voices from natural objects. Notwithstanding the many differences between these two films, *We All Loved Each Other So Much* and *La Strada*, both female characters eventually die: one lets herself go after Zampanò has killed the Fool; the other (Elide) commits suicide after her husband's last refusal to communicate with and thus love her. In both circumstances, the women are victims and display signs of humanity. Elide's 'real' suicide is also a detour from the destiny of Antonioni's many female characters who never quite reach such an extreme decision: they may dissolve in the surrounding landscape (like Anna in *L'Avventura*), but they never quite choose to terminate their 'fictional' existence. Contrary to Scola's characters, who are constantly aware that they are primarily fictional elements of an equally fictional construct, Antonioni's characters are fragments of reality constantly seeking meaning and a sense of continuity with the world of experience.

The third and most important cinematic reference in *We All Loved Each Other So Much* is Fellini's *La Dolce Vita*. No longer a citation or a digression, Fellini's film is a true metadiscoursive strategy as the film is represented in its making: a true film within the film, or better, filming within the filming. *We All Loved Each Other So Much* unfolds before our eyes as it reaches the end of the fifties, and we are called to witness the making of the soon-to-be-famous sequence of the Trevi fountain in *La Dolce Vita*, one of the most overpowering mythic images in film history and in Western culture. We are also allowed to peep behind the scenes and watch Fellini in the act of filming; more importantly, we see Marcello Mastroianni as he watches the celebrated sequence being filmed without Anita Ekberg and himself. We are thus shown the 'lie' behind the illusion of reality. We, the audience, together with the many other witnesses inside the film *We All Loved Each Other So Much*, are confronted with the fictionality of hyper-realism. Significantly, *La Dolce Vita* was also the film with which Fellini closed his own long and conflictual dialogue with the heritage of neorealism. Widening the scope, Fellini portrayed the collapse of Western civilization characterized by the progressive lowering and contamination of sacred values. The film becomes a powerful statement on the disintegration of the neorealistic trust in an unambiguous representation of reality. *La Dolce Vita* is undoubtedly one of the most self-reflexive moments in Fellini's career, a powerful statement on contemporary Italy and the cinema that reflects and comments upon it. After this, Fellini went on to a novel approach to filmmaking with the landmark work, *8½*. Fellini – the magician who can create illusions of reality, the alchemist who can freely transform substance, the prince and master of ceremony, the wonderful illusionist who can make you dream and believe the dream is true – is unquestionably the primary inspiration for a film like *We All Loved Each Other So Much*, a work that continually denounces its own fictionality and thus 'unreliability.'

As previously noted, Scola's film begins three times in the present time of filmmaking and flashes back to the years of the Resistance. In a documentary-like sequence, the first narrator, Nicola, begins telling his own story, a story that, as the viewer will soon find out, is thoroughly connected to that experience and to the cinema that was fostered by the ideals of the partisan movement. With the liberation of Italy, Antonio takes over and narrates the years of reconstruction characterized by a pervasive optimism and trust in change and renewal. Then, with the loss of the leftist coalition in the 1948 elections, Gianni's narration appropriately begins as he stands for the middle class's betrayal of Resistance ideals. In two hours, the audience witnesses the passing of three decades in the history of contemporary Italy, and yet the narration is entirely subjective and set forth by the three protagonists who are alternatively characters and narrators. In this film, like in so many others in his rich filmography, Scola sets History in a dialogic relationship with personal history and chronicle. The narration of Italian history is eccentric and unreliable when narrated from three totally different and thoroughly subjective points of view. Through a series of self-reflexive and metadiscoursive strategies, the integrity of the narrative structure is also fundamentally altered: rather than being the recording of a choral experience, the film becomes the fragmented narration of three different narrative 'possibilities.' Neither of the narrators can be identified with an all-knowing presence, since each story is constantly fragmented by the others' narration, and thus by an increasing irony. In *We All Loved Each Other So Much*, the narrative becomes progressively hypercritical and self-reflexive, forcing a sense of contemporaneity over the viewing experience. The audience is called to a thorough re-evaluation of the history of the country, and of the development of Italian cinema, but also of his or her own personal history. In a thoroughly humoristic process, the activity of reflection modifies the traditional comedic structure, and the film unquestionably and consciously initiates a new season in the history of the genre as well as in the history of Italian cinema as a whole. The 'comedy Italian style,' degenerate daughter of neorealism, is fundamentally and forever deconstructed by revisiting the heritage of neorealism, by placing it at a reasonable distance and finally demystifying the myth.

Significantly, in 1976 Scola filmed *Down and Dirty*, a paradoxical remake of De Sica's *Miracle in Milan*, the film that unquestionably initiated the new 'comic imagination' in an Italian context, and injected fantasy and utopia in the neorealistic tale.

Mais l'art du comique selon Scola est l'art du paradoxe: en noircissant les traits des personnages on éclaire leur esprit; en remplissant leur comportement d'aberrations et de nuissances, on fait émerger leur tragédie individuelle; en les faisant vivre dans la pourriture on en exalte la pureté.[57]

But the art of comedy according to Scola is the art of paradox: by darkening the traits of the characters, one elucidates their spirit; by filling their behaviour with aberrations and nuisances, one lets their individual tragedies surface; by making them live in corruption, one exhalts their purity.

Thus, Scola promotes a kind of comicality that opposes the optimism and candour of De Sica's fairy tale as inspired by Zavattini's surrealistic narrations. There is no innocence in the folly of Scola's characters, while there is in De Sica's. While goodness triumphs at the end of *Miracle in Milan*, in *Down and Dirty* a dismal and gloomy vision prevails. The story of Giacinto, played by Nino Manfredi (Antonio in *We All Loved Each Other So Much*), embodies one of the many narrative 'possibilities' for the proletarian character after the immediate postwar years. Giacinto's fundamental corruption mirrors that of Romolo Catenacci, Aldo Fabrizi's character in *We All Loved Each Other So Much*, and, later in the same film, Gianni's. The progressive loss of values has touched every segment of society, and salvation is given to nobody. It is relevant to note that Aldo Fabrizi played the courageous priest in Rossellini's *Rome Open City* who is shot by the Germans at the end of the film as he refuses to betray the partisans. It is also appropriate to note that the scene of his shooting is witnessed by a group of youths led by Romoletto: Fabrizi's character in *We All Loved Each Other So Much* is called Romolo; he is then a possible grown-up and degenerate version of Romoletto.[58] *Rome Open City* is thus a clear internal citation for both *We All Loved Each Other So Much* and *Down and Dirty*. In the 1974 film, the citation is activated through the character played by Aldo Fabrizi; in *Down and Dirty*, *Rome Open City* is quoted and truly 'evoked' through many internal references, the strongest of which, besides the character of Giacinto, come from the children. Unlike the children in Rossellini's neorealistic masterpiece, these children are no longer 'fighters for freedom' but, enclosed in a 'concentration camp,' have become the victims of a failed dream for freedom and social renewal. They are guarded by a little girl, an innocent onlooker, who is the leitmotiv in the film. She is the silent virgin who introduces each new day in the grotesque story of Giacinto and his family of outcasts, the vestal who goes for water in the morning and then leads the children to their day camp. She is the one who, one last morning, exits the hovel to go for water, and, now pregnant and forever violated, stands in the foreground as St Peter's Cathedral is set far and truly unreachable in the background. While *Rome Open City* ended with the image of the children holding each other and walking toward the cathedral in a last image of hope, *Down and Dirty* concludes with a message of pervasive pessimism.

The discouraging and cynical message in the closing sequence of *Down and Dirty* constitutes the necessary preface to *The Terrace*, a companion piece to *We All Loved Each Other So Much* in Scola's complex social and cinematic metadiscourse. With the 1979 film, the director virtually closed a season in his rich production, somewhat liquidating recent Italian history. After *The Terrace*, Scola focused on personal history and chronicle in such films as *Passione d'amore* (*Love Passion*, 1981), *The Family*, and *Che ora è* (*What Time It Is*, 1989); gazed in a distant or foreign past in such films as *Il mondo nuovo* (*The New World*, 1982) and *Le Bal*; or revisited personal memory with clear Fellinian overtones in *Splendor*, a film that unmistakably reminds one of *Amarcord*. His recent work, *Mario, Maria e Mario* (*Mario, Maria and Mario*, 1993), on the contrary, is a disappointing attempt to reconnect with *The Terrace*, and does not seem to have the same ability to read and interpret reality and history. This inability derives from society's loss of ideals, which had already been denounced in *We All Loved Each Other So Much*, but especially in *The Terrace*, a film that in more than one way was the testament of a generation in society as well as in the history of cinema. Yet, in a moment of great confusion in recent Italian history, a time in which the country seemed to be on the verge of a reactionary overturn, perhaps Scola felt the need to raise the conscience of the people to renewed ideals.

The Terrace thus occupies a central position in Scola's filmography: it comes half-way in his career; it offers a thorough commentary on Italian society as the expression of middle-class values; and it implicitly provides a comprehensive evaluation of the state of the cinema that better reflects this society. Furthermore, *The Terrace* is a poignant statement on the role of cinema in social and cultural history as well as an extensive theoretical re-evaluation of Italian cinematic comedy. *The Terrace* is perhaps the most comprehensive statement, almost a manifesto, of that Pirandellian mode in Italian cinema whose map we have tried to draw in the present study. A long underestimated film, *The Terrace* is far from being 'un quadretto della condizione pseudointellettuale e sostanzialmente piccolo-borghese dell'intellettualità cinematografara' ('a diminishing picture of the pseudo-intellectual and petit-bourgeois condition of the film intelligentsia'), as Lino Miccichè stated in his review of the film for the socialist newspaper *Avanti!* on 17 February 1980.[59] Gian Piero Brunetta's assessement of *The Terrace* moves closer to the truth when he states that the film 'non è da classificarsi tra i massimi risultati di quegli anni, ma coglie con il tempismo del tempo aureo della commedia, il momento di stasi nell'attività intellettuale e politica delle sinistre, il prevalere dei discorsi fatici e inconcludenti, del vuoto sulle capicità progettuali e sull'intelligenza della realtà'[60] ('cannot be classified among the best achievements of those years, but with the brilliant intuition of the best comedy it catches the stasis in the intellectual and political activity of the left, the prevalence of fatic and inconclusive speeches, the void now overpowering the projectual ability and the intelligence of reality'). Despite its pessimism, *The Terrace* must be interpreted under the 'sign of comedy' since the film works within the boundaries of that 'critical humour' that informs a large segment of the best Italian cinematic production since the 1960s.

The Terrace moves extremely close to *We All Loved Each Other So Much* and realizes the narrative possibilities left undeveloped by the previous film. Three of the actors from the 1974 film reappear on the terrace, which becomes the stage for the collective trial, the catalyst of everyone's narration, and the most important character in the story. The theatrical setting of the film is reminiscent of Pirandello's Villa degli Scalognati in the most notable of his 'theatrical myths,' *The Giants of the Mountain*, since, like the *Arsenale delle Apparizioni* ('the Arsenal of the Apparitions') standing at the centre of the villa, the terrace becomes 'un autentico trovarobado per *trances* audiovisive ... spazio labirintico cinto da muri equivoci, che ruotano nella furiosa dialettica tra *desiderio d'immagini* ed *immagini del desiderio*' ('an authentic prop storehouse for audiovisual *trances* ... a labyrinthine space surrounded by equivocal walls that move around in the furious dialectic between *desire for images* and *images of desire*') where the night and the filmic medium meet in an explosive manner.[61] The terrace also reminds one of Jean Renoir's *La règle du jeu* (*The Rules of the Game*, 1939), where in the central sequence in the villa the French director provides a large satiric fresco of the bourgeoisie. In *The Terrace*, as in Renoir's film, narration relies less on action than on the 'tempi morti,' that is, on those dramatically static situations in which the characters can better reveal their existential and social identity. As Jean Gili stated in his 1984 review of Scola's *Le bal*:

De film en film, Ettore Scola affectionne toujours davantage les espaces clos où se déroule la majeure partie de l'action ... Le monde extérieur bouge, change, s'agite mais ce qui intéresse Scola, ce sont les échos de cette agitation, les rumeurs qui parviennent sur les lieux où se concentre le récit.[62]

From film to film, Ettore Scola progressively takes advantage of the enclosed spaces where the most part of the action unfolds ... The outside world moves, changes, agitates, but what interests Scola are the echoes of this turmoil, the noises that reach the place where narration concentrates.

As in *The Rules of the Game*, the camera thus becomes extremely fluid and mobile; the actors move freely in the enclosed space, and the characters proliferate since they are unmistakably 'one, nobody, and one hundred thousand' – that is, faces of the same 'character without an identity.'[63]

The story unfolds on the terrace of a luxury Roman penthouse where friends and acquaintances – all belonging to the same left-wing political and cultural circles – periodically meet, chatting constantly about the same issues, and making the same comments. Repetitiousness is the fundamental trait of their lives and thus of their meetings on the terrace, as the story begins several times, or at least as many times as the tales told or projected on the large, invisible screen constituted by their collective unconscious. The narrative structure of the film is extremely fragmented to augment the sense of 'chorality': *The Terrace*, like *We All Loved Each Other So Much*, is a collective trial, although more gruesome and pessimistic. At the end of the 1974 film, one wondered what would have happened if the Gianni Peregos had not sold out to money and power. In *The Terrace*, that question is answered: nothing, absolutely nothing would have changed. There is no hope left. The character can take whatever direction he or she likes, but the reality is always dismal. The loss of identity that comes from the loss of an ideological and existential as well as psychological and social centre is unrecoverable.

As the crowd meets on the terrace, the film follows the stories of only five characters, since they are characteristic of the cinematic, cultural, and political history of the country. First, we witness the drama of Enrico, played by Jean-Louis Trintignant (significantly, one of the two protagonists of Dino Risi's *The Easy Life*), a scriptwriter of traditional comedies 'Italian style,' who is now unable to write stories that 'make one laugh.' A central section in this narrative segment is devoted to Enrico's fight with Tizzo, a film critic who accuses him of writing only comic films for entertainment and thus weakening people's capacity to think critically. Significantly, Tizzo is played by Stefano Satta Flores, the same actor who played Nicola, the would-be film critic, in *We All Loved Each Other So Much*. This character *has* indeed founded his film journal, and lives with his wife. Nevertheless he is a 'ridiculous' man; his condition is 'humoristic' since an unrecoverable gap exists between his mask and his face, a gap that he is yet unaware of. Only the viewer is given the chance to detect the discrepancy as the camera unmasks his fundamental loss of contact with reality. The process of unmasking unfolds through Enrico's dramatic tale, as he, in the frantic attempt to write and to define the essence of his work with a new interpretation of humour, drives himself insane and chops his finger in an electric sharpener.

The film then slides into the life story of Luigi, a once-famous journalist who is now unable to make sense of his professional and personal life. This idle character, significantly, is played by Marcello Mastroianni, the unforgettable journalist, Marcello, in Fellini's *La Dolce Vita*. The character of Luigi embodies a narrative alternative to the one offered by Marcello in Fellini's gloomy vision; yet, the outcome is dramatically the same. The condition of the *vitellone*, that is, the Subject that does not want to take on responsibility in life, presents no feasible alternative and thus no escape, since it is not merely a contingent but a true historical condition. Unlike Marcello in *La Dolce Vita*, who cannot escape being a 'servant of the idles' and never manages to become a writer, Luigi is a famous journalist, but in both his professional and personal life he still is a loser, an anachronism, basically a 'ridiculous man.' At the newspaper, he is emptied of value as the new generation takes over, accusing him of never taking sides and promoting an escapist and superficial interpretation of reality; in his personal life, he loses his wife to television and to the new world of women's liberation. In Fellini's filmography, beginning with *Ginger and Fred*, the written tradition comes to share a similar space with the cinema, for both are juxtaposed with and ultimately overpowered by the apocalyptic world of television, as it is further exemplified by *Interview* and by the disquieting ending of *The Voice of the Moon*, when the much-longed-for Aldina/the Moon utters 'Pubblicità!' ('Commercial time!'). In Scola's career, such an investigation began with *We All Loved Each Other So Much*, and thereafter continued, especially in *The Terrace* and *Splendor*.

From the tragicomic story of Luigi, we are led into the tragic tale of Sergio, once a cherished writer and now an unappreciated manager of RAI, the Italian national television network. He is to coordinate the production of a television version of *Il viaggio di capitan Fracassa* (*The Journey of Captain Fracassa*). (It is relevant here to remember that, in the endless internal citation characteristic of Scola's filmography, a paramount example is his 1990 film, *The Journey of Captain Fracassa*, which obviously referred back to this episode in *The Terrace*.) Yet the script submitted for Sergio's consideration is greatly different from the first text in form and substance: the original seven characters have become fifty-three, since the young author (and director) of the TV production has added a chorus to the story. The function of the chorus is to give voice to the thoughts of the mythic hero, since, as the young director states,

Il viaggio di capitan Fracassa come romanzo d'avventure ironiche e poetiche ... non interessa me e non interessa i giovani, gliel'assicuro. Io intendo esplorare il mito moderno di Fracassa e dei suoi girovaghi che cercano un inserimento diverso nella realtà del teatro che è appunto un momento di grossa riflessione sul nuovo ruolo dell'attore nel territorio.[64]

The journey of Captain Fracassa interpreted as a tale of ironic and poetic adventures ... does not interest me or the youth, I assure you. I intend to explore the modern myth of Fracassa and his itinerant actors who look for a different introduction/role in the reality of theatre that is, in fact, a moment of thorough rethinking of the role of the actor in the territory.

The literary source has undergone a thorough process of interpretation or, rather, 'overinterpretation'; the story of captain Fracassa has been actualized to the point of clashing with Sergio's nostalgic vision of the past. The irreconcilable nature of his relationship to the present becomes quite clear when he replies,

Sì, intendo la sua posizione, ma i fatti, almeno quelli, forse, non andavano cambiati. La bellissima scena di Matamoro che muore di freddo e d'inedia nella neve, qui, ad esempio, non c'è.[65]

Yes, I understand what you are saying, yet the facts, at least those, perhaps, should have not been changed. The awesome scene when Matamoro dies of cold and hunger in the snow, here, for instance, cannot be found.

The irreparable fracture between past and present, between old and new interpretations, as well as between fiction and reality is emphasized by the young author/director's reply, 'C'è, c'è ... la neve c'è' ('It is there, it is there ... the snow is there'). The director goes on to hint at the political intention behind the decision to produce his adaptation, and thus the 'vulgarization' of the original text. There is no alternative left to Sergio but to let himself die of starvation; like, or better, as Matamoro, he falls dead and disappears in the fictional snow while the shooting of the film continues. Engulfed by fiction, for a last moment Sergio becomes the field of ambiguity and irresolution – that is, he states that he is just *a character* in an 'ironic and poetic tale,' but at the same time, like Pirandello's characters in 'search of an author,' he becomes the field of the opposition between being and appearing, and of the unresolved conflict between life that is flux and art that is form. At the end of Pirandello's play, *Six Characters in Search of an Author*, the Son – the character who had constantly refused to act – shoots himself in the reality of fiction or in the fiction of reality. This sense of irresolution is mirrored in the words of the actors witnessing the characters' tale: 'Finzione? Realtà! realtà! E' morto! ... No! Finzione! Finzione! ... Ma che finzione! Realtà, realtà, signori! realtà'[66] ('Fiction? Reality! reality! He is dead! ... No! Fiction! Fiction! ... What fiction! Reality, reality, ladies and gentlemen! reality!').[67] The words the Son utters in the few moments immediately preceding his final 'act/ion' seem prophetic: 'Le par possibile che si viva davanti a uno specchio che, per di più, non contento di agghiacciarci con l'immagine della nostra stessa espressione, ce la ridà come una smorfia irriconoscibile di noi stessi?'[68] ('Do you think that it is possible to go on living facing a mirror that not only freezes our expression in an image, but also gives it back to us as an unrecognizable grimace of ourselves?')[69] Incapable of facing his own unrecognizable grimace, as he is reduced to a ridiculous puppet in the hands of a heartless master, Sergio *becomes* or, better, *is* Matamoro and dies in the snow, in the fiction of reality but forever lives in the reality of fiction.

Nothing can be saved from the voracious present. Yet, the past was no better, as is further exemplified by the next story, that of Amedeo, a producer with limited scruples, poor syntax, and many matrimonial problems. Fundamentally opposed to novelty, for many years he has produced second-rate comedies with screenplays written by Enrico. He progressively drives Enrico insane, and is led by his wife to produce an avant-garde film. However, this time he turns out to be right, and the film is revealed as a bluff. Past, present, and future are caught in the same dilemma, since the loss of values cannot be recovered.

The gallery of existential, cultural, and even historical fiascos concludes with Mario, the communist member of parliament, played by Vittorio Gassman. The actor also starred in *We All Loved Each Other So Much*, where he played Gianni Perego, the character who started out as a hero of the Resistance and the kind of man who could have made society more just had he not sold out to power and money. Significantly, Gassman was and is an icon in the Italian collective unconscious, as he has become one of the most recognizable 'faces' of the so-called 'comedy Italian style'; traditionally, he has played unpleasant and compromising, selfish and self-absorbed character types as exemplified by his roles in Mario Monicelli's *The Great War* and Risi's *The Easy Life*. Yet Mario embodies the wished-for future, a narrative avenue quite different from the one taken by Gianni; Mario is the outcome of a diverse existential and ideological choice, and yet the dilemma he eventually has to face when forced to choose between the young woman he has fallen in love with and his past – his wife and the party – echoes Gianni's in the 1974 film: 'Sceglieremo di essere onesti o felici?' ('Will we choose to be honest or happy?'). With this question, Gianni's narrative begins in *We All Loved Each Other So Much*, while in *The Terrace* the question virtually closes Mario's segment as he addresses the congress of the Italian Communist Party. In a dreamlike sequence, he imagines expressing his thoughts and doubts to the crowd, thus using a theatrical convention similar to that used in *We All Loved Each Other So Much*; but, as in the previous film, the response to his quest for help is silence.

Of the four actors who played leading roles in *We All Loved Each Other So Much*, three reappear in *The Terrace*: Stefano Satta Flores, formerly Nicola, now Tizzo; Vittorio Gassman, Gianni in the earlier film and now Mario; and Stefania Sandrelli, who played the female lead in the 1974 film, and in *The Terrace* stars as Giovanna, married to a petit bourgeois and having a love affair with Mario. In a moment of fundamental dissatisfaction with his public role – his 'mask' – she triggers in Mario a reconsideration of his entire life; and yet once again she is 'betrayed,' as he now, like fifteen years earlier, cannot find the courage to make a choice for happiness. Now and again, Scola states the inevitability of the outcome, whatever narrative stance or existential choice one chooses to take.

Interestingly enough, one of the male leads in *We All Loved Each Other So Much* has vanished as actor and as character: there is no Nino Manfredi and no Antonio in *The Terrace*. The disappearance of both has metadiscoursive implications in a social as well as in a cinematic context. In the long journey that led Italy out of the war, away from the postwar years, and into the late seventies, the country's social organization changed forever. The privileged subject of Italian cinematic neorealism has progressively disappeared from the scene; along with the proletariat and all its Antonios, the pervasive optimism in a better and more just society and in a cinema committed to change and renewal has also vanished. Moving from *Bicycle Thieves*, as an 'ideal' point of departure insofar as De Sica's film already contained the seeds for a fundamental criticism of the ideals of the Resistance, to *We All Loved Each Other So Much*, *Down and Dirty*, and then ultimately to *The Terrace*, Ettore Scola's cinema has moved toward a thorough critique of the social and cinematic past, and has arrived at a pervasive pessimism. Yet, his work is thoroughly grounded in comedy, and thus could not reach the apocalyptic visions one finds, for instance, in Pasolini's late films, such as *Salò o Le 120 giornate di Sodoma* (*Salò or the 120 Days of Sodom*, 1975). In collecting the heritage of the genre, Scola eventually developed a novel approach to comedy through the elaboration of a 'critical humour' that owes much to Pirandello's theoretical and creative writings.

A large segment of *The Terrace*, and truly its most relevant subtext, is essentially the definition of a contemporary form of humour in an Italian context and the evaluation of the role of cinema in society. With Antonio, the character played by Manfredi in *We All Loved Each Other So Much*, neorealism disappeared from the horizon, while, with the vanishing of Nino Manfredi, a specific tendency within the tradition of Italian cinematic comedy – the escapist and optimistic 'commedia di costume' – has also disappeared.

Il mondo della commedia di costume è decisamente abbandonato ed il nuovo continente da esplorare si rivela quello delle contraddizioni storico-sociali.[70]

The world of situation comedy is decisively abandoned and the new continent that awaits to be explored is that of social and historical contradictions.

Significantly, Gassman still holds his place on the stage of the collective trial of Italian contemporary society, which had begun with the 'monstrosities' of Dino Risi's films. Yet, the focus has shifted to the intellectuals as creators of meanings and interpretations, and also to the film establishment as producer of contemporary myths. The victims are the artists, characters like Enrico and Sergio, who are unmistakably caught in the clash between their ideals and the materialistic needs of a greedy society. All these characters are, however, 'humorists,' no longer heroes but 'anti-heroes,' contradictory embodiments of the same individual, of the same feeling.

Enrico, the writer, the modern artist and humorist, is the one who has the responsibility to reflect on the nature of comedy. The leitmotiv of his narrative segment, of his character and his own persona is: 'Is it funny? Does it make you laugh?' Such an apparently innocent question becomes increasingly cruel and gruesome as he rapidly shifts into madness and reappropriates his fictional place. Enrico's is the first tale that unfolds on the terrace as he submits to the pressures acted on him by Amedeo and the others, among these Tizzo. The producer and the critic force the writer, the artist, outside the stage, the terrace, and into a rethinking of the nature of his work. Once at home, unable to write, Enrico is also pressured by the ghosts of the many humorists that have influenced his life and work – Diderot, Charlot, Totò – and by the phantoms of his 'authorities' – Stalin and the Communist dream, Verdi and the Italian melodrama, and Marilyn Monroe and the myth of cinema.

Enrico's segment begins with an argument with the critic on the terrace. Pressured by Amedeo, who asks about his new script, Enrico mumbles about the comic nature of his new work being the result of a rethinking of the exaggerated self-criticism that had characterized their work up to that point. Tizzo thus attacks him, stating, 'Tu fai caricature senza problematica' ('You draw caricatures without depth'). To this, Enrico promptly responds: 'E no, questo è provincialismo culturale. Io voglio fare della caricatura e della satira, non dei ritrattini problematici' ('Well no, this is cultural provincialism. I want to make caricatures and satire, and not some problematic petty portraits'). Tizzo rails at him: 'Perchè non li sai fare' ('Because you don't know how to do them'). Enrico's angry reply sets the framework for his interpretation of comedy: 'Ma nemmeno Molière li voleva fare' ('Not even Molière intended to do them'). And then he continues, 'La verità è questa: che la perfida intolleranza di voi critici è la prova che non amate il cinema' ('The truth is this: the critics' cruel intolerance is the proof that you don't love the cinema'). Tizzo then suggests that Enrico read Nietzsche's appraisal of irony, but Enrico puts an end to their theoretical argument by reminding everybody of Wittgenstein's famous aphorism, 'La gabbia del linguaggio si distrugge anche con il comico' ('The cage of language can be destroyed even with comedy'). Enrico closes his first assessment of the nature of comedy by actualizing it into an Italian context, and states 'Guarda Totò' ('Look at Totò'). Totò's surreal and fabulatory comedy certainly was the founding antecedent of traditional 'comedy Italian style' as it developed in the postwar years.

Following this outburst, Enrico leaves and spends the night strenuously attempting to write a comic script on contemporary taboos. He is surrounded by sheets of paper scribbled with statements and questions on the topic of comedy. One note emphasizes the person who laughs, thus the viewer, as it wonders, 'Riderà non riderà?' ('Will he/she laugh?'); another outlines the fundamental dilemma differentiating the two traditional interpretations of comedy: 'Risata come trasgressione o come consenso' ('Laughter as transgression or as consensus'). Here Scola reflects on the differing interpretations of laughter in modernity, such as Bergson's recovery of a positive function of laughter in society, and conversely, Baudelaire's and later Pirandello's siding with the 'negative' or, rather, subversive nature of laughter in society and in art. Undoubtedly, Italian comedy had for many years attempted to provide a faithful and thus consensual portrayal of contemporary society. In his argument with Tizzo, Enrico, however, states that even the 'commedia di costume' contributed to the formation of a democratic awareness. Tizzo's response provokes Enrico's departure: 'Come si potrebbe fare un ritratto drammatico a una macchietta, a una marionetta, a un pulcinella come te?' ('How could one draw a dramatic portrayal of a character/caricature, of a marionette, of a Pulcinella like yourself?'). In fact, this swift questioning reply summarizes the development and the true essence of humour in an Italian context, since Italian film comedy progressively assumed dramatic overtones and developed by displaying an inner tension toward the transgression of traditional narrative and dramatic, as well as social and political, strategies. The facile optimism of 1940s 'neorealismo rosa' ('pink neorealism'), headed by filmmakers such as Renato Castellani, but also Dino Risi and Luigi Comencini, was soon dismissed, and, under the sign of comedy, Italian directors produced their increasingly pessimistic critiques of contemporary Italian society.

In his investigation of the nature of comedy and the social function of laughter, Enrico evokes diverse interpretations of comedy, from Molière to Diderot and Wittgenstein. It is appropriate here to note a passage in Denis Diderot's *Paradoxe sur le comédien*:

Dans la grande comédie du monde, celle à laquelle j'en reviens toujours, toutes les âmes chaudes occupent le théâtre; toutes les hommes de génie sont au parterre. Les premieres s'appelent des fous, les seconds, qui s'occupent à copier leurs folies, s'appelent les sages. C'est l'oeil du sage qui saisit le ridicule de tant de personnages divers, qui le peint, et qui vous fait rire, et de ces fâcheux originaux dont vous avez été la victime, et de vous-même. C'est lui qui vous observait, et qui traçait la copie comique et du fâcheux et de votre supplice.[71]

In the grand comedy of the world, the one to which I am constantly referring to, the stage is held by the fiery souls, while the orchestra is filled with the men of genius. The former (the actors) are called fools; and as they copy their follies, the latter (the spectators) are called sages. And it is the eye of the sage that catches the ridicule at work in so many diverse characters, that represents it for you and makes you laugh both at those fastidious originals who have victimized you, and at yourself. He is the one who observes you, and sketches a comic imitation of both your nuisance and your torment.[72]

According to Guido Neri, in this passage Diderot was referring to a minor work by Molière himself entitled *Les Fâcheux*, which, instead of focusing on plot, concentrates on presenting a veritable gallery of characters, and precisely of bores and nuisances.[73] Thus, the constellation of Baudelaire and Pirandello previously discussed in this volume stretches its boundaries and comes to include Molière, Diderot, and Wittgenstein by identifying humour as a fundamentally transgressive strategy in art and in society.

After a delirious phone conversation with Amedeo, the producer, who is constantly pressuring him to write comic scripts, Enrico receives a visit from Galeazzo, a friend just returned from Venezuela, 'attor giovane di teatro, cinema e rivista dei ruggenti anni '50' ('young actor in the theatre, cinema, and variety shows of the roaring 1950s'). The friend begs Enrico to include him in his new and 'plural' film, but the bewildered writer makes an astonishing revelation to the equally astonished Galeazzo: 'Non posso scrivere cose che non fanno ridere ... Guarda, ho scritto anche un saggio sulle diverse maniere di far ridere' ('I cannot write things that don't make people laugh ... Look, I even wrote an essay on the different techniques of laughter'). The essay is made up of ten chapters, each discussing various subjects related to laughter – laughter and social classes, laughter as transgression or as consensus to power – and the different kinds of comedy, from humor to irony, from satire to farce, concluding with a chapter on death and laughter. His tearing apart of the book declares him totally insane; it is reminiscent of the fatal 'strappo nel cielo di carta' ('tear in the paper sky') in Pirandello's *The Late Mattia Pascal*, when Orestes is declared forever Hamlet, perhaps the first self-conscious 'humorist.'

The many references to Pirandello in *The Terrace* make the film, in many ways, a manifesto of Italian contemporary filmmaking. All five major characters are unquestionably Pirandellian, typical 'humorists,' or, as Mario states at the end of his last meeting with Giovanna, 'Comunque si è personaggi drammatici che si esprimono comicamente' ('No matter what we do, we are dramatic characters that express themselves comically'). In an unexpected moment of self-awareness, Mario seems to be looking back at Gianni in *We All Loved Each Other So Much* and answering the question that may have seemed so basic and fundamental earlier on, but that now reveals its internal inconsistency: 'What if ...?' Whatever narrative stance a character takes, whatever existential or political choice an individual makes, the outcome is the same. No hope is left either to contemporary human beings or characters: they are all ridiculous individuals caught in the cage of language, trapped in an endless game of signification and interpretation. Humour seems to be the only alternative, the only tool that will allow the transgression and eventually the subversion of a given order of things. The five characters are ridiculous, and yet their audiences – the audience in the film and the audience outside the movie – are also ridiculous. As we watch *The Terrace* approach its choral ending, we are also forced to face a frozen image, a distorted reflection of ourselves.

It is certainly not by chance that in their last meeting, this time at a new party, on the same terrace, the five characters begin their conversation, this time all together and not fragmented, by discussing the most celebrated example of the 'processo umoristico' ('humoristic process') that Pirandello provides in his essay *On Humor*: the case of the old woman who smears her face with make-up and would make us laugh in comedy, but would only make us smile in humour. In fact, the act of reflection forces one 'to see' that she turns herself into a 'mask of youth' quite *consciously* in order to preserve the love of her younger husband. By overtly evoking Pirandello on the screen, Scola is not only establishing the source of his own 'poetics,' but because of the metadiscoursive and self-reflexive nature of his entire filmography, he is also assessing the primary inspiration of that *certain Italian cinema* growing out of the rubble of the neorealistic experience and within which his own cinematic discourse has unfolded. Not only, then, is *The Terrace* 'il testamento della commedia all'italiana. E' il film che chiude un *genere*'[74] ('the testament of the "comedy Italian style." It is the film that closes a *genre*'); it is also the film with which Scola states the ethical and aesthetic intentions of his own filmmaking and provides a thorough and comprehensive assessment of a large segment of Italian cinematic production. Such filmic experience has developed within the domain of a typically Italian 'comic imagination'; it is characterized by internal doublings and mirrorings; it pursues the contamination of diverse levels of consciousness as well as different genres; and can be comfortably defined as 'humoristic.'

After this biting statement on both contemporary reality and its artistic representation, Scola's cinema has moved inwards and become increasingly claustrophobic, as exemplified in such films as *The Family* and *Le Bal*, but also in two of his latest films, *Splendor* and *What Time It Is*. These latter two films are connected by the presence of Marcello Mastroianni, the actor of Scola's passage from *genre film* to *auteur cinema*, and the unforgettable protagonist of his first investigation of the interplay between diverse levels of consciousness, *May I? Rocco Papaleo*. It is with this film that Scola unquestionably proceeded to the disintegration of the traditional generic categories typical of the so-called 'comedy Italian style,' and moved toward the acquisition of new narrative spaces as well as of original discursive strategies.

Splendor is a journey into the history of Italian cinema from the early days through the years of Fellini's *La Dolce Vita* up to the present as it is exemplified by Carlo Mazzacurati's film, *Notte italiana (Italian Night)* (this film was made in 1987 and was produced by Nanni Moretti, the director who can, in many ways, be defined as the founding father of the 'New Italian Cinema'). The film takes place in a little town in the Italian province; the protagonists are a passionate owner of a movie theatre called Splendor, Marcello Mastroianni, and his projectionist, played by Massimo Troisi (one of the 'new comedians' of Italian contemporary filmmaking, an actor and director who died in June 1994). The film is the story of the nearly thirty-year relationship between these two men, the story of their love for the same woman, and the story of their love affair with the cinema. The movie is also a nostalgic and melancholic meditation on the history of the filmic event as it became progressively menaced and fundamentally undermined by the advent of television. *Splendor* is a film of Fellinian memory, as it can easily be compared to *Amarcord*, but also to *Ginger and Fred* and *Interview*. Furthermore, Scola's movie is a companion piece to one of the most acclaimed examples of the 'New Italian Cinema,' Giuseppe Tornatore's *Nuovo Cinema Paradiso*.[75]

Unlike Tornatore's film, in which the closing of the movie theatre is inevitable, and unlike Fellini's last films, in which the atmosphere has become increasingly gloomy and deadly, Scola's movie ends with a miracle. The ending has much in common with the miraculous intervention that saves the life of the protagonist in Frank Capra's *It's a Wonderful Life*: 'forse egualmente scaturito, come quello, da un'atmosfera di favola ma, se non vero, possibile, come nelle favole è sempre possibile la speranza'[76] ('like that, perhaps equally born of a fairy-tale atmosphere; yet, if not true, at least possible, insofar as in fairy-tales hope is always possible'). It also recalls the miracle that closes Vittorio De Sica's *Miracle in Milan*. At the end of de Sica's 1950 film, people fly on broomsticks to a world where 'Good Morning really means *Good Morning*,' a world where people really care for one another. De Sica's flight into fantasy and utopia was one of the films that marked the end of 'traditional neorealism'; but, most importantly, it virtually initiated the journey into that 'comic imagination' that was to inform a large segment of Italian postwar cinema. With *Splendor*, Scola offers a thorough revisitation of that particular, extremely *Italian* – that is, national and popular – mode of filmmaking, and ideally reconnects with the miraculous event that closed De Sica's film. It is time for the last show at the movie theatre Splendor: the next day everything will be dismantled and brought away. Jordan, the owner, watches the last projection and revisits his entire life in the cinema that was his life: the loves, wars, sorrows, and joys experienced through the magic images running on the screen; film after film, evening after evening through time, from black and white to colour and back; from the 'golden age' in which crowds poured into the theatre eager to dream, to the 'dark ages' of the advent of television when people started deserting the factory of dreams. Everything has changed but Jordan, Chantal, the cashier, and Luigi, the projectionist, and their love for the dream world of the movies.

Yet people do not want to dream any more, and tomorrow the cinema Splendor will be shut down. But, wouldn't it be wonderful if, like in Capra's film, a miracle took place and everything went back to what used to be? ... Wouldn't it be wonderful if people retrieved their desire to dream? ... And all of a sudden, while workers are dismantling the movie theatre under the petrified supervision of the protagonists of the story, the people of the town begin pouring in and take a seat in silence. When the theatre is completely full, the three main characters walk in front of the audience, back to the screen. After a moment of almost magic silence, the crowd starts singing the song that accompanied the closing sequence of Frank Capra's *It's a Wonderful Life*. Then an equally magic and almost miraculous snow descends on the scene. Silence and darkness prevail as the screen lights up and the image of a child, little Jordan, watching a screen standing in a public square closes the film and concludes Scola's most touching declaration of love for the cinema.

Wolfgango (Giulio Base) carries Michele's (Giuseppe Pianviti) dead body out of the gym in the hopeless ending of Giulio Base's *Crack* (1991), a film about squalor, drugs, and despair in suburban Rome

Young Totò (Salvatore Cascio) and Alfredo, the projectionist (Philippe Noiret), in the old movie theatre projection room in Giuseppe Tornatore's *Cinema Paradiso* (1989)

A moment of awe as Alfredo (Philippe Noiret) and Totò (Salvatore Cascio) look outside the window in Giuseppe Tornatore's *Cinema Paradiso* (1989).

Grown-up Totò (Marco Leonardi) and his girlfriend Elena (Agnese Nano) tenderly kiss in Giuseppe Tornatore's *Cinema Paradiso* (1989)

Director Giuseppe Tornatore and actor Marcello Mastroianni on the set of
Everybody's Fine (1990)

Matteo Scuro (Marcello Mastroianni) in a city square during one of the stops on his trip through Italy to rejoin his children in Giuseppe Tornatore's *Everybody's Fine* (1990)

Director Maurizio Nichetti playing himself in his *Icicle Thief* (1989)

Antonio, the father (Maurizio Nichetti himself), and Bruno, the son, in
Maurizio Nichetti's parodic remake of De Sica's *Bicycle Thieves*

The stolen object in De Sica's film was a bicycle, here replaced by a chandelier
in Maurizio Nichetti's *Icicle Thief* (1989)

Director Gabriele Salvatores and actor Diego Abatantuono at the Milan airport after receiving the Academy Award for *Mediterraneo* in 1992

Diego Abatantuono plays the lead in Gabriele Salvatores' postmodern film
Puerto Escondido (1992), a contamination of thriller, road movie, and love story

A dramatic scene in Gabriele Salvatores' *Sud* (1993) as two of the desperate protagonists, an African immigrant and an unemployed union leader, break into a
polling station in a small southern town

The three stranded travellers in Gabriele Salvatores' *Puerto Escondido* (1992), the last chapter of the director's trilogy of 'road movies'

Director Gabriele Salvatores on the set of *Puerto Escondido* (1992)

In Gabriele Salvatores' *Sud* (1993), police obstruct a rally in support of the gang that has seized the polling station

Pietro Monti, a Milanese worker, and Pabe, the young gypsy, embrace in Silvio
Soldini's *A Split Soul* (1993)

Nanni Moretti in his first Super 8 film, *I Am an Autarkic* (1977)

Director Nanni Moretti on the set of his first feature film, *Ecce Bombo* (1978)

Michele Apicella (Nanni Moretti), the typical 'bombo character,' smokes
neurotically while in the car with a girlfriend (Carola Stagnaro) in Nanni
Moretti's *Ecce Bombo* (1978)

Don Giulio, the priest, in Nanni Moretti's *The Mass Is Over* (1985)

Nanni Moretti on the set of *Red Lob* (1989)

A surreal and oneiric scene in the pool in Nanni Moretti's cinematic extrava-
ganza, *Red Lob* (1989)

Nanni Moretti in the first episode, 'On the Scooter,' of his latest film, *Dear Diary* (1993)

Unable to write in the city, Moretti and a friend look for peace on an island in the second episode, 'Islands,' of *Dear Diary* (1993)

Moretti submits to one of the many therapies doctors suggest as a cure for his disease in the third episode of *Dear Diary* (1993), entitled 'Doctors'

Nanni Moretti smiling at us and, thus, at the future in *Dear Diary* (1993), a perfect closing for this book and a celebration of his twenty years in filmmaking with the new Italian cinema

6 The New Italian Cinema: Restoration or Subversion?

Until a few years ago, the film world was mourning the death of Italian cinema. It seemed that the long 'crisis of the seventies' had left nothing but an irreparable void.[1] Then, in 1989, a 'miracle' occurred: Giuseppe Tornatore's *Nuovo Cinema Paradiso* (*Cinema Paradiso*, 1988) received the grand prize of the jury at the Cannes Film Festival; it was nominated for and eventually won an Academy Award as best foreign film. The Italian film industry began to record a considerable increase in production, and Italian films received great recognition abroad. France, always attentive to Italian films, paid homage to the new Italian cinema, and Nanni Moretti's *Palombella rossa* (*Red Lob*, 1989) was given front-page coverage in the prestigious French film journal *Cahiers du cinéma* and the daily paper *Libération*. Since 1989, Italian film has been increasingly acclaimed as one of the more vital of the national cinemas. In 1993, I collaborated with the Toronto International Film Festival of Festivals in organizing a special section on 'very young Italian filmmakers' and a retrospective of Nanni Moretti's filmography; both events received public and critical acclaim because of the freshness and originality of this new generation of filmmakers. After decades of consistent critical denial, Italian cinema is experiencing a rebirth, if not a true 'renaissance.'

To talk about the 'new Italian cinema' – the cinema of the 1980s and 1990s – is challenging, partly because of the difficulty in assuming a critical distance from something that is so close to us, and partially because the generation of young filmmakers who are presently working in the industry come from diverse and quite fragmented backgrounds. To draw a comprehensible map of such a 'polyphonic' reality is complicated by the fact that many of the so-called 'young' filmmakers belong to different generations, since some were born as early as 1945, and many in the 1950s or 1960s. Moreover, within a general history of Italian cinema, they can be defined as 'a generation of *orphans*,' as Lino Miccichè observes in his postscript to the volume *Una generazione in cinema*. Indeed, Miccichè adds that even though, in many ways all generations are orphans,

la generazione degli anni '80 ... vive un'*orfanità* assoluta, totale, irrimediabile, e al contempo, necessaria e inevitabile: ammesso che a uno stato di privazione si addicano superlativi, questa generazione è più orfana che mai, e lo è, per così dire, diacronicamente e sincronicamente.[2]

the generation of the 1980s ... lives an absolute, total, irreparable, and at the same time, necessary and inevitable condition of being orphan: if one accepts the possibility of making an absolute (superlative) statement of a condition of deprivation, one must say that this generation is more orphan than ever, and it is so both diachronically and synchronically, so to speak.

Thus, the directors who came of age as filmmakers in the late seventies and early eighties are preceded by no father or affluent brother they could follow, imitate, or reject. There seems to be no common ethical or aesthetic project for them to pursue. Therefore, the distinctive characteristic of those individuals who made their directorial début in the last two decades is,

la perdita progressiva di quella progettualità, tensione, senso di appartenenza, denominatore comune che aveva accompagnato per un lungo tratto gli autori italiani del dopoguerra.[3]

the progressive loss of that projectuality, tension, *feeling of belonging*, a common denominator that had accompanied for a long time the Italian authors of the postwar years.[4]

The fundamental difference between the filmmakers of the postwar years and those who made their directorial débuts at the end of the 1960s and in the early 1970s was that the former shared the same project – to build a new cinema for a new country – while the latter did not feel any sense of togetherness. Yet, being preceded by a powerful past, both generations could reject and move away from their 'fathers': the necessary condition for growth and development to reach ethical and aesthetic maturity. For instance, in the 1950s the generation of directors who came of age during neorealism had to eventually distance themselves from this glorious yet overpowering heritage. After the disintegration of the 'neorealistic body' in the complex system created by *genre film* and *auteur cinema*, directors as diverse as Federico Fellini and Michelangelo Antonioni, but also Roberto Rossellini and Vittorio De Sica, the so-called masters of cinematic neorealism, were able to contribute profusely to the history of Italian cinema as they developed a critical assessment of the premises of neorealism, and set the foundations for its overcoming.

Filmmakers who began working in the years immediately following 1968 were also able to deal with the authoritarian past, yet they were unable to contribute substantially to its overcoming. Both generations 'dovevano/potevano compiere un gesto edipico concreto: padri e fratelli maggiori erano lì, tuttora incalzavano ed era comunque alla loro scuola che i nuovi cineasti si erano formati, idealmente e operativamente'[5] ('had to/could perform a concrete Oedipal gesture: their fathers and big brothers were there, they still pressured them and, in any case, all the new filmmakers came of age, ideally and practically, under their teachings'). As Gian Piero Brunetta suggests, the filmmakers of the late sixties and those of the postwar generation, notwithstanding their many differences, had certain common traits: both attempted to obscure the difference between *genre film* and *auteur cinema* and both pursued

il policentrismo narrativo, l'opzione a favore di un costante disgregarsi dell'unità e della linearità a favore di una deambulazione in più direzioni.[6]

narrative polycentrism, the option in favour of a constant disintegration of unity and linearity so as to obtain a meandering in different directions.

As previously argued in this study, Italian cinema as it developed from 1945 to the late sixties constantly chose to reflect the multifaceted reality of a young nation 'in search of an identity' – to mirror all the different and possible gazes expressed by a fragmented country striving to build a sense of belonging and togetherness. The two generations of filmmakers seemed to share similar aesthetic and ethical beliefs, since the younger generation grew and developed under the auspices of the older one.

A drastic change occurred in the 1970s as Italian society and, consequently, its cinema experienced a difficult crisis:

Tutte le realtà sembrano dissolte, tutte le sicurezze appaiono frantumate, tutte le problematiche diventano indefinite, tutti i nodi risultano sfuggenti.[7]

All realities seem to have dissolved, all certainties appear to be shattered, all the problematics have become indefinite, all the knots have proven to be fleeting.

Hence, abnormal products flourished – for instance, the reduction of ideology to pure spectacle in Bernardo Bertolucci's *Novecento* (*1900,* 1976), or the anachronistic dramatizing of suffering as purging in Ermanno Olmi's *L'albero degli zoccoli* (*The Tree of the Wooden Clogs,* 1978), as Miccichè pointedly observed.

In Rossellini's *Rome Open City,* the dichotomy between good and evil produced a Manichean portrayal of the war years, in which the Nazis and Fascists, seen as ideological perverts, were thus depicted as sexual perverts; this analogical theorem is maintained in *1900.* Yet, in Bertolucci's Italian, or rather 'padana,'[8] version of *Gone with the Wind,* such juxtaposition is filtered through a spectacularization of Marxism. The film follows the lives of two people from 1900 to 1945: a landowner, Alfredo Berlinghieri, and the bastard son of Leo, Olmo Dalco, a peasant. The film *1900* is the story of a master–slave relationship as it undergoes fundamental changes during the first half of the twentieth century. Unfortunately, the film is impoverished by a pervasive sense of self-pity, and thoroughly lacks a sense of self-irony. The film thus mirrors the decay of an ideology, Marxism, at a difficult time in the history of Western communist parties, including the Italian one, and reflects the repentance of one of the many sons of the neorealistic 'lie,' Bernardo Bertolucci.[9]

Even though a far better film, Olmi's *The Tree of the Wooden Clogs* displays the same lack of irony that characterizes Bertolucci's *1900.* Olmi's work follows the lives of farmers and their families at the close of the nineteenth century with a linear narration that progresses chronologically. *The Tree of the Wooden Clogs* obviously moves within the boundaries of cinematic realism, and connects back with the Italian literary tradition by recalling Alessandro Manzoni's celebrated novel, *I promessi sposi (The Betrothed).* However, the film's magic realism also echoes Italian popular oral tradition.[10] The return to the past, typical of both films, is the result of a profound dissatisfaction with the present; the staging of the past is not aimed at building a sense of continuity, and thus it is no place of redemption or a milestone on which to construct a better future.

While for a few decades after neorealism the old and the new stood in a dialectic relationship, thus creating a fecund link between tradition and innovation, in the 1970s Italian cinema seemed to have exhausted the heritage of the tradition without laying the foundations for a new ethical and aesthetic discourse.[11] Thus, the directors who came to filmmaking in the 1980s felt they had been preceded by a threatening 'void.' While the Italian film industry was facing a serious crisis, the new filmmakers found themselves in a sort of 'protostoria cinematografica'[12] ('cinematographic protohistory') where the past was too far away to constitute anything more than a myth. In the late 1970s, consequently, Italian cinema became confined within the limits of a fairly respectful imitation of the past, or attempted to escape from that past by resorting to 'autobiography,' effortlessly trying to build a personal 'year zero.' It is, thus, reasonable to state that the Italian cinema of the 1970s recorded its own global isolation.[13]

This conclusion, however, is plausible only if one applies the ethical and aesthetic paradigms drawn from the neorealistic heritage, or those based on the syntactical and morphological categories defined by 'traditional' interpretations of genre. While it may be accurate to maintain that the filmmakers of the new Italian cinema are a generation without fathers or affluent brothers, it is more relevant to underline the fact that they found themselves in the grip of an old and still pending matter, 'la questione neorealista' ('the neorealistic problem'), an issue that the members of preceding generations failed either to address or to resolve.

Even though it was a grand and unquestionably important cinematic and literary glory of the postwar period, Italian neorealism was already holding back Italian cinema in the late 1950s. It inhibited the growth and development of a new wave in Italian filmmaking in the 1960s,[14] and eventually 'contaminated' the Italian cinematic panorama until the 1970s. Undoubtedly, it gave film history one of its best moments, and provided Italian cinema with a number of internationally renowned 'authors.' Neorealism also represented a major step forward in the overcoming of the provincialism and solipsism Italian society had been forced into during the Fascist regime.[15]

However, over the years, neither directors nor film critics ever managed to deal with the neorealistic lesson successfully. From its outset, neorealism had been turned into a myth, transformed in an aesthetic and ideological category for Italian cinema to follow. Miccichè intuitively observes that for decades, a strict and rigid interpretation of the neorealistic lesson unfortunately inhibited any possibility of linguistic and stylistic innovations, breachings into the fantastic, escapes from ideology, and narrative experimentations. In short, it impeded the delineation of new avenues that could provide an alternative route to those defined by direct derivation/citation or deviation/digression from neorealism itself. The few exceptions – such as the cinema of Federico Fellini but also the best protagonists of the so-called 'comedy Italian style' – have been marginalized, isolated, or, as in the case of Carmelo Bene, forced to silence in a sterile and impossible relationship with the impoverished audience of commercial cinema.[16]

The same neorealistic paradigms that proved to be inadequate to comprehend the 1970s are now unthinkable interpretative tools for the 1980s and the 1990s. Those who began filmmaking in the late 1970s, then, were apparently the 'heirs of nothingness,' and were forced to build their cinematic discourse in a virtual void. Consequently, young Italian cinema almost constantly defined itself as 'un cinema dell'asocialità e dell'implosione'[17] ('a cinema of asociality and implosion'). The Italian cinema that developed from the *Ceneri di Gramsci*[18] – that is, from the débris of a leftist project for political change and social reform, from the vanishing of a dream for a utopian reality – became nothing but the recording of the various symptoms of a generational malaise. The new reality could only produce fatic and inconclusive discourses, since 'la parola e lo sguardo, impoveriti di socialità e caricati di pura essenzialità, non hanno più echi e riflessi'[19] ('the word and the gaze, impoverished of sociality and charged with pure essentiality, have no reflections or echoes'). If the present has no past and the future is thoroughly enigmatic – that is, if one lives in a time apparently 'without History' – it becomes difficult to tell stories. The cinema that grew of age in the late 1970s was characterized by insecurity and discomfort as it reflected but could hardly comment upon a society without certainties. Miccichè concludes his brief, yet substantial discussion by stating that the films of this critical period in the recent history of Italian cinema infrequently make a cohesive statement; they mostly mumble or merely wink at the spectator, never providing a satisfying conclusion.

Nineteen hundred and seventy-eight can easily be taken as the 'founding year' of the 'New Italian cinema.'[20] It was around this time that such diverse and important films as Nanni Moretti's *Ecce Bombo*, Maurizio Nichetti's *Magic Show* and *Ratataplan* (1979), Gianni Amelio's *La morte al lavoro* (*Death at Work*) and *Effetti speciali* (*Special Effects*) were made. When asked to comment on his film *Special Effects*, Gianni Amelio made a revealing and intriguing statement: 'Ritorna qui, come nel primo capitolo di questa serie [*La morte al lavoro*], il cinema come mito al tramonto che tenta una sua estrema sopravvivenza'[21] ('As in the first chapter of this series [Death at Work], here returns the cinema as a myth at its sunset in a last attempt to survive'). Thus, the objective of Amelio's movie and the films of the other young directors was to bring back cinema to full existence, to save it from death. What they did not yet feel then, while they certainly do now, was the need to find what Gabriele Salvatores has termed as a new 'pensiero cinema'[22] ('cinema thought') – that is, an extensive and original idea about cinema, something comparable in intention and scope to the neorealist project, yet something substantially different that would reflect and comment upon a thoroughly new and diverse country.

In Death at Work, the protagonist is a director of horror movies. He has nourished himself with images, and he has built his existence on a dream up to the point of believing it to be a reality; he has played with shadows and death, and at the end of the film those shadows penetrate him and the screen truly becomes his ultimate scene. Approaching its sunset boulevard, the cinema attempts its own ultimate rescue by staging its own making, and thus by unmasking its own inner secrets. This beautiful statement by one of the most talented protagonists of the new season in Italian filmmaking unveils a newly acquired awareness of the essence of cinema as the fabricator of 'dangerous' dreams. Such cinematic dreams obscure the borders between fiction and reality, and make a distinction between the two utterly impossible. This proximity leads the director as 'dream maker,' as well as the viewer, to death.

Unquestionably, the difficult relationship between life and art, between reality and its cinematic representation, together with the role of cinema in society, brought to the foreground by the neorealists, continue to be focal points of the emergent Italian cinema. Both issues were considerably complicated by the intervention of public television in the 1950s and then by the introduction of private network stations in the 1970s. The threatening and contaminating power of television has 'indirectly' inspired several films that addressed the death of the cinematic age, such as Fellini's Interview, Ginger and Fred, and The Voice of the Moon; Scola's Splendor and The Terrace; Tornatore's Nuovo Cinema Paradiso; and Maurizio Nichetti's Ladri di saponette (Icicle Thief, 1989).

After years of debate on the so-called 'crisis of Italian cinema,' the late 1980s and early 1990s witnessed clear signs of rebirth, a renaissance that is unquestionably the product of a newly found capacity to effectively address the age-old question of the neorealistic heritage. It is not by chance that at the 1991 Venice Film Festival, Giuseppe Piccioni, one of the 'novissimi'[23] (the generation of filmmakers who began working for the industry in the 1980s), declared: 'Meglio essere *carini* che neorealisti'[24] ('Better to be *cute* than neorealist'). Leaving aside its apparent polemical undertones, one should note the significance of this statement in its assessment of the situation in which the 'very new' Italian filmmakers find themselves. Even though it is the prevailing critical opinion that neorealism has been forever buried, to deal successfully with the glorious and yet extremely authoritarian neorealistic tradition still seems to be the obligatory premise for the creation of a new and forceful ethical and aesthetic discourse in Italian cinema.

Twenty years ago, Ettore Scola's *We All Loved Each Other So Much* attempted to bring the myth of neorealism to a manageable distance. This film aimed at placing the neorealistic heritage in a thoroughly knowable place and in an equally familiar time-frame that would allow for a profitable reconsideration of its ethical and aesthetic foundations. By inserting neorealism within the larger flow of Italian postwar cinema, Scola unquestionably called for its final and irrevocable overcoming.[25] A number of years, however, had to pass and many films had to be made before Scola's investigation, enriched with the experience of other directors, was thoroughly understood, interiorized, and brought to a satisfactory solution.

It is undeniable, for instance, that several directors of the new generation still dialogue with the neorealistic tradition, assessing new ways of visiting the avenues of realism in the cinema. While avoiding direct imitation, a number of films made in the last decade exhibit a citational, commemorative, and, at times, thoroughly 'nostalgic' vein in their homage to the ethical foundations of neorealism and its urge for truth and social commitment. This particular trend in Italian contemporary filmmaking is epitomized by the works of Gianni Amelio.

Amelio's career began in 1970 with *La fine del gioco* (*The End of the Game*), a low-budget, black and white short film shown on Italian public television in a series titled 'Programmi sperimentali' ('Experimental Programs'). In 1976, Amelio shot a film on the making of Bertolucci's *1900*, and in an interview made revealing statements on the nature of his cinema as well as of filmmaking in general. He consciously revealed his debt to Bertolucci: 'Perchè Bertolucci? Per stima certo, o per affinità'[26] ('Why Bertolucci? Certainly because of respect, or affinity'). The lesson of the 'masters' of Italian cinematic neorealism is filtered through Bertolocci's interpretation in several of Amelio's most celebrated films, such as *Porte aperte* (*Open Doors*, 1990), *Colpire al cuore* (*To Aim at the Heart*, 1982), and *I ragazzi di Via Panisperna* (*The Boys in Panis-*

perna Road, 1988). In the same interview Amelio also reflected on the art of filmmaking and its relationship to reality, as well as the very essence of the filmic experience: '*Il cinema è un furto* – ha detto qualcuno. Quale furto più scoperto che girare un film su un film, fare del cinema su chi fa del cinema?'[27] ('The cinema is a theft – someone said. What theft is more overt than shooting a film on a film, making cinema on someone who makes cinema?'). While his previous films freely borrowed or literally stole images and rhythms from Bertolucci's filmography, with *Ladro di bambini* (*Stolen Children*, 1992) Amelio developed his own personal reassessment and true retrieval, no longer a 'theft,' of the neorealistic mandate.

Stolen Children is thoroughly indebted to the ethical paradigms of neorealism, in particular, those exemplified by De Sica's work, insofar as it denounces a historical and yet also existential condition. While in De Sica's *Bicycle Thieves* the social and existential denunciation was 'plural,' here the thief is unmistakably only 'one' – in fact, the Italian title of the film literally reads *Thief of Children*. While in the 1948 film what is stolen is a bicycle – an object, or better, a means of production – in Amelio's 1992 film two children are 'stolen.' Yet there is no parodic or satiric intention in Amelio's work; on the contrary, the film records the ultimate defeat of the ideals of social change and renewal and human solidarity that animated Italian neorealist cinema. This is the profound link between Amelio's and De Sica's cinema. Through the story of a father and son, De Sica's film narrated, on the one hand, the failure of the ideals that animated the Resistance – the partisan movement for the liberation of Italy – and, on the other, the dismal reality of the years of the reconstruction: the hope for change and for a bright future that closed Rossellini's 1945 film, *Rome Open City*, in De Sica's 1948 work gives way to disillusionment and despair.

A similar disillusionment inspires Amelio's tale of the meeting of three individuals and their escape down south. It is a journey of discovery, that is a true reversal of the journey in Rossellini's *Paisan*, in which true communication is ultimately built among the various cultural and linguistic identities; in *Stolen Children* no communication or understanding grows between the three protagonists and the outside world. Indeed, as the journey progresses, the distance between them and the others increases. Amelio's represents a fatal 'singularization' of De Sica's statement on a collective condition in *Bicycle Thieves*. As mentioned, the thief is unmistakably 'one' in Amelio's tale of the 'theft' of two children by a young *carabiniere* who is supposed to take them to an institution after their mother has been arrested for having forced the little girl into prostitution. At the film's opening, they are all 'personaggi fuori chiave' ('characters out of key'): the two children forced to grow up too fast by a corrupted and dismal social reality, the 'grown-up' cop compelled to be a child by a system that requires him not to think and thus not to make choices in life. As the film progresses, the transformation is twofold: the children regain access to childhood, and the young man travels a journey toward maturity. The same sense of solidarity that developed between Antonio, the bicycle thief, and Bruno, his son, at the end of *Bicycle Thieves*, here grows between the two children and the *carabiniere*.

In the 1990s, emphasis is once again placed on childhood: the privileged subject of many Italian films of the neorealistic period has gone through decades of corruption and exploitation; children now need to be 'stolen' from society, and brought to a virgin and untouched landscape where they can regain their place as our last hope for a better future.[28] Yet, *Stolen Children* ends on a deserted southern road with no conclusive statement and a definite sense of detachment; the film records our failure to build a better society and a cohesive sense of human solidarity. At the end of Amelio's journey, no definite solution is to be found; unlike De Sica's film, which suggested the possibility of finding a solution to social and political malaise in human solidarity, *Stolen Children* progressively records the increasing isolation of the three travellers from the others and from themselves. At the end of the film, the children are also visually separated from the *carabiniere*, and all three of them are placed at an irrecoverable distance from everything and everybody else. A similarly devastating commentary on society's inability to communicate and build a fairer world can be found in Amelio's latest film, *Lamerica* (*Lamerica*, 1994), a gripping portrayal of the dismal conditions in contemporary Albania and a relentless critique of a Western culture built on exploitation and imperialism.

Working within a similar retrieval of the ethical mandate of Italian cinematic neorealism, Marco Risi has come to occupy an important place in contemporary Italian cinema as well. The son of one of the 'fathers' of the so-called 'comedy Italian style,' Dino Risi, Marco is in his early forties. After an apprenticeship in commercial film comedies – from *Vado a vivere da solo* (*I Am Going to Live on My Own*, 1982) to *Soldati 365 all'alba* (*Soldiers 365 Days Before Discharge*, 1987) – Risi found his own truer cinematic voice with films that display an overt undercurrent of neorealism and social denunciation. Yet, while in Amelio's cinema the ethical lesson of the masters of neorealism is filtered through Bertolucci's interpretation, Marco Risi's films owe much to Francesco Rosi's 'cinema of denunciation' and Pasolini's investigation of the subproletarian culture of large urban aggregations. These directors are the most powerful inspiration of Risi's diptych on the underground world of Sicilian cities: *Mery per sempre* (*Mery Forever*, 1989) and *Ragazzi fuori* (*Boys Out*, 1990). The two films, co-written with Aurelio Grimaldi, depict the lives of a group of youths forced to live in the streets of Palermo. Facing unemployment, they are compelled to find alternative ways to make a living in a world dominated by 'other cultures': those of the gangs and of the Mafia. Responsible for having opened the way to the so-called 'nuovo realismo'[29] ('new realism'), Risi did not live up to the expectations created with these two impressive works, and his subsequent film, *Muro di gomma* (*Rubber Wall*, 1991), displayed weaknesses in both form and content. From a technical standpoint, the movie has the flat and unappealing look of a television production; it is also marred by a limited interpretation of the air tragedy that took place in Ustica in the 1970s. Unquestionably, Risi's cinema declares the urgency of the cinematic quest for a better society but also speaks of a generalized inability to read and interpret reality due to the thorough loss of ideals that had created a threatening void in public and personal life in the 1970s. Consequently, his subsequent film, *Nel continente nero* (*In the Dark Continent*, 1992), is the story of a journey in a foreign country, Africa, and is somewhat reminiscent of Scola's 1968 African trip of discovery, *Will Our Heroes Manage to Find Their Friend Mysteriously Disappeared in Africa?*, and yet constitutes a true reversal of Scola's earlier film. Risi's movie articulates a pervasive feeling of defeat in the face of reality and of a growing desire to escape, a recurrent theme in many films of the young generation, namely, Gabriele Salvatores' *Mediterraneo* (*Mediterraneo*, 1991) and Pasquale Pozzessere's *Verso Sud* (*Towards the South*, 1992), a promising first feature about a couple of young misfits who try to escape a deteriorating and corrupt northern urban life by attempting to reach an Eden-like south.

The journey of discovery and self-discovery has traditionally been the Italian answer to the loss of an ideal and personal centre since neorealism, in particular, since Rossellini's *Paisan*. Many are the journeys in the new Italian cinema, as young filmmakers try to make sense of a reality in which all certainties – geographical, cultural, and existential – have dissolved. While the journey previously brought increased knowledge and understanding of a given reality, now, in most cases, it brings no conclusive endings as the circle of knowledge can no longer be completed, or, once the hermeneutic circle is closed, the journey discloses an irrecoverable loss of meaning in the hopeless condition of contemporary humankind.

Films such as Giulio Base's *Crack* (*Crack*, 1991) and Ricky Tognazzi's *Ultrà* (*Ultrà*, 1991) and *La scorta* (*The Bodyguards*, 1993) are also marked by an overt retrieval of the neorealistic mandate. These works are thoroughly indebted to the ethical and aesthetic discourse of neorealism, again filtered through subsequent interpretations of that heritage, such as Francesco Rosi's and Elio Petri's. Although these films display clear signs of directorial maturity and avoid direct imitation, they unequivocably exhibit a citational and commemorative vein as they pursue the neorealist mandate for truth and realism. The Zavattinian 'tailing' of the character as he or she strives to survive in an unfriendly environment is literally assumed in these works, notwithstanding their profound differences in theme and ideology.

Giulio Base's *Crack* is a nocturnal and turbid film that portrays the ambiguous and dismal reality of a suburban boxing school where drugs become a factor in the story's progression toward its tragic ending. Ricky Tognazzi's *Ultrà*, a far better film, displays powerful visual and thematic tones as it follows a group of subproletarian Roman youth in their 'violent life,'[30] which eventually leads to tragedy and death during a soccer game.

In his late thirties, and the eldest son of the late and much-beloved actor Ugo Tognazzi, one of the unforgettable protagonists of Italian postwar cinema, Ricky Tognazzi first worked as an assistant to directors Sergio Leone,[31] Pupi Avati,[32] and Luigi Comencini, one of the 'masters' of Italian cinematic comedy. He also starred in films by Ettore Scola and Giuliano Montaldo.[33] Tognazzi's latest film, *The Bodyguards*, is a tightly paced and engaging political thriller that draws its inspiration and strength from contemporary Italian life, specifically the fight against political corruption and the Mafia. It is the story of a state attorney, working on a delicate political case in Sicily, who is brutally assassinated; a magistrate, played by Carlo Cecchi,[34] comes from northern Italy to continue the investigation. He is given a group of bodyguards who follow him at all times. In this tense tale of informers and hitmen, fear and violence, the director also describes the personalities of the bodyguards as they develop respect and trust for the magistrate. Parallel in theme but far more convincing than Margarethe von Trotta's *Il lungo silenzio* (*The Long Silence*, 1993),[35] Tognazzi's movie uses the genre of the fast-paced thriller to engage the viewer in the powerful and convincing message that human solidarity is the only effective answer to a violent and corrupt reality.

In addition to a renewed call for social and political commitment, the most important contribution these films bring to film history is undoubtedly the reintroduction of *tragedy* to the Italian screen after its virtual absence from the 1950s to the 1970s. Yet, this newly found sense of the tragic is 'frozen': it is not supported by a convincing value system that differentiates the good and evil in life and society; these contemporary forms of tragedy find no cathartic resolutions, and leave the audience with a sense of detachment and inconclusiveness.

While it is difficult to make sense of the disquieting body of diversified utterances that strive to coalesce in a coherent and comprehensive form within the troubled panorama of the new Italian cinema, one can thus discern a number of works that are guided by the desire to retrieve not only the ethical but also the aesthetic mandate of neorealism. While attempting to account for the new linguistic and cultural perspectives now emerging in Italy, these works still aim at building a sense of belonging and a feeling of identity. Such an urge finds a thoroughly nostalgic expression in the films of directors such as Giuseppe Tornatore and Francesca Archibugi, even though they differ in style and intent.

An extreme instance of the citational and commemorative vein in contemporary Italian cinema is the use of *nostalgia*, in which comedy and melodrama freely contaminate each another, and citation and digression enter a 'conservative' relationship. *Cinema Paradiso*, Giuseppe Tornatore's Academy Award–winning film, is the forerunner of this particular vein in Italian contemporary filmmaking as it strenuously attempts to recover the glorious past of Italian cinematic tradition from its early days to the present. In his thorough revisitation of film history, Tornatore adopts the perspective and the discoursive strategies of Italian *auteur cinema*. The past here is mythical – a metaphorical place where cinema was a magic fabricator of dreams, and where good feelings prevailed. *Cinema Paradiso* nostalgically connects back to Fellini's *Amarcord* but without that director's unmistakable humour and irony. Thus, despite superficial similarities, the film distances itself from Fellini's work insofar as it proposes a thorough understanding of a place – the past – that is, in Fellini's filmography, not thoroughly understandable because it is constantly being reinvented and thus fictionalized.

Cinema Paradiso can be also compared to Ettore Scola's *Splendor*, as both films revisit the history of Italian cinema from the 1930s to the present. Yet, while Scola's film links back to De Sica's *Miracle in Milan* and thus states the possibility of an almost miraculous retrieval of a collective knowledge, Tornatore's film, despite its visual seductiveness, remains confined to a personal, and thus thoroughly nostalgic, revisitation of the past. While Scola's film is the story of a movie theatre called Splendor, and thus of Italian filmmaking from its glory days in the 1930s through the 1950s and 1960s to the dismal reality of the present time where television has undermined cinema's very existence, *Cinema Paradiso* is only apparently the story of a movie theatre in a little town in Sicily, Giancaldo,[36] that is eventually destroyed by a fire. The film is largely a flashback in which Salvatore is not merely the protagonist but the only source of discourse. The collective life of the small town is revisited through his inner eyes; the same can be said for the life of Alfredo, the movie operator (reminiscent of Pirandello's cameraman, Serafino Gubbio) who, at the film's close, 'vindicates' his mechanical condition by giving back to Salvatore the missing links of his existence, the filmic kisses subtracted from his experience by the benevolent censorship of the town priest. The life of cinema and of one of its 'temples' is also experienced through Salvatore's eyes.

The film opens with a sun-bathed shot of a fishing boat standing still in the glittering ocean. The camera zooms back to a balcony and then to the inside of an apartment where an old woman is talking on the phone asking about her son. She begs the stranger to inform her son of the death of Alfredo. The opening sequence, reminiscent of the Taviani Brothers' *Kaos* (*Kaos*, 1984), in which an aged Pirandello talks to his dead mother, is the first of many of the film's internal citations. The following sequence shows us a middle-aged, handsome man as he returns home at night and is told by a half-asleep woman about the news of Alfredo's death. The darkness of the room is perforated by the rays of the moon that generate strange shadows; the silence of the night is broken by a magic, twinkling sound. Shadows and sounds trigger Salvatore's memory, and the movie proceeds to an extensive flashback of his life in the small town of Giancaldo until the day he left for the Continent and Rome to pursue a career in the movies.

We witness Salvatore's initiation to the magic world of the movies by Alfredo, masterfully played by Philippe Noiret, and of love by Elena, a beautiful and tender girl he meets during his high-school years. The two loves go hand in hand and make for the film's most lyrical moments. On Salvatore's departure from Giancaldo, after Elena had vanished from the scene, at the train station Alfredo ordered him never to come back; yet the news of Alfredo's death triggers a remembering of his past and brings him back to Giancaldo. When he gets back to his hometown for Alfredo's funeral, the movie regains linearity and continuity as Salvatore meets his old 'friends' and wanders about the locales of his remembrance. Present reality, though, is dismal as Alfredo is dead, the others are visibly aged, and the movie theatre Cinema Paradiso is destroyed after years of neglect and is about to be replaced by a parking lot. Salvatore is given a last present from Alfredo's wife: a film the aged and blind man had made for him, perhaps knowing that, in the end, Salvatore would indeed return. Back at his studios in Rome, the now-famous director experiences the most tender and lyric moment in his life as he watches a film made of all the 'stolen kisses' Alfredo had pieced together for him. In this ultimate moment of retrieval of the missing links of his life, Salvatore is given the chance to close his personal circle of knowledge, and we as audience witness one of the most nostalgic moments in the history of contemporary Italian cinema.

Giuseppe Tornatore's longing revisitation of the past aims to close the hermeneutic circle as in this film there is no crisis of reason. Citation and digression are here caught in the bracketing of time. The title, for instance, does not simply signal an object of Proustian descendance that would initiate the involuntary remembering of the Subject; on the contrary, it is an internal citation in a 'Platonic' sense, a narrative element with a reversed temporality: by moving from the present of the 'remembering,' it gives form and substance to the 'remembered.' That which is recollected is not simply the field of the opposition between old and new, tradition and innovation; it is a narrative and cognitive strategy. In *Cinema Paradiso*, the Subject is fully reinstated at the centre of experience and as a source of signification; the movement of subtraction operating at the level of the fabula is forcefully contrasted by an ultimate act of addition that at the closing of the film translates with Salvatore's being given back everything that was 'stolen' from him during his childhood. Tornatore's journey into the past is, thus, a traditional *bildungsroman*, or an *éducation sentimentale* of its protagonist from childhood to maturity as he is given the chance to relive his two loves, his two biggest dreams: Elena and the cinema. They are not experienced intermittently but are inserted in the larger flow of remembering. Memory, though, is like a dream, and dream is like a film. Consequently, Tornatore's film implicitly states the irreparable loss of our ability to dream: we no longer have access to the darkness of the Platonic cave on whose walls shadows and dreams originate. Our time is irreparably lit 'da una continua, lattiginosa, elettronica luce indifferente'[37] ('by a continuous, whitish, electronic and indifferent light'), the light of television.

Born and raised in the small town of Bagheria in Sicily, Tornatore came to directing after years of odd jobs, from projectionist to photo-reporter, from carpenter to bartender. His directorial début, *Il camorrista* (*The Camorra Man*, 1985), was a typical example of *cinéma verité*, a fast-paced docudrama starring Ben Gazzarra and based on the book by Giuseppe Marrazzo, a television journalist and Mafia expert, who disappeared in 1986.

Cinema Paradiso, Tornatore's second feature film, had a troubled life. When it first appeared, it was a 'flop' both at the box office and with the critics. Having withdrawn the film from the market in its first and longer version,[38] Tornatore began working on his third feature, *Stanno tutti bene* (*Everybody's Fine*, 1990). However, he was soon encouraged to re-edit *Cinema Paradiso*, and in its second and shorter version the film gained popular and critical acclaim around the world. The latest version of the film is, thus, the result of a thoroughly 'public' surgical operation: what is normally done behind doors was executed in the open, and this is unquestionably what makes this tender and lyrical tale filled with nostalgic memories of a life with the cinema so singular.

The melancholic dimension of *Cinema Paradiso* also characterizes Tornatore's third feature, *Everybody's Fine*, which was conceived during the troubled moments the director experienced with *Cinema Paradiso* before its international acclaim. *Everybody's Fine* describes a journey from south to north taken by an aged Marcello Mastroianni playing Matteo Scuro, a civil servant in Sicily for twenty-five years (now retired) and lover of opera for twice as long. For years, his five grown children, scattered throughout Italy, have paid him an annual visit on his birthday. But this year, one and all advise him that they cannot come. A staunch optimist, Matteo suddenly decides to pay his children a surprise visit and gather them around the same table once again. He thus leaves his little town in Sicily heading for the 'continent' – that is, Italy for the Sicilians. From the very beginning, as Matteo crosses a noisy, crazy, and troubled country, the trip turns into an investigation filled with unsettling and surprising twists. Wearing thick glasses that dilate his gaze to the point of making it unnatural, Matteo 'sees' through contemporary Italy: 'Attraverso gli occhi di quest'uomo scorre tanta Italia di oggi. E c'è tanto bisogno di raccontarla, quest'Italia, attraverso lenti diverse da quelle sempre più cupe del telegiornale'[39] ('Through this man's eyes flows much of today's Italy. And there is a tremendous need to narrate this Italy through lenses that are different from the increasingly gloomy ones of television news').

Matteo visits six locales, which were shot in a cinematic tour de force in eighteen places and with seventy-five different scenes. The film is an emotional tour de force as well, recording the interior solitude of protagonists who appear and disappear like phantoms of Matteo's imagination. After all, even what people say is often 'quello che potrebbero dire, cioè è lui, Matteo, che lo immagina'[40] ('what they could say, not what they do say; that is, it is him, Matteo, the one who imagines what they say'), and they all 'lie' in order not to destroy Matteo's dream. Tornatore warns against a realistic interpretation of the film, stating that 'non bisogna guardare questo film in chiave realistica perchè è un film paradossale e grottesco'[41] ('one should not interpret this film on a realistic level because it is a paradoxical and grotesque film'). Yet, *Everybody's Fine* is also a film about 'ordinary people,' or as Tornatore puts it, 'quelli che non fanno mai notizia, non fanno mai cronaca. Quelli che non sono assassini ma neanche assassinati. Sono anime del purgatorio' ('those who never make newspaper front-page or headline news; those who are neither assassins nor assassinated. They are souls in purgatory'). Through Matteo's thick and distorting lenses – a kind of Pirandellian reversed telescope, the film shows its way to the director and to the audience: 'Mi piace che siano i film ad impormi cosa devo fare e dove devo andare'[42] ('I would rather have the films impose on me what I have to do and where I have to go'). In *Everybody's Fine*, the world is characterized by a cruel and grotesque interplay of illusion and reality, and ultimately appearance *has to be* the only possible reality. When Matteo finally returns to his village, the station master greets him and asks, 'Did you have fun? Did you enjoy playing the tourist?' With a melancholic smile, Matteo replies, 'It was nice.' Then, the old friend asks, 'And how are all your children doing?' An overtly aged Matteo can hardly hide the sadness that overtakes him, and replies, 'Everybody's fine.' He picks up his suitcase, and slowly walks away.

With *Cinema Paradiso* and *Everybody's Fine*, Tornatore participates in that nostalgic retrieval of the past, both thematically and stylistically, that preoccupies a large segment of contemporary Italian cinema. This trend is not generated by a tension toward the acquisition of new and original narrative and discoursive strategies; rather, it aims at reconnecting with the tradition, insofar as it travels the avenue of masterful authorial voices and grand story-tellers, such as Federico Fellini and the Taviani brothers. Furthermore, this cinema is a non-ironic and citational commemoration of the grand tradition of Italian film comedy that developed from the neorealistic experience. When asked about the films that most influenced him, Tornatore makes his inspiration apparent as he names De Sica's *Miracle in Milan* and Fellini's *8½* among his favourites, next to Charlie Chaplin's *Modern Times* and Orson Welles's *Citizen Kane*.[43] As stated in previous chapters, *Miracle in Milan* was the film with which De Sica anticipated the overcoming of 'traditional cinematic neorealism' by favouring fantasy and utopia, and initiated what I have termed a new 'comic imagination' in Italian filmmaking. On the other hand, *8½* was a true watershed in Fellini's filmography, a film with which the director, after a long interest in exploring the nature of the cinematic character, began a long-lasting investigation of the new possibilities provided by the reciprocal contamination of different levels of consciousness or diverse modes of reality. Furthermore, beginning with *8½* Fellini aimed at, and indeed succeeded in subverting traditional narrative strategies, leaving a lasting effect on the history of world cinema.

Despite Tornatore's overt attempt to connect with that particular trend in Italian filmmaking that strove to blur the boundaries between the various genres and to undermine the author as a reliable source of discourse, his films seemed to move safely within the realm of 'imitation' and failed to bring an innovative stance to the new Italian cinema. Yet, his 1993 film, *Una pura formalità (A Mere Formality)*, displays a novel approach that will likely take him away from an acritical retrieval of the past into a fertile ground of thematic and stylistic innovation as it tests the narrative possibilities offered by the fantastic and the surreal.

On the other end of the spectrum of contemporary Italian cinema, one finds films that rely heavily on parodic discourse. A number of Italian directors share one of modern artists' main understandings: they 'have recognized that change entails continuity,' and attempt to offer us a new model for the process of the transfer and reorganization of the past.[44] Thus, a significant portion of recent Italian filmmaking relies heavily on parody as a mode of coming to terms with all the texts of the rich yet intimidating legacy of neorealism as well as of the subsequent cinematic tradition of the so-called comedy 'Italian style.'

As Linda Hutcheon observes in her study of parody as the privileged form of twentieth-century artistic discourse, modern double-voiced parodic forms play on the tension created by historical awareness. They signal the artists' desire 'to refunction' their predecessors' artistic forms to their own needs.[45] Thus, 'parody is fundamentally double and divided: its ambivalence stems from the dual drives of conservative[46] and revolutionary[47] forces that are inherent in its nature as authorized transgression.'[48] In its pursuit of repetition with difference and its ironic playing with multiple conventions, in its double-voiced nature as both a critique and an homage to the past, parody has come to be the privileged discoursive strategy of a considerable segment of contemporary Italian filmmaking.

By embracing the conservative drive inherent in parodic discourse, parody has often come to characterize the most commercial manifestations of this national cinema, such as Neri-Parenti's *Le comiche* (*Silent Comics*, 1990). At other times, by playing on the double tension created by its inner conservative and revolutionary forces, parody becomes a mode of perception and reception, a true and complex genre in terms of its form and ethos. Parody, then, becomes 'a mode of self-reflexivity, though not a true paradigm of fictionality or the fiction making process.'[49]

In this particular instance, parody, then, is characterized by the productive interplay of different moods and infinite variations of the precarious balance between citation and imitation, or citation and digression.[50] Digression here has a threefold nature: first 'as *mark* of the complex intertextual situations governing the process'[51] of viewing/reception;[52] second, as an internal structural *deviation*, that is, a straying away from the spoken discourse as a formative element of the textual production; and last, as a form of *distraction*, that is, a key dynamic of reception in mass culture.[53]

The reciprocal interaction and at times true contamination between citational and digressive instances that constitute the qualifying trait of contemporary parody characterizes a large segment of contemporary Italian filmmaking in a wide range of outcomes – from the ironic and playful to the scornful and ridiculing, from the sublime to the profane, to the farcical and the burlesque. Films as diverse as Daniele Luchetti's *Domani accadrà* (*It Will Happen Tomorrow*, 1988), Sergio Rubini's *La stazione* (*The Station*, 1990), Pappi Corsicato's *Libera* (*Libera*, 1992), Neri-Parenti's *Silent Comics*, but especially Maurizio Nichetti's *Icicle Thief*, all participate to varying degrees and in different ways in this particular mode of discourse, which is defined by exploring all forms of contemporary parody.

Irony is the cognitive strategy and prevailing modulation of Daniele Luchetti's It Will Happen Tomorrow, a road movie set around 1848 (in the troubled years preceding the unification of the country) that revisits, with intelligence and originality, the tradition of Italian cinematic comedy. The witty story of the escape of two butteri (cowboys), Edo and Lupo, from the Tuscan Maremma region after an unsuccessful and grotesque robbery attempt becomes a vivid portrait of the ideas, conflicts, and atmosphere of nineteenth-century Italian society. A picaresque story is successfully combined with fairy-tale undertones, historical elements, and philosophical notations. This historical, philosophical, and utopian fantasy has the freshness of nineteenth-century travellers' stories and the rhythm of an oral tale narrated by a creative story-teller.

No easy autobiographism or minimalist flair due to a lack of ideas – unfortunately two qualifying traits of a number of films of the new generation – can be found in Sergio Rubini's The Station. Despite the fact that the film is an adaptation of a play by Umberto Marino with the same title, that the actors starring in the film are the same who brought the play to the stage, and that Rubini, before becoming famous as the young Fellini in the director's Interview, was a theatre actor, The Station cannot be defined 'filmed theatre.'[54] In the film, the respect for the unity of time and space is indeed theatrical: the action unfolds in one night in a small station of southern Italy. There are only three characters: the stationmaster, Domenico (Sergio Rubini), the glaring Fulvia (Margherita Buy), and her fiancé, Danilo (Ennio Fantastichini). One night, a dazzling and mysterious woman breaks the monotony of the station and its master's life by storming in looking for a train to Rome after a fight with Danilo. From the realistic portrayal of provincial life, the movie soon progresses into a surrealistic comedy that successfully combines melancholy and irony. Although it is not theatrical in intention, the film's greatest originality lies in its investigation of original avenues for a reciprocal contamination of filmic and theatrical discoursive strategies.

Pappi Corsicato's directorial début, Libera, is also characterized by an overt tension toward the transfer and reorganization of the past, which in this instance is the grand tradition of Italian film comedy. In the fifties, Vittorio De Sica made an episodic film on Naples entitled L'oro di Napoli (The Gold of Naples), a vivid and humorous portrayal of Neapolitan life starring two of Italy's most popular actors, Totò and Sophia Loren. Since Rossellini's Paisan, where Naples appeared violated and destroyed as it was exiting the war, this city has given Italian cinema a powerful and convincing metaphor for a degraded and corrupt country. A similar destiny awaits Naples in Corsicato's film, where the city is not only the locale but the true protagonist of the story. A Neapolitan, Corsicato was one of the many surprises in the Italian cinematic scene in 1993. Like Rubini, Corsicato also comes from the theatre, with a background in dance and music as well. His film is polyhedric, a work that uses, and almost 'abuses,' a visual and sonic multilinguism. The movie presents three episodes involving three female characters: Aurora, Carmela, and Libera. However, there is only one story: the tale of Naples (and perhaps of Italy as well, since this is the name of one of the film's many characters, one who is deflowered by her shoe heel in a grotesque scene where she falls down a stair on her wedding day). The three women embody different aspects of a single beautiful female lavishly stretched out along the Tirrenean coast line: Naples, the city that has often been violated and indeed 'deflowered' in the course of modern Italy's troubled history.

The film, then, is the story of three women, or three stories of one woman. Corsicato has stated in an interview that 'La donna è più interessante dell'uomo. Mentre infatti egli è falsamente complicato e facilmente leggibile, la donna è più vaga, più vera, più profonda'[55] ('A woman is more interesting than a man. While he is falsely complicated and easily understandable, woman is more vague, more authentic and more profound').

Corsicato's film could easily have exploited a woman's body as a forum for a discussion of Italian politcs, but it does not. On the contrary, the movie wilfully parodies a practice that has produced many celebrated Italian films, from Rossellini's *Paisan* to Scola's *We All Loved Each Other So Much* and, to a certain extent, the recent *Mediterraneo* by Gabriele Salvatores. In all these films, a woman – Francesca in *Paisan*, Luciana in *We All Loved Each Other So Much*, and Vassilissa in *Mediterraneo* – is transformed into a large metaphor for Italy itself or for an ideal of freedom and liberation. In Corsicato's film, the parodic intention is openly stated in the title itself. The movie is made of three episodes, each of which could easily develop within the realm of tragedy and are instead narrated with pervasive irony, with that ambivalence and detachment that constitute one of the most original stylistic features of the 'very new' Italian cinema.

Silent Comics is a typical 'Christmas film,'[56] directed by Neri-Parenti as a mere vehicle for Paolo Villaggio. An example of 'vulgarized' modern – or, better, postmodern – parodic discourse, the film is a 'trash' comedy that nonetheless uses the forms of learned literary and cinematic citation. *Lowered* to the level of pure contamination, the citations here remain constrained within the boundaries of an imitative mode of discourse and do not give way to creative digressive openings. Nevertheless, through the obvious citational strategy, one can retrace the cultural patterns of mass comedy, a kind of comedy that looks back to Buster Keaton rather than Charlie Chaplin, to the grand tradition of American cinematic comedy from the silent era to the comedy of ambiguity and role-playing. Such a comedy is characterized by a vulgarization of a Pirandellian interplay between illusion and reality, and stands as the inspirational motif of Woody Allen's *The Purple Rose of Cairo*, a film that *Silent Comics* almost directly evokes. One can conclude that Neri-Parenti's 1990 film is an example of 'postmodern' parody, a thoroughly kitsch text that erases the boundaries between high and low culture, and turns citation and digression into active parts of a process of global commodification.

Thus, a large segment of contemporary Italian cinema is grounded exactly on the idea of 'cinema as theft,' as constant citation of an 'original' source and digression from a stated intention. There are two conspicuous examples of 'theft' from one of the masterpieces of Italian cinematic neorealism, De Sica's *Bicycle Thieves*: Gianni Amelio's *Stolen Children*, a film that nostalgically reappropriates the ethical mandate of the earlier work, and Maurizio Nichetti's *Ladri di saponette* (1989). The film's Italian title was given a mixed translation in English as *Icicle Thief*: on the one hand, the use of the word 'icicle' instead of 'soap' is appropriate as it preserves the 'sound effect' of the original title reminiscent of 'bicycle'; on the other hand, Nichetti's film also found the same fate as De Sica's movie in that the Italian 'thieves' become one 'thief' in the English translation. In the 1948 film, this singularization deprived the film of its choral dimension, its denunciation of a collective condition, making De Sica's work the tale of one individual. In turn, Nichetti's film was deprived of its parodic intention, since the film is truly the tale of only *one* thief.[57]

Icicle Thief is the story of a movie director whose film is presented on television, and who, after entering the film in order to fix the damage done by the continuous fragmentations and interruptions of his work, remains imprisoned inside the television set. *Icicle Thief* is the story of a film irreparably modified by the commercials that eventually contaminate it and turn it into a totally different work. *Icicle Thief* is the story of six characters – a mother, a father, their two children, a priest, and an American TV commercial actress – whose fictional 'lives' become a tireless escape from their author's. *Icicle Thief* is made of all these stories and many more as the film avoids unambiguous meanings and unequivocal significations.

Unlike Tornatore's *Cinema Paradiso* – a perfect example of what Fredric Jameson would call 'nostalgic postmodernism' – in *Icicle Thief* not only is the Subject no longer a coherent source of signification; it is also no longer a comprehensible source of enunciation, and it soon reaches the point of being silenced. In fact, this Subject is progressively emptied, without nostalgia, and with an apocalyptic irony, an integral and global dissociation. As Maurizio Nichetti, the director and the traditional source of signification and enunciation, is caged inside the television set, the film concludes with the liquidation and the true bracketing of the Subject. Furthermore, *Icicle Thief* plays on multiple conventions and genres; it is internally and structurally double and divided, and pursues a fertile contamination between different media. The film is thus far from predicting the nostalgic and apocalyptic end of the cinema, like Scola's *Splendor* and Tornatore's *Cinema Paradiso*. Nichetti here exploits all possible forms of parody, and constructs a witty and original self-parody that seeks a 'happy contamination' between citation and digression. *Icicle Thief* is a true container – a filmic realization of Marshall McLuhan's celebrated axiom: the medium is the message.

Nichetti's cinema clearly pursues a form of resistance to the generalized feeling of loss and estrangement that the Italian cinematic scene has been experiencing for a number of years. As early as the late seventies, together with a few other directors, he had proposed new avenues for Italian cinema:

Negli anni Settanta la nuova generazione cominciava a non essere più maschilista, viriloide, aggressiva, furba, individualista come poteva essere stata la generazione precedente. La commedia all'italiana non si è accorta di questi fermenti nuovi ed è andata avanti per altri dieci anni a rappresentare le corna, le donne inquadrate da sotto una scala, tutta una serie di cose che non appartenevano più neanche alla fantasia dei giovani.[58]

In the seventies the new generation was ceasing to be chauvinist, 'viriloid,' aggressive, shrewd, individualistic like the previous generation was. Comedy Italian style did not perceive these new ideas, tensions etc. and for ten more years it continued to represent people cheating on each other, women shot from underneath a ladder, a whole series of things that no longer belonged even to the imagination of youth.

The new Italian comic cinema thus entered an immediate critical dialogue with the tradition and aimed at subverting the well-established paradigms on which the tradition was built. The cinema of Nichetti as well as that of the early Moretti, despite their many differences, share the same project as they both avoid the acritical imitation of the tradition like others did and still do;[59] they do not portray negative heroes who pitifully survive because of their shrewdness in cheating on others. This new Italian comedy owes much to the grand tradition of silent comedies, and thus to Charlot, Keaton, Lloyd, Oliver and Hardy, but also to the 'prince' of the Italian screen, Totò. Their characters are funny and clownish, but they are always the victims, not the protagonists, of a swindle or a cheating. Subverting the pervasive tendency of the traditional comedy Italian style to portray cynical and shrewd social climbers who provide the audience with negative models of behaviour, the comic films of the generation that came of age in the late seventies depict tender, clownish figures who make one laugh but never ridicule either themselves or reality. In so doing, the young filmmakers, somewhat unconsciously, have participated in the history and development of that 'certain Italian cinema' that is characterized by a specifically Italian 'comic imagination' and that pursues the reciprocal contamination of the various genres as well as the subversion of traditional modes of discourse in art and society. This national and popular cinema, here labelled humoristic, is defined by a mode of discourse that is internally doubled, self-reflexive, and self-critical. Generally speaking, this cinema is also constantly 'autobiographical,' but not anedoctal, as it thoroughly reflects on generational, geographic, and existential issues that qualify, if not an individual's life, then the largely cultural journey of a specific segment of Italian society.

Gabriele Salavatores is a young director whose work bridges the gap between the generally 'realistic' vein, the nostalgic mode, and the 'cinema of resistance,' a largely humoristic and thus self-reflexive and internally subversive mode of filmmaking. Salvatores' films are journeys of self-enunciation as they attempt to design the koine of a generation that was in its twenties in the late 1970s. In the good company of Maurizio Nichetti, Nanni Moretti, and Gianni Amelio, Salvatores has been defined as a 'young filmmaker' only because of a certain critical laziness that for decades has refused to acknowledge the new energies that were being expressed in Italian cinema. In fact, only after gaining international recognition with his Academy Award–winning film *Mediterraneo* is Salvatores now receiving attention and his early films undergoing critical scrutiny.

Born in 1950 in Naples, Salvatores moved to Milan to study at the Accademia d'Arte Drammatica of the 'Piccolo Teatro di Milano.' In 1972, he was one of the founders of the Teatro dell'Elfo, a theatrical experience that soon became the point of reference for an entire generation of spectators. Today, the Teatro dell'Elfo is considered one of the most important agencies of theatrical production in the country. Salvatores has directed over twenty works for the theatre, and made his first film in 1982, *Sogno di una notte d'estate (Dream of a Summer Night)*, a rock musical freely adapted from Shakespeare's text. The world of theatre has strongly infiltrated Salvatores' filmography, beginning with his second full-length film, *Kamikazen, ultima notte a Milano (Kamikazen, Last Night in Milan*, 1987).

The film displays a Pirandellian flare as a group of comic actors are asked to perform a play upon which their entire destiny depends. Some cannot face the hardship of the task and fall apart on the stage; some refuse to act, but others manage to make the audience laugh and are hired for a popular TV program, *Drive In*. It is relevant to remember here that these are the conflicts around which Pirandello constructed his three most impressive theatrical works, the famous trilogy of the 'theatre within the theatre';[60] he did so at a time when European theatre was experiencing a radical expressive revolution prompted by several factors, most important of which was the development of the cinema.

Salvatores' film dialogues with the grand tradition of the Italian cinematic comedy that grew out of neorealism and addressed social issues through the vehicle of comedy. *Kamikazen* is the name of the horse that loses the race that generates the entire story; this easily brings to mind another famous horse race in Italian film history: the opening sequence in De Sica's *Shoeshine*. Indeed, the film is filled with citations from the history of that particular 'comic imagination' that began with neorealism, especially with De Sica's works, and developed with the masters of the so-called 'comedy Italian style,' such as Risi, Comencini, and Monicelli.[61]

Salvatores' later films also exploit the paradigms of that tradition as it has been reinterpreted and redirected by filmmakers such as Ettore Scola. This is quite evident in Salvatores' trilogy of 'road movies': *Marrakech Express (Marrakech Express*, 1989), *Turnè (Turnè*, 1990), and *Puerto Escondido (Puerto Escondido*, 1992), but also *Mediterraneo*. The latter film attempts to rewrite modern Italian history by revisiting the various cinematic interpretations of that history, such as Rossellini's *Paisan*, Scola's *We All Loved Each Other So Much*, and Monicelli's *The Great War*. *Mediterraneo* takes place during the Second World War; it is the story of a battalion of misfits who are sent by the Fascist regime to 'conquer' an isolated Greek island, and are eventually won over by the island and its inhabitants. In its rich network of internal citations aimed at designing a generational portrait, the story of *Mediterraneo* was prefigured in the earlier *Marrakech Express*. In that film, four friends embark on a journey to rescue their former mate Rudy, now lost in Africa.[62] As they are sailing toward Morocco, the character played by Diego Abatantuono[63] narrates one of their previous journeys, one that took them to a Greek island where they met a beautiful girl everyone fell in love with. This story obviously foreshadows *Mediterraneo* in that repetitiousness becomes a true discursive strategy as Salvatores continues the counter-tradition of humoristic filmmaking. The innumerable internal references and citations in Salvatores' filmography serve to enunciate the existential, psychological, and social identity of an entire generation. Salvatores' triptych of 'road movies' is interrupted by *Mediterraneo*, which, by revisiting Italy's modern history as represented in its cinema, provides the ideological justification for the trilogy itself, as the film is dedicated to those who are escaping. Furthermore, the film identifies escape as the only way to survive and go on dreaming. To dream is the only possible answer to the irreparable loss of subjectivity that marks an age dominated by the hyperreality of technological media.

Salvatores' trilogy of 'road movies' ends with *Puerto Escondido*, a free adaptation of a novel by the Bolognese writer, Pino Cacucci. While the book narrates the story of a man who lives in Bologna, without money, without a job, and without certainties, Enzo Monteleone's screenplay is the tale of an Italian yuppie who lives in Milan and has a life filled with things and certainties. Suddenly, because of strange circumstances, he finds himself in another world, Mexico; that is, as Salvatores once remarked: 'Uno dei posti mitici della mia generazione, che prima è fuggita verso l'Oriente, verso l'India, e quando è andata ad Occidente si è andata a riparare in Messico'[64] ('One of the mythical places of my generation that first escaped toward the East, toward India, and when it moved West, found a shelter in Mexico'). A journeying to distant, foreign places is Salvatores' strategy for gaining the critical distance necessary to gaze at Italy with honesty, but also for drawing a larger map of the world and ultimately leaving behind the provincial and narrow perspective that has characterized a large segment of this national cinema.

Puerto Escondido racconta in particolare proprio il passaggio da un mondo ad un altro di un rappresentante del mondo occidentale ... Là in Messico, si dovrà porre, per la prima volta, il problema di sopravvivere più che di vivere.[65]

Puerto Escondido precisely narrates the passage from one world to another of a representative of the West ... There in Mexico, for the first time, he will have to face the problem of surviving more than that of living.

Survival is the central theme of Salvatores' latest film *Sud* (*Sud*, 1993), a work that removes itself from the 'road movies' triptych insofar as it takes place in a single location, a small town in the south of Italy, and over a brief span of time, a few hours. The spatial dimension of the film becomes increasingly claustrophobic as a group of social outcasts seize a polling station and barricade themselves against the outside. Their desperate venture is an act of revolt against the generalized corruption of an archaic electoral system in which votes are stolen or faked, and which has brought to power the same political parties for decades. It is such a system that allowed the south of Italy to be exploited and impoverished. Elia, Michele, and Munir (a Northern African man) are led by Ciro, an unemployed union leader (played by Silvio Orlando, one of the most talented actors of the new generation) who, in his alienation and diversity, possesses the gift of special sight: through his eyes we are given an estranged gaze onto the world, a peculiar meeting of fiction and reality as things are distorted and action is slowed down. The four characters are a strange bundle of human destinies who attempt to build an alternative to the dominant discourse in life and society, and forge a different spatial and time dimension in which all diverse linguistic and cultural identities can live together in respect through a fruitful process of reciprocal interaction. The film itself is characterized by linguistic contamination as the director pursues a fluid movement from one genre to another, especially when Ciro's gaze affects the diegesis of the text. Exemplary is the moment when Ciro exits the polling station to discuss the situation with the head of police. Saturated with his desire to experience a moment of glory, the scene is shot like a dramatic duel in the classic western tradition of Fred Zinnemann's *High Noon* (1952), yet also in slow motion to emphasize its subjective quality. Linguistic as well as cultural contamination are also stressed by the peculiar musical score, which employs different and at times divergent themes as well as fine examples of recent Italian rap music.

To confront a foreign culture, to draw alternative existential paths, and thus to survive, are recurrent themes in the young Italian cinema as it attempts to reflect and comment upon a society in rapid change. The reality of immigration, and thus the potential contamination of the existing culture by alien cultures is new to a relatively young country that has not yet found its own identity. These thematic elements can be found in many films, especially Carlo Mazzacurati's *Un'altra vita* (*Another Life*, 1992), in which a Roman dentist falls in love with an attractive and enigmatic Russian girl, and Silvio Soldini's *Un'anima divisa in due* (*A Split Soul*, 1993), in which a neurotic Milanese desperately falls in love with an intriguing and equally enigmatic gypsy.

In Soldini's film, the encounter of the two cultures is not only the theme but also the structuring principle of the narrative: the movie is virtually divided in two segments that are stylistically quite different from each other. The first segment is about Pietro Monti, the head of security at a large downtown Milan department store. Originating from his distorted and somewhat ill vision, the narrative is fragmented, characterized by swift and accelerated editing as glimpses of random scenes run through his head. He gazes at an alienating and alienated city life, staring in bewilderment at the bustle of contemporary life. When Pietro meets the young gypsy who has been caught stealing in the department store, the film shifts to a narrative tempo and representation of space that reflects gypsy culture: fast-paced cutting is replaced by longer shots and a slower rhythm. The unstoppable process of contamination, though, brings an irreparable feeling of loss.

These films participate in a general tendency expressed by the young Italian filmmakers to subvert traditional forms of cinematic representation by connecting with the pressing extradiegetic concerns expressed by a society in transformation. Furthermore, they also connect to the healthiest segment of Italian filmmaking that has conventionally advocated the free contamination of traditional narrative strategies, a mode of discourse that is double-voiced, ambivalent, self-critical, and self-reflexive, and that we have defined as 'humoristic.'

Within this specific framework are Nanni Moretti's autobiographical films. Moretti's work is somehow parallel to Salvatores' but filled with anger, aggressiveness, and a pervasive self-irony. Within a cinema that has been rightly defined as 'Pirandellian,'[66] humour is the structuring principle and the true 'poetics' of Moretti's filmography as it constantly attempts to draw the profile of an entire generation and eventually investigate the new avenues that this generation can take.

Forse sto solo cercando di capire dove va questa generazione. Però con due punti fermi: uno senza troppi compiacimenti, senza troppi lamenti. Infatti io credo che quando si parla di se stessi l'ironia e quindi l'autoironia sia obbligato-ria ... L'unica maniera di prendersi sul serio sia prendersi in giro. All'inverso se ci si prende troppo sul serio poi si diventa ridicoli.[67]

Perhaps I am only trying to understand where this generation is going. But with two fixed points: one is without excessive complacency, without too much whining. In fact I believe that whenever one talks about oneself, irony and thus self-irony is obligatory ... The only way to take yourself seriously is to make fun of yourself. On the contrary if you take yourself too seriously then you become ridiculous.

In 1986, Moretti similarly stated that in autobiographical films comedy is the vehicle to exorcize what is represented, yet a comedy that is based on irony and distance.[68] This new comedy clearly places itself closer to humour than to traditional comic strategies; in so doing, it connects with that 'certain Italian cinema' that has developed from the work of directors such as Fellini and Scola. Humour is a discursive strategy that, by exploiting estrangement instead of empathy, produces an act of reflection in the source of discourse, the humorist. Thus, Moretti's films are hypercritical and self-reflexive as they expose the proximity between the enunciating and the enunciated Subject. By blurring the boundaries between traditionally separated fields of discursive production and reception, they constantly provide a 'cruel' self-portrait of their author and consequently of a segment of Italian society that is homogeneous from a social, generational, and political point of view.[69]

Holding a critical position toward the so-called 'comedy Italian style' as it developed in the 1960s and 1970s, and in an open dialogue with the lesson of the Italian film *auteurs*, Moretti has forcefully and consciously attempted to found a new mode of discourse in Italian filmmaking. In 1981, when asked if one could indeed talk of a 'new Italian cinema,' Nanni Moretti stated, 'Io non credo che esista un nuovo cinema italiano: mancano nuovi autori, un nuovo modo di fare cinema'[70] ('I do not believe that a new Italian cinema exists: there are no new authors, nor a new way of making movies'). Yet, when asked the same question in 1993, the director replied:

E' cambiata la situazione nel frattempo ... Allora portavamo gli spettatori al cinema, ma era ancora un po' presto per parlare di nuovo cinema italiano. Ora mi sembra che ci siano registi nuovi come Francesca Archibugi e non nuovi ma molto bravi come Gianni Amelio che è stato dai più scoperto solo adesso mentre aveva già fatto tanti bei film ... C'è qualche nuovo produttore, qualche nuovo regista, qualche nuovo sceneggiatore.[71]

In the meanwhile the situation has changed ... Then we managed to bring the spectators to the movie theatres, but it was too early to speak of a new Italian cinema. Now it seems to me that there are new directors like Francesca Archibugi and not-so-new but extremely skilled like Gianni Amelio, a director whom most people have only now discovered even though he has already directed many good films ... There are some new producers, some new directors, some new screenwriters.

Moretti's early films participated in the founding of a 'new Italian filmmaking' insofar as they aimed not only at breaking away from the authoritarian but no longer intimidating past of neorealism, but also defining their own specific cinematic discourse as self-ironic, self-critical, and self-reflexive. Such a discourse is internally ambivalent and fragmented; even editing serves no dramatic function but only works as a process of assembly of apparently discontinuous images and then sequences.

Donc dans mes premiers films, il y avait beaucoup d'allusions au cinéma comme absence, comme négation de ce que j'avais vu et que je ne voulais pas qu'il y ait dans mes films.[72]

Thus in my early films, there were numerous allusions to a cinema of absence, a cinema of negation of what I had seen and what I did not want to be in my films.

From his first films, Moretti seemed to understand that a coherent 'pensiero cinema' ('cinema thought') was needed to allow Italian filmmaking to move into the twenty-first century. Moretti's first acclaimed Super 8 film *Io sono un autarchico* (*I Am an Autarkic*, 1977) and his first feature *Ecce Bombo* (*Ecce Bombo*, 1978) both denounce the overall loss of ideals as well as of an ideal centre in Italian cinema and society in the late 1970s; however, in both films the depiction of an existential and ideological solitude is pervasively ironic and self-reflexive. Using the premises established in *I Am an Autarkic*, *Ecce Bombo* creates a true fracture between itself and codified genres. In this sense, it is truly a film 'without memory'[73] as, through the story of its protagonist, Michele Apicella, it tries to draw the geography of the *Bombi*'s space. Placed in a humorous framework – that is, a narrative space emptied of the empathy and sense of superiority characteristic of traditional comedy – the *Bombo* is a character or a type without an a priori fixed model. Thoroughly self-reflexive and hypercritical, Moretti's privileged 'type' is simultaneously subject and object, enunciator and enunciated, connecting back to Pirandello's many humorists, but particularly to Henry IV, who, like Michele Apicella, is an 'estrema declinazione del tipo del Pazzo, come folle e come *fool*, ossia matto ed attore'[74] ('extreme stance of the Mad Man, as foolish and *fool*, that is, character and actor'). Similar to the progression of Pirandello's narrative works, from *The Late Mattia Pascal* to *Notebooks of Serafino Gubbio, Cameraman* and then especially to *One, Nobody, and One Hundred Thousand*, Moretti's cinematic journey builds a filmic specificity, a personal 'idea' of the cinema, that 'restringe il campo a un profilmico ridotto al corpo dell'attore parlante'[75] ('restricts the field to a profilmic essence reduced to the body of the speaking actor'), and, moving even further, confines it to the body of the uttering actor/author/character of Nanni Moretti/Michele Apicella.

Born in 1953, Nanni Moretti made his directorial début in 1973 with a short colour Super 8 film, *La sconfitta (The Defeat)*, and continued thereafter to the produce films with impressive internal coherence up to his latest film, *Caro diario (Dear Diary*, 1993),[76] which, on the contrary, displays signs of novelty and difference. By beginning directing in the early 1970s, Moretti was witness to and protagonist in an extremely critical period in the recent history of this national cinema. In more than one way he was a 'precursor' of the Italian cinema that saw its beginning after 1977, a cinema whose qualifying trait was the total loss of a unifying productive and aesthetic centre. Yet, in the good company of directors Maurizio Nichetti and Gianni Amelio, and even when choosing thoroughly different avenues, Moretti was responsible for proposing original solutions to the ethical, aesthetic, and productive crisis Italian cinema was facing in the late seventies. Despite Moretti's distaste for the so-called 'cinema civile' ('political/civil cinema'), his work shares with that genre the attempt to make a cinema committed to social, political, and cultural critique and change, one that can be defined as a 'cinema of resistance.' Moretti's cinematic gaze is forcefully moral as it constantly traverses the ambiguous space between comedy and drama, pursuing the juxtaposition of opposites and constructing itself into a regime of discontinuity.

On rit chez Moretti comme on rit chez Buñuel; chez eux, les choses et les mots sont à prendre au pied de la lettre; on joue sur l'absurde, la dérision, on quitte une scène pour une autre selon un régime de discontinuité, pour mieux embarquer dans des moments plus graves, où le sujet bascule dans la souffrance.[77]

One laughs with Moretti as one laughs with Buñuel; with them, things and words ought to be taken literally; one plays on the absurd and derision, one leaves a scene to go to another according to a regime of discontinuity, to better embark on more serious moments where the subject is immersed in suffering.

The painful feeling of an existential otherness and a social estrangement produces innumerable juxtapositions and doublings, and parallels the fundamental condition of the Pirandellian humorist, an extension and extreme embodiment of the Baudelairean *flaneur* as discussed in previous chapters. The strategy is also humoristic, and aims at resisting and eventually subverting traditional modes of discourse in art and society. In most of his films, especially in *Red Lob*, Moretti liquidates his ever-conflictual relationship with contemporary Italy, a country characterized by 'les faux-semblantes, les mots vulgaires, la "culture médiatique," la perte de goût, le renoncement idéologique et moral, la pseudo "modernité"'[78] ('the false appearances, the vulgar words, the media culture, the loss of taste, the ideological and moral giving up, the pseudo-modernity').

Moretti's resistance proposes the abandonment of *genre film* and of the traditional narrative strategies of *auteur cinema*. Stylistically, his films privilege a horizontal construction and thus resist the paradigmatic construction of generic cinema; they are also characterized by an internal editing defined by movement within the image so as to create multi-levelled and confusing planimetries;[79] moreover, the soundtrack reflects the same multidiscoursive strategy, as the dialogue ceases to be communicative, and instead pursues a neurotic and obsessive affabulation of the subject/object. Michele Apicella is the everpresent, proteiform, and overpowering protagonist of all Moretti's films but his last one as he progressively takes on all the possible 'roles' played by an entire generation, and Moretti's cinematic language increasingly becomes 'un fait de résistance: résister à la modernité, aux choses faciles'[80] ('an instance/fact of resistance: to resist modernity and easy solutions').

Red Lob is a watershed work in Moretti's filmography. In this film, Michele Apicella plays an amnesiac who finds himself in a swimming pool where he has to play a game of water polo with the strangest of teams made up of people from diverse age groups. Even though cinema is directly evoked only on a TV screen as David Lean's 1965 classic *Doctor Zhivago* unfolds, *Red Lob* is unquestionably the most self-reflexive film Moretti has ever made. It is a film on film language itself, a cinematic work that reflects on its own status as well as on its own making process. Despite the proliferation of linguistic utterances as Michele tries to recover a remembrance of things past and the ability to interpret that past, *Red Lob* is mostly an oneiric film that seems to make a forceful statement in favour of a silent cinema, a cinema of movement and images or, rather, of 'movement-images.'[81]

Once the troubled discourse over the relationship between reality and its cinematic representation, and between words and images in film, seemed to be exhausted, Moretti decided to deal once and for all with the equally troubled planimetry of memory and the complicated issue of autobiography in his latest movie, *Dear Diary*. A tripartite work, the film is heterogeneous in form and content as it revisits Moretti's various personae: the viewer/spectator, the author/director, and the subject/character. The movie immediately displays its metadiscoursive strategy as it reviews the various forms of autobiography, or rather, the cinematic recollection of a past that in reality unfolded in reverse order from that depicted in the film. In Moretti's life, the events narrated in the final episode, 'Medici' ('Doctors'), came first; the second episode, 'Isole' ('Islands'), was scripted when he had recovered from his illness; the first, 'In vespa' ('On the Scooter'), was shot as the movie *Dear Diary* was in the making and is thoroughly scriptless. 'On the Scooter' is literally a film and a life in the making as it emphasizes the ability to look at things in a fresh, new way, retrieving the enchantment of our first glance at the world and the awe that is typical of an age of innocence. 'Islands' is the only thoroughly scripted episode[82] of the triptych. Here Moretti casts himself, the author/director, as the 'speaking' narrator in search of a story, a place and a character in detached and peripheral surroundings. No place and no character are to be found, since Eden is lost forever in the time and space of *The Bold and the Beautiful*. Perhaps, though, new narrative possibilities and strategies can be delineated since what matters here is not the destination but the journey itself, and specifically the 'timelessness' and 'spacelessness' between the Mediterranean islands. In the third episode, 'Doctors,' Moretti relates his battle with cancer. This story is recounted not with anger but with a surprising detachment, notwithstanding the employment of extremely subjective inserts of Super-8 shooting. Heterogeneity and heteroglossia are the stylistic traits of a tale of alienation and fear that eventually leads to self-knowledge: Moretti's body, previously expropriated by his alter-ego Michele Apicella, is now reappropriated by the director himself and is no longer a war machine, but an unrenounceable place of departure for a thorough remapping of the world of experience. Moretti unbound from Apicella is free to catalogue and restructure objects, to rewrite his *Erlebnis*. Freed from the cage of language, Moretti is ultimately able to record thought and emotion merely through the intensity of his images,[83] bringing to full fruition Pirandello's dream for the art of film-making:

Je crois que le Cinéma, plus facilement, plus complètement que n'importe quel autre moyen d'expression artistique, veut nous donner la vision de la pensée ... le Rêve, le Souvenir, l'Hallucination, la Folie, le Dédoublement de la personnalité! Si les cinégraphistes voulaient, il y aurait de si grandes choses à faire![84]

I believe that cinema, more easily, more completely than any other means of artistic expression, will give us the vision of thought ... dream, memory, hallucination, madness, personality doubling! If the cinematographers want it, they'll have grand things to do!

At last, then, irony and humour prevail over the anger and fury that characterized Moretti's cinema before such films as *La messa è finita* (*The Mass Is Over*, 1985) and *Red Lob*; the director seems to have found a new and energetic vision, one that stands in a harmonious relationship with his previous position as he constantly strove, and strives, to define a coherent and innovative 'cinema thought' – one that resists and subverts outmoded and authoritarian strategies in film and society.

On the other hand, Moretti's film practice also proposes alternative modes of production and distribution in answer to an industry that has been traditionally far too receptive to the pressures of the Hollywood model. In 1986, Moretti and Angelo Barbagallo founded the Sacher production company, named after Moretti's favourite cake, the luscious chocolate Sacher-torte. The production company soon became a distribution agency as well, and in 1991 Moretti and Barbagallo also renovated a popular movie theatre in Trastevere, a central neighbourhood in Rome made famous by Fellini's *La Dolce Vita*. The theatre was dubbed the 'Nuovo Sacher,' and soon became one of the city's most popular film haunts primarily because of its intelligent programming. The project was then and is now a global intervention on the filmic event in its totality.

Ho deciso di fare il produttore perchè ... sono convinto che bisogna *fare qualcosa* e, forse questo è l'elemento davvero decisivo, perchè mi danno tanto fastidio le inutili chiacchere, i lamenti, i gemiti, le tavole rotonde e i convegni sulla crisi del cinema italiano: quelli che possono fare qualcosa di concreto – cioè fare dei film – lo facciano prima che sia troppo tardi. Io posso fare qualcosa, qualcosa di piccolo, e lo faccio.[85]

I decided to become a producer because ... I am convinced that *something must be done* and – perhaps this is really the decisive factor – because I hate useless chatterings, moanings, and wailings, round-tables and conferences on the crisis of Italian cinema. Those who can concretely do something – that is, make movies – must do it, before it is too late. I can do something, something modest, and I do.

The ethical message Moretti has delivered in twenty years of filmmaking, producing, and distributing constitutes a 'legacy' that directors of the latest generation in Italian filmmaking do not hesitate to recognize. Even when organizing their discourses along fresh and original lines, they still propose a cinema that is 'independent' at every stage of its development, from the original conception to the post-production phase, and that 'resists' outmoded cinematic and social strategies. This general tendency, which began with neorealism, but was later abandoned under the pressures of generic productions – with few notable exceptions, such as the cinema of Federico Fellini – became not only a characteristic but a true manifesto of Moretti's cinema. During a press conference at the 1993 Toronto International Film Festival of Festivals, five representatives of the 'very young' Italian cinema – Pappi Corsicato, Giulio Base, Francesco Martinozzi, Vito Zagarrio, and Silvio Soldini – all agreed that Nanni Moretti was the 'father' of this generation of filmmakers insofar as he proposed alternative models of film production and distribution, as well as a convincing ethical message, to a cinema that seemed to have lost focus and strength. Mostly in their late twenties and early thirties, these young directors recognized the unparalleled contribution of the former generation to freeing Italian cinema from the shackles of the past. The stringent boundaries between genres have blurred, those between *genre film* and *auteur cinema* have been removed, and all dues have been paid. Now freed from the past and thus from any autobiographical stance, Italian cinema can proceed in the present toward the future. And the story continues ...

Notes

INTRODUCTION   Why Pirandello and the Cinema?

1   To date, the only essay translated into English is *On Humor*, translated and edited by Antonio Illiano and Daniel P. Testa (Chapel Hill, NC: University of North Carolina Press, 1974). However, since the rights to Pirandello's works have recently expired, new translations and editions are being pursued.

2   On this subject, see also Gian Piero Brunetta, *Intellettuali, cinema e propaganda fra le due guerre* (Bologna: Patron, 1972).

3   He is best known in the English-speaking world for his famous trilogy of the 'theatre in the theatre,' as he himself defined it in the preface to the definitive Italian edition of his complete theatrical works. I am referring to *Sei personaggi in cerca d'autore* (*Six Characters in Search of an Author*, 1921), *Ciascuno a suo modo* (*Each in His Own Way*, 1924), and *Stasera si recita a soggetto* (*Tonight We Improvise*, 1930). However, his theatrical production includes more than forty plays collected in two volumes with the title Pirandello himself gave the collection, *Maschere nude* (*Naked Masks*) (1958; Milan: Mondadori, 1978).

4   Pirandello wrote seven novels collected in two volumes by Mondadori and edited by Giovanni Macchia, *Tutti i romanzi* (1973; Milan: Mondadori, 1984). The most famous of his novels are *Il fu Mattia Pascal* (*The Late Mattia Pascal*, 1904), *Quaderni di Serafino Gubbio operatore* (*Shoot!*, 1916; 1925) and *Uno, nessuno e centomila* (*One, Nobody, and One Hundred Thousand*, 1926). I include the date of first publication in volume for each of the three novels; note, however, that all of them were first published in serial form in weekly journals.

5   Pirandello was always quite active in both critical and theoretical specula-

tion from his university years onward. One of his best-known essays, one that has always been well received, quoted, and is still studied in the English-speaking world is his study of humour, *L'umorismo (On Humor)* first published in 1908. In many ways, *On Humor* can be considered a manifesto of Pirandello's aesthetic and existential beliefs, a statement on his poetics, and a philosophical investigation on the relationship between art and life, and between reality and its artistic representation. This essay serves as the foundation of Pirandello's revolutionary narrative and dramatic works and is the only working key to this thoughts on the cinema.

6   Pirandello wrote several poems, which are collected in a volume together with his theoretical essays and critical writings edited by Manlio Lo Vecchio-Musti, *Saggi, poesie scritti varii* (Milan: Mondadori, 1960).

7   On Pirandello's venture into painting, see Antonio Alessio, *Pirandello pittore* (Agrigento: Edizioni del Centro nazionale studi pirandelliani, 1984).

8   As I shall discuss later in my study, Pirandello not only scripted screenplays but also adapted several of his narrative and dramatic works for the screen.

9   Ricciotto Canudo was born in Gioia del Colle on 2 January 1879. A poet and a journalist, he was in many ways the first true film theorist. He moved to Paris in 1908 and died there on 10 November 1923.

10   In his volume *Pirandello e il cinema* (Venice: Marsilio, 1991, 17), Francesco Càllari maintains that in 1941, Ugo Ojetti told him that he had invited Pirandello to the Italian première of twelve short films by Louis Lumière at the photographic studio Le Lieure in Rome on 13 March 1896. The publication of this book together with the two beautiful volumes edited by Nino Genovese and Sebastiano Gesù, *La musa inquietante di Pirandello: Il Cinema* (Palermo: Bonanno Editore, 1990), has strengthened my discourse, bringing new evidence to support my argument, and at times reaching similar conclusions.

11   For a discussion of the novel *Shoot!* see Chapter 2. For Pirandello's fascination with the new technology, see *Pirandello capocomico: La compagnia del teatro d'arte di Roma, 1925–1928,* ed. Alessandro Tinterri (Rome: Sellerio, 1987).

12   Pierre Leprohon, *Le cinéma italien* (1966; Paris: Éditions d'Aujourd'hui, 1978), 18.

13   Guido Aristarco, 'L'oltre del linguaggio cinematografico in Pirandello,' *Rivista di studi pirandelliani* V.3 (June 1985), 47. It may be relevant to remember here that the Marxist film critic and historian was the founder of one of Italy's most celebrated film journals, *Cinema Nuovo.* Aristarco was also responsible for the establishment of film studies as an academic sub-

ject by having it accepted in Italy's most prestigious learned society, the Accademia dei Lincei.

14 I used this definition in my Ph.D. dissertation *The Pirandellian Mode in European Cinema: Luigi Pirandello and Federico Fellini* (Indiana University, 1989), from which much of this discussion is taken. Two years later, Nino Genovese also used this particular expression in his article 'Quel ragno nero sul treppiedi. Analisi dei rapporti tra Pirandello e il cinema,' included in the first volume of *La musa inquietante*, 14.

15 Gaspare Giudice, *Luigi Pirandello* (1963; Turin: UTET, 1980).

16 New light is now being shed on Pirandello's life and career, and especially on his ever-conflicting attitude toward theatre. See, for instance, Alessandro D'Amico's on-going critical edition of Pirandello's collection of theatrical works, *Maschere nude* (*Naked Masks*) for the Mondadori in the series called *I Meridiani*, and Claudio Vicentini, *Pirandello. Il disagio del teatro* (Venice: Marsilio, 1993).

17 Giudice, *Luigi Pirandello*, 511.

18 I shall discuss this particular issue in detail in Chapter 2.

19 Jennifer Stone, 'Cinéastes' Texts,' *The Yearbook of the British Pirandello Society* 3 (1983), 45.

20 Giudice, *Luigi Pirandello*, 520.

21 For further discussion on this matter, see Chapter 1.

22 Giovanni Verga (1840–1922) was a Sicilian intellectual who promoted the literary movement called *verismo*, an Italian version of French naturalism, which pursued the representation of truth in art in the second half of the nineteenth century.

23 Genovese, 'Quel ragno nero sul treppiedi,' 14.

24 Before De Castris's work, the field of Pirandello studies had become quite obsolete, as a number of prejudices persisted due primarily to Pirandello's membership in the Fascist party. After the Second World War, it was hard for Italians to accept and recognize artists who displayed an 'ambiguous' attitude toward fascism. This led to the 'ostracism' of many intellectuals and artists. For a thorough discussion of this matter, see Gian Franco Vené, *Pirandello fascista. La coscienza borghese tra ribellione e rivoluzione* (1971; Venice: Marsilio, 1981), and Olga Ragusa, 'Pirandello's *Teatro d'Arte* and a New Look at His Fascism,' *Italica* LV.2 (1978), 236–53.

25 Arcangelo Leone De Castris, *Storia di Pirandello* (1962; Bari: Laterza, 1986), 127n20.

26 See Genovese, 'Quel ragno nero sul treppiedi,' 12.

27 See Genovese, 'Quel ragno nero sul treppiedi,' 15. I shall develop these concepts in Chapter 2 of the present study.

28 Two books recently published deserve special mention as well: Franca Angelini's *Serafino e la tigre. Pirandello tra scrittura teatro e cinema* (Venice: Marsilio, 1990), and Sergio Micheli's *Pirandello e il cinema. Da 'Acciaio' a 'Káos.'* (Rome: Bulzoni, 1989).

29 Maurizio Del Ministro, *Pirandello scena personaggio e film* (Rome: Bulzoni, 1980).

30 See Genovese, 'Quel ragno nero sul treppiedi,' 16.

31 See De Castris, *Storia di Pirandello*, 127n20.

32 This statement is also contained in note 20 of De Castris, *Storia di Pirandello*, 127.

33 See the anthology edited by Enzo Lauretta, *Pirandello e il cinema* (Agrigento: Centro Nazionale di Studi Pirandelliani, 1978), and Paolo Puppa, *Fantasmi contro giganti: scena e immaginario in Pirandello* (Bologna: Pàtron, 1978); Claudio Vicentini, *L'estetica di Pirandello* (Milan: Mursia, 1970), in particular, section V, with special attention to 'Cinema e teatro' (202–7) and 'Il cinematografo' (228–30). See also Jennifer Stone's insightful article 'Cinéastes' Textes,' and Gavriel Moses' many valuable essays on this subject, as well as several important works by de Castris, Tessari, Cudini, Aristarco, and others. See bibliography for a full account of the many publications on this subject.

34 See Tullio Kezich, 'Mattia Pascal: uno, due, tre,' in *Omaggio a Pirandello*, ed. Leonardo Sciascia (Milan: Bompiani, 1986), 80.

35 See, in particular, Del Ministro, *Scena, personaggio e film*.

36 See also Nino Genovese and Maurizio Del Ministro, in Genovese and Gesù's *La musa inquietante di Pirandello: Il cinema*.

CHAPTER 1   He Lost It at the Movies: A Love-Hate Relationship of Over Thirty Years

1 Pierre Leprohon, *Le cinéma italien* (Paris: Éditions Séghers, 1966), 7.

2 Leprohon, *Le cinéma italien*, 7.

3 For a comprehensive account of the early days of Italian cinema, see Gian Piero Brunetta, *Storia del cinema italiano 1895–1945* (Rome: Editori Riuniti, 1979); Pierre Leprohon, *Le cinéma Italien* (1966); Vernon Jarrat, *The Italian Cinema* (London: Falcon Press, 1951); Aldo Bernardini, *Cinema muto italiano*, 3 vols (Rome-Bari: Laterza, 1980–2); and Peter Bondanella, *Italian Cinema: From Neorealism to the Present* (New York: Frederick Ungar, 1984), 1–30. For the early days of the movies, see Georges Sadoul, *Storia generale del cinema. Le origini (1909–1920)*, vols I–II (Turin: Einaudi, 1975).

4   Leprohon, *Le cinéma italien*, 229.
5   I have already mentioned the fact that he conceived a novel on the film world as early as 1903.
6   For a full account of Pirandello's theatrical journey, see Luigi Pirandello, *Maschere nude*, ed. Alessandro D'Amico (Milan: Mondadori, 1994). See also Claudio Vicentini's most recent study of Pirandello's theatre, *Pirandello. Il disagio del teatro* (Venice: Marsilio, 1993).
7   The play was written in 1892 and published with the title *L'epilogo* in the journal *Ariel* on 20 March 1898. It was never staged until the performance at Martoglio's company Teatro Minimo at the Teatro Metastasio in Rome on 9 December 1910.
8   Several works have aided me in the compilation of this section on Pirandello's 'love–hate' relationship with the cinema. Among them, special mention goes to Gaspare Giudice's biography, but also Francesco Càllari's many essays on the subject, especially his most recent book *Pirandello e il cinema*. Also indispensable have been the two volumes by Nino Genovese and Sebastiano Gesù, op. cit.
9   Ippolito Nievo was one of the most notable representatives of those Italian writers who came of age during the Risorgimento, the movement that led to the unification of Italy in the nineteenth century. His novel *Le Confessioni di un Italiano* was written in 1858 and published posthumously with the title *Le Confessioni di un ottuagenario*.
10 Lucio D'Ambra refers to this in his article 'Sette anni di cinema,' which appeared in *Cinema* 14 (25 January 1937). On this matter, see Càllari, *Pirandello e il cinema*, 25, and the chronology by D'Amico in *Maschere nude* (1994), xliii.
11 This letter and the following were published in *Cinema* (25 December 1936).
12 It was originally a short story that appeared in the review *Marzocco* in 1904.
13 From a letter published in the journal *Cinema* on 25 December 1936, a few days after Pirandello's death on 10 December.
14 Enrico Roma, 'Pirandello e il cinema,' *Comoedia* (15 July–15 August 1932), 20.
15 For information about this period, see Lucio D'Ambra, 'Sette anni di cinema,' *Cinema* (25 January 1937), and Arnaldo Frateili, 'Pirandello e il cinema,' *Cinema* (25 December 1936).
16 Orio Vergani, 'Ritratto di Pirandello,' *Rivista d'Italia* (28 February 1919).
17 Roma, 'Pirandello e il cinema,' 20.
18 Roma, 'Pirandello e il cinema,' 20.

19   Franca Angelini, 'Si gira ...: L'ideologia della macchina in Pirandello,' in *Il romanzo di Pirandello*, ed. Enzo Lauretta (Palermo: Palumbo, 1976), 150.

20   The letter written by Pirandello was published by Mario Verdone in *Anton Giulio Bragaglia* (Rome: Bulzoni, 1965), 11. We have proof of two projected film adaptations of Pirandello's *Six Characters in Search of an Author* by two directors of the French *nouvelle vague*. In 1961 Jean-Luc Godard planned to cast Anna Magnani, the unforgettable female lead in Roberto Rossellini's *Roma, città aperta* (*Rome Open City*, 1945), in the role of the Mother. The second project came a year later from François Truffaut. See Càllari, op. cit., 73.

21   Although written in 1899, the play was based on a dramatic text written in 1895 and entitled *Il nido*. The title was eventually changed to *Il nibbio* in 1896 and then to *La ragione degli altri* in 1921.

22   For a long time scholars believed that Pirandello scripted nine silent films. An important correction has recently come from Francesco Càllari who, in his *Pirandello e il cinema*, states that 'quelle mute che sono otto e non nove, come alcuni tuttavia ritengono, essendo *Il crollo* e *Lumíe di Sicilia* due titoli del medesimo film di Mario Gargiulo' (31) ('the silent films are eight and not nine, as some nevertheless maintain, since *The Downfall* and *Lights in Sicily* are two titles for the same film directed by Mario Gargiulo').

23   As Sebastiano Gesù informs us, the film has been almost 'miraculously' found at the Gosfilmofond, the main film library in the former Soviet Union. The movie was screened for the first time at the 1989 edition of the Giornate del cinema muto in Pordenone, Italy, within a restrospective of Augusto Genina's work. A copy of the film is now available at the Museo nazionale del cinema in Turin. For further details, see Sebastiano Gesù, '*Lo scaldino* di A. Genina: Un prezioso ritrovamento,' in *La musa inquietante di Pirandello: Il cinema*, ed. N. Genovese and S. Gesù, I, 437–41.

24   Pirandello is probably referring to the unrealized Paramount film project for *Henry IV*; it was never made because the author refused to accept the producers' request to turn the dénouement of the original into a typical Hollywood happy ending by having Henry IV marry Matilde Spina.

25   Reprinted in Georges Sadoul, *Storia generale del cinema: l'arte muta (1919–1929). I. Il dopoguerra in Europa* (Turin: Einaudi, 1978), 83. Italics are mine.

26   Both quotes are taken from Jennifer Stone, 'Cineastes' Texts,' *The Yearbook of the British Pirandello Society* 3 (1983), 46.

27   Nöel Burch, *Marcel L'Herbier* (Paris: Seghers, 1973), 91.

28   Published in Berlin by Reimar Hobbing in 1930.

29   For further information about this film project, including the scenario itself, see 'Pirandello's Film Project for *La nuova colonia*,' ed. Giovanni

Bussino and Antonio Illiano, *Canadian Journal of Italian Studies* 6(22–3) (1983), 111–30. For a discussion of Pirandello's long venture into a film adaptation of *Six Characters in Search of an Author* and for a comprehensive remapping of the various film projects based on his most famous play, see Càllari, *Pirandello e il cinema*, 34–74.

30   With 'the new Cines studios' Pirandello refers to the fact that Stefano Pittaluga had just moved into the facilities of the old Cines, which closed down at the outset of World War I. *Love Song* was the first film Pittaluga made in that studio, which Pirandello continued to refer to as Cines, although that name was not officially used for it again until 1949.

31   Roma, 'Pirandello e il cinema,' 21.

32   Giulio Caprin, 'Colloqui con Pirandello,' *La lettura*, 27(3) (1 March 1927), 161–8.

33   Giudice, *Luigi Pirandello*, 518.

34   Roma, 'Pirandello e il cinema,' 22.

35   Roma, 'Pirandello e il cinema,' 22.

36   Roma, 'Pirandello e il cinema,' 22.

37   For information about Walter Ruttmann's career within the general history of German cinema, see Sigfried Kracauer, *Cinema tedesco: dal 'Gabinetto del Dottor Caligari' a Hitler* (1954; Milan: Mondadori, 1977).

38   Kracauer, *Cinema tedesco*, 192.

39   Interview appeared in *L'Italia letteraria* (27 October 1935).

40   Giudice, *Luigi Pirandello*, 519.

41   Corrado Alvaro, 'Pirandello e gli sceneggiatori,' in *Cinema* (10 November 1938).

42   Giudice, *Luigi Pirandello*, 519–20.

43   For more information on both film versions of *The Late Mattia Pascal*, see Osvaldo Campassi and Virgilio Sabel, 'Chenal, L'Herbier e *Il fu Mattia Pascal*,' in *Cinema* 117 (10 May 1941).

44   Giuseppe Petronio, 'Pirandello e il cinema,' in Enzo Lauretta, ed., *Pirandello e il cinema*, 31–50.

45   For a comprehensive list of the film adaptations of Pirandello's works, see Francesco Càllari, 'Films Based On Works by Pirandello,' *The Yearbook of the British Pirandello Society* 6 (1986), 65–76. See also Càllari's most recent volume, *Pirandello e il cinema* as well as Genovese and Gesù's two volumes on the general subject.

CHAPTER 2   Pirandello and the Theory of the Cinema

1   The neologism 'theatrality' is used here instead of the usual term 'theatri-

cality' for several reasons. 'Theatrality' is directly borrowed from Jean Alter's article 'From Text to Performance: Semiotics of Theatrality,' *Poetics Today* 2(3) (1981), 113–39. As Alter maintains, the concept of 'theatricality' is relatively new and not uniformly defined, and within its linguistic and conceptual confusion, it already has undesirable connotations that 'theatrality' helps to avoid. The neologism has been inspired in Alter by the French word 'théâtralité' (translated in Italian as 'teatralità'), which, in modern critical practice, antedates 'theatricality' and has gained widespread acceptance. With the neologism 'theatrality,' Alter refers to total theatre, that is, a system composed of two categories of signs, corresponding to its two pragmatic media of expression: text and performance. I maintain that Pirandello's conception of theatre as a total artistic experience accounted for both of these two media.

2 Luigi Pirandello, 'Per il film italiano. Intervista con Pirandello,' ed. Testor, *La stampa* (9 December 1932).

3 Luigi Pirandello, 'Se il film parlante abolirà il teatro,' *Saggi, poesie scritti varii* (Milan: Mondadori, 1960), 996.

4 Pirandello, 'Se il film parlante abolirà il teatro,' *Saggi, poesie scritti varii*, 996.

5 Pirandello, *L'umorismo*, in *Saggi, poesie scritti varii*, 17–160.

6 That is, the set of elements that form cinema's *specific* language, later to be defined as the 'cinematic apparatus.'

7 Emilio Garroni, *Semiotica ed estetica* (Bari: Laterza, 1968). In particular, see the chapter titled 'L'eterogeneità del linguaggio e il linguaggio cinematografico.'

8 Christian Metz, *Langage et cinéma* (Paris: Librairie Larousse, 1971). The Italian version bears the title *Linguaggio e cinema*, trans. Alberto Farassino (Milan: Bompiani, 1977).

9 See Franco Ferrini in his introduction to Christian Metz, *Semiologia del cinema* (Milan: Garzanti, 1980), 15. The original French is entitled *Essais sur la signification au cinéma*, 2 vols. (Paris: Éditions Klincksieck, 1971).

10 Luigi Pirandello, *Quaderni di Serafino Gubbio operatore*, in *Tutti i romanzi* (Milan: Mondadori, 1984) II, 519.

11 Pirandello, *The Notebooks of Serafino Gubbio or (Shoot!)*, trans. C.K. Scott Moncrieff (Langford Lodge: Dedalus, 1990), 3–4.

12 Franca Angelini, '*Si gira* ...: L'ideologia della macchina in Pirandello,' in *Il romanzo di Pirandello*, ed. Enzo Lauretta (Palermo: Palumbo, 1976), 143. See also Franca Angelini, *Serafino e la tigre. Pirandello tra scrittura teatro e cinema* (Venice: Marsilio, 1990); Giancarlo Mazzacurati, *Pirandello nel romanzo europeo* (Bologna: Il Mulino, 1987); and Giacomo Debenedetti, *Il romanzo del novecento* (1971; Milan: Garzanti, 1987), 256–80.

13   Pirandello, *Quaderni di Serafino Gubbio operatore*, in *Tutti i romanzi*, II, 521.
14   Pirandello, *The Notebooks of Serafino Gubbio*, 6.
15   Pirandello, *Quaderni di Serafino Gubbio operatore*, in *Tutti i romanzi*, II, 523.
16   Pirandello, *The Notebooks of Serafino Gubbio*, 8.
17   Angelini, *'Si gira ...*: L'ideologia della macchina in Pirandello,' 143.
18   Frank Allen Nulf, 'Luigi Pirandello and the Cinema: A Study of His Relationship to Motion Pictures and the Significance of That Relationship to
Selected Examples of His Prose and Drama,' diss., Ohio University, 1969,
98.
19   Nulf, 'Luigi Pirandello and the Cinema,' 99.
20   My analysis of cinematic structure of *Shoot!* is thoroughly indebted to
Frank Nulf's 'pioneering' study.
21   Pirandello, *Quaderni di Serafino Gubbio operatore*, in *Tutti i romanzi*, II, 565.
22   Pirandello, *The Notebooks of Serafino Gubbio*, 73.
23   Pirandello, *Quaderni di Serafino Gubbio operatore*, in *Tutti i romanzi*, II, 566.
24   Pirandello, *The Notebooks of Serafino Gubbio*, 77.
25   Nulf, 'Luigi Pirandello and the Cinema,' 101.
26   Walter Benjamin, *Das Kunstwerk im Zeitalter seiner technischen Reproduzierbarkeit*, in *Illuminationen: Ausgewählte Schriften* (Frankfurt: Suhrkamp Verlag, 1961), 169. The essay was first published in *Schriften* (Frankfurt:
Suhrkamp Verlag, 1955).
27   Walter Benjamin, *The Work of Art in the Age of Mechanical Reproduction* in *Illuminations*, ed. Hannah Arendt, trans. Harry Zohn (New York: Harcourt,
Brace & World, Inc., 1968), 237. For the Italian translation, see *L'opera d'arte
nell'epoca della sua riproducibilità tecnica*, trans. Enrico Filippini (Turin: Einaudi, 1966), 40.
28   Benjamin, *Das Kunstwerk*, 169–70.
29   Benjamin, *The Work of Art*, 238; for the Italian translation, see *L'opera d'arte
nell'epoca della sua riproducibilità tecnica*, 41.
30   Benjamin, *Das Kunstwerk*, 170.
31   Benjamin, *The Work of Art*, 238; for the Italian translation, see *L'opera d'arte*,
41.
32   Benjamin, *Das Kunstwerk*, 170.
33   Benjamin, *The Work of Art*, 239; for the Italian translation, see *L'opera d'arte*,
43.
34   As for the importance Eisenstein granted to Dickens' narrative technique,
see Sergei M. Eisenstein, 'Dickens, Griffith, and the Film Today,' *Film
Form: Essays in Film Theory*, trans. Jay Leyda (New York: Harcourt, Brace
Jovanovich & World, 1949) 195–255. The Italian version bears the title
'Dickens, Griffith e noi' and is published in *Forma e tecnica del film e lezioni
di regia* (Turin: Einaudi, 1964), 172–237.

35 George Bluestone, *Novels into Film* (Berkeley and Los Angeles: University of California Press, 1957), 24.

36 Bluestone, *Novels into Film*, 25.

37 Béla Balázs, *Theory of the Film* (London: Dobson, 1952), 118.

38 Eisenstein, *The Film Sense* (New York: Meridian Books, 1957), 4.

39 Eisenstein, *The Film Sense*, 7–8.

40 Pirandello, 'Foglietti editi da Corrado Alvaro,' *Saggi, poesie scritti varii*, 1218.

41 Pirandello, 'Foglietti editi da Corrado Alvaro,' 1219.

42 Luigi Pirandello, 'Discorso al Convegno Volta sul teatro drammatico (Roma, 8–14 ottobre 1934),' *Saggi, poesie scritti varii*, 1005–6.

43 Metz, *Essais sur la signification au cinéma*, I, 13; for the Italian translation, see *Semiologia del cinema*, 31.

44 Angelini, '*Si gira* ...: L'ideologia della macchina in Pirandello,' 150.

45 Angelini, '*Si gira* ...: L'ideologia della macchina in Pirandello,' 151.

46 Mario Verdone, *Anton Giulio Bragaglia* (Rome: Bulzoni, 1965), 11.

47 Here my discussion of the two theory types is thoroughly indebted to Brian Henderson, 'Two Types of Film Theory,' in *Movies and Methods: An Anthology*, ed. Bill Nichols (Berkeley: University of California Press, 1976), 388–400.

48 The essay was first published in the newspaper *Corriere della sera*, Milan, 16 June 1929. On 28 July 1929, it appeared as a feature article in *The New York Times*. It is included in the volume edited by Manlio Lo Vecchio-Musti, *Saggi, poesie scritti varii*, 996–1002.

49 Translated into Italian and published under the title 'Dramma e sonoro,' with an introduction by Renato Giani, in *Cinema* 17 (10 November 1939), 277–8.

50 As the text demonstrates, Pirandello was aware of the strong ideological nature of the cinematic discourse, which eventually makes one of the most powerful mythmakers of modern society.

51 Italics are mine.

52 Roma, 'Pirandello e il cinema,' 21–2.

53 Pirandello, 'Dramma e sonoro,' 277–8.

54 Giovanni Bussino and Antonio Illiano, eds, 'Pirandello: Progetti filmici sui *Sei personaggi*,' *Forum Italicum* 16 (1982), 119.

55 Pirandello, 'Se il film parlante abolirà il teatro,' *Saggi, poesie scritti varii*, 1002.

56 Pirandello, 'Se il film parlante abolirà il teatro,' 1002.

57 Christian Metz, *The Imaginary Signifier: Psychoanalysis and the Cinema*, trans. Celia Britton, Annwyl Williams, Ben Brewster and Alfred Guzzetti (Bloomington: Indiana University Press, 1982), 139.

58   Metz, *Essais sur la signication au cinéma*, I, 97; in *Semiologia del cinema*, 143.

59   Nulf, 'Luigi Pirandello and the Cinema,' 43.

60   Nulf, 'Luigi Pirandello and the Cinema,' 43.

61   Pirandello, 'Se il cinema parlante abolirà il teatro,' *Saggi, poesie scritti varii*, 1001.

62   Sergei Eisenstein, in *The New York Sun* (5 June 1930).

63   Pirandello, 'Per il film italiano. Intervista con Pirandello,' *La stampa* (9 December 1932).

64   Béla Balázs, *Theory of the Film*, 41.

65   Herbert Read, 'Towards a Film Aesthetic,' *Cinema Quarterly* 1(1)(Autumn 1932), 8.

66   For Bergman's ideas concerning the affinities between film and music, see the introduction to Ingmar Bergman, *Four Screenplays of Ingmar Bergman* (New York: Simon and Schuster, 1960), and 'My Need to Express Myself in a Film,' an Interview with Bergman by Edwin Newman in *Film Comment* 4(2–3) (Fall/Winter, 1967), 58–62.

67   René Clair, *Reflections on the Cinema*, trans. Vera Traill (London: Kinber, 1953), 96.

68   Pirandello, 'Se il film parlante abolirà il teatro,' in *Saggi, poesie scritti varii*, 1000.

69   Pirandello, *Quaderni di Serafino Gubbio operatore*, in *Tutti i romanzi*, II, 585–6. Here Pirandello takes a position in favour of theatre, which was discussed, for instance, by Umberto Artioli in *L'officina segreta di Pirandello* (Rome-Bari: Laterza, 1989).

70   Pirandello, *The Notebooks of Serafino Gubbio or (Shoot!)*, trans. C.K. Scott Moncrieff (Lagford Lodge: Dedalus, 1990), 105–7.

71   Benjamin, *Das Kunstwerk*, 151.

72   Benjamin, *The Work of Art*, 222; for the Italian translation, see *L'opera d'arte*, 22.

73   Benjamin, *Das Kunstwerk*, 152.

74   Benjamin, *The Work of Art*, 223; *L'opera d'arte*, 23.

75   Benjamin, *Das Kunstwerk*, 161.

76   Benjamin, *The Work of Art*, 231; *L'opera d'arte*, 32.

77   Paolo Puppa, *Fantasmi contro giganti. Scena e immaginario in Pirandello* (Bologna: Pàtron, 1978), 223.

78   Benjamin, *Das Kunstwerk*, 163.

79   Benjamin, *The Work of Art*, 232; *L'opera d'arte*, 34.

80   For the theme/strategy of the mirror, see Corrado Donati, *La solitudine allo specchio* (Rome: Lucarini, 1980).

81   Peter Szondi's *Theorie des modernen Dramas* first appeared in 1956, and was revised in 1959. Here I shall refer to the 1974 edition by Suhrkamp Verlag.

The text was translated into English quite late, and was published by the University of Minnesota Press in 1987. The Italian edition was published by Einaudi in 1976.

82 Szondi, *Theorie des modernen Dramas*, 98.

83 Szondi, *Theory of Modern Drama*, ed. and trans. Michael Hays (Cambridge: Polity Press, 1987), 59.

84 Szondi, *Theorie des modernen Dramas*, 61–2, 66; in the English edition, 34–5, 37–8.

85 These and other concepts are investigated throughout Szondi's work. For a critical synopsis of this seminal study on modern drama, see Cesare Cases' preface to the Italian edition (1976).

86 Szondi, *Theorie des modernen Dramas*, 13. Szondi here borrows the expression 'subject of the epic form' from György Lukács, *Die Theorie des Romans* (1920) and the term 'epic I' from Robert Petsch, *Wesen und Formen der Erzählkunst* (1934).

87 Szondi, *Theory of the Modern Drama*, 6.

88 Wladimir Krysinski, *Le paradigme inquiet. Pirandello et le champ de la modernité* (Montréal: Le Préambule, 1989), 55.

89 Krysinski, *Le paradigme inquiet*, 55.

90 Krysinski, *Le paradigme inquiet*, 55.

91 Of particular interest to a study of the relationship between Pirandello, Brecht, and Artaud is Roger Copeland, 'Brecht, Artaud and the Hole in the Paper Sky,' *Theater* 9(3) (Summer 1978), 42–9.

92 Several scholars have discussed the relationship between Luigi Pirandello and Bertolt Brecht. I will here only mention some of the most interesting contributions: Paolo Chiarini, 'Brecht e Pirandello,' *Atti del congresso internazionale di studi pirandelliani. Venezia 2–5 ottobre 1961* (Venice: Marsilio, 1967); Paolo Valesio, 'Del classico Bertolt Brecht' (28–43) and Luigi Gozzi, 'Dall'ideologico al popolare' (3–20), *Verri* V.4 (August 1961); Silvio Gaggi, 'Brecht, Pirandello and Two Traditions of Self-Critical Art,' *Theatre Quarterly* 8 (Winter 1979), 42–6; and André Bouissy, 'Pirandello et le théâtre de son temps – Notes de lectures,' *Lectures Pirandelliennes* (Abbeville: F. Paillart, 1978), 253–69. Particularly valuable for my discussion have been Wladimir Krysinski's latest work on Pirandello, *Le paradigme inquiet* as well as some of the essays included in *Pirandello e il teatro*, ed. Enzo Lauretta (Palermo: Palumbo, 1985).

93 Mention of these authors is made in Pirandello's well-known essay on humour, *L'umorismo*, in *Saggi, poesie, scritti varii* (1960), 15–160.

94 André Bouissy, 'Pirandello et le théâtre de son temps,' 267.

95 For a comprehensive account of Pirandello's fortune in Germany, see

Michele Cometa, *Il teatro di Pirandello in Germania* (Palermo: Novecento, 1986).

96 Benjamin, *Das Kunstwerk*, 162.

97 Benjamin, *The Work of Art*, 231.

98 Pirandello, *Sei personaggi in cerca d'autore*, in *Maschere nude* (1958; Milan: Mondadori, 1978) I, 65.

99 Pirandello, *Six Characters in Search of an Author* in *Naked Masks*, ed. Eric Bentley (New York: E.P. Dutton, 1969), 224.

100 Pirandello, *Sei personaggi* in *Maschere nude*, I, 72.

101 Pirandello, *Six Characters* in *Naked Masks*, 231.

102 For a discussion of Pirandello's definition of new and subversive strategies in narrative and in society, see my article 'From Pascal to Moscarda: Pirandello's Narrative within and beyond Modernism,' in *Forum Italicum* 22(2) (Fall 1988), 176–86.

103 On this subject, see Luigi Gozzi, 'Dall'ideologico al popolare,' and Silvio Gaggi, 'Brecht, Pirandello and Two Traditions of Self-Critical Art.'

104 On the development of political theatre, see Massimo Castri, *Per un teatro politico Piscator Brecht Artaud* (Turin: Einaudi, 1973) and Martin Esslin, *Brecht, a Choice of Evils: A Critical Study of the Man, His Work and His Opinions* (1953; London: Eyre Methuen, 1980).

105 Giorgio Barberi Squarotti, 'La trilogia pirandelliana e il rinnovamento del teatro,' in *Pirandello e il teatro*, ed. Enzo Lauretta (Palermo: Palumbo, 1985), 69.

106 Barberi Squarotti, 'La trilogia pirandelliana,' 72.

107 In particular, see the second version of Walter Benjamin's famous essay 'Was ist das epische Theater?' included in the volume *Versuche über Brecht* (Frankfurt am Main: Suhrkamp Verlag, 1966), 22–30. In English, see 'What Is Epic Theater?' in *Understanding Brecht* (London: Verso, 1983), 15–22.

108 See Jennifer Stone, *Pirandello's Naked Prompt. The Structure of Repetition in Modernism* (Ravenna: Longo, 1989).

109 Important in this respect would be an analysis of Pirandello's *Sei personaggi in cerca d'autore*. See Stone, *Pirandello's Naked Prompt*.

110 Romano Luperini, *L'allegoria del moderno. Saggi sull'allegorismo come forma artistica del moderno e come metodo di conoscenza* (Rome: Editori Riuniti, 1990), 221–58.

111 Pirandello, *I giganti della montagna*, in *Maschere nude*, II, 1337.

112 John Willett, *Brecht in Context: Comparative Approaches* (London and New York: Methuen, 1984), 219.

113 The essay was written in 1937, and published for the first time in the weekly journal *Sontag* in January 1954. It was later included in Brecht's fa-

mous *Schriften zum Theater 1937–1951*, which first appeared in 1957 and was reprinted in 1963 by Suhrkamp Verlag (Vol. 5, 166–82). In English, the essay is included in *Brecht on Theater. The Development of an Aesthetic*, ed. and trans. John Willett (London: Methuen, 1964), 91–9. In French, the essay was translated as 'Effets de distanciation dans l'art dramatique chinois,' and is included in Bertolt Brecht, *Écrits sur le théâtre*, vol. I , trans. Jean Tailleur et al. (1963; Paris: L'Arche Éditeur, 1972), 590–601.

114   Willett, *Brecht in Context*, 220.
115   Willett, *Brecht in Context*, 220.
116   See Lucio Lugnani's masterful study 'Teatro dello straniamento ed estraniazione dal teatro in *Questa sera si recita a soggetto*,' in *Pirandello e il teatro*, ed. Enzo Lauretta (Palermo: Palumbo, 1985), 309–70.
117   Cometa, *Il teatro di Pirandello in Germania*, 56.
118   That is, the world of the characters.
119   That is, the world of author, director, actors, and spectators.
120   Lugnani, 'Teatro dello straniamento,' 328.
121   On Brecht's revolutionary dramaturgy, see Claudio Meldolesi and Laura Olivi, *Brecht regista. Memorie del Berliner Ensemble* (Bologna: Il Mulino, 1989).
122   Krysinski, *Le paradigme inquiet*, 55.
123   Mikhail Bakhtin, *Problems in Dostoevsky's Poetics* (1984; Minneapolis: University of Minnesota Press, 1985).
124   Umberto Eco, 'The Frames of Comic Freedom' in U. Eco, V.V. Ivanov and M. Rector, *Carnival* (New York: Mouton Publishers, 1984), 8. In this essay, Eco defines the constitutive elements of Pirandello's concept of humour, outlining the differences between the modalities of comedy, tragedy, and humour.
125   Charles Baudelaire, *De l'essence du rire et généralement du comique dans les arts plastiques*, in *Oeuvres complètes de Baudelaire* (Paris: Gallimard, 1951), 702–20.
126   Baudelaire, *De l'essence du rire*, 708.
127   Baudelaire, *De l'essence du rire*, 709.
128   Baudelaire, *De l'essence du rire*, 709.
129   Baudelaire, *De l'essence du rire*, 709.
130   On the Pirandellian humorist as *raisonneur*, see Paolo Puppa's numerous studies of Pirandello's narrative and dramatic writings, two of which are relevant here: *Fantasmi contro giganti* and *Dalle parti di Pirandello*.
131   Baudelaire, *De l'essence du rire*, 710.
132   Pirandello, *L'umorismo*, in *Saggi, poesie scritti varii*, 127.
133   Baudelaire, *De l'essence du rire*, 712.

134 Baudelaire, *De l'essence du rire*, 720.
135 Baudelaire, *De l'essence du rire*, 720.
136 Umberto Artioli, *Teatro e corpo glorioso. Saggio su Antonin Artaud* (Milan: Feltrinelli, 1978), 85n51.
137 See the above-mentioned essay by Lucio Lugnani, 'Teatro dello straniamento ed estraniazione dal teatro in *Questa sera si recita a soggetto*,' in Lauretta, *Pirandello e il teatro* (1985), 309–70.
138 On the loss of the *aura*, see Walter Benjamin, *The Work of Art in the Age of Mechanical Reproduction*, in *Illuminations* (1968).
139 Jürgen Habermas, *Etica del discorso* (Rome-Bari: Laterza, 1985), 17. See also his *Il discorso filosofico della modernità* (Rome-Bari: Laterza, 1987).
140 On this matter, Romano Luperini's long essay on Pirandello included in his volume *L'allegoria del moderno* (1990), 221–58, is illuminating. See also, by the same author, 'L'atto del significare allegorico in *Sei personaggi* e in *Enrico IV*,' in *Rivista di studi pirandelliani* 3(6/7) (June-December 1991), 9–19, and *Introduzione a Pirandello* (Rome-Bari: Laterza, 1992).
141 Walter Benjamin, *Angelus Novus. Saggi e frammenti* (Turin: Einaudi, 1976), 85–154.
142 See Luperini, *L'allegoria del moderno.*
143 Baudelaire, *De l'essence du rire*, 720.
144 For example, see Gavriel Moses, 'Film Theory as Literary Genre in Pirandello and the Film-Novel,' *Annali d'Italianistica* 6 (1988), 38–65.
145 Pietro Ferrua, 'Incontri di Pirandello col cinema,' *Canadian Journal of Italian Studies* 3 (1979), 108–13.
146 René Jeanne, 'Cinq minutes avec Pirandello,' *Les Nouvelles Littéraires* (15 November 1924), 8.
147 Jeanne, 'Cinq minutes avec Pirandello,' 8.
148 Jeanne, 'Cinq minutes avec Pirandello,' 8.
149 Jeanne, 'Cinq minutes avec Pirandello,' 8. Italics are mine.
150 Alexandre Astruc, 'The Birth of a New Avant-Garde: La Caméra-Stylo,' in *The New Wave*, ed. Peter Graham (London: Secker and Warburg; New York: Doubleday Cinema One Series, 1968). Trans. from *Écran Français* 144 (30 March 1948).
151 Astruc, 'The Birth of a New Avant-Garde.'
152 Roma, 'Pirandello e il cinema,' 22.
153 Federico Fellini, *Fare un film* (Turin: Einaudi, 1980), 42.

CHAPTER 3   The Origins of the Myths: From Pirandello to Fellini

  1 Italics are mine. In the same section of this long interview, Fellini also lists

his many likings, which include Matisse, the Marx Brothers, 'waiting for dates and hoping that the other person won't come (even if it's a beautiful woman)' (151), Totó, 'not having been there' (151), Homer, Ariosto, Raymond Chandler, Simenon, Dickens, Kafka, and Jack London; empty places, deserted restaurants, squalor, empty churches, silence; Bologna, Venice, all of Italy, and Vienna, even though he has never been there; vaudeville before a film, Laurel and Hardy, soubrettes, and ballerinas.

2   Federico Fellini, *Comments on Film*, ed. Giovanni Grazzini, trans. Joseph Henry (Fresno, CA: The Press at California State University, 1988), 151.

3   Federico Fellini, *Fellini on Fellini*, ed. Anna Keel and Christian Strich, trans. Isabel Quigly (London: Eyre Methuen, 1976), 49.

4   Cited in Suzanne Budgen, *Fellini* (London: British Film Institute, 1966), 92.

5   Peter Bondanella, *The Cinema of Federico Fellini* (Princeton, NJ: Princeton University Press, 1992), xix.

6   The so-called 'comedy Italian style' is discussed in Chapter 5 of this volume.

7   Pietro Pintus, 'Ombre e luci di un paese che cambia,' in *Commedia all'italiana. Angolazioni e controcampi*, ed. Riccardo Napolitano (Rome: Gangemi Editore, 1986), 18.

8   Roberto Campari, 'Commedia italiana e commedia americana,' in *Commedia all'italiana*, ed. Napolitano, 30.

9   Franco La Polla, 'Non é piú tempo d'eroi, ovvero: su alcuni limiti della macchina da presa, oggi,' *Cinema e cinema* 10(37) (1983), 48.

10   Maurizio Casadei, *Ipotesi sul cinema* (Bologna: Patron, 1978), 84.

11   Mikhail Bakhtin, *Problems of Dostoevsky's Poetics* (1984; Minneapolis: University of Minnesota Press, 1985).

12   Umberto Eco, 'The Frames of Comic *Freedom*,' in Umberto Eco, V.V. Ivanov, and Monica Ractor, *Carnival* (New York: Mouton Publishers, 1984).

13   Eco, 'The Frames of Comic *Freedom*,' 6.

14   Eco, 'The Frames of Comic *Freedom*,' 7.

15   Eco, 'The Frames of Comic *Freedom*,' 8.

16   Bondanella, *The Cinema of Federico Fellini*, 26.

17   Fellini's wife, and the unforgettable female lead in some of his best films such as *La strada* (*La Strada*, 1954), *Le notti di Cabiria* (*The Nights of Cabiria*, 1957), and *Giulietta degli spiriti* (*Juliet of the Spirits*, 1965).

18   Others have remarked on the 'Pirandello–Fellini connection'; see Tullio Kezich's biography of Fellini, *Fellini* (Milan: Camunia, 1987) and Bernardino Zapponi as cited in Françoise Pieri, 'Federico Fellini écrivain du *Marc'Aurelio*,' *Positif* 244–5 (1981), 20–32. In this study of Fellini's sto-

ries written for the famous Roman satirical journal, Zapponi emphasizes the similarities between the *Piccoli fidanzati* cycle (*Little Fiancés*, six tales written between 29 March 1941 and 1 July 1942) and an early short story that Pirandello eventually turned into a play, *Lumíe di Sicilia (Limes of Sicily)*, which was first staged by Nino Martoglio at the Teatro Metastasio in Rome on 9 December 1910.

19 Bakhtin, *Problems of Dostoevsky's Poetics*, 122–37. The similarities between Pirandello's interpretation of 'umorismo' and Bakhtin's definition of 'carnivalization' have been analysed in Elio Gioanola's introductory chapter to his volume *Pirandello la follia* (Genova: Il Melangolo, 1983), 7–37.

20 Giovanni Macchia, *Pirandello o la stanza della tortura* (1981; Milan: Mondadori, 1986), 66.

21 I shall use the neologism 'de-centredness' in opposition and in relation to 'centredness.' To explain the meaning of the neologism is one of the primary tasks of this section of my work.

22 Federico Fellini, *Fellini on Fellini*, ed. Anna Keel and Christian Strich, trans. Isabel Quigly (London: Eyre Methuen, 1976), 154.

23 As to the question of Fellini's being a provincial artist, see Barthélelemy Amengual, 'Fin d'itinéraire: du "côté de Lumière" au "côté de Méliès,"' *Études cinématographiques* 127–30 (1981), 93.

24 Macchia, *Pirandello o la stanza della tortura*, 21.

25 Luigi Pirandello, 'La tragedia di un personaggio,' *Novelle per un anno*, 2 vols (1956; Milan: Mondadori, 1986) I, 713–19.

26 Macchia, *Pirandello o la stanza della tortura*, 29.

27 Federico Fellini, *Fare un film* (Turin: Einaudi, 1980), 9.

28 For more information about the role that Rimini played in Fellini's life and artistic career, see Federico Fellini, *La mia Rimini* (Bologna: Cappelli, 1967); see also, Tullio Kezich, *Fellini* (1987), especially the first chapter, 'Tema della famiglia e della fuga,' 15–36.

29 Fellini, *Fare un film*, 19; italics are mine.

30 Peter Bondanella, 'Early Fellini: Variety Lights, The White Sheik, The Vitelloni,' in *Federico Fellini: Essays in Criticism*, ed. Peter Bondanella (New York: Oxford University Press, 1978), 231–2; the essay on *The White Sheik* has been reprinted with modifications in Peter Bondanella, *Italian Cinema: From Neorealism to the Present* (New York: Frederick Ungar, 1984), 118–24.

31 It is interesting to note that according to Pirandello the dualistic nature of art happens to be one of the most important characteristics of a work of art.

32 In Italy, the 'trattoria' is a family-run restaurant characterized by simple menus and low prices.

33 The novel was written in the summer of 1893 and titled *Marta Ajala*. It was then published in 1901 with the new title.

34 Fellini, *Fare un film*, 11.

35 Fellini is here referring to his childhood, of course. In Italy, children were taught to write by drawing pot-hooks first and then the letters of the alphabet; boys were given little toy soldiers to play with.

36 Federico Fellini, *E la nave va*, screenplay by Federico Fellini and Tonino Guerra, ed. Gianfranco Angelucci (Milan: Longanesi, 1983), 170.

37 Fellini, *Fellini on Fellini*, 6.

38 Luigi Pirandello, *Il fu Mattia Pascal* in *Tutti i romanzi*, ed. Giovanni Macchia, 2 vols. (Milan: Mondadori, 1984) I, 444–5.

39 Pirandello, *Il fu Mattia Pascal* in *Tutti i romanzi*, I, 429.

40 Pirandello, *The Late Mattia Pascal*, trans. William Weaver (New York: Anchor Books, 1966), 108.

41 Pirandello, *Quaderni di Serafino Gubbio operatore* in *Tutti i romanzi*, II, 522.

42 Pirandello, *The Notebooks of Serafino Gubbio or (Shoot!)*, 8.

43 As to the existence of a long tradition of discourse on Rome's symbolic history in political and/or ethical terms as well as in art, see Peter Bondanella, *The Eternal City: Roman Images in the Modern World* (Chapel Hill: University of North Carolina Press, 1987).

44 Amengual, 'Fin d'itinéraire,' 81–111.

45 Amengual, 'Fin d'itinéraire,' 81.

46 Pirandello, *Il fu Mattia Pascal* in *Tutti i romanzi*, I, 431.

47 Pirandello, *The Late Mattia Pascal*, 111.

48 Fellini, *Fare un film*, 145.

49 As for the question of *Fellini's Roma* being the perfect metaphor of the myth of foundation, see Walter C. Foreman, 'Fellini's Cinematic City: Roma and the Myths of Foundation,' *Forum Italicum* 14 (1980), 78–97.

50 All the dialogue related to the film *Fellini's Roma* is cited directly from the American print of the film.

51 For an exhaustive theory of the fairy tale, see Vladimir Propp, *Morphology of the Folktale*, 2nd ed., trans. Lawrence Scott (Austin: University of Texas Press, 1968); for the Italian translation, see *Morfologia della fiaba* (Turin: Einaudi, 1966).

52 Pirandello, *Il fu Mattia Pascal* in *Tutti i romanzi*, I, 447.

53 Pirandello, *The Late Mattia Pascal*, 126–7.

54 The definition of Rome as 'bella totalità' is taken from George Simmel as cited in Massimo Cacciari, *Metropolis* (Rome: Bulzoni, 1973), 189.

55 Luigi Pirandello, 'Lettere ai famigliari,' *Terzo Programma* 3 (1961), 284; italics are mine.

56   Pirandello, 'Triste,' *Saggi*, 492–3.
57   Giovanni Marchi, 'La Roma di Pirandello. Una, nessuna e centomila,' *Studi Romani* 25 (1977), 45–65.
58   Pirandello, 'Un'altra allodola,' *Novelle*, II, 342.
59   Pirandello, *Novelle*, II, 342.
60   Pirandello, *Novelle*, II, 343.
61   Pirandello, *Novelle*, II, 343.
62   The dialogue is directly quoted from the soundtrack of the film; italics are mine.
63   Pirandello, *Suo marito* in *Tutti i romanzi*, I, 593.
64   Pirandello, *Suo marito* in *Tutti i romanzi*, I, 593; italics are mine.
65   Pirandello, *Suo marito* in *Tutti i romanzi*, I, 594.
66   Pirandello, *Suo marito* in *Tutti i romanzi*, I, 595.
67   Pirandello, *Suo marito* in *Tutti i romanzi*, I, 595.
68   Franca Angelini, '*Si gira* ...: L'ideologia della macchina in Pirandello' in *Il romanzo di Pirandello*, ed. Enzo Lauretta (Palermo: Palumbo Editore, 1976) 143–60.
69   Pirandello, *Quaderni di Serafino Gubbio operatore* in *Tutti i romanzi*, II, 524.
70   Pirandello, *The Notebooks of Serafino Gubbio*, 10–11.

CHAPTER 4   Character and Discourse from Pirandello to Fellini: Defining a Countertradition in an Italian Context

1   See Peter Szondi, *Theorie des modernen Dramas 1880–1950* (Frankfurt am Main: Suhrkamp Verlag, 1974); in English, *Theory of the Modern Drama* (Cambridge: Polity Press, 1987)
2   Wladimir Krysinski, *Le paradigme inquiet. Pirandello et le champ de la modernité* (Montréal: Les Éditions du Préambule, 1989), 55. See translation in Chapter 2, page 59, of this text.
3   On this matter, see Umberto Eco, 'The Frames of Comic Freedom,' 8.
4   I refer here to one of Baudelaire's lesser-known essays, *De l'essence du rire* (1855). For a thorough investigation of the similarities between this text and Pirandello's *On Humor*, see my 'Effetti di straniamento come strategia della messa in scena nella trilogia: appunti e spigolature sulla poetica della scena di Luigi Pirandello,' in *Il teatro di Pirandello*, ed. Enzo Lauretta (Milan: Bompiani, 1993), 335–42.
5   Umberto Artioli, *Teatro e corpo glorioso. Saggio su Antonin Artaud* (Milan: Feltrinelli, 1978), 85n51.
6   Peter Bondanella, *Italian Cinema from Neorealism to the Present* (1983; New York: Continuum, 1993).

7   These are dates normally associated with neorealism. Yet it is now common knowledge that a tendency toward realism in the cinema began much earlier than 1945, precisely during the Fascist period; it then continued beyond the official ending date, extending to the present in the films of directors such as Gianni Amelio and Marco Risi.

8   Robert Hughes, ed., *Film: Book One* (New York: Grove Press, 1959).

9   Naturally, the same can be said for *The Late Mattia Pascal*, which is central to our present argument.

10   Paolo Puppa, *Dalle parti di Pirandello* (Rome: Bulzoni, 1987), 42.

11   Federico Fellini, telephone interview with Tullio Kezitch, 25 December 1985, in Tullio Kezich, *Fellini*, 5.

12   Part of the present discussion of Pirandello's concept of character was published as 'From Pascal to Moscarda: Pirandello's Narrative within and beyond Modernism,' *Forum Italicum* 22(2) (Fall 1988), 176–86.

13   Pirandello, *Il fu Mattia Pascal* in *Tutti i romanzi*, 320.

14   Pirandello, *The Late Mattia Pascal*, trans. William Weaver (New York: Anchor Books, 1966), vii.

15   Pirandello, *Il fu Mattia Pascal* in *Tutti i romanzi*, 578.

16   Pirandello, *The Late Mattia Pascal*, 255.

17   Roland Barthes, *Le plaisir du texte* (Paris: Éditions du Seuil, 1973), 70; for the Italian translation, see *Il piacere del testo* (Turin: Einaudi, 1975), 43.

18   Barthes, *The Pleasure of the Text*, trans. Richard Miller (New York: Hill & Wang, 1975), 43.

19   For an exhaustive definition of 'being' *(Sein)* and 'being there' *(Dasein)*, see Martin Heidegger, *Being and Time*, trans. John Macquarrie and Edward Robinson (New York: Harper & Row, 1962).

20   Federico Fellini, 'Intervista di Aldo Tassone a Federico Fellini' in *Casanova rendez-vous con Federico Fellini*, ed. Liliana Betti and Gianfranco Angelucci (Milan: Bompiani, 1975), 142.

21   Federico Fellini, 'Intervista di Aldo Tassone,' 140.

22   See Chapter 3, p. 98 and note 36, for bibliographical reference.

23   Mikhail Bakhtin, *Problems in Dostoevsky's Poetics*, ed. and trans. Caryl Emerson (Minneapolis: University of Minnesota Press, 1984), 122–37. The similarities between Pirandello's definition of 'umorismo' and Bakhtin's definition of 'carnivalization' have been analysed by Elio Gioanola in the introductory chapter of his book *Pirandello la follia* (Genova: Il Melangolo, 1983).

24   Bakhtin, *Problems of Dostoevsky's Poetics*, 122.

25   Pirandello, *L'umorismo* in *Saggi*, 160.

26   Pirandello, *On Humor*, trans. Antonio Illiano and Daniel P. Testa (Chapel Hill, NC: University of North Carolina Press, 1974), 145.

27 Pirandello, *L'umorismo*, 134.
28 Pirandello, *On Humor*, 120.
29 For a discussion of postmodern narrative discourse with particular reference to Pirandello's narrative works, see Manuela Gieri, 'From Pascal to Moscarda: Pirandello's Narrative within and beyond Modernism,' *Forum Italicum* 22(2) (1988), 176–86; Jennifer Stone, *Pirandello's Naked Prompt. The Structure of Repetition in Modernism* (Ravenna: Longo, 1989); and Wladimir Krysinski, *Le paradigme inquiet. Pirandello et le champ de la modernité* (Montréal: Le Préambule, 1989). Even though many others exist, three landmark studies provide us with different and yet complementary perspectives of both postmodernism as an aesthetic movement and postmodernity as a historical category: Ihab Hassan, *The Dismemberment of Orpheus. Toward a Postmodern Literature* (New York: Oxford University Press, 1971); Fredric Jameson, *Postmodernism, or, The Cultural Logic of Late Capitalism* (Durham: Duke University Press, 1991); and Jean-François Lyotard, *The Postmodern Condition: A Report on Knowledge*, trans. Geoff Bennington and Brian Massumi (Minneapolis: University of Minnesota Press, 1984).
30 Cited in Roy Armes, *Patterns of Realism: A Study of Italian Neo-Realist Cinema* (South Brunswick and New York: A.S.Barnes, 1971), 199.
31 Bakhtin, *Problems in Dostoevsky's Poetics*, 48.
32 Bakhtin, *Problems in Dostoevsky's Poetics*, 48–9.
33 Paolo Puppa, *Dalle parti di Pirandello*, 152. As for the de-symbolized narration within the stream of consciousness, see Walter Benjamin's comments to Döblin's *Berliner Alexander Platz* in the chapter on the crisis of the novel in *Avanguardia e rivoluzione*, trans. A. Marietti (Turin: Einaudi, 1973), 93–100. As for a Lacanian re-reading of the Saussurean terms *langue* and *parole*, see Massimo Franciani, *Psicoanalisi linguistica ed epistemologia in Jacques Lacan* (Turin: Boringhieri, 1978).
34 Puppa, *Dalle parti di Pirandello*, 153.
35 Puppa, *Dalle Parti di Pirandello*, 153.
36 Pirandello, *L'umorismo*, 147.
37 Pirandello, *On Humor*, 133.
38 Pirandello, *L'umorismo*, 148.
39 Pirandello, *On Humor*, 134.
40 For the question of the function of the mirror and of mirroring in this particular novel see Gianpaolo Biasin, 'Lo specchio di Moscarda,' *Paragone* 268 (1972), 44–68. More generally, see Umberto Eco, *Sugli specchi* (Milan: Bompiani, 1985), 9–37; and Lacan's 'The Mirror Stage as Formative of the Function of the I,' in Jacques Lacan, *Écrits: A Selection*, trans. Alan Sheridan (New York: W.W. Norton, 1977), 1–7.

41 Pirandello, *L'umorismo*, 148.
42 Pirandello, *On Humor*, 134.
43 Pirandello, *L'umorismo*, 149. For the English, see *On Humor*, 134.
44 Federico Fellini, 'Intervista di Aldo Tassone,' 145.
45 Fellini, '*Casanova*: An Interview with Aldo Tassone,' in *Federico Fellini. Essays in Criticism*, ed. Peter Bondanella (New York: Oxford University Press, 1978), 35.
46 For a comprehensive study and a full definition of the difference between 'schizoid' and 'schizophrenic,' see R.D. Laing, *The Divided Self: An Existential Study in Sanity and Madness* (London: Tavistock Publications, 1969); for the Italian translation, see *L'io diviso* (Turin: Einaudi, 1969).
47 Gioanola, *Pirandello la follia*, 12.
48 Pirandello, *L'umorismo*, 41.
49 Pirandello, *On Humor*, 23.
50 Macchia, *La stanza della tortura*, 28.
51 Fellini, *Fare un film*, 156.
52 Italics are mine. It is relevant to note the proximity with Pirandello's essay on humour.
53 Pirandello, *L'umorismo*, 127.
54 Pirandello, *On Humor*, 113.
55 Fellini, *Fellini on Fellini*, 154.
56 It must be noted that both Pirandello and Fellini at some point mentioned Dostoevsky.
57 Pirandello, *La casa del Granella* in *Novelle*, 303–23.
58 Cited from *8½: Federico Fellini, Director*, ed. Charles Affron (New Brunswick: Rutgers University Press, 1987), 132.
59 Jacques Lacan, *Écrits: A Selection*, trans. Alan Sheridan (New York: W.W. Norton, 1977). In particular, see the essays 'The Mirror Stage as Formative of the Function of the I' (1–7), 'The Function and Field of Speech and Language in Psychoanalysis' (30–113), 'The Agency of the Letter in the Unconscious or Reason since Freud' (146–78), and 'On the Question Preliminary to Any Possible Treatment of Psychosis' (179–225).
60 Pirandello, *La tragedia di un personaggio* in *Novelle*, I, 713.
61 Cited from the American print of the film.
62 Joseph McBride, 'The Director as Superstar,' *Sight and Sound*, 41(2) (1972), 78–81; republished in *Federico Fellini: Essays in Criticism*, ed. Peter Bondanella (New York: Oxford University Press, 1978), 152–60.
63 Pirandello, *La tragedia di un personaggio* in *Novelle per un anno*, I, 719.
64 The dialogues are cited directly from the American print of the film.
65 Pirandello, *Illustratori, attori e traduttori* (1908) in *Saggi*, 215.
66 Bakhtin, *Problems of Dostoevsky's Poetics*, 150.

67 On the clown as metaphor for both the character and the author/artist and their respective discourses, see Jean Starobinski, *Portrait de l'artiste en saltimbanque* (Genève: Éditions d'Art Albert Skira, 1971); Richard Pearce, *Stages of the Clown. Perspectives on Modern Fiction from Dostoevsky to Beckett* (Carbondale and Edwardsville: Southern Illinois University Press, 1970); and, especially relevant to our discussion of this issue in an Italian context, Gianni Celati, 'Dai giganti buffoni alla coscienza infelice' in *Finzioni occidentali. Fabulazione, comicitá e scrittura* (1975; Turin: Einaudi, 1986), 51–101.

68 Federico Fellini, 'The Genesis of *La Strada*,' in *'La Strada': Federico Fellini, Director*, ed. Peter Bondanella and Manuela Gieri (New Brunswick: Rutgers University Press, 1987), 182–3; first appeared in Federico Fellini, *Fare un film*, 57–60.

69 Pirandello, *L'umorismo*, 158.

70 Pirandello, *On Humor*, 143.

71 Pirandello, *L'umorismo*, 158.

72 Pirandello, *On Humor*, 143.

73 Gioanola, *Pirandello la follia*, 20–21.

74 On this matter, see Gioanola, *Pirandello la follia*, 7–37; Lacan, *Écrits*, 40–113 and 292–325; and Jameson, *The Political Unconscious: Narrative as a Socially Symbolic Act* (Ithaca, NY: Cornell University Press, 1981).

75 Pirandello, *Saggi*, 865–80.

76 Gioanola, *Pirandello la follia*, 21.

77 Gioanola, *Pirandello la follia*, 21.

78 It is interesting to note that Fellini had meant to make a film adaptation of Kafka's novel for a long time, and that one of his last films, *Interview*, unfolds during the 'making' of this 'film to be.'

79 Michel Foucault, *Histoire de la folie à l'âge classique* (Paris: Gallimart, 1972), 259.

80 It may be relevant here to reconsider Jacques Lacan's 'return to Freud.' For a discussion of this important segment of Lacan's investigation, see Shoshana Felman, 'The Originality of Jacques Lacan,' *Poetics Today* 2.1b (Winter 1980/81), 45–57. For a discussion of schizophrenic behaviours as psychological answers but also as direct products of capitalistic society, see Gilles Deleuze and Felix Guattari, *Capitalisme et schizophrenie* (1972; Paris: Éditions de Minuit, 1980).

81 Puppa, *Dalle parti di Pirandello*, 203.

82 For a thorough study of this concept, see Giacomo Debenedetti, *Il romanzo del Novecento* (1987), in particular, the chapter 'Adriano Meis e la mancata "epifania" del personaggio,' 362–90.

83 Pirandello, *L'umorismo*, 151. In the second part of this famous essay, Piran-

dello provides a full definition of his own conception of humour, and, I believe, of his overall world view, by using the word 'flux' as a key concept: 'La vita è un flusso continuo che noi cerchiamo d'arrestare, di fissare in forme stabili e determinate, dentro e fuori di noi ... Le forme in cui noi cerchiamo d'arrestare, di fissare in noi questo flusso continuo sono i concetti ... tutte le finzioni che ci creiamo, le condizioni, lo stato in cui tendiamo a stabilirci. Ma dentro di noi stessi, in ciò che noi chiamiamo anima, e che è la vita in noi, il flusso continua, indistinto, sotto gli argini, oltre i limiti che noi imponiamo, componendoci una coscienza, costruendoci una personalità' (151). From the English edition, *On Humor*: 'Life is a continual flux which we try to stop, to fix in stable and determined forms, both inside and outside ourselves ... The forms in which we seek to stop, to fix in ourselves this constant flux are the concepts ... all the fictions we create for ourselves, the conditions, the state in which we tend to stabilize ourselves. But within ourselves, in what we call the soul and is the life in us, the flux continues, indistinct under the barriers and beyond the limits we impose as a means to fashion a consciousness and a personality for ourselves' (137).

84 On the Name-of-the-Father (agency of the symbolic, or dead, Father), see Lacan, *Écrits*, 69, 199, 217, 310.

85 See Roland Barthes, *Mythologies*, trans. Annette Lavers (New York: Hill and Wang, 1972). Barthes states that the bourgeoisie is the class that does not want to be named, that then 'ex-nominates' itself, and that this middle-class strategy aims at transforming man into the Eternal Man. Barthes then points out that this strategy leads to a twisting of the once-revolutionary bourgeois ideology (that mankind can change nature through reason) to its opposite, thus emphasizing the permanent quality of nature, of the human condition in the bourgeois social organization. Pirandello, although certainly not aligned with any leftist belief, provides that strategy a new revolutionary power, although I understand that his position can also be easily interpreted as neo-liberal.

86 It must be noted that *Interview*, one of Fellini's last films, ends on this note. The director imagines his producer complaining about another film without hope and asking for a *raggio di sole* – a ray of light/hope. Then, Fellini shoots a beam of light in *Teatro 5*, and it is the conclusion of the film.

87 Barthes, *Le plaisir du texte*, 75–6; for the Italian translation, see *Il piacere del testo*, 46.

88 Barthes, *The Pleasure of the Text*, 47.

89 Lacan, *Écrits*, 2.

90 Bakhtin, *Problems of Dostoevsky's Poetics*, 137.

CHAPTER 5   Ettore Scola: A Cinematic and Social Metadiscourse

1   Henri Bergson, *Le rire, essai sur la signification du comique* (Paris: Presses Universitaires de France, 1967), 152–3. Bergson's essay first appeared in instalments in *Revue de France* in 1899 and was then published in 1900. It was translated into English as *Laughter. An Essay on the Meaning of the Comic*, trans. Cloudesley Brereton and Fred Rothwell (London: Macmillan, 1911). For an English translation of this quotation, see the Macmillan edition, page 200.

2   Four texts are of utmost importance to a discussion of laughter in modernity: Charles Baudelaire's *De l'essence du rire et généralement du comique dans les arts plastiques*, published in 1855; Henry Bergson's *Le rire*; and Sigmund Freud's essay on jokes, *Der Witz uns seine Beziehung zum Unbewussten*, published in 1905, only three years before Pirandello's *On Humor*.

3   The film stands in open dialogue with the first important journey in the history of Italian postwar cinema: *Paisan* by Roberto Rossellini. While the 1946 film was a journey of discovery of the geographical and social parts of Italy that had never before been shown on the screen, *Voyage to Italy* is a 'journey' through the inner landscape of the characters, and in many ways is the precursor of Michelangelo Antonioni's many investigations of the mind. For a further discussion of this matter, see Chapter 4 in this volume.

4   Under the sign of 'comedy' and beginning with this film, Italian cinema will then investigate the mystery of life and its many *miracles*. The interplay between fable and mystery, comedy and tragedy, will constitute a large segment of Italian cinematic production to the point of eventually exploring the possibilities offered by *fantasy* and *utopia*.

5   *Miracle in Milan* was made in 1950, *Voyage to Italy* in 1951.

6   Gian Piero Brunetta, *Cent'anni di cinema italiano* (Bari: Laterza, 1991), 394.

7   Brunetta, *Cent'anni di cinema italiano*, 397.

8   Brunetta, *Cent'anni di cinema italiano*, 400.

9   Brunetta, *Cent'anni di cinema italiano*, 77; italics are mine.

10   Maurizio Grande elaborates Northrop Frye's formula as expressed in *Anatomy of Criticism: Four Essays* (Princeton: Princeton University Press, 1957). See Maurizio Grande, *Il cinema di Saturno. Commedia e malinconia* (Rome: Bulzoni, 1992), 9.

11   On 28 August 1978, the French weekly magazine *L'Express* published a cover story entitled 'La comedie à l'italienne,' declaring the success of the 'comedy Italian style.' However, French critics had already 'discovered' this national comedy in the beginning of the 1970s. On this matter, see Morando Morandini, 'Dal 1968 ai giorni nostri agonia, morte e resur-

rezione,' in *Commedia all'italiana. Angolazioni e controcampi*, ed. Riccardo Napolitano (Rome: Gangemi, 1986), 87–94.

12   Tullio Masoni and Paolo Vecchi, 'Degeneri e scostumati: commedia, satira e farsa nel cinema sonoro italiano,' in *Commedia all'italiana*, ed. Napolitano, 75.

13   Lorenzo Pellizzari, 'Dal cinismo al civismo, e ritorno: libera escursione nel cinema "romano" tra eventi, ceti, classi e personaggi,' in *Commedia all'italiana*, ed. Napolitano, 117.

14   Brunetta, *Cent'anni di cinema italiano*, 426.

15   Ettore Scola as quoted in Roberto Ellero, *Ettore Scola* (Florence: La Nuova Italia, 1988), 9.

16   Vittorio Metz, as cited in *Era Cinecittà*, ed. Oreste Del Buono and Lietta Tornabuoni (Milan: Almanacco Bombiani, 1980).

17   Brunetta, *Cent'anni di cinema italiano*, 306–7.

18   Brunetta, *Cent'anni di cinema italiano*, 332.

19   Pellizzari, 'Dal cinismo al civismo,' in *Commedia all'italiana*, ed. Napolitano, 116.

20   Pellizzari, 'Dal cinismo al civismo,' in *Commedia all'italiana*, ed. Napolitano, 116–17.

21   '8½' *Federico Fellini, Director*, ed. Affron, 45–6.

22   For a classical discussion of *auteur cinema*, see François Truffaut, 'Une certaine tendance du cinéma français,' *Cahiers du Cinéma* 31 (January 1954), and Andrew Sarris, 'Notes on the Auteur Theory in 1962,' *Film Culture* 27 (Winter 1962–3).

23   For a thorough discussion of this matter, see previous chapters of the present volume.

24   Cited in Brunetta, *Cent'anni di cinema italiano*, 331.

25   Peter Bondanella, 'La comédie "métacinématographique" d'Ettore Scola,' *CinémAction* 42 (1987), 91–9.

26   Fellini was born in 1920 in Rimini, while Scola was born in 1931 in Trevico, a little town in Irpinia.

27   For a complete filmography, see Bondanella, *The Cinema of Federico Fellini*, 335–44.

28   Brunetta, *Cent'anni di cinema italiano*, 330.

29   Ettore Scola, as cited in Ellero, *Ettore Scola*, 5.

30   This synopsis of Ettore Scola's career as scriptwriter is indebted to the complete filmography provided by Roberto Ellero under the supervision of Scola himself in Ellero, *Ettore Scola*, 92–109.

31   Before making his cinematic début in Alessandro Blasetti's *Nerone* (*Nero*, 1930), Ettore Petrolini was one of Italy's most celebrated comedians. He

trained for a long time in the variety shows, but he wore the multiple masks and characters of Italian theatre from Terentius to the Commedia dell'arte, as well as dialect poetry. His acting was anachronistic and contemporary, as well as surreal and nonsensical. In his performances, one found the same commitment to social critique and the same elements that would later characterize the acting of such Italian film comedians as Totò, Alberto Sordi, Roberto Benigni, and Massimo Troisi.

32 Totò – his name itself is a strange mixture of fiction and reality – was and still is one of the most beloved comedians of the Italian scene. His thoroughly idiosyncratic comedy collects elements from all forms of spectacle, from the characters of the Commedia dell'arte, such as Pulcinella and Arlecchino, to Pierrot and Captain Fracassa. He has been defined as a 'hybrid' (Brunetta, 209) who has learned acting from improvised farces on Neapolitan stages. His acting technique is characterized by irregularities, dissymmetries, and arhythmic tempos (see Goffredo Fofi, *Totò* [Rome: Savelli, 1975]). Because of 'the Prince,' as he was also called, dodecaphonic music as well as cubist and surrealist painting have entered the Italian theatrical and cinematographic scene (Brunetta, 209). Totò has influenced many actors, especially one of the most impressive representatives of the new generation of film actors and directors, Massimo Troisi.

33 The eighteenth-century Italian comic tradition of itinerant theatrical companies whose improvised performances took place on and around a simple canvas or 'canovaccio.'

34 Brunetta, *Cent'anni di cinema italiano*, 428.

35 Age, as quoted in *L'avventurosa storia del cinema italiano raccontata dai suoi protagonisti. 1935–1959*, ed. Franca Faldini and Goffredo Fofi (Milan: Feltrinelli, 1979), 397.

36 Brunetta, *Cent'anni di cinema italiano*, 599.

37 Brunetta, *Cent'anni di cinema italiano*, 602.

38 Ellero, *Ettore Scola*, 21.

39 Brunetta, *Cent'anni di cinema italiano*, 603.

40 It is interesting to observe that Tullio Pinelli co-scripted all Fellini's films up to *Toby Dammit*, an episode in *Tre passi nel delirio* (*Spirits of the Dead*, 1968), while Bernardino Zapponi was intermittently present in Fellini's career thereafter.

41 Brunetta, *Cent'anni di cinema italiano*, 547.

42 Paradoxically, a parallel discussion of Scola's *Will Our Heroes ...?* and Antonioni's *L'avventura* (1959) could be quite profitable in an understanding of the two discursive strategies that I have targeted as qualifying features of Italian postwar cinema: the 'melodramatic' (Antonioni) and the 'hu-

moristic' (Scola). The constellation to which Antonioni's *L'avventura* belongs is that of Rossellini's *Voyage to Italy*; Scola's 1968 film moves within
the domain of comedy but profits from the contribution of the melodramatic and the tragic to produce a discourse that is internally doubled and
self-reflexive. A reversal of the neorealistic theory of the *pedinamento* operates in both films; yet in Antonioni's film, a complete defeat is declared
since there is the conviction that there is truth in the surface of the world;
in Scola's film, this belief is fundamentally undermined. Following
Fellini's predicament, attention is given to the mysterious but equally
'real' side of the human experience.

43 Scola, as cited in Ellero, *Ettore Scola*, 3.
44 Scola, as cited in Ellero, *Ettore Scola*, 6.
45 For an interesting discussion of Scola's directorial career and the develop-
    ment of his personal interpretation of cinematic comedy, see Giuseppe
    Panella, 'Dalla farsa della società alla commedia della storia: Ettore Scola,
    1964/1984,' in *Si fa per ridere ... ma è una cosa seria*, ed. Sandro Bernardi
    (Milan: La Casa Usher, 1987), 89–93.
46 Ellero, *Ettore Scola*, 5.
47 See Ellero, *Ettore Scola*, 77.
48 Ellero, *Ettore Scola*, 83.
49 Ellero, *Ettore Scola*, 83.
50 Brunetta, *Cent'anni di cinema italiano*, 603.
51 Peter Bondanella, *Italian Cinema: From Neorealism to the Present* (New York:
    Frederick, 1983), 374.
52 Millicent Marcus, *Italian Film in the Light of Neorealism*, 421.
53 Scola as quoted in Ellero, *Ettore Scola*, 5; italics are mine.
54 Scola as cited in Ellero, *Ettore Scola*, 49; italics are mine.
55 It must be noted here that Vittorio Gassman played the lead in Mario
    Monicelli's *The Great War* and Dino Risi's *The Easy Life*, two masterpieces
    of the genre that, however, begin the internal transformation of the genre
    itself.
56 For a convincing discussion of Antonioni's cinema, see Seymour Chat-
    man, *Antonioni or, The Surface of the World* (Berkeley: University of Califor-
    nia Press, 1985). For an analysis of the 'great tetralogy,' see 51–135.
57 Luigi Codelli, '... et dangereux (affreux, sales et méchants),' *Positif* 189
    (January 1977), 61.
58 In Italian, *Romoletto* is a diminutive of *Romolo*.
59 Cited in Ellero, *Ettore Scola*, 68.
60 Brunetta, *Cent'anni di cinema italiano*, 604.
61 Puppa, *Dalle parti di Pirandello*, 28.

62 Jean Gili, '*Le Bal*. Une humanité condamnée à tourner en rond,' *Positif* 276 (February 1984), 54.
63 For an intriguing discussion of Renoir's masterpiece, see Gianni Rondolino, 'Il cinema francese del Fronte Popolare,' in *Storia del cinema. Dall'affermazione del sonoro al neorealismo*, ed. Adelio Ferrero (Venice: Marsilio, 1978), 97–112.
64 Quoted directly from the film *The Terrace*.
65 Quoted directly from the film *The Terrace*.
66 Pirandello, *Sei personaggi in cerca d'autore* in *Maschere nude*, I, 115.
67 This translation is mine. A published English translation can be found in *Naked Masks. Five Plays by Pirandello*, trans. Eric Bentley (New York: E.P. Dutton, 1969), 276.
68 Pirandello, *Sei personaggi in cerca d'autore* in *Maschere nude*, I, 113.
69 Translation is mine. For the English translation, see *Naked Masks*, ed. Bentley, 274.
70 Panella, 'Dalla farsa della società alla commedia della storia,' 92.
71 Denis Diderot, *Paradoxe sur le Comédien* (Paris: Société Française d'Imprimerie et de Livrairie, 1902), and especially the 'Manuscrit de Saint-Pétersbourg,' 98.
72 The English translation is mine. For the Italian see, Denis Diderot, *Paradosso sull'attore* (Rome: Editori Riuniti, 1993), 80. For a published English translation, see Denis Diderot, *Paradox of Acting*, trans. Walter Herries Pollock (New York: Hill and Wang, 1965), 18.
73 Denis Diderot, *Scritti di estetica*, ed. Guido Neri (Milan: 1957), 9.
74 Natalino Bruzzone, 'C'eravamo tanto filmati,' in *I film e le sceneggiature di Ettore Scola*, ed. Antonio Maraldi (Cesena: Quaderni del Centro Cinema, 1982), 14.
75 The film is discussed in Chapter 6 of this book.
76 Gian Luigi Rondi, '*Splendor* di Ettore Scola,' *Rivista del cinematografo* 59(3) (1989), 11.

CHAPTER 6   The New Italian Cinema: Restoration or Subversion?

1 At the end of the 1970s, a lively and forceful debate over the 'crisis' of Italian cinema engaged critics and filmmakers. The various film journals in Italy became a forum for such discussion. For instance, see the inserts 'Cineasti italiani allo specchio,' *Cinemasessanta* 125 (January-February 1979), 4–27, and 126 (March-April 1979), 30–39, including interviews with Bernardo Bertolucci, Luigi Comencini, Francesco Maselli, Cesare Zavattini, Giuseppe Bertolucci, and Nanni Moretti, as well as an interesting essay by Otello Angeli, 'Anatomia della crisi.'

2   Lino Miccichè, 'Gli eredi del nulla. Per una critica del giovane cinema ita-
    liano,' in *Una generazione in cinema. Esordi ed esordienti italiani 1975–1988*,
    ed. Franco Montini (Venice: Marsilio, 1988), 252. For a discussion of the
    new Italian cinema, see also Mario Sesti, *Nuovo cinema italiano. Gli autori i
    film le idee* (Rome-Naples: Theoria, 1994); *Il cinema italiano degli anni ottanta
    ... ed emozioni registiche*, ed. Vincenzo Camerino (Lecce: Piero Manni,
    1992). See also the entire issue of *Segnocinema* 13(64) (November-Decem-
    ber 1993), especially Flavio De Bernardinis, 'Caro cinema italiano ...'
    (11–13), and Giorgio Simonelli, 'Proposta decente' (14–16); *Segnocinema*
    10(41) (January 1990), especially Marcello Walter Bruno, 'Introduzione al
    nemico. Televisione, pubblicità e nuove tecnologie nel cinema italiano
    degli anni '80' (11–15) and Marcello Cella, 'La natura indifferente. Il pae-
    saggio nel cinema italiano degli anni Ottanta' (16–20). See also Marcello
    Walter Bruno, 'Meta in Italy. La via nazionale al cinema-sul-cinema,' *Seg-
    nocinema* 11(51) (September-October 1991), 10–13; Morando Morandini, 'Il
    regista è finito? Breve viaggio intorno agli autori del cinema italiano degli
    anni '80,' *Segnocinema* 6(22) (March 1986), 4–6. See also *Cineforum* 29(10)
    (October 1989) and 30(7/8) (July-August 1990), which are devoted to the
    young Italian cinema and bear the title 'Sperduti nel buio.' For a discus-
    sion of the renaissance in contemporary Italian cinema, see interviews
    with Italian directors, 'Il "che fare" per il cinema italiano,' in a special
    issue of *Cinema nuovo* 41(1) (January-February 1992), 13–31.
3   Gian Piero Brunetta, 'La polvere di Kantor,' in *Cent'anni di cinema italiano*
    (Bari: Laterza, 1991), 625.
4   Italics are mine.
5   Miccichè, 'Gli eredi del nulla,' 253.
6   Brunetta, *Cent'anni di cinema italiano*, 625.
7   Miccichè, 'Gli eredi del nulla,' 253.
8   The well-fed and somewhat 'vulgar' region of the Po Valley that gave
    birth to many famous Italian directors such as Bertolucci, Fellini, Anto-
    nioni, Bellocchio, and Avati.
9   Significantly, Bertolucci is 'literally' a son of neorealism as he was born in
    1941. For an analysis of Bertolucci's career, see Francesco Casetti, *Bernardo
    Bertolucci* (Florence: La Nuova Italia, 1978).
10 An interesting discussion of Ermanno Olmi's film can be found in Jeanne
    Dillon, *Ermanno Olmi* (Florence: La Nuova Italia, 1985).
11 Notable exceptions to this general argument are the cinema of the Taviani
    Brothers on the one hand, and the many examples of a cinema of overt po-
    litical and social commitment such as that of Francesco Rosi, Gillo Pon-
    tecorvo, and Elio Petri together with that of Pier Paolo Pasolini. Such cine-

matic experiences, even though noteworthy, cannot be properly understood within the framework of the 'humoristic filmmaking' that is under discussion at this time. This study is not concerned either with a specific tradition that I have generally termed the 'melodramatic imagination,' which is especially evident in the films of Michelangelo Antonioni and Luchino Visconti.

12 Miccichè, 'Gli eredi del nulla,' 254.
13 Miccichè, 'Gli eredi del nulla,' 255.
14 For instance, Italy never saw anything comparable to the French *nouvelle vague*, the innovative cinematic movement developed by directors such as François Truffaut and Jean-Luc Godard beginning in 1959.
15 Miccichè, 'Gli eredi del nulla,' 254–5.
16 See Miccichè, 'Gli eredi del nulla,' 255. It is only quite recently that directors such as Dino Risi, one of the great 'masters' of the 'comedy Italian style,' received critical recognition in Italy.
17 Miccichè, 'Gli eredi del nulla,' 256.
18 This is the title of one of Pier Paolo Pasolini's most celebrated collections of poems, *Le ceneri di Gramsci* (1957).
19 Miccichè, 'Gli eredi del nulla,' 256.
20 The expression was coined in the late seventies with the débuts of such filmmakers as Nanni Moretti, Maurizio Nichetti, Gianni Amelio, Carlo Verdone, and Giuseppe Bertolucci.
21 Gianni Amelio as cited in 'Emozioni al lavoro,' ed. Claver Salizzato, *Cinecritica* 14(19–20) (October 1990/March 1991), 23.
22 As he stated in a long interview given to me at the 1994 Toronto International Film Festival.
23 This label was coined by Franco Montini in the preface to his *I novissimi. Gli esordienti nel cinema italiano degli anni '80* (Turin: Nuova ERI, 1988), 7–20.
24 As quoted in Maria Fotia, 'I giovani autori italiani: due anime,' *Mass Media* X(4) (September-October 1991), 24.
25 For a thorough discussion of this matter, see Chapter 5 of this book. See also Millicent Marcus, *Italian Film in the Light of Neorealism* (Princeton, NJ: Princeton University Press, 1986).
26 Gianni Amelio as cited in 'Emozioni al lavoro,' ed. Salizzaro, 20.
27 Amelio as quoted in 'Emozioni al lavoro,' ed. Salizzaro, 20; italics are mine.
28 Recently, another Italian film has dealt with the theme of childhood in a corrupted and violent environment: Carlo Carlei's *La corsa dell'innocente* (*The Flight of the Innocent*, 1992). In his early thirties and born in Calabria,

Carlei has received little attention in Italy, but enormous public acclaim in North America; MGM has not only bought the film, but also hired the director for two more projects, one of which he is presently shooting.

29   Rosario Lizzio, *Passi sulla luna. Mappa tendenziosa del nuovo cinema italiano* (Catania: Quaderni di 'Zéro de conduite,' Azdak, 1991), 22.

30   I am borrowing the title of one of Pasolini's novels, *Una vita violenta* (*A Violent Life*, 1959), since Tognazzi's youth unquestionably reminds one of Pasolini's personal interpretation of neorealism in the depiction of these Roman contemporary 'ragazzi di vita.'

31   The celebrated director of the so-called 'spaghetti Westerns,' with such unforgettable films as *Per un pugno di dollari* (*A Fistful of Dollars*, 1964), *Per qualche dollaro in più* (*For a Few Dollars More*, 1965), and *Il buono, il brutto, il cattivo* (*The Good, the Bad and the Ugly*, 1966).

32   Almost an 'unidentified object' in the recent history of Italian cinema, Giuseppe Avati, called 'Pupi,' began filmmaking in 1968 with *Balsamus, l'uomo di Satana* (*Balsamus, the Man of Satan*), but received public acclaim only in 1976 with his *La casa dalle finestre che ridono* (*The House with Laughing Windows*) and in 1980 with *Aiutami a sognare* (*Help Me to Dream*), a gentle remembrance of the war years. One of his best films, though, is *Regalo di Natale* (*Christmas Present*, 1986), a nocturnal and surreal tale of a strange card game on Christmas Eve.

33   One of the representatives of Italian political cinema as it developed in the seventies, and the author of such excellent films as *Sacco e Vanzetti* (*Sacco and Vanzetti*, 1971).

34   Carlo Cecchi also plays the leading role in Mario Martone's outstanding directorial début, *Morte di un matematico napoletano* (*Death of a Neapolitan Mathematician*, 1992).

35   A few years ago, Margarethe von Trotta, the famous German director, moved to Italy, where she now lives and works. Among her most celebrated films are *Die verlorene Ehre der Katharina Blum* (*The Lost Honor of Katharina Blum*), which she co-directed with Volker Schlöndorff in 1975, and *Rosa Luxemburg* (1986). Her Italian filmmaking began in 1988 with *Paura e amore* (*Fear and Love*). *The Long Silence*, made in the wake of 1992's slaying of two of Italy's anti-Mafia investigators, Giovanni Falcone and Nino Borsellino, is a chilling portrait of the life of those who fight against corruption at great personal cost. While Tognazzi's *The Bodyguards* focuses on the 'guardian angels' of a magistrate, von Trotta's film is told from the perspective of a magistrate's wife after her husband is killed and she finds herself in a desperate predicament. Despite Carla Gravina's outstanding performance, the film is self-indulgent and unconvincing.

36 The name is probably nothing more than a pseudonym for Bagheria, Tornatore's hometown.

37 Vincenzo Consolo, 'La cuna del sogno,' in Giuseppe Tornatore, *Nuovo Cinema Paradiso* (Palermo: Sellerio, 1990), 170.

38 In its first version, the film contained a narrative segment in which an aged Salvatore encounters an equally aged but still beautiful Elena; they revisit past events and discover that Alfredo had orchestrated the 'failed' meeting that changed their entire life. Stylistically, the roughly twenty-minute sequence is characterized by an impoverished and melodramatic imagination that spoils the evocative and lyrical nature of the whole film.

39 Giuseppe Tornatore as cited in Silvia Tortora, 'San Giuseppe. Parla Tornatore, il regista della resurrezione italiana,' *Epoca* (24 December 1989), 87.

40 My interview with Giuseppe Tornatore on 7 September 1990, when he presented *Everybody Is Fine* at the Toronto International Film Festival of Festivals.

41 Interview with Giuseppe Tornatore, 7 September 1990.

42 Inteview with Giuseppe Tornatore, 7 September 1990.

43 All these films could be justly taken as examples of that particular mode of filmmaking that I have termed as *Pirandellian* or *humoristic*. For a discussion of Pirandello and Welles, see Maurizio De Ministro, *Pirandello scena personaggio e film* (Rome: Bulzoni, 1980), 157–81.

44 Linda Hutcheon, *A Theory of Parody. The Teachings of Twentieth-Century Art Forms* (1985; New York and London: Methuen, 1986), 4.

45 Hutcheon, *A Theory of Parody*, 4.

46 Roland Barthes, in *S/Z* , trans. Richard Miller (New York: Hill & Wang, 1974), and Julia Kristeva, in *Semiotike. Recherches pour une sémanalyse* (Paris: Seuil, 1969), support the concept that because of its reverential and mocking aspects parody can be seen as a conservative force.

47 Mikhail Bakhtin in *Rabelais and His World*, trans. Hélène Iswolsky (Cambridge, MA: MIT Press, 1968), maintains that parody can also be a genuinely revolutionary genre.

48 Hutcheon, *A Theory of Parody*, 26.

49 Hutcheon, *A Theory of Parody*, 28.

50 For a discussion of 'digression,' see Barbara Klinger, 'Digression at the Cinema: Commodification and Reception in Mass Culture,' in *Modernity and Mass Culture*, ed. James Naremore and Patrick Bratlinger (Bloomington: Indiana University Press, 1991), 117–34.

51 Klinger, 'Digression at the Cinema,' 119.

52 This interpretation of digression relies heavily on a semiotic approach to the problem as exemplified in the works of Roland Barthes and Umberto

Eco. Both theorists have treated digression 'as a part of the reading process that attests strongly to the profound intertextual location of text and reader' (Klinger, 118). On this subject, see Barthes, *S/Z*, and Eco, *The Role of the Reader* (Bloomington: Indiana University Press, 1979).

53   This definition was provided by the Frankfurt School: 'According to Benjamin, Kracauer, Adorno and Horkheimer, mechanical reproduction within the capitalist regime transforms reception from a state of absorption in the totality of the art work to one of inattentiveness, resulting in the atomization of the work. Adorno's perspective on the culture industry in particular links distraction to procedures of commodification which define a work for consumption in the *age of mechanical reproduction*' (Klinger, 119).

54   Maria Fotia, '*La stazione* di Sergio Rubini,' *Rivista del Cinematografo* 60(11) (November 1990), 14.

55   Interview given to me on 11 September 1993, during the 18th Toronto International Film Festival of Festivals.

56   Box-office enterprises that are normally released in Italy at Christmas time to entertain families and whose aesthetic and ethical value is close to nil.

57   In the Italian title, 'thief' is, in fact, ironically, 'plural': 'ladri' and not 'ladro.' It is ironic since only one thief is identified, while many are the thefts perpetrated in this postmodern divertissement.

58   Interview with Maurizio Nichetti published in Nuccio Orto, *Maurizio Nichetti: un comico, un autore* (Chieti: Métis, 1990), 54.

59   It is sufficient here to mention directors Carlo Verdone, Francesco Nuti, and some of the films starring Paolo Villaggio.

60   Specifically, *Six Characters in Search of an Author*, *Each in His Own Way*, and *Tonight We Improvise.*

61   See previous chapter for a discussion of the so-called 'comedy Italian style,' and its overcoming.

62   This topos clearly reminds one of Ettore Scola's 1968 film, *Will Our Heroes …?*; Salvatores, however, operates a reversal of the singular condition of Scola's film, and proposes a pluralization of the earlier situation, a true collective experience.

63   Diego Abatantuono is not only one of Salvatores' best friends but also one of his dearest companions in his cinematic journey, together with Fabrizio Bentivoglio, Giuseppe Cederna, and Gigio Alberti. Abatantuono has played many central roles in Salvatores' films, beginning with *Marrakech Express*; in *Mediterraneo*, he plays the macho and Fascist lieutenant, in *Turnè*, he is one of the two male leads, and in *Puerto Escondido* he is the sole protagonist.

64   As cited in *Gabriele Salvatores*, ed. Flavio Merkel (Rome: Dino Audino Editore, 1992), 59.

65   As cited in Merkel, ed., *Gabriele Salvatores*, 59.

66   'E' popolato di ombre il cinema pirandelliano di Nanni Moretti, il "così è se vi pare" del personaggio in cerca d'autore, dell'autore in cerca di personaggio' ('Nanni Moretti's Pirandellian cinema is crowded with shadows, the "it is so if you think so" of the character in search of an author, of the author in search of a character'), states Fabio Bo in his 'La massa è finita,' *Filmcritica* 40(399) (November 1989), 583.

67   My interview with Nanni Moretti during the 18th Toronto International Film Festival of Festivals (1993).

68   See Flavio De Bernardinis, *Nanni Moretti* (1987; Florence: La Nuova Italia, 1994), 4.

69   Cited in De Bernardinis, *Nanni Moretti*, 6.

70   Cited in De Bernardinis, *Nanni Moretti*, 9.

71   My interview with Nanni Moretti during the 18th Toronto International Film Festival of Festivals (1993).

72   Jean A. Gili, 'Des films pour exorciser mes obsessions. Entretien avec Nanni Moretti,' *Positif* 311 (January 1987), 15.

73   De Bernardinis, *Nanni Moretti*, 40.

74   De Bernardinis, *Nanni Moretti*, 42.

75   Marcello Walter Bruno, 'Perchè Moretti non è un regista,' *Segnocinema* 10(41) (January 1990), 5.

76   Quite recently Nanni Moretti has received a burst of critical attention in Italy and abroad. De Bernardinis' volume has been revised and published in a new edition in 1994, and another monographic study has been edited by Paola Ugo and Antioco Floris and published with the title *Facciamoci del male. Il cinema di Nanni Moretti* (Cagliari: CUEC Editrice, 1990). Numerous articles have appeared in non-Italian film journals.

77   Serge Toubiana, 'Le regard moral,' *Cahiers du Cinéma* 425 (November 1989), 20–1.

78   Toubiana, 'Le regard moral,' 20.

79   This is a common strategy in Fellini's filmography.

80   Toubiana, 'Entretien avec Nanni Moretti,' *Cahiers du Cinéma* 425 (November 1989), 23.

81   Here I borrow the term 'movement-image' from Gilles Deleuze, *Cinema 1. The Movement-Image* (Minneapolis: University of Minnesota Press, 1989). Since the film is not presently distributed in North America, it seems useless to discuss it further at this time. However, I would like to mention a few excellent essays on *Palombella*, such as the above-mentioned 'Le re-

gard moral' by Serge Toubiana; Fabio Bo, 'La massa è finita,' 582–9; and Marcello Walter Bruno, 'Perchè Moretti non è un regista'; Thierry Jousse's essay, 'Le corps du défi,' *Cahiers du Cinéma* 426 (December 1989), 42–4; Gustavo Micheletti, 'Una palombella tra Habermas e Foucault,' *Cinemasessanta* 31(1/190) (January-February 1990), 9–10; and Franco La Polla's discussion of the film in *Cineforum* 29(10) (October 1989), 61–7.

82   Nanni Moretti explained the pre-production process in an interview he gave to me in September 1994 as he was presenting the film in Toronto.

83   See Emanuela Martini, '*Caro Diario* di Nanni Moretti,' *Cineforum* 33(11) (November 1993), 61.

84   René Jean, 'Cinq minutes avec Pirandello,' *Les nouvelles littéraires* (15 November 1924), 8.

85   Cited in De Bernardinis, *Nanni Moretti*, 9.

Bibliography

WORKS BY LUIGI PIRANDELLO

Pirandello, Luigi. 'Dramma e sonoro.' Introduction by Renato Giani. *Cinema* 17 (10 November 1939): 277–8
- *The Late Mattia Pascal*. Trans. William Weaver. New York: Anchor Books, 1966
- 'Lettere ai famigliari.' *Terzo Programma* 3 (1961): 284–8
- *Le maschere nude*. 2 vols. 1958. Milan: Arnoldo Mondadori Editore, 1978
- *Maschere nude*. Ed. Alessandro D'Amico. Milan: Mondadori, 1994
- *Naked Masks. Five Plays by Pirandello*. Trans. Eric Bentley. New York: E.P. Dutton, 1969
- *The Notebooks of Serafino Gubbio or (Shoot!)*. Trans. C.K. Scott Moncrieff. Langford Lodge: Dedalus, 1990
- *Novelle per un anno*. 2 vols. 1956. Milan: Arnoldo Mondadori Editore, 1986
- *On Humor*. Trans. and Ed., Antonio Illiano and Daniel P. Testa. Chapel Hill, NC: The University of North Carolina Press, 1974
- 'Per il film italiano. Intervista con Luigi Pirandello.' Ed. Testor. *La stampa* (9 December 1932)
- *Saggi, poesie, scritti varii*. Milan: Arnoldo Mondadori Editore, 1960
- *Tutti i romanzi*. Ed. Giovanni Macchia. 2 vols. 1973. Milan: Arnoldo Mondadori Editore, 1984
Pirandello, Luigi, and Adolf Lantz. '*Sei personaggi*: una storia per lo schermo.' Ed. Rossano Vittori. *Cinema nuovo* (Giugno 1984): 27–55

WORKS ON LUIGI PIRANDELLO

Adler, Thomas P. 'The Mirror as a Stage Prop in Modern Drama.' *Comparative Drama* 14 (1980–1): 355–73

Alberti, Guglielmo. '*Acciaio.*' *Scenario* (April 1933): 187–91

Alessio, Antonio. *Pirandello pittore.* Agrigento: Edizioni del Centro Nazionale Studi Pirandelliani, 1984

Alonge, Roberto. *Pirandello tra realismo e mistificazione.* Naples: Guida Editori, 1972

Alonge, Roberto, et al. *Studi pirandelliani. Dal testo al sottotesto.* Bologna: Pitagora, 1986

Angelini, Franca. *Serafino e la tigre. Pirandello tra scrittura teatro e cinema.* Venice: Marsilio, 1990

Alvaro, Corrado. 'Pirandello e gli sceneggiatori.' *L'Italia letteraria* (27 October 1935)

Anceschi, Luciano, ed. *L'idea del teatro e la crisi del Naturalismo: Studi di poetica dello spettacolo.* Bologna: Edizioni Calderini, 1971

Andersson, Gösta. *Arte e teoria. Studi sulla poetica del giovane Luigi Pirandello.* Stockholm: Almqvist & Witksell, 1966

– 'Verso un teatro nuovo: Luigi Pirandello sull'arte del dramma.' *Studi urbinati di storia, filosofia e letteratura* 47 (1973): 253–300

Argenziano Maggi, Maria. *Il motivo del viaggio nella narrativa pirandelliana.* Naples: Liguori Editore, 1977

Aristarco, Guido. 'L'*oltre* del linguaggio cinematografico in Pirandello.' *Rivista di studi pirandelliani* V(3) (June 1985): 42–56

Artioli, Umberto. *L'officina segreta di Pirandello.* Rome-Bari: Laterza, 1989

Aste, Mario. *La narrativa di Pirandello: Dalle Novelle al Romanzo 'Uno, nessuno e centomila.'* Madrid: Studia Humanitatis, 1979

Atti del Congresso Internazionale di Studi Pirandelliani. Venezia 2–5 Ottobre 1961. Perugia: Le Monnier, 1967

Barilli, Renato. *La barriera del Naturalismo: studi sulla narrativa italiana contemporanea.* 1964. Milan: Mursia, 1980

– *La linea Svevo-Pirandello.* 2d. ed. Milan: Mursia, 1977

– *Pirandello. Una rivoluzione culturale.* Milan: Mursia, 1986

Barker, Clive, and Susan Bassnett. 'Locating Pirandello in the European Theatre Context.' *The Yearbook of the British Pirandello Society* 5 (1985): 1–19

Bassnett, Susan. 'Interview with Luigi Pirandello.' *The Yearbook of the British Pirandello Society* 4 (1984): 48–55

Bentley, Eric. 'The Pirandello Commentaries.' *Pirandellian Studies* 1 (Winter 1985): 1–73

Biasin, Gian Paolo. *Literary Diseases: Theme and Metaphor in the Italian Novel.* Austin: University of Texas Press, 1975

– *Malattie letterarie.* Milan: Bompiani, 1976

– 'Lo specchio di Moscarda.' *Paragone* 268 (1972): 44–68

Biasin, Gian Paolo, and Nicolas J. Perella, eds. *Pirandello 1986*. Rome: Bulzoni, 1987

Borlenghi, Aldo. *Pirandello o dell'ambiguità*. Padua: Edizioni R.A.D.A.R., 1968

Borsellino, Nino. *Immagini di Pirandello*. Cosenza: Edizioni Lerici, 1979

Boschetto, Sandra. 'Luigi Pirandello: "La tragedia di un personaggio" and the Genesis of *Sei personaggi in cerca d'autore*.' *Proceedings of the Pacific Northwest Conference of Foreign Languages* 30(1–2) (1979): 87–90

Bottoni, Luciano. 'Il saggio e la scienza: l'umorismo di Pirandello.' *Intersezioni* 1 (1985): 155–71

Bouissy, André. 'Pirandello, "psychologue de la décadence."' *Revue des Études Italiennes* 26(2–4) (1980): 173–94

– 'Pirandello et le théâtre de son temps – Notes de lecture.' *Lectures Pirandelliennes*. Abbeville: F. Paillart, 1978

Briosi, Sandro. 'Un autore in cerca d'autore.' *The Yearbook of the British Pirandello Society* 2 (1982): 57–65

Brunetta, Gian Piero. 'La conquista dell'impero dei sogni: D'Annunzio e Pirandello.' *Annali d'Italianistica* 6 (1988): 18–37

Brustein, Robert. *The Theatre of Revolt: An Approach to Modern Drama*. Boston: Little, Brown, 1964

Bussino, Giovanni R., and Antonio Illiano, eds. 'Pirandello's Film Project for *La nuova colonia*.' *Canadian Journal of Italian Studies* 6(22–23) (1983): 111–30

– 'Pirandello: Progetti filmici sui *Sei personaggi*.' *Forum Italicum* 16 (1982): 119–45

Caesar, Michael. 'Enrico's Foil: the Function of Belcredi in *Enrico IV*.' *The Yearbook of the British Pirandello Society* 2 (1982): 48–54

Càllari, Francesco. 'Films Based on Works by Pirandello.' *The Yearbook of the British Pirandello Society* 6 (1986): 65–76

– 'Pirandello-cinema, cinema-Pirandello.' *Bianco e nero* XXXIX(2) (1978): 119–25

– *Pirandello e il cinema. Con una raccolta completa degli scritti teorici e creativi*. Venice: Marsilio, 1991

Cambon, Glauco, ed. *Pirandello: A Collection of Critical Essays*. Englewood Cliffs, NJ: Prentice-Hall, 1967

Camerini, Claudio, ed. *'Acciaio.' Un film degli anni trenta. Pagine inedite di una storia italiana*. Turin: Nuova ERI, 1990

Campassi, Osvaldo, and Virgilio Sabel. 'Chenal, L'Herbier e *Il fu Mattia Pascal*.' *Cinema* 117 (10 May 1941)

Caprin, Giulio. 'Colloqui con Pirandello.' *La lettura* 27(3) (1 March 1927): 161–8.

Carrabino, Victor. 'Pirandello's Drama: A Phenomenology of the Theatre.' *Claudel Studies* 9(2) (1982): 53–60

Caserta, Ernesto. 'Croce, Pirandello e il concetto di umorismo.' *Canadian Journal of Italian Studies* 6 (1983): 103–10

Cavalluzzi, Raffaele. 'Le aporie del superfluo. Cinema e romanzo nei *Quaderni di Serafino Gubbio operatore.' Lavoro critico* 23 (1981): 57–74

Corrigan, Beatrice. 'Pirandello as a Director.' *Theater Research* 12 (1972): 155–63

Corsinovi, Graziella. *Pirandello e l'espressionismo.* Genoa: Tilgher, 1979

– *Pirandello: Tradizione e trasgressione. Studi su Pirandello e la letteratura italiana tra '800 e '900.* Genoa: Tilgher, 1983

Chiarini, Paolo. 'Brecht e Pirandello.' *Atti del convegno internazionale di studi pirandelliani. Venezia 2–5 ottobre 1961.* Venice: Marsilio, 1967

Cometa, Michele. *Il teatro di Pirandello in Germania.* Palermo: Novecento, 1986

Cousin, Geraldine. 'Stanislavsky and Pirandello: from Text to Performance.' *The Yearbook of the British Pirandello Society* 5 (1985): 43–59

Crespi, Stefano. 'L'esperienza cinematografica in Pirandello.' *Vita e pensiero* 50 (1967): 847–53

Crifò, Cosmo. *Dalle origini a 'Il fu Mattia Pascal.'* Vol. 1 of *I volti di Pirandello.* Palermo: Manfredi Editore, 1977

– *Dalla 'Vita nuda' alla Realtà del Mito.* Vol. 2 of *I volti di Pirandello.* Palermo: Manfredi Editore, 1979

Cuminetti, Benvenuto. 'Indicazioni su *Quaderni di Serafino Gubbio operatore.' Vita e pensiero* 50 (1967): 854–65

D'Alberti, Sarah. *Pirandello romanziere.* Palermo: S.F. Flaccovio Editore, 1967

D'Ambra, Lucio. 'Sette anni di cinema.' *Cinema* (25 January 1937)

D'Amico, Alessandro, and Alessandro Tinterri, eds. *Pirandello capocomico. La compagnia del Teatro d'Arte di Roma. 1925–28.* Palermo: Sellerio, 1987

Debenedetti, Giacomo. *Personaggi e destino: la metamorfosi del romanzo contemporaneo.* Milan: Il Saggiatore, 1977

– *Il romanzo del Novecento.* Milan: Garzanti, 1981

De Castris, Arcangelo Leone. *Il decadentismo italiano: Svevo, Pirandello, D'Annunzio.* Bari: De Donato Editore, 1974

– *Storia di Pirandello.* Bari: Editori Laterza, 1986

Del Ministro, Maurizio. *Pirandello: scena, personaggio e film.* Rome: Bulzoni Editore, 1980

– 'La presenza di Pirandello nella poetica di Ingmar Bergman.' *Quaderni dell'Istituto di Studi Pirandelliani* 1 (1973): 201–10

Di Giammatteo, Fernaldo. 'Pirandello e il cinema mancato.' *La nuova rivista europea* IV(15) (1980): 95–102

Di Sacco, Paolo. *L'epopea del personaggio: uno studio sul teatro di Pirandello.* Rome: Luciano Lucarini Editore, 1984

– 'Pirandello e il cinema.' *Cultura oggi* 1(4) (1983): 5–17

Dombroski, Robert S. 'Laudisi's Laughter and the Social Dimension of *Right You Are (If You Think So).' Modern Drama* 16 (1973): 337–46

- *Le totalità dell'artificio: ideologia e forma nel romanzo di Pirandello.* Padua: Liviana Editrice, 1978
Donati, Corrado. *Bibliografia della critica pirandelliana 1962–1981.* Florence: Editrice La Ginestra, 1986
- *La solitudine allo specchio: Luigi Pirandello.* Rome: Luciano Lucarini Editore, 1980
- 'L'umorismo di Pirandello e il dialogismo di Bachtin.' *Letteratura italiana contemporanea* IV(9) (1983): 381–96
Donati, Corrado, and Anna T. Orsani, eds. *Pirandello nel linguaggio della scena. Materiali bibliografici dai quotidiani italiani (1962–1990).* Ravenna: Longo Editore, 1993
Eco, Umberto. *Sugli specchi.* Milan: Bompiani, 1985
Esslin, Martin. *Brief Chronicles: Essays on Modern Theatre.* London: Temple Smith, 1970
Federici, Corrado. 'Per un'ipotesi di lettura platonica de *Il fu Mattia Pascal.*' *Quaderni d'italianistica* 4(1) (1983): 99–110
Ferroni, Giulio. *Il comico nelle teorie contemporanee.* Rome: Bulzoni Editore, 1974
Ferrua, Pietro. 'Incontri di Pirandello col cinema.' *Canadian Journal of Italian Studies* 3 (1980): 108–13
Ferrucci, Franco. 'Pirandello e il palcoscenico della mente.' *Lettere Italiane* 36(2) (1984): 219–25
Frateili, Arnaldo. 'Pirandello e il cinema.' *Cinema* (25 December 1936)
Gardair, Jean-Michel. *Pirandello: fantasmes et logique du double.* Paris: Librairie Larousse, 1972
Genot, Gérard, ed. *Pirandello (1867–1967).* Paris: Lettres Modernes Minard, 1968
Genovese, Nino, and Sebastiano Gesù, eds. *La musa inquietante di Pirandello: il Cinema.* 2 vols. Palermo: Bonanno Editore, 1990
Gieri, Manuela. 'Character and Discourse from Pirandello to Fellini: Defining a Countertradition in an Italian Context.' *Quaderni d'italianistica* xiii(1) (1992): 43–55
- 'Effeti di straniamento come strategia della messa in scena nella trilogia: Appùnti e spigolatura sulla "poetica della scena" di Luigi Pirandello.' *Pirandello e il teatro.* Ed. Enzo Lauretta. Milan: Mursia, 1993.
- 'From Pascal to Moscarda: Pirandello's Narrative Within and Beyond Modernism.' *Forum Italicum* 22(2) (Fall 1988): 176–86
Gioanola, Elio. *Pirandello la follia.* Genoa: Il Melangolo, 1983
Giovanelli, Paola Daniela, ed. *Pirandello saggista.* Palermo: Palumbo, 1982
Gioviale, Fernando. *La poetica narrativa di Pirandello: tipologia e aspetti del romanzo.* Bologna: Pàtron Editore, 1984
Giudice, Gaspare. *Luigi Pirandello.* 1963. Turin: UTET, 1980

Guglielmi, Guido. 'Satira, mito e utopia (nota sull'ultimo Pirandello).' *Verri* 26–27 (1983): 51–67

Guglielminetti, Marziano. *Struttura e sintassi del romanzo italiano del primo Novecento*. Milan: Silva Editore, 1964

Hölz, Karl. 'Doppelsinn und Widerspruch: Theorie und Praxis der Modernität im Werke Luigi Pirandello.' *Germanisch-Romanische Monatsschrift* 31(2) (1981): 173–90

Illiano, Antonio. *Introduzione alla critica pirandelliana*. Verona: Fiorini, 1976
– 'Una novella da recuperare. Luigi Pirandello: "Personaggi."' *Italica* 56 (1979): 230–36

Jeanne, René. 'Cinq minutes avec Pirandello.' *Les Nouvelles Littéraires* (15 November 1924): 8

Katz Sanguineti, Giuliana. 'La pazzia di Enrico IV.' *The Yearbook of the British Pirandello Society* 6 (1986): 50–64

Krysinski, Wladimir. 'La dislocation des codes, le croisement des récits et la brisure de la représentation dans *Six personnages en quête d'auteur* de L. Pirandello.' *Études Littéraires* 13(3) (1980): 495–514
– *Le paradigme inquiet. Pirandello et le champ de la modernité*. Montréal: Les Éditions du Préambule, 1989

Lauretta, Enzo. *Luigi Pirandello: Storia di un personaggio 'fuori di chiave.'* Milan: Mursia, 1980
– ed. *Pirandello e il cinema*. Agrigento: Edizione del Centro Nazionale Studi Pirandelliani, 1978
– ed. *Pirandello e il teatro*. Palermo: Palumbo, 1985
– ed. *Pirandello e il teatro*. Milan: Mursia, 1993
– ed. *Il romanzo di Pirandello*. Palermo: Palumbo Editore, 1976
– ed. *Il romanzo di Pirandello e Svevo*. Agrigento: Vallecchi Editore, 1984
– ed. *La trilogia di Pirandello*. Agrigento: Edizione del Centro Nazionale Studi Pirandelliani, 1977

Licastro, Emanuele. *Luigi Pirandello dalle novelle alle commedie*. Verona: Fiorini, 1974

Livio, Gigi. *Il teatro in rivolta: Futurismo, grottesco, Pirandello e pirandellismo*. Milan: Mursia, 1976

Lucente, Gregory. *Beautiful Fables: Self-Consciousness in Italian Narrative from Manzoni to Calvino*. Baltimore: The Johns Hopkins University Press, 1986
– "Non conclude': Self-Consciousness and the Boundaries of Modernism in Pirandello's Narrative.' *Criticism* 26(1) (1984): 21–47

Macchia, Giovanni. *Pirandello o la stanza della tortura*. Milan: Arnoldo Mondadori Editore, 1982

McDonald, David. 'Heidegger's Theatre of the Double Concealment: Claudel and Pirandello.' *Claudel Studies* 7(2) (1980): 57–78

McDowell, Danièlle. 'Le Masque de Protée: Le dramaturge à la conquête de ses doubles.' *Claudel Studies* 7(2) (1980): 90–100

Maira, Salvatore. 'Ideologia e tecnica nella narrativa di Pirandello.' *Nuovi Argomenti* 29–30 (1972): 187–224

Marchese, Angelo. '*Il fu Mattia Pascal* dal romanzo al palcoscenico.' *Humanitas* 30 (1975): 611–18

Marchi, Giovanni. 'La Roma di Pirandello. Una, nessuna e centomila.' *Studi romani* 25 (1977): 45–65

Maslanka, Maria. 'Il problema della morte psicologica nella narrativa di Luigi Pirandello.' *Pirandellian Studies* 2 (Spring 1988): 1–33

Massi, Lucia. 'Pirandello's Theory of "Modern Myths."' *The Yearbook of the British Pirandello Society* 6 (1986): 1–18

Mazzacurati, Giancarlo. *Pirandello nel romanzo europeo.* Bologna: Il Mulino, 1987

Micheli, Sergio. *Pirandello e il cinema. Da 'Acciaio' a 'Káos.'* Rome: Bulzoni, 1989

Milioto, Stefano, ed. *Gli atti unici di Pirandello (tra narrativa e teatro).* Agrigento: Edizioni del Centro Nazionale Studi Pirandelliani, 1978

– ed. *Pirandello e il teatro del suo tempo.* Agrigento: Sarcuto, 1983

– ed. *Studi pirandelliani a Malta.* Palermo: Palumbo, 1985

Milioto, Stefano, and Enzo Scrivano, eds. *Pirandello e la cultura del suo tempo.* Milano: Mursia, 1984

Moestrup, Jorn. *The Structural Patterns of Pirandello's Work.* Odense: Odense University Press, 1972

Moses, Gavriel. 'Film Theory as Literary Genre in Pirandello and the Film Novel.' *Annali d'Italianistica* 6 (1988): 38–65

– "Gubbio in gabbia': Pirandello's Cameraman and the Entrapments of Film Vision.' *MLN* 94 (1979): 36–60

– 'Irrealtà e ironia del fatto filmico in Pirandello.' *Inventario* XIX(1) (1981): 74–96

Mundula, Anna Paola. *Pirandello e le violazioni del proibito.* Rome: Lucarini, 1986

Nardelli, Federico Vittore. *L'uomo segreto: Vita e croci di Luigi Pirandello.* Milan: Arnoldo Mondadori Editore, 1932

Nelson, Robert J. *Play within the Play. The Dramatist's Conception of His Art: Shakespeare to Anouilh.* New Haven: Yale University Press, 1958

Nencioni, Giovanna. 'L'interiezione nel dialogo teatrale di Pirandello.' *Studi di grammatologia italiana* 6 (1977): 227–63

Nulf, Frank Allen. 'Luigi Pirandello and the Cinema: A Study of His Relationship to Motion Pictures and the Significance of That Relationship to Selected Examples of His Prose and Drama.' Diss. Ohio University, 1969

Oliver, Roger. *Dreams of Passion: The Theater of Luigi Pirandello*. New York: New York University Press, 1979

Pacifici, Sergio, ed. *From Verismo to Experimentalism: Essays on the Modern Italian Novel*. Bloomington: Indiana University Press, 1969

Paolucci, Anne. 'The Birth of Drama: Monolog Theatre in Claudel and Pirandello.' *Claudel Studies* 7(2) (1980): 6–17

– 'Pirandello and the Waiting Stage of the Absurd (With Some Observations on a New 'Critical Language').' *Modern Drama* 23 (1980): 102–11

– 'Pirandello: Experience as the Expression of Will.' *Forum Italicum* 7 (1973): 404–14

– *Pirandello's Theater: The Recovery of the Modern Stage for Dramatic Art*. Carbondale: Southern Illinois University Press, 1974

Pennica, Gilda, ed. *Pirandello e la Germania*. Palermo: Palumbo, 1984

Pestarino, Paola. 'Ipotesi sulle redazioni manoscritte di *Uno, nessuno e centomila*.' *Rassegna della letteratura italiana* 82 (1978): 442–65

Piroué, Georges. *Pirandello*. Palermo: Sellerio Editore, 1975

Procaccini, Alfonso. 'Pirandello and the Enigma of Non-Sense.' *Quaderni d'italianistica* 3(1) (1982): 51–62

Puppa, Paolo. *Dalle parti di Pirandello*. Rome: Bulzoni Editore, 1987

– *Fantasmi contro giganti. Scena e immaginario in Pirandello*. Bologna: Pàtron, 1978

Radcliff-Umstead, Douglas. *The Mirror of Our Anguish: A Study of Luigi Pirandello's Narrative Writings*. London: Associated University Presses, 1978

Ragusa, Olga. *Luigi Pirandello*. New York: Columbia University Press, 1968

– *Luigi Pirandello: An Approach to His Theatre*. Edinburgh: Edinburgh University Press, 1980

– 'Pirandello's Haunted House.' *Studies in Short Fiction* 10 (1973): 235–42

– 'Pirandello's *Teatro d'Arte* and a New Look at His Fascism.' *Italica* LV(2) (1978): 236–53

Rey, John B. 'A Case of Identity: The Source of Pirandello's *As You Desire Me*.' *Modern Drama* 15 (1973): 433–39

Roffarè, Francesco. *L'essenzialità problematica e dialettica del teatro di Pirandello*. Florence: Le Monnier, 1972

Roma, Enrico. 'Pirandello e il cinema.' *Comoedia* 14(7) (1932–3): 19–22

Salinari, Carlo. *Luigi Pirandello*. Naples: Liguori, 1968

Sani Fink, Daniela. 'Pirandello a New York nei documenti della stampa americana.' *Quaderni di teatro* 10 (1980): 123–41

Sciascia, Leonardo. *Alfabeto pirandelliano*. Milan: Adelphi, 1989

– ed. *Omaggio a Pirandello*. Milan: Bompiani, 1986

– *Pirandello e la Sicilia*. Caltanisetta-Rome: Salvatore Sciascia Editore, 1961

Scrivano, Enzo, ed. *Pirandello e la drammaturgia fra le due guerre*. Agrigento: Edizioni del Centro Nazionale Studi Pirandelliani, 1985

Sogliuzzo, Richard A. *Luigi Pirandello Director: The Playwright in the Theatre.* Metuchen, NJ: The Scarecrow Press, 1982

Spizzo, Jean. 'Répétition et réformation du texte pirandellien *Tutto per bene*: De la forme narrative à la forme dramatique.' *Revue des Etudes Italiennes* 20 (1974): 74–104

Starkie, Walter. *Luigi Pirandello 1867–1936.* Berkeley: University of California Press, 1965

Stewens, Dorothea. 'The Character as Director: From *Leonora addio!* to *Questa sera si recita a soggetto.*' *The Yearbook of the British Pirandello Society* 2 (1982): 66–72

– *Pirandello: scrittura e scena.* Agrigento: Edizioni del Centro Nazionale Studi Pirandelliani, 1983

Stocchi-Perucchio, Donatella. *Pirandello and the Vagaries of Knowledge. A Reading of* Il fu Mattia Pascal. Saratoga, CA: Anma Libri, 1991

Stone, Jennifer. 'Cineastes' Texts.' *The Yearbook of the British Pirandello Society* 3 (1983): 45–66

– 'Double Exposure: Pirandello, Mosjoukine and Casanova.' *The Yearbook of the British Pirandello Society* 4 (1984): 56–66

– *Pirandello's Naked Prompt. The Structure of Repetition in Modernism.* Ravenna: Longo, 1989

– 'Pirandello's Picassos.' *The Italianist* 2 (1982): 15–39

– 'Pirandello's Scandalous Docile Bodies.' *The Yearbook of the British Pirandello Society* 4 (1984): 21–35

Styan, J. L. *The Dark Comedy: The Development of Modern Comic Tragedy.* 2d ed. London: Cambridge University Press, 1968

Tessari, Roberto. *Il mito della macchina. Letteratura e industria nel primo Novecento italiano.* Milan: Mursia, 1973

Vené, Gian Franco. *Pirandello fascista. La coscienza borghese tra ribellione e rivoluzione.* 1971; Venice: Marsilio, 1981

Vergani, Orio. 'Ritratto di Pirandello.' *Rivista d'Italia* (28 February 1919)

Vicentini, Claudio. 'Dalla filosofia di Pirandello alla culturologia di Barilli.' *Rivista di estetica* 17 (1972): 232–7

– *L'estetica di Pirandello.* Milan: Mursia, 1970

– *Pirandello. Il disagio del teatro.* Venice: Marsilio, 1993

– 'Pirandello and the Problem of Theatre as an Impossible Art.' *The Yearbook of the British Pirandello Society* 4 (1984): 1–20

– 'La trilogia pirandelliana del teatro nel teatro e le proposte della teatralità futurista.' *The Yearbook of the British Pirandello Society* 3 (1983): 18–32

Zangrilli, Franco. *L'arte novellistica di Pirandello.* Ravenna: Longo Editore, 1983

WORKS BY FEDERICO FELLINI

Fellini, Federico. *Amarcord*. Milan: Rizzoli, 1974
– *Amarcord: Portrait of a Town*. New York: Berkley Windhover Books, 1975
– *Il Casanova*. Ed. Gianfranco Angelucci and Liliana Betti. Bologna: Cappelli, 1977
– *Casanova: sceneggiatura originale*. Screenplay by Federico Fellini and Bernardino Zapponi. Turin: Einaudi, 1976
– *La città delle donne*. Milan: Garzanti, 1980
– *I clowns*. Ed. Renzo Renzi. Bologna: Cappelli, 1970
– *Comments on Film*. Ed. Giovanni Grazzini. Trans. Joseph Henry. Fresno, CA: The Press at California State University, Fresno, 1988
– *La dolce vita*. Screenplay by Federico Fellini, Ennio Flaiano, and Tullio Pinelli. Milan: Garzanti, 1981
– *La Dolce Vita*. Trans. Oscar DaLiso and Bernard Shir-Cliff. New York: Ballantine Books, 1961
– *Early Screenplays: Variety Lights, The White Sheik*. Trans. Judith Green. New York: Grossman Publishers, 1971
– *8½ [Otto e mezzo]*. Ed. Camilla Cederna. Bologna: Cappelli, 1965
– *E la nave va*. Screenplay by Federico Fellini and Tonino Guerra. Ed. Gianfranco Angelucci. Milan: Longanesi, 1983
– *Fare un film*. Turin: Giulio Einaudi Editore, 1980
– *Fellini on Fellini*. Trans. Isabel Quigly. Ed. Anna Keel and Christian Strich. London: Eyre Methuen, 1976
– *Fellini Satyricon*. Ed. Dario Zanelli. Bologna: Cappelli, 1969
– *Fellini's Satyricon*. Ed. Dario Zanelli. Trans. Eugene Walters and John Matthews. New York: Ballantine Books, 1970
– *Fellini TV. Block-notes di un regista. 'I clowns.'* Ed. Renzo Renzi. Bologna: Cappelli, 1972
– *'Ginger e Fred': Rendiconto di un film*. Ed. Mino Guerrini. Milan: Longanesi, 1986
– *Giulietta degli spiriti*. Ed. Tullio Kezich. Bologna: Cappelli, 1965
– *Intervista sul cinema*. Ed. Giovanni Grazzini. Bari: Laterza, 1983
– *Juliet of the Spirits*. Ed. Tullio Kezich. Trans. Howard Greenfield. Transcription of final screenplay by John Cohen. Trans. Cecilia Perrault. New York: Ballantine Books, 1966
– 'The Long Interview.' *Juliet of the Spirits*. Ed. Tullio Kezich. Trans. Howard Greenfield. New York: Ballantine Books, 1966: 17–64
– *La mia Rimini*. Ed. Renzo Renzi. Bologna: Cappelli, 1967
– *'Moraldo in the City' and 'A Journey with Anita.'* Ed. and trans. John C. Stubbs. Urbana: University of Illinois Press, 1983

- *Le notti di Cabiria*. Screenplay by Federico Fellini, Ennio Flaiano, and Tullio Pinelli. Milan: Garzanti, 1981
- *Il primo Fellini: Lo sceicco bianco, I vitelloni, La strada, Il bidone*. Ed. Liliana Betti and Eschilo Tarquini. Bologna: Cappelli, 1969
- *Prova d'orchestra*. Milan: Garzanti, 1980
- *Quattro film*. Introduction by Italo Calvino. Turin: Einaudi, 1974
- *Roma*. Ed. Bernardino Zapponi. Bologna: Cappelli, 1972
- *Lo sceicco bianco*. Milan: Garzanti, 1980
- *La strada*. Screenplay by Federico Fellini and Tullio Pinelli. Rome: Edizioni Bianco e Nero, 1955
- 'La Strada.' *L'Avant-Scène du Cinéma* 102 (April 1970): 7–51
- 'La strada': *Un film de Federico Fellini*. Paris: Éditions du Seuil, 1955
- 'La Strada': *Federico Fellini, Director*. Ed. Peter Bondanella and Manuela Gieri. New Brunswick: Rutgers University Press, 1987
- *The Sweet Beginnings*. New York: Atlas, 1982
- *Three Screenplays: 'I Vitelloni,' 'Il Bidone,' 'The Temptations of Doctor Antonio.'* Trans. Judith Green. New York: Orion Press, 1970

WORKS ON FEDERICO FELLINI

Agel, Geneviève. *Les chemins de Fellini*. Paris: Les Éditions du Cerf, 1956
Alpert, Hollis. *Fellini, A Life*. New York: Atheneum, 1986
Amengual, Barthélemy. 'Fin d'itinéraire: Du "côté de Lumière" au "côté de Méliès."' *Études cinématographiques* 127–30 (1981): 81–111
Angelini, Pietro. *Controfellini: Il fellinismo tra restaurazione e magia bianca*. Milan: Ottaviano, 1974
Benderson, Alpert E. *Critical Approaches to Federico Fellini's '8½.'* New York: Arno Press, 1974
Betti, Liliana. *Fellini: An Intimate Portrait*. Trans. Joachim Neugroschel. Boston: Little, Brown, 1979
Betti, Liliana, and Gianfranco Angelucci, eds. '*Casanova' rendez-vous con Federico Fellini*. Milan: Bompiani, 1975
Bispuri, Ennio. *Federico Fellini: Il sentimento latino della vita*. Rome: Ventaglio, 1981
Bondanella, Peter. *The Cinema of Federico Fellini*. Princeton, N.J.: Princeton University Press, 1992
- ed. *Federico Fellini: Essays in Criticism*. New York: Oxford University Press, 1978
Bondanella, Peter, and Cristina Degli Esposti, eds. *Perspectives on Federico Fellini*. New York: G.K. Hall, 1993
Boyer, Deena. *The Two Hundred Years of '8½.'* New York: Garland, 1978

Budgen, Suzanne. *Fellini*. London: British Film Institute, 1966

Burke, Frank. *Federico Fellini: 'Variety Lights' to 'La Dolce Vita.'* Boston: Twayne, 1984

Costello, Donald P. *Fellini's Road*. Notre Dame: University of Notre Dame Press, 1983

Delouche, Dominique. 'Journal d'un bidoniste.' In Geneviève Agel, *Les chemins de Fellini*, 99–159. Paris: Les Éditions du Cerf, 1956

De Miro, Ester, and Mario Guaraldi, eds. *Fellini della memoria*. Florence: La Casa Usher, 1983

De Santi, Pier Marco. *I disegni di Fellini*. Rome: Laterza, 1982

Estève, Michel, ed. *Federico Fellini: Aux sources de l'imaginaire. Études cinématographiques*, 127–30. Paris: Lettres Modernes Minard, 1981

– ed. *Federico Fellini: '8½.' Études Cinématographiques*, 28–9. Paris: Lettres Modernes Minard, 1963

Fava, Claudio. *I film di Federico Fellini*. Rome: Gremese Editore, 1981

– *The Films of Federico Fellini*. Trans. Shula Curto. Secaucus, NJ: Citadel Press, 1985

Foreman, Walter C. 'Fellini's Cinematic City: *Roma* and Myths of Foundation.' *Forum Italicum* 14 (1980): 78–97

Ketcham, Charles B. *Federico Fellini: The Search for a New Mythology*. New York: Paulist Press, 1976

Kezich, Tullio. *Fellini*. Milan: Camunia, 1987

Mollica, Vincenzo, ed. *Scenari: Il fumetto e il cinema di Fellini*. Montepulciano: Editori del Grifo, 1984

Murray, Edward. *Fellini the Artist*. New York: Frederick Ungar, 1985

Pecori, Franco. *Fellini*. Florence: La Nuova Italia, 1974

Perry, Ted. *Filmguide to '8½.'* Bloomington: Indiana University Press, 1975

Pieri, Françoise. 'Federico Fellini écrivain du *Marc'Aurelio.'* *Positif* 244–5 (1981): 20–32

Pillitteri, Paolo. *Appunti su Fellini*. Milan: Cooperativa Libraria I.U.L.M., 1986

Prats, A. J. *The Autonomous Image: Cinematic Narration & Humanism*. Lexington: The University Press of Kentucky, 1981. [Chapters on *The Clowns* and *Fellini: A Director's Notebook*]

Price, Barbara Anne, and Theodore Price. *Federico Fellini: An Annotated International Bibliography*. Metuchen, NJ: The Scarecrow Press, 1978

Rondi, Brunello. *Il cinema di Fellini*. Rome: Edizioni di Bianco e Nero, 1965

Rosenthal, Stuart. *The Cinema of Federico Fellini*. South Brunswick: A.S. Barnes, 1976

Salachas, Gilbert. *Federico Fellini*. Paris: Seghers, 1963

- *Federico Fellini: An Investigation into His Films and Philosophy*. Trans. Rosalie Siegel. New York: Crown Publishers, 1969
Sarris, Andrew. 'Notes on the Auteur Theory in 1962.' *Film Culture* 27 (Winter 1962–3)
Schoonejans, Sonia. *Fellini*. Rome: Lato Side, 1980
Slike, James R., ed. *Fellini*. Beverly Hills, CA: American Film Institute, 1970
Solmi, Angelo. *Fellini*. Trans. Elisabeth Greenwood. London: Merlin, 1967
- *Storia di Federico Fellini*. Milan: Rizzoli, 1962
Stubbs, John C. *Federico Fellini: A Guide to References and Resources*. Boston: G.K. Hall, 1978
Truffaut, François. 'La politique des auteurs.' *Cahiers du Cinéma* 31 (January 1954)
Wall, James M., ed. *Three European Directors: Truffaut, Fellini, Buñuel*. Grand Rapids: Eardmans, 1973

WORKS OF GENERAL INTEREST

Alberti, Alberto Cesare. *Il teatro nel fascismo. Pirandello e Bragaglia*. Rome: Bulzoni, 1974
Alonge, Roberto. *Teatro e spettacolo nel secondo ottocento*. Rome-Bari: Laterza, 1988
Alter, Jean. 'From Text to Performance: Semiotics of Theatrality.' *Poetics Today* 2(3) (1981): 113–39
Angelini, Franca. *Teatro e spettacolo nel primo novecento*. Rome-Bari: Laterza, 1988
- *Teatro del Novecento da Pirandello a Fo*. Rome-Bari: Laterza, 1990
Armes, Roy. *Patterns of Realism: A Study of Italian Neo-realist Cinema*. South Brunswick: A.S. Barnes, 1971
Artioli, Umberto. *Teatro e corpo glorioso. Saggio su Antonin Artaud*. Milan: Feltrinelli, 1978
Astruc, Alexandre. 'The Birth of a New Avant-Garde: La Caméra- Stylo.' *The New Wave: Critical Landmarks*. Ed. Peter J. Graham. London: Secker and Warburg, 1968. Trans. from *Écran Français* 144 (30 March 1948)
Bachelard, Gaston. *On Poetic Imagination and Reverie: Selections from the Works of Gaston Bachelard*. Trans. Colette Gaudin. Indianapolis: Bobbs-Merrill, 1971
Bakhtin, Mikhail. *The Dialogic Imagination*. Ed. Michael Holquist. Trans. Caryl Emerson and Michael Holquist. Austin: University of Texas Press, 1986
- *L'opera di Rabelais e la cultura popolare*. Turin: Einaudi, 1979
- *Problems of Dostoevsky's Poetics*. Ed. and trans. Caryl Emerson. Minneapolis: University of Minnesota Press, 1985

– *Rabelais and His World*. Trans. Helene Iswolsky. Cambridge, MA: MIT, 1968
Balázs, Béla. *Theory of the Film*. London: Dobson, 1952
Barthes, Roland. *Mythologies*. Trans. Annette Lavers. New York: Hill and Wang, 1972
– *Le plaisir du texte*. Paris: Éditions du Seuil, 1973
– *The Pleasure of the Text*. Trans. Richard Miller. New York: Hill and Wang, 1975
– *S/Z*. Trans. Richard Miller. New York: Hill & Wang, 1974
Baudelaire, Charles. *De l'essence du rire et généralement du comique dans les arts plastiques*. In *Oeuvres complètes de Baudelaire*. Paris: Gallimart, 1951: 702–20
Bazin, André. *What Is Cinema?* Trans. Hugh Gray. Forward by François Truffaut. 2 vols. Berkeley: University of California Press, 1972
Benjamin, Walter. *Angelus Novus. Saggi e frammenti*. Turin: Einaudi, 1976
– *Avanguardia e rivoluzione*. Trans. Aldo Marietti. Turin: Einaudi, 1973
– 'Das Kunstwerk im Zeitalter seiner technischen Reproduzierbarkeit.' *Illuminationen: Ausgewählte Schriften*. 1955. Frankfurt am Main: Suhrkamp Verlag, 1961. 148–84
– *L'opera d'arte nell'epoca della sua riproducibilità tecnica*. Trans. Enrico Filippini. Turin: Einaudi, 1966
– *Understanding Brecht*. Trans. Anna Bostock. London: Verso, 1983
– *Versuche über Brecht*. Frankfurt am Main: Suhrkamp Verlag, 1966
– 'The Work of Art in the Age of Mechanical Reproduction.' *Illuminations*. Trans. Harry Zohn. Ed. Hannah Arendt. New York: Harcourt, Brace & World, 1968. 219–53
Bergman, Ingmar. *Bergman on Bergman*. Trans. Paul Britten Austin. London: Secker & Warburg, 1973
– *Four Screenplays of Ingmar Bergman*. New York: Simon and Schuster, 1960
– Interview. 'My Need to Express Myself in a Film.' By Edwin Newman. *Film Comment* 4(2–3) (Fall/Winter, 1967): 58–62
Bergson, Henri. *Laughter, An Essay on the Meaning of the Comic*. New York: Macmillan, 1911
– *Rire, essai sur la signification du comique*. Paris: Alcan, 1908
– *Il riso. Saggio sul significato del comico*. 1916; Rome-Bari: Laterza, 1991
Bernardini, Aldo. *Cinema muto italiano*. 3 vols. Rome-Bari: Laterza, 1980–2
Bernardi, Sandro, ed. *Si fa per ridere ... ma è una cosa seria*. Milan: La Casa Usher, 1987
Blau, Herbert. *The Eye of Prey: Subversion of the Postmodern*. Bloomington: Indiana University Press, 1987
Bluestone, George. *Novels into Film*. Berkeley: University of California Press, 1957
Bo, Fabio. 'La massa è finita.' *Filmcritica* 40(399) (November 1989): 582–9

Bondanella, Peter. 'La comédie 'métacinématographique' d'Ettore Scola.' *Ciné-mAction* 42 (1987): 91–9
– *The Eternal City: Roman Images in the Modern World*. Chapel Hill: The University of North Carolina Press, 1987
– *Italian Cinema: From Neorealism to the Present*. 1983; New York: Continuum, 1993
– *The Films of Roberto Rossellini*. Cambridge: Cambridge University Press, 1993
Brecht, Bertolt. *Brecht on Theatre. The Development of an Aesthetic*. Ed. and Trans., John Willett. London: Methuen, 1964
– *Schriften zum Theater 1937–1951*. 1957; Frankfurt am Main: Suhrkamp Verlag, 1963
Brunetta, Gian Piero. *Cent'anni di cinema italiano*. Bari: Laterza, 1991
– *Intellettuali, cinema e propaganda fra le due guerre*. Bologna: Pàtron, 1972
– , ed. *Letteratura e cinema*. Bologna: Zanichelli, 1976
– *Storia del cinema italiano 1895–1945*. Rome: Editori Riuniti, 1979
Brunette, Peter. *Roberto Rossellini*. New York and Oxford: Oxford University Press, 1987
Bruno, Marcello Walter. 'Introduzione al nemico. Televisione, pubblicità e nuove tecnologie nel cinema italiano degli anni '80.' *Segnocinema* 10(41) (January 1990): 11–15
– 'Meta in Italy. La via nazionale al cinema-sul-cinema.' *Segnocinema* 11(51) (September-October 1991): 10–13
– 'Perchè Moretti non è un regista.' *Segnocinema* 10(41) (January 1990): 5–6
Burch, Nöel. *Marcel L'Herbier*. Paris: Seghers, 1973
Cacciari, Massimo. *Metropolis*. Rome: Bulzoni, 1973
Calinescu, Matei. *Five Faces of Modernity: Modernism, Avant- Garde, Decadence, Kitsch, Postmodernism*. Durham: Duke University Press, 1987
Camerino, Vincenzo, ed. *Il cinema italiano degli anni ottanta ... ed emozioni registiche*. Lecce: Piero Manni, 1992
Casadei, Maurizio. *Ipotesi sul cinema*. Bologna: Pàtron, 1978
Casetti, Francesco. *Bernardo Bertolucci*. Florence: La Nuova Italia, 1978
Castri, Massimo. *Per un teatro politico. Piscator Brecht Artaud*. Turin: Einaudi, 1973
Celati, Gianni. *Finzioni occidentali. Fabulazione, comicità e scrittura*. 1975; Turin: Einaudi, 1986
Cella, Marcello. 'La natura indifferente. Il paesaggio nel cinema italiano degli anni Ottanta.' *Segnocinema* 10(41) (January 1990): 16-20
Chatman, Seymour. *Antonioni or, The Surface of the World*. Berkeley: University of California Press, 1985
Cineforum. 'Sperduti nel buio.' 29(10) (October 1989)

– 'Sperduti nel buio.' 30(7/8) (July-August 1990)

Cinema nuovo. 'Il "che fare" per il cinema italiano.' 41(1) (January-February 1992): 13–31

Cinemasessanta 125 (January- February 1979): 4–27

– 126 (March-April 1979): 30–9

Clair, René. *Reflections on the Cinema*. Trans. Vera Traill. London: Kinber, 1953

Codelli, Lorenzo. '… et dangereux (affreux, sales et méchants).' *Positif* 189 (January 1977): 61–2

Cohen, Keith. *Cinema e letteratura: le dinamiche di scambio*. Turin: ERI, 1982

Con Davis, Robert, ed. *Lacan and Narration: The Psychoanalytic Difference in Narrative Theory*. Baltimore: The Johns Hopkins University Press, 1985

Copeland, Roger. 'Brecht, Artaud and the Hole in the Paper Sky.' *Theater* 9(3) (Summer 1978): 42–9

Dällenbach, Lucien. *Le récit spéculaire: Essai sur la mise en abyme*. Paris: Éditions du Seuil, 1977

Debenedetti, Giacomo. *Il romanzo del Novecento*. Milan: Garzanti, 1987

De Bernardinis, Flavio. 'Caro cinema italiano …' *Segnocinema* 13(64) (November-December 1993): 11–13

– *Nanni Moretti*. 1987; Florence: La Nuova Italia, 1994

Del Buono, Oreste, and Lietta Tornabuoni, eds. *Era Cinecittà*. Milan: Almanacco Bompiani, 1980

Deleuze, Gilles. *Cinema 1. The Movement-Image*. Minneapolis: University of Minnesota Press, 1989

Deleuze, Gilles, and Felix Guattari. *Capitalisme et schizophrenie*. 1972; Paris: Éditions de Minuit, 1980

De Marinis, Marco. *Capire il teatro. Lineamenti di una nuova teatralogia*. Florence: La Casa Usher, 1988

Derrida, Jacques. *De la Grammatologie*. Paris: Éditions de Minuit, 1967

Diderot, Denis. *Paradosso sull'attore*. Rome: Editori Riuniti, 1993

– *The Paradox of Acting*. Trans. Walter Herries Pollock. 1957; New York: Hill and Wang, 1965

– *Paradoxe sur le comédien*. Paris: Société Française d'Imprimerie et de Livrairie, 1902

– *Scritti di estetica*. Ed. Guido Neri. Milan: Bompiani, 1957

Dillon, Jeanne. *Ermanno Olmi*. Florence: La Nuova Italia, 1985

Eco, Umberto. *The Role of the Reader*. Bloomington: Indiana University Press, 1979

Eco, Umberto, V.V. Ivanov, and Monica Rector. *Carnival*. New York: Mouton Publishers, 1984

Eisenstein, Sergei. *Film Form: Essays in Film Theory*. Trans. and ed. Jay Leyda. New York: Harcourt, Brace & World, 1949

– *The Film Sense*. Trans. and ed. Jay Leyda. New York: Harcourt, Brace & World, 1975

– *Forma e tecnica del film e lezioni di regia*. Turin: Einaudi, 1946

Ellero, Roberto. *Ettore Scola*. Florence: La Nuova Italia, 1988

Esslin, Martin. *Brecht, a Choice of Evils: A Critical Study of the Man, His Work and His Opinions*. 1953; London: Eyre Methuen, 1980

– *Reflections: Essays on Modern Theatre*. Garden City, NY: Doubleday, 1969

Felman, Shoshana, ed. *Literature and Psychoanalysis: The Question of Reading, Otherwise*. Baltimore: The Johns Hopkins University Press, 1982

– 'The Originality of Jacques Lacan.' *Poetics Today* 2(1b) (Winter 1980/81): 45–57

Ferrero, Adelio, ed. *Storia del cinema italiano. Dall'affermazione del sonoro al neorealismo*. Venice: Marsilio, 1978

Fink, Guido, and Antonio Miccolo, eds. *Cinema e teatro: verso una 'totalità' dello spettacolo e una partecipazione critica del pubblico*. Florence: Guaraldi, 1977

Fofi, Goffredo. *Totò*. Rome: Savelli, 1975

– 'La comédie du miracle.' *Positif* 60 (April–May 1964): 14–27

Fofi, Goffredo, and Franca Faldini, eds. *L'avventurosa storia del cinema italiano raccontata dai suoi protagonisti. 1935–1959*. Milan: Feltrinelli, 1979

Fotia, Maria. 'I giovani autori italiani: due anime.' *Mass Media* X(4) (September–October 1991): 24–7

– '*La stazione* di Sergio Rubini.' *Rivista del Cinematografo* 60(11) (November 1990): 14

Foucault, Michel. *Histoire de la folie à l'âge classique*. Paris: Gallimart, 1972

Franciani, Massimo. *Psicoanalisi linguistica ed epistemologia in Jacques Lacan*. Turin: Boringhieri, 1978

Frye, Northrop. *Anatomia della critica: teoria dei modi, dei simboli, dei miti e dei generi letterari*. Turin: Einaudi, 1969

– *Anatomy of Criticism: Four Essays*. Princeton: Princeton University Press, 1957

Gaggi, Silvio. 'Brecht, Pirandello and Two Traditions of Self-Critical Art.' *Theatre Quarterly* 8 (Winter 1979): 42–6

Garroni, Emilio. *Semiotica ed estetica*. Bari: Laterza, 1968

Gili, Jean A. 'Des films pour exorciser mes obsessions.' *Positif* 311 (January 1987): 14–19

– '*Le bal*. Une humanité condamnée à tourner en rond.' *Positif* 276 (February 1984): 54–5

Girard, René. *Deceit, Desire, and the Novel: Self and Other in Narrative Structure*. Baltimore: The Johns Hopkins University Press, 1965

Gozzi, Luigi. 'Dall'ideologico al popolare.' *Il Verri* V(4) (August 1961): 3–20

Graff, Gerald. *Literature against Itself*. Chicago: The University of Chicago Press, 1979

Grande, Maurizio. *Abiti nuziali e biglietti di banca. La società della commedia nel cinema italiano*. Rome: Bulzoni, 1986

– *Il cinema di Saturno. Commedia e malinconia*. Rome: Bulzoni, 1992

Guidorizzi, Ernesto. *La narrativa italiana e il cinema*. Florence: Sansoni, 1973

Habermas, Jürgen. *Il discorso filosofico della modernità*. Rome-Bari: Laterza, 1987

– *Etica del discorso*. Rome-Bari: Laterza, 1985

Hassan, Ihab. *The Dismemberment of Orpheus. Toward a Postmodern Literature*. New York: Oxford University Press, 1971

Hassan, Ihab, and Sally Hassan, eds. *Innovation/Renovation: New Perspectives in the Humanities*. Madison: The University of Wisconsin Press, 1983

Heath, Stephen. *Questions of Cinema*. Bloomington: Indiana University Press, 1981

Heidegger, Martin. *Being and Time*. Trans. John Macquarrie and Edward Robinson. New York: Harper & Row, 1962

Hughes, Robert, ed. *Film: Book One*. New York: Grove Press, 1959

Hume, Kathryn. *Fantasy and Mimesis: Responses to Reality in Western Literature*. New York: Methuen, 1984

Hutcheon, Linda. *Narcissistic Narrative: The Metafictional Paradox*. New York: Methuen, 1984

– *A Theory of Parody. The Teachings of Twentieth-Century Art Forms*. 1985; New York and London: Methuen, 1986

Iser, Wolfgang. *The Implied Reader: Patterns of Communication in Prose Fiction from Bunyan to Beckett*. 4th ed. Baltimore: The Johns Hopkins University Press, 1987

Jameson, Fredric. *The Political Unconscious: Narrative as a Socially Symbolic Act*. Ithaca, NY: Cornell University Press, 1981

– *Postmodernism, or, The Cultural Logic of Late Capitalism*. Durham, NC: Duke University Press, 1991

Jakobson, Roman, and Grete Lübbe-Grothues. 'The Language of Schizophrenia.' *Poetics Today* 2 (1980): 137–44

Jarrat, Vernon. *The Italian Cinema*. London: The Falcon Press, 1951

Jousse, Thierry. 'Le corps du défi.' *Cahiers du cinéma* 426 (December 1989): 42–4

Kaminsky, Stuart M., ed. *Ingmar Bergman: Essays in Criticism*. New York: Oxford University Press, 1975

Kawin, Bruce F. *The Mind of the Novel: Reflexive Fiction and the Ineffable*. Princeton: Princeton University Press, 1982

Kolker, Robert P. *The Altering Eye: Contemporary International Cinema.* New York: Oxford University Press, 1983

Kracauer, Sigfried. *Cinema tedesco: dal 'Gabinetto del Dottor Caligari' a Hitler. 1954.* Milan: Arnoldo Mondadori Editore, 1977

– *Theory of Film: The Redemption of Physical Reality. 1960.* New York: Oxford University Press, 1972

Kristeva, Julia, Josette Rey-Debove, and Donna Jean Umiker, eds. *Essais de Sémiotique.* The Hague: Mouton, 1971

– *Semiotiké: Recherches pour une sémanalyse.* Paris: Éditions du Seuil, 1969

Lacan, Jacques. *Écrits: A Selection.* Trans. Alan Sheridan. New York: W.W. Norton, 1977

– *The Four Fundamental Concepts of Psycho-Analysis.* New York: W. W. Norton, 1981

Laing, R.D. *The Divided Self: An Existential Study in Sanity and Madness.* London: Tavistock Publications, 1969

– *L'io diviso.* Turin: Einaudi, 1969

La Polla, Franco. 'Non è più tempo d'eroi, ovvero: su alcuni limiti della macchina da presa, oggi.' *Cinema e cinema* 10(37) (1983): 42–9

– 'Palombella rossa.' *Cineforum* 29(10) (October 1989): 61–7

Lecercle, Jean-Jacques. *Philosophy through the Looking Glass: Language, Nonsense, Desire.* La Salle, IL: Open Court, 1985

Leprohon, Pierre. *Le cinéma italien.* Paris: Séghers, 1966

Lizzio, Rosario. *Passi sulla luna. Mappa tendenziosa del nuovo cinema italiano.* Catania: Quaderni di 'Zero de conduite,' Azdak 1991

Luperini, Romano. *L'allegoria del moderno. Saggi sull'allegorismo come forma artistica del moderno e come metodo di conoscenza.* Rome: Editori Riuniti, 1990

– 'L'atto del significare allegorico in *Sei Personaggi* e in *Enrico IV*.' *Rivista di studi pirandelliani* 3(6/7) (June-December 1991): 9–19

– *Introduzione a Pirandello.* Rome-Bari: Laterza, 1992

Lyotard, Jean-François. *La condizione postmoderna.* Milan: Feltrinelli, 1987

– *The Postmodern Condition: A Report on Knowledge.* Trans. Geoff Bennington and Brian Massumi. Forward Fredric Jameson. Minneapolis: University of Minnesota Press, 1984

– *Le Postmoderne expliqué aux enfants: Correspondance 1982–1985.* Paris: Éditions Galilée, 1986

Maraldi, Antonio, ed. *I film e le sceneggiature di Ettore Scola.* Cesena: Quaderni del Centro Cinema, 1982

Marcus, Millicent. *Italian Film in the Light of Neorealism.* Princeton, NJ: Princeton University Press, 1986

Martini, Emanuela. '*Caro diario* di Nanni Moretti.' *Cineforum* 33(11) (November 1993): 58–63

Meldolesi, Claudio. *Fondamenti del teatro italiano. La generazione dei registi.* Florence: Sansoni, 1984

Meldolesi, Claudio, and Laura Olivi. *Brecht regista. Memorie del Berliner Ensemble.* Bologna: Il Mulino, 1989

Merkel, Flavio, ed. *Gabriele Salvatores.* Rome: Dino Audino Editore, 1992

Metz, Christian. *Essais sur la Signification au Cinéma.* 2 vols. Paris: Éditions Klincksieck, 1971

– *The Imaginary Signifier: Psychoanalysis and the Cinema.* Trans. Celia Britton, Annwyl Williams, Ben Brewster, and Alfred Guzzetti. Bloomington: Indiana University Press, 1977

– *Langage et cinéma.* Paris: Librairie Larousse, 1971

– *Linguaggio e cinema.* Trans. Alberto Farassino. Milan: Bompiani, 1977

– *Semiologia del cinema.* Trans. Adriano Aprà and Franco Ferrini. Introduction by Franco Ferrini. Milan: Garzanti, 1980

Micheletti, Gustavo. 'Una palombella tra Habermas e Foucault.' *Cinemasessanta* 31(1/190) (January-February 1990): 9–12

Momo, Arnaldo. *Brecht, Artaud e le avanguardie teatrali: teatro divertimento-teatro gioco.* Venice: Marsilio Editore, 1976

Monaco, James. *The New Wave: Truffaut, Godard, Chabrol, Rohmer, Rivette.* New York: Oxford University Press, 1976

Montini, Franco, ed. *Una generazione in cinema. Esordi ed esordienti italiani 1975–1988.* Venice: Marsilio, 1988

– *I novissimi. Gli esordienti del cinema italiano degli anni '80.* Turin: Nuova ERI, 1988

Morandini, Morando. 'Il regista è finito? Breve viaggio intorno agli autori del cinema italiano degli anni '80.' *Segnocinema* 6(22) (March 1986): 4–6

Morris, Cyril Brian. *This Loving Darkness: The Cinema and Spanish Writers 1920–1936.* New York: Oxford University Press, 1980

Mukarovsky, Jan. *Il significato dell'estetica.* Turin: Einaudi, 1973

Muscio, Giuliana. *Scrivere il film. Sceneggiatura e sceneggiatori nella storia del cinema.* Milan: Savelli, 1981

Napolitano, Riccardo, ed. *Commedia all'italiana. Angolazioni e controcampi.* Rome: Gangemi, 1986

Naremore, James, and Patrick Bratlinger, eds. *Modernity and Mass Culture.* Bloomington: Indiana University Press, 1991

Nichols, Bill. *Movies and Methods.* 2 vols. Berkeley: University of California Press, 1976–1985

Orto, Nuccio. *Maurizio Nichetti: un comico, un autore.* Chieti: Métis, 1990

Pasolini, Pier Paolo. 'The Scenario as a Structure Designed to Become Another Structure.' Trans. Michèle S. de Cruz-Sáenz. *Wide Angle* 2 (1977): 40–7

Pearce, Richard. *Stages of the Clown. Perspectives on Modern Fiction from Dostoevski to Beckett.* Carbondale and Edwardsville: Southern Illinois University Press, 1970

Piro, Sergio. *Il linguaggio schizofrenico.* Milan: Feltrinelli Editore, 1967

Porro, Marzio. 'Le pagine morte, nota sulla sceneggiatura.' *Autografo* 3 (1984): 26–36

Propp, Vladimir. *Morfologia della fiaba.* Turin: Einaudi, 1966

– *Morphology of the Folktale.* Trans. Lawrence Scott. 2d ed. Austin: University of Texas Press, 1968

Proust, Marcel. *Remembrance of Things Past.* Trans. C.K. Scott Moncrieff. 2 vols. London: Chatto and Windus, 1925

Puppa, Paolo. *Teatro e spettacolo nel secondo Novecento.* Rome-Bari: Laterza, 1990

Read, Herbert. 'Towards a Film Aesthetic.' *Cinema Quarterly* 1(1) (Autumn 1932): 7–11

Ricardou, Jean. *Le Nouveau Roman.* Paris: Éditions du Seuil, 1973

– *Pour une théorie du nouveau roman.* Paris: Éditions du Seuil, 1971

– *Problèmes du nouveau roman.* Paris: Éditions du Seuil, 1967

Robbe-Grillet, Alain. *For a New Novel: Essays on Fiction.* Trans. Richard Howard. New York: Grove Press, 1965

– *Pour un nouveau roman.* Paris: Les Éditions de Minuit, 1963

Rondi, Gian Luigi. '*Splendor* di Ettore Scola.' *Rivista del Cinematografo* 59(3) (1989): 11

Rossellini, Roberto. *Il mio metodo. Scritti e interviste.* Ed. Adriano Aprà. Venice: Marsilio, 1987

Sadoul, George. *Storia generale del cinema. Le origini (1909–1920).* Turin: Einaudi, 1975

– *Storia generale del cinema. L'arte muta (1919–1929).* Turin: Einaudi, 1978

Salizzaro, Claver, ed. 'Emozioni al lavoro.' *Cinecritica* 14(19–20) (October 1990/March 1991): 17–44

Sarris, Andrew. 'Notes on Auteur Theory in 1962.' *Film Culture* 27 (Winter 1962/63): 1–8.

Sears, Sallie, and Georgianna W. Lord, eds. *The Discontinuous Universe: Selected Writings in Contemporary Consciousness.* New York: Basic Books, 1972

Sesti, Mario. *Nuovo cinema italiano. Gli autori i film le idee.* Rome-Naples: Theoria, 1994

Simonelli, Giorgio. 'Proposta decente.' *Segnocinema* 13(64) (November-December 1993): 14–16

Starobinski, Jean. *Portrait de l'artiste en saltimbanque*. Genève: Éditions d'Art Albert Skira, 1971

Steiner, George. *Martin Heidegger*. New York: Penguin Books, 1980

Sturrock, John, ed. *Structuralism and Since: From Lévi-Strauss to Derrida*. New York: Oxford University Press, 1979

Szondi, Peter. *Theorie des modernen Dramas. 1850–1950*. Frankfurt am Main: Suhrkamp Verlag, 1974

– *Teoria del dramma moderno 1880–1950*. 1962; Turin: Einaudi, 1976

– *Theory of the Modern Drama*. Ed. and trans. Michael Hays. Cambridge: Polity Press, 1987

Tornatore, Giuseppe. *Nuovo Cinema Paradiso*. Palermo: Sellerio, 1990

Tortora, Silvia. 'San Giuseppe. Parla Tornatore, il regista della resurrezione italiana.' *Epoca* (24 December 1989): 87

Toubiana, Serge. 'Le regard moral.' *Cahiers du Cinéma* 425 (November 1989): 20–1

– 'Entretien avec Nanni Moretti.' *Cahiers du cinema* 425 (November 1989): 22–32

Truffaut, François. 'Une certaine tendance du cinéma français.' *Cahiers du Cinéma* 6(31) (January 1954): 15–29

Ugo, Paola, and Antioco Floris, eds. *Facciamoci del male. Il cinema di Nanni Moretti*. Cagliari: CUEC Editrice, 1990

Valesio, Paolo. 'Del classico Bertolt Brecht.' *Il Verri* V(4) (August 1961): 28–43

Verdone, Mario. *Anton Giulio Bragaglia*. Rome: Bulzoni, 1965

– *Poemi e scenari cinematografici d'avanguardia*. Rome: Officina, 1975

Waugh, Patricia. *Metafiction: The Theory and Practice of Self-Conscious Fiction*. New York: Methuen, 1984

Willett, John. *Brecht in Context: Comparative Approaches*. London and New York: Methuen, 1984

– *The Theatre of Bertolt Brecht: A Study from Eight Aspects*. 1959; London: Methuen, 1960

Zavattini, Cesare. *Diario cinematografico*. Milan: Mursia, 1991

Index